GHOSTS OF
AFGHANISTAN

ALSO BY JONATHAN STEELE

Eastern Europe Since Stalin

Socialism with a German Face

Limits of Soviet Power

Eternal Russia

Defeat

GHOSTS OF AFGHANISTAN

THE HAUNTED BATTLEGROUND

JONATHAN STEELE

Portobello
BOOKS

Published by Portobello Books 2011

Portobello Books
12 Addison Avenue
London
W11 4QR
UK

Copyright © Jonathan Steele 2011

Published in the United States by Counterpoint

The right of Jonathan Steele to be identified as the author of this work has been asserted
by him in accordance with the Copyright, Designs and Patents Act 1988

A CIP catalogue record is available from the British Library

9 8 7 6 5 4 3 2 1

ISBN 978 1 84627 430 5

www.portobellobooks.com

Printed and bound by CPI Group (UK) Ltd, Croydon, CR0 4YY

FOR RUTH

CONTENTS

CONTENTS

THIRTEEN MYTHS
ABOUT AFGHANISTAN

MYTH NUMBER ONE:

The Taliban have little popular support. (CHAPTER ONE, PAGE 43)

MYTH NUMBER TWO:

The Soviet invasion was an unprovoked attack designed to capture new territory. (CHAPTER TWO, PAGE 63)

MYTH NUMBER THREE:

The Soviet invasion led to a civil war and Western aid for the Afghan resistance. (CHAPTER TWO, PAGE 78)

MYTH NUMBER FOUR:

The USSR suffered a massive military defeat in Afghanistan at the hands of the mujahedin. (CHAPTER THREE, PAGE 108)

MYTH NUMBER FIVE:

Afghans have always beaten foreign armies, from Alexander the Great to modern times. (CHAPTER THREE, PAGE 109)

I

MYTH NUMBER SIX:

The CIA's supply of Stinger missiles to the mujahedin forced the Soviets out of Afghanistan. (CHAPTER THREE, PAGE 112)

MYTH NUMBER SEVEN:

After the Soviets withdrew, the West walked away. (CHAPTER FOUR, PAGE 136)

MYTH NUMBER EIGHT:

In 1992 the mujahedin overthrew Kabul's regime and won a major victory over Moscow. (CHAPTER FOUR, PAGE 143)

MYTH NUMBER NINE:

Soviet shelling destroyed Kabul. (CHAPTER FIVE, PAGE 165)

MYTH NUMBER TEN:

The Taliban were by far the harshest government Afghanistan has ever had. (CHAPTER SIX, PAGE 200)

MYTH NUMBER ELEVEN:

The Taliban invited Osama bin Laden to use Afghanistan as a safe haven. (CHAPTER SIX, PAGE 204)

MYTH NUMBER TWELVE:

The Taliban are uniquely harsh oppressors of Afghan women. (CHAPTER THIRTEEN, PAGE 364)

MYTH NUMBER THIRTEEN:

Banning girls from school is a Taliban trademark. (CHAPTER THIRTEEN, PAGE 369)

CHRONOLOGY

1747	Afghanistan founded by Ahmad Shah Durrani as modern state
1839–42	First Anglo-Afghan War
1878–80	Second Anglo-Afghan War
1919	Third Anglo-Afghan War leads to independence
1919–29	Reign of Amanullah, who seeks and fails to modernize country; assassinated
1933–73	Reign of Zahir Shah
1973–78	Rule of Mohammed Daoud Khan, who proclaims republic and one-party state; mujahedin groups start armed struggle: beginning of civil war
1978	Coup by People's Democratic Party of Afghanistan (PDPA)
1979	Arrival of Soviet troops in large numbers, Babrak Karmal installed
1985	Mikhail Gorbachev, new Soviet leader, decides on phased withdrawal of troops

1986	Karmal replaced by Mohammed Najibullah
1988	U.S.-Soviet Geneva accords on withdrawal of Soviet troops
1989	FEBRUARY 15, last Soviet troops leave: civil war intensifies
1992	APRIL: Najibullah government falls: mujahedin forces enter Kabul
1996	MAY: Osama bin Laden invited by mujahedin to return to Afghanistan
	SEPTEMBER: Taliban enter Kabul, but civil war continues in north; bin Laden moves to Kandahar in Taliban heartland
2001	SEPTEMBER: Taliban refuse to hand over Osama bin Laden after 9/11 attacks in the United States
	OCTOBER: George W. Bush launches attack on Afghanistan
	DECEMBER: Taliban toppled
2002	JUNE: Loya Jirga selects transitional government
2004	Hamid Karzai elected president
2009	MARCH: Barack Obama announces first surge of 19,000 extra U.S. troops
	NOVEMBER: Karzai elected to second five-year term
	DECEMBER: Second surge of 30,000 troops announced
2011	JUNE: Obama announces withdrawal of 33,000 troops by September 2012; first contacts between U.S. and Taliban officials are confirmed

DRAMATIS PERSONAE

ABDULLAH ABDULLAH, Tajik, foreign minister 2001 to 2005, runner-up in 2009 presidential election

MULLAH MOHAMMED OMAR AKHUND, Pashtun, founder of Taliban who ruled between 1996 and 2001, now head of Taliban leadership in exile, known as Quetta Shura

HAFIZULLAH AMIN, Pashtun, Afghan president September to December 1979, invited Soviet troops to support government, assassinated by Soviet forces

MOHAMMED DAOUD KHAN, Pashtun, overthrew the monarchy of his first cousin Mohammed Zahir Shah in 1973, promulgated a republic and declared himself president, assassinated in April 1978 during coup by People's Democratic Party of Afghanistan (PDPA)

ABDUL RASHID DOSTUM, Uzbek, militia leader who supported the Soviet-backed government in Kabul, and later defected to the muja-hedin. Founder of Junbesh-i Milli-ye Islami (National Islamic Front), a secularist party based in northern Afghanistan

JALALUDDIN HAQQANI, Pashtun, former mujahedin leader against Soviets, now heads insurgent network based in Pakistan with day-to-day operations run by his son, Sirajuddin

GULBUDDIN HEKMATYAR, Pashtun, leader of Hezb-i Islami (Islamic Party), fundamentalist mujahedin commander, member of Peshawar Seven, against Soviet occupation and currently against Afghan forces and U.S. occupation

BABRAK KARMAL, leader of PDPA from December 1979 to May 1986 under Soviet occupation

HAMID KARZAI, Pashtun, served briefly as deputy foreign minister in Burhanuddin Rabbani's government, nominated by Taliban as UN representative in 1996, declined post. In December 2001 selected to lead interim administration, elected president of Afghanistan in 2004 and reelected in 2009

AHMAD SHAH MASSOUD, Tajik, mujahedin commander from northeastern Afghanistan, known as Lion of Panjshir in fight against Soviet occupation, assassinated by al Qaeda on September 9, 2011

MOHAMMED NAJIBULLAH, Pashtun, leader of PDPA from May 1986 and president of Afghanistan from 1987 to 1992, executed by Taliban September 1996

BURHANUDDIN RABBANI, Tajik, leader of Jamiyat-i Islami (Islamic Society) and one of Peshawar Seven mujahedin leaders, president of Afghanistan 1992 to 1996, member of Parliament since 2005, appointed by Karzai to head the High Peace Council in 2010

ABDUL RASUL SAYYAF, Pashtun, Wahhabi fundamentalist, former commander of mujahedin group Ittehad-al-Islami (Islamic Union for the Liberation of Afghanistan), one of Peshawar Seven, invited Osama bin Laden to Afghanistan in 1996, member of Parliament since 2005

ZAHIR SHAH, Pashtun, king overthrown in 1973, lived in exile in Rome until 2002, returned to Kabul as "Father of the Nation," died in 2007

NUR MOHAMMED TARAKI, Pashtun, leader of People's Democratic Party of Afghanistan from 1965 to 1979, became Afghan president after coup of April 1978, murdered in September 1979

ANATOMY OF AFGHAN SOCIETY

POPULATION:

Estimates of the population of Afghanistan range from 29 to 30 million. The last official census, in 1979, counted 15.5 million.

ETHNIC GROUPS (IN PERCENT):

Pashtun: 42

Tajik: 27

Hazara: 9

Uzbek: 9

Aimak: 4

Turkmen: 3

Baluch: 2

LANGUAGES (IN PERCENT):

There are over forty languages and 200 different dialects. The main languages are:

Dari (Persian): 50

Pashto: 35

Uzbek/Turkmen: 11

POVERTY:

Afghanistan is the poorest country in the world. It ranks 135 out of 135 countries on the United Nations Human Poverty Index. Its annual per capita income is $906, and its GDP is $27 billion.

MORTALITY:

Afghans' life expectancy at birth is the lowest in the world: 44.6 years. Twenty percent of the children die before the age of five.

EDUCATION:

Mean years of schooling completed: three years and three months.

POTENTIAL:

In 2010, American geologists and Pentagon officials estimated that Afghanistan's vast untapped mineral riches in Afghanistan were worth $1 trillion.

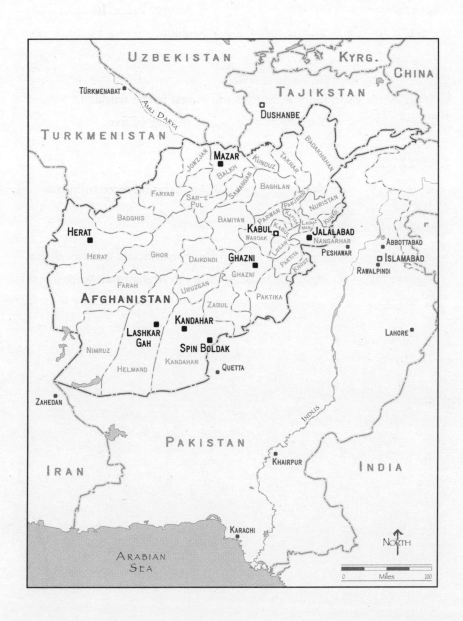

INTRODUCTION

"A confused silence greeted the Vietnam reference. 'Ghosts,' Obama whispered."

—BOB WOODWARD, *OBAMA'S WARS*

AFGHANISTAN HAS BEEN part of my life for the past thirty years. I have reported from the country in each of its turbulent modern phases, starting with the Soviet occupation and the ensuing war between Western-backed Islamist warlords in the mid-1990s to five years of oppressive Taliban rule and, most recently, the American effort to pacify the country in the face of a powerful Taliban resurgence.

I sometimes feel haunted. Memories of Afghanistan and the people I have met there float into my head at home in London or wherever else I happen to be. Memories and questions.

What is it that keeps tempting powerful foreign states to spend soldiers' lives in seeking to control a country that is landlocked, not endowed with oil and much poorer than its less invaded neighbors?

Why does a society that so clearly needs economic progress and development always take up arms whenever a few of its leaders try to bring reform? Why does it succeed in forcing them to retreat?

In spite of Afghanistan's deep ethnic divisions and decades of civil war, how come no movement for secession has ever appeared? Can its majestic natural beauty and rich cultural heritage be the glue that holds Afghanistan together? There must be deeper and more complex reasons.

The ghosts of this book's title are not just my wandering thoughts. They are the ghosts of catastrophic mistakes made by earlier invaders that haunt Obama's war today. I saw the blunders the Soviets made in the 1980s and have watched most of them repeated in recent years. Anger and hubris that lead to a misguided mission of revenge. Regime change that slips, undebated, into nation building. Surging more troops because those who died must not have lost their lives in vain.

The principal ghosts of Afghanistan are the dead on every side. In thirty-five years of unfinished civil war, made worse by foreign intervention, close to 15,000 Soviet dead, over 1,500 Americans, nearly 400 British and more than 500 from other countries. Above all, the lost sons and daughters of Afghanistan itself: some 20,000 troops, and as many as two million civilians.

"Ghosts"—*dukhi*—also happens to be the name Soviet troops gave their Afghan opponents—elusive, ever-moving and hard to pin down. Wearing no uniform, they struck from ambushes by day, and after dark they delivered "night letters" to warn fellow Afghans not to collaborate with the infidels. The Americans and British use different names for those who resist today's occupation. But the urge to dehumanize their shadowy opponents is as strong as it was with the Russians. Today's war is also just as asymmetric. Heavily equipped high-tech forces try to grapple with a guerrilla enemy that wears civilian clothes and never comes head-on. State-of-the-art night-vision goggles are no use for detecting ghosts, and U.S. troops may go through an entire six-month tour of combat without ever knowingly seeing an insurgent alive or dead. Pilots of attack drones, sitting in air-cooled bases in Nevada, never even touch the terrain on which they kill.

The Soviet Union's Afghan agony hovers over the U.S. war. Obama may sense ghosts from Vietnam when he ponders how long to keep troops there or how fast to take them out. But lessons of greater relevance emerge from the Central Asian quagmire that trapped his country's Cold War rival. In 1979, former U.S. national security adviser Zbigniew Brzezinski hoped Afghanistan would become the Soviet Union's Vietnam. Now the Soviet Union's Vietnam has become America's Afghanistan.

So a central theme of this book is the similarity of the Soviet and U.S. interventions and the lessons that ought to be learned. Described as wars of necessity, they were really wars of choice. In each case the decision to invade was made on the grounds of protecting national security but with little thought of the consequences. Could non-Muslim outsiders expect support if they stayed for more than a few months in a country that had never welcomed foreign armies? Was there not a substantial risk that the mission would increase rather than lesson the dangers of terrorism.

The wars became unpopular, and new leaders emerged in Moscow and Washington who had to weigh the wisdom of continuing the struggle. Mikhail Gorbachev and Barack Obama each inherited a war their predecessors had begun too lightly. The Soviet leader decided the war could not be won and opted for a negotiated troop withdrawal, initially hoping to persuade Pakistan and the United States to end their support for the mujahedin insurgents. When this proved unreachable, he pressed his Kabul allies to talk to the opposition with a view to a cease-fire and a government of national unity. He was even willing to urge his Afghan clients to resign in the name of national reconciliation.

But the withdrawal of Soviet troops and an end to his predecessors' adventure were Gorbachev's overriding aim. In spite of failing to defeat the mujahedin, the Soviet leadership had the sense to change course. As a result, it emerged from its nine-year occupation without a major loss of dignity. The tragedy of the Soviet withdrawal came later.

Afghanistan's numerous warring parties as well as the country's neighbors failed to agree on a peace deal as the Russians left or in the months that followed. Illusions of imminent victory swamped the imperative of national reconciliation and doomed Afghanistan to another two decades of civil war.

Obama's strategy has been different from Gorbachev's. Allowing military commanders to persuade him that military success was possible, he launched two large surges of extra U.S. troops and brought the number of foreign forces to well above the Soviet figure. As for the notion of talks with the insurgents, the U.S. president has only recently started to pay lip service to the idea but not yet dropped the doomed strategy of building up local Afghan forces to prolong the civil war.

The biggest lesson of recent Afghan history is that it is wrong for foreigners to arm factions engaged in civil war. For foreigners then to intervene with their own troops is even greater folly. The only way to end thirty-five years of war is through a negotiated peace in which the main fighting groups and their political allies are included. Obama needs to change course, as Gorbachev did. Washington and the government of Hamid Karzai must make a sustained effort to negotiate local cease-fires with the Taliban, leading to a nationwide halt in the fighting and a complete American withdrawal in parallel with a power-sharing deal among the key sectors of Afghan society, no doubt with a substantial devolution of power to the provinces. Pakistan, India, Iran and other regional neighbors need to be part of a companion deal in which their interests in a sovereign but neutral Afghanistan are preserved.

It will not be easy, but if peace is to be restored, there is no other way. The Americans have already been in Afghanistan longer than the Soviets were. The victory that eluded Moscow will not be achieved by Washington.

Ghosts of Afghanistan is based on my eyewitness impressions from visiting Afghanistan at regular intervals over the past thirty years as well as on dozens of interviews with Afghans, including their leaders from the Soviet period, the Taliban time and today. I have conducted new interviews with key Afghan experts and United Nations negotiators. I have gained much from Kremlin, U.S. State Department and British Foreign Office documents released over the last two decades as well as the treasure trove of contemporary U.S. diplomatic cables and war logs that a brave whistleblower passed to WikiLeaks, which shared them with the *Guardian*, the *New York Times* and *Der Spiegel*.

That stunning archive consisted of "ghost" matter, reports and cables that were initially invisible and beyond the world's reach. Had it not been for the leak, the biggest unauthorized disclosure of official documents in history, the citizens of the world's largest democracy and its allies, as well as those of Iraq and Afghanistan, would not have known the truth that hovered over their battlegrounds, unseen. As one of the first journalists who had the chance to read the leaked reports, I saw the gap that separated public statements of policy from the motives that really drove it.

One reason why the United States has repeated so many Soviet mistakes is that much of the West's conventional wisdom on Afghanistan rests on myths. Policy makers and the media peddle an inaccurate view of Afghanistan's history. In this book I hope to set the record straight.

One myth, pushed by former mujahedin leaders and the Taliban as well as by Osama bin Laden, right up to his death in May 2011—and accepted without question as part of the standard Western narrative—is that the Soviet Union suffered military defeat in Afghanistan. The reality is that the Russians suffered heavy casualties but never lost a pitched battle. They could have stayed in Afghanistan for several more years. Their defeat was political. They chose to abandon their initial goals and leave.

According to another more dangerous myth, "the West walked away after the Russians left." The implication is that Afghanistan was abandoned to its fate instead of being showered with aid. The record is the opposite. After 1989, Western governments not only continued to arm and support the mujahedin, they urged them to prolong the civil war and reject Najibullah's offers of talks. The result was three more years of fighting, a chaotic transfer of power in 1992 in which mujahedin leaders turned their artillery on each other and killed tens of thousands of the luckless people of Kabul—and the emergence of the Taliban. The Soviet Union bears the greatest responsibility for the misery and war that Afghans suffered in the 1980s. But the United States and its allies should acknowledge their guilt for the misery and war that Afghans suffered in the 1990s. Unless that truth is recognized, there will be little moral incentive for Western leaders, this time, to help bring Afghans together in order to end the civil war.

Myths may seem as fleeting as ghosts. But they always do more harm.

[1] WHERE ARE WE NOW?

"What we figured out is that people really aren't anti-U.S. or anti-anything; they just want to be left alone. Our presence is what's destabilizing this area."

—U.S. MILITARY OFFICIAL,
EASTERN AFGHANISTAN, FEBRUARY 2011

WEDGED INTO FLAK jackets with helmets at the ready, Sean Smith, a *Guardian* photographer, and I wait in the parking lot of a twenty-first-century fortress. Bristling with communications antennae, its high walls consist of tier upon tier of wired sacks of stones and concrete rubble, known as Hesco barriers, a vastly improved variant of the ancient sandbag. Nearby stand huge vehicles with reinforced steel floors to protect against mines and metal mesh over their windows to block shrapnel. A security contractor directs us to a line of armor-plated LandCruisers with darkened windows.

It is October 2010, and we are in Lashkar Gah at the headquarters of Task Force Helmand, a key unit of the International Security Assistance Force (ISAF), the coalition of forty-eight troop-contributing countries, which the U.S. leads in Afghanistan. In Helmand the dominant ISAF presence is U.S. and British with small contingents from

Denmark and Estonia. Elsewhere in southern Afghanistan, the Dutch have a contingent of several thousand in Uruzgan and the Canadians in Kandahar. The Germans have almost 5,000 troops in the more peaceful north. No Afghan province has received as high an American and British investment of troops and treasure as Helmand, a largely semi-desert region that with its neighbor Kandahar has become the epicenter of the Taliban insurgency. The U.S. connection with the area goes back decades before the emergence of the Taliban in the early 1990s. Most of Helmand's one and a half million people depend for their livelihoods on irrigation schemes donated by the United States in the 1950s during the Cold War. Afghanistan, a strategic crossroads of Central Asia, was at peace, but Moscow and Washington competed for the country's allegiance with development projects.

Now the region is suffering through its worst war. A combined force of 9,000 American and 9,500 British troops is embattled in this one province, roughly a seventh of the total number of 142,000 foreign soldiers in Afghanistan's thirty-four provinces. As for foreign aid aimed at winning hearts and minds, if Helmand were a country, it would be the fifth biggest recipient in the world.

So the success or failure of the U.S. war in Afghanistan depends heavily on what happens there. Thirty years ago Soviet forces found Helmand and the nearby province of Kandahar the toughest region to hold. Nothing has changed.

We are about to drive from the ISAF fortress in Lashkar Gah, the capital of Helmand, to the shooting range where American and British advisers train Afghan police. The city has hosted U.S. Marines for over a year and British troops for more than four, so you might think the two-mile journey would be an easy commute.

Think again. The security guard and our driver, both former soldiers and each armed with a rifle and a revolver, take their places in front. Similar teams—Europeans or Americans on contract—clamber into two identical LandCruisers behind ours. Three-car convoys are standard for trips into town, they tell us. The armored glass in the side window of our vehicle sports an ominous perforated crack like a starburst. "I see you've taken at least one bullet," I comment after the guard finishes briefing us on how to operate the two-way radio in case he and his colleague are incapacitated.

"Actually it was just a stone," he says, laughing. "Small boys throw them. They take time to aim so it's better to be in the lead vehicle. You usually get past before they're ready." The car zigzags through a series of fortified gates and checkpoints and suddenly we are in an untidy world. Motorbikes with turbaned riders are bumping over the uneven ground. A few young men are sitting by a mud-brick wall and chatting. They turn their heads as we lumber past. Battered cars with men at the wheel and women and children in the backseat lurch from alleys between mud-brick houses and follow our convoy toward the tarmac road a hundred yards away. The women are covered head to toe in blue burqas.

As we reach the smoother ground and drive past a row of shops, the guard picks up his handset to launch into a running commentary of potential threats for the benefit of the cars behind. "Static tuc-tuc [three-wheeler] on right. White Toyota no license plate approaching from side road. Multiple pax [passengers]. Tuc-tuc on left, has eyes on us. No pax."

Our convoy reaches the shooting range. The policewomen we meet look chic in their light blue knee-length coats and trousers. But what is most striking is their headgear—scarves covering the chin as well as the hair and wraparound reflecting sunglasses give them a totally anonymous appearance, like ninjas.

As if that were not disguise enough, I notice folded-up burqas on the bench where we sit to enjoy soft drinks before the training starts. Roshan Zakia, the senior officer, sees my quizzical look. She explains that although "Lashkar Gah has sixteen policewomen, only three are willing to wear their uniforms" on their commute between home and

work. The rest don the traditional Afghan woman's head-to-toe covering before going home. Like resistance movements throughout history,
the Taliban often kill people they accuse of collaborating with foreign
forces. Those who join the police are especially vulnerable.

I was not expecting such insecurity in Helmand's capital. The
twenty-minute helicopter ride from the huge transit airfield at Camp
Bastion in northern Helmand that all visitors to the region have to
make when they arrive had ended with heart-stopping swerves and
tilts at little more than fifty feet above Afghan family compounds on
Lashkar Gah's outskirts. In order to make it harder for insurgents to get
the helicopters in their sights, pilots make a series of irregular maneu-
vers. At one moment you tip left and see the helicopter's shadow racing
across the tops of fruit trees almost close enough to touch. The next
minute you tip right and see nothing but deep blue sky. But once on the
ground in Lashkar Gah I had thought to find a town that would be safe.

I have been to Afghanistan fourteen times over the past thirty years,
but this was my first embed with British troops in Helmand since they
arrived in 2006. The British and Americans had claimed that their forces
and those of the Afghan Government controlled most of the province.
These claims were, I now saw, exaggerated.

Countless TV and newspaper reports on the war in southern
Afghanistan and the work of individual platoons have provided a
graphic glimpse of small corners of the battlefield and highlighted the
courage of frontline soldiers. But what does not come through is what
I now saw: the 18,500 American and British troops are actually confined
to garrisons near the few towns in this largely rural province. The situation is the same in Kandahar, Uruzgan and Zabul, the other provinces
of the south.

Soldiers sit in a chain of security bubbles labeled main bases, forward operating bases (FOBs) and patrol bases, of respectively diminishing size, with the last type occupied by anything from a dozen to a
hundred troops. They make forays along the network of canals that cut

through fields of wheat, onions and poppy but return to their heavily fortified sanctuaries after grim hours of dismantling or avoiding improvised explosive devices (IEDs). From 2010 on, they have conducted more and more nighttime raids on farmhouses and family compounds suspected of sheltering Taliban commanders.

The surge of American troops in 2010 allowed a new tactic: the erection of checkpoints, each one in sight of the next so that travelers are always watched. These checkpoints are usually manned by Afghan police. The aim is to revive the flow of commerce and prevent insurgents from planting booby-trap bombs. U.S. forces have blown up hundreds of empty houses to prevent them from being used as hiding places for ambushers and snipers. The Americans uproot trees, dynamite farm buildings and flatten agricultural walls, using an awesome machine called the MICLIC, the M58 Mine Clearing Line Charge—a chain of explosives tied to a rocket that can destroy everything in a swath 30 feet wide and 325 feet long. But what they gain in military security they lose in local goodwill when farmers who flee the American offensives return to find their homes destroyed.

ISAF's pervasive sense of anxiety reminds me of the Soviet garrison mentality I encountered during three reporting assignments in occupied Afghanistan in the 1980s. The technology of the Soviets was less advanced, but they and their Afghan Government allies were also based in the main towns with little control over the villages where most Afghans lived. They also set up outposts, or *zastavas*, along the roads to try to protect their supply convoys. They too faced an insurgency whose main appeal to local people was its promise to expel foreigners and their infidel troops from the country. When I reread my dispatches from those trips, I am struck by the Soviet ghosts that haunt ISAF today.

How was it the Americans did not think more carefully before they plunged into war in Afghanistan? Had they really forgotten what had happened little more than a decade earlier when the Russians learned they could never beat a local insurgency? The Americans were deeply involved in helping that insurgency so they should have foreseen the problem.

Ten years after George W. Bush launched Operation Enduring Freedom, as he billed his attack on Afghanistan, the war has never been as intense as it is today. The Taliban were forced out of power within two months of the start of the American military campaign but they were not defeated in a major battle on the ground. They withdrew from Kabul, the capital and largest city, and Kandahar, the second largest city, to escape U.S. bombing and missile strikes. Within two years the Taliban, who mainly come from Afghanistan's biggest ethnic group, the Pashtun, were able to revive and regroup in the southern part of the country, the traditional homeland of the Pashtun. The fighting has intensified every year since then. The year 2010 was the bloodiest so far. Some 711 foreign troops died, including 499 Americans and 103 British—199 more than the year before. The estimated number of IEDs that were planted climbed to 14,661, a rise of 62 percent. They killed 268 U.S. troops in 2010, about as many as in the three previous years combined.

With more than 2,770 civilians killed, the year 2010 was also the deadliest for ordinary Afghans since the U.S.-led invasion began. Although Taliban and other insurgents were responsible for more than 60 percent of the civilian deaths, those caused by U.S. and other coalition forces have more political resonance, forcing President Hamid Karzai to express great anger whenever a wedding party or other large group of Afghans is bombed by unmanned drones or aircraft. About 730,000 Afghans fled their homes between 2006 and 2010, mostly due to military operations by foreign forces, according to the Oslo-based Internal Displacement Monitoring Center (IDMC), an affiliate of the Norwegian Refugee Council.

As of July 2011, ten years of war in Afghanistan have taken the lives of 1,556 U.S. troops. The war costs the U.S. taxpayer more than

$100 billion a year—$1 million per soldier per year—and yet the Taliban have a presence in more provinces than they did in 2009. Starting in the south and the southeast in 2003, they have moved up to the center and since 2009 have conducted military operations in parts of the north and west which only have small Pashtun populations. In Baghlan, a province in northern Afghanistan where security deteriorated in 2010, Munshi Abdul Majid, the provincial governor, told reporters in January 2011, "I can tell you this very clearly: fifty percent of the people who are working with the Afghan government, their hearts are with the Taliban." Two United Nations maps, one showing the security situation in March and the other in October 2010, highlighted a decline in sixteen districts in nine provinces in the north and west. Only two districts previously deemed high-risk—one in Kunduz in the north and another in Herat in the west—received a safer rating.

The Pentagon's annual report to Congress for 2010, "Progress Toward Security and Stability in Afghanistan," conceded that the Taliban had "a ready supply of recruits, drawn from the frustrated population where insurgents exploit poverty, tribal friction, and lack of governance to grow their ranks." Their numbers were estimated to have grown to 35,000 fighters. It also noted that the Taliban's "operational reach are qualitatively and geographically expanding." Their tactics and procedures for conducting attacks were increasing in sophistication. On the political front, the shadow governments that the Taliban had appointed in several provinces were having an increasing effect in undermining the authority of President Hamid Karzai's government.

The Pentagon report frequently dropped into bureaucratese, saying that "insurgents continue to leverage their religious, ethnic, and tribal affinities with local Afghans for recruitment, resources, and freedom of movement." In plain English this means that "the Taliban are Afghans and Muslims and get support for that reason." Although joblessness and poverty may be motives for people to join the Taliban, the hard truth is that most are also, or even primarily, motivated by patriotism. They resent being occupied by foreign troops. A poll conducted in July 2010 in Helmand and Kandahar found that 68 percent rejected the claim that ISAF was protecting local people. As many as 74 percent thought it was wrong to collaborate with foreign forces.

In spite of extensive media coverage of Afghanistan, the ISAF propaganda machine's constant stream of optimistic statements is effective in hiding the true state of the war, in particular the limits on U.S. and British movement in southern Afghanistan. In Helmand around 150 U.S. and British advisers form what is called the Provincial Reconstruction Team (PRT). Almost every Afghan province has a PRT. Hunched over computers in their fortress of camouflaged watchtowers, tents and air-conditioned trailers, they supervise the aid and development arm of the U.S.-led counterinsurgency program. Within Lashkar Gah, their travel is confined to armed convoys of the kind that took us to the police shooting range. Trips to any of Helmand's district centers is by helicopter only. Advisers who work on logistics, finance and administration never leave the fortified garrison.

Freight convoys between Afghanistan's provinces go by road and are mainly subcontracted to private companies that charge heavily for security in addition to the transportation costs. The fact that this often means they pay money to local tribal leaders who are linked to the Taliban is well documented.

PRT officials and NATO military spokesmen deliberately use vague phrases to define success in Helmand and Kandahar. The Afghan Government has "extended its reach" or "can now exert influence" or "has a presence" in this or that new district. Every press release makes the same point. The unspoken assumptions are that the coalition is playing a zero-sum game, and territory won from the Taliban is territory denied to them. But this is asymmetric warfare, and those Taliban—the majority—who are local farmers usually disperse before major operations begin. They pursue the struggle by other means, planting IEDs and firing sniper rifles from ambush positions, or intimidating government officials with assassinations and night letters delivered to people's doors warning them not to work with foreigners. The mujahedin used the same tactic when Soviet troops occupied Helmand.

Reporting from Helmand and Kandahar is difficult. Independent travel to the province is seriously dangerous. A quick in-and-out trip within a day accompanied by a local fixer can be risked, but an overnight stay in a hotel or guesthouse will attract immediate attention and may lead to kidnap and murder. Being embedded with American or British troops offers the only means of staying for some days or weeks, but the vantage point is inevitably limited, and contact with independent Afghans to assess their opinions is virtually impossible.

Taking shelter with the British is particularly challenging. I was invited by the British Department for International Development (DFID), but everything I wrote had to be submitted to the Ministry of Defence and cleared for publication. Britain claims to be bringing good governance to the people of Afghanistan, and this includes respect for press freedom. But before journalists can be embedded with the British in Helmand, they must agree to a complicated set of procedures. All text, audio and pictures have to be submitted for approval before publication. A soldier must sit in on reporters' interviews. No wonder most American journalists decline to report on the British. The U.S. Government makes no such demands of the embedded press. But other pressures inhibit all journalists, including Americans. Reporting that the Pentagon considers too critical is likely to mean an end to future embeds.

The U.S. counterinsurgency strategy of "clear, hold, build, and transfer to the Afghans" aims to bring services to ordinary people within weeks, if not days, of the military's advances. Before troops go into an area, the plan is to have a "district delivery package" geared up and ready to follow. This consists of basic services, good governance and rule of law. Install a district governor and key officials, set up a community council, offer cash-for-work programs, open health clinics and schools, appoint officials to handle local disputes and put police, judges and prosecutors in place to deal with crime.

Eleven of Helmand's fourteen districts had a governor and some officials at work in October 2010, when I was there, compared to only five districts two years earlier. Schools had reopened with almost 80,000 children enrolled, virtually double the number of 2007. Police were being trained at the rate of 150 new recruits every month. ISAF forces were trying to pave the way for economic development and the resumption of trade. They were removing IEDs from the main roads, mounting regular patrols and making it possible for bazaars to reopen and commerce to revive. DFID and the U.S. Agency for International Development (USAID) were funding a program that gives wheat seed to farmers to replace opium-poppy production. Loans were going to small businesses.

The downside was that the Taliban were constantly devising new ways to undermine any ISAF sense of success. The latest resistance pinprick was the stoning of Afghan Government and foreign vehicles, as I discovered when I sat in on an hour-long Pashtu for Beginnners class for British troops at one FOB. Offering language tips was an intelligent move, and attendance was impressive. On a blisteringly hot afternoon, almost 15 young men turned up, perhaps aided by the fact that their instructor, a fellow soldier in combat fatigues, was an attractive blonde. After we had rehearsed several standard phrases—"How are you?", "I'm not an enemy," "I'm a British soldier"—a sergeant asked her, "What's the Pashtu for 'Stop throwing stones at us'?"

We had a starker illustration of the point on a visit to a girls' high school in Lashkar Gah. The school also teaches boys up to the age of twelve. Dozens of boys were racing around as our armored convoy entered the dusty compound and parked in the shade of the playground's only tree, close to a sign saying that USAID had helped to rebuild the school. The PRT considered the school a success story. Enrollment was up sharply, and teachers had to operate in three shifts so that more children could attend for a few hours each day. Some female pupils were in their twenties, having missed out during Taliban rule, the deputy headmistress told me. Twenty minutes into my interview with her, one of our security guards came in and warned us that we might have to leave soon. Boys were starting to stone the expensive LandCruisers and had already caused hundreds of dollars of damage.

The deputy headmistress and several other women teachers who were listening with interest to the interview showed no sign of shock or alarm. The guard left but none of the school staff went outside to stop the attack or warn the boys. We resumed the interview, but after five minutes the guard came back and ordered us to don our helmets. He instructed us to run to the cars, which they had managed to move closer to the building. As we prepared to retreat, a teacher told me the children also stoned Afghan Government cars when officials visited. Her worry appeared to be that we might think the kids were violating the rules of Pashtun hospitality and only targeting foreign guests. As our convoy moved off through the playground, the boys carried on stoning. We felt like Gulliver among the Lilliputians, with our dignity in tatters and defenseless against a swarm of little people.

Back at the PRT fortress, officials downplayed the incident, calling it a onetime piece of mindless delinquency. Our soldier minder confessed he had thrown stones at cars when he was a kid in England. After further inquiries we discovered that the widespread scale of the stoning was new. It had the hallmarks of being organized, presumably by the Taliban, a PRT source told us. Like many officials we met, he did not wish to be quoted by name.

To beam propaganda messages to local people, the Americans and British have set up radio stations in several Helmand bases. Staffed by carefully vetted Afghans, the stations never reveal they are located on a coalition base for fear of losing credibility. A radio producer said that among the new messages he was asked to broadcast was one urging local people not to let their children help the Taliban.

Most Helmandis live in the province's fertile central strip along the Helmand river and the adjacent irrigation canals, which survive from an earlier period of peacetime aid, provided by the Eisenhower administration. Locals have long called the strip the green zone because of the contrast with the khaki desert. The name's aptness strikes all visitors as they suddenly find themselves above productive land after flying over huge expanses of parched earth where camel-trains walk and nomads plant their tents. For Americans and British the name is a reminder of Baghdad's green zone, where many of them did earlier service as diplomats or contractors. That zone's green was code for relative safety, but the hallmarks of foreign officials' lives in both Helmand and Baghdad are the same: isolation from local people other than the political elite, and constant fear.

Talking to Helmandis in the green zone's villages is as difficult for embedded journalists as it is for officials and U.S. troops. But we asked to meet with Afghan nongovernmental organizations (NGOs), in spite of knowing that conversation would be limited while a soldier sat beside us. The request ran into problems. "They won't come to the PRT and they don't want to have vehicles from the PRT coming to their offices," we were told. The PRT's Afghan interpreters, all of whom are men, have a similar fear of being linked to the occupation. They mainly come from Kabul and sleep in the Lashkar Gah compound, not daring to go into town off duty in case of reprisals. On the job some wear baseball caps and scarves around their faces to avoid identification. One reason that the PRT is so full of U.S. and British advisers is that it is hard to recruit qualified Afghan engineers and other professionals to supervise projects. In spite of high salaries, they are too scared to come.

In the rest of Helmand beyond Lashkar Gah, the lack of security is even greater. Afghan Government offices are located in heavily guarded compounds where for safety reasons officials often live as well as work. A British military minder took me from Lashkar Gah to Nad

Ali, a district center considered a model for other centers to follow as the Americans and British capture districts from the Taliban. Here too safety precautions were massive. Although Nad Ali is only nine miles from Lashkar Gah, travel was by helicopter. Kicking up clouds of dust, we landed beside a compound of ancient mud-brick walls. Until the British arrived, it was used as the town's livestock market. Now it is known as FOB Shawqat. Its crumbling walls are encased within a new fortress of Hesco barriers, steel freight containers, large communal tents and camouflaged watchtowers.

Two weeks before our visit, the Taliban had launched a two-hour attack on one of the watchtowers. The daily security advice note posted outside the meal tent warned troops that the risks of direct fire and suicide attacks on Shawqat were substantial. Under heavy guard, we were allowed to walk fifty yards from the base to watch the district governor cut the ribbon to open a roofed area of open space meant to house a new bazaar. When we went to his office later, two hundred yards away, it was in armored vehicles. Security officials also insisted vehicles were necessary to travel a short distance to the old bazaar, where I was allowed to dismount briefly to conduct stilted interviews with shopkeepers while armed guards stood by.

One of Helmand's toughest areas is Sangin, in the north. Since arriving there in October 2010, U.S. Marines have patrolled more aggressively than the British, who had been in the province since 2006. According to a U.S. diplomatic cable released by WikiLeaks in 2010, Helmand's governor, Gulab Mangal, felt the change of tactics was essential. Accompanied by U.S. advisers, he visited Sangin in January 2009, when it was still in the British area of operations. He was shocked to discover that he was only allowed about 200 yards beyond the FOB. British officers warned him not even to walk through the bazaar. Infuriated, he told British officials, "Stop calling it the Sangin District and start calling it the Sangin Base. All you have done here is build a military camp next to the city. I asked you people to do reconstruction and yet the District Governor remains in the FOB and how can you expect a city to recover if the bazaar is not in the security zone?"

A few days later, Mangal played a role in inspiring new U.S. tactics. The U.S. vice president–elect, Joe Biden, was visiting Afghanistan with senior officers shortly before his and Barack Obama's inauguration. Mangal told the Americans he was disappointed with the British. The governor's anger and similar stories of inadequate performance by British troops helped to convince the Obama administration to mount its first surge of an extra 17,000 U.S. combat troops in February 2009.

Responding to Governor Mangal's appeals for more energetic military activity in Sangin, the Americans used air strikes and mortars to dislodge the Taliban from their bunkers and compounds. The Taliban replied by spreading allegations that U.S. Marines were killing scores of civilians. The marines broadcast denials from the radio station in their base, but they commanded less credibility than the Taliban's accusations. "They will send people down to the bazaar to say, 'Have you heard what's going on in X, Y, Z places? It's terrible'," said Phil Weatherill, a British adviser in Sangin. "It just needs one flicker and it will spread like wildfire."

The marines tried to sway public opinion in Sangin by completing new development projects. But it soon became clear that better roads and new flood walls along the Helmand river would not change attitudes if locals believed the marines were a source of death and destruction. "The people say we don't need any help, just stop injuring and killing our civilians," said Mira Jan Aka, a village elder who along with other complainants met the marines. Assuming the elders had been coached by the Taliban, the marines dismissed their statements. Mullah Abdul Wali, a landowner from Sangin who fled with his family to Lashkar Gah, told reporters aggressive attacks by the marines had killed dozens of civilians. "The foreign troops should leave Sangin," he insisted. "They are bringing disaster to the area."

Marines' foot patrols met fierce resistance. The British had found Sangin the most lethal district in Helmand. In four years, 106 soldiers lost their lives, making it the most dangerous place in the whole of Afghanistan. In the first three months after taking over from the British, the marine battalion in Sangin lost more than 20 percent of its combat power through death and injury. Twenty-seven had died and more than 140 had been injured.

A BBC reporter wondered whether the marines had thought their strategy through. One foot patrol route, code-named Pharmacy Road, had been cleared of IEDs by the British eighteen months earlier. They had then established a patrol base so as to watch the area, a maze of alleys and high walls called Wishtan. When the Americans took over, they abandoned Wishtan, thinking that too many bases would spread them too thin. Weeks later they decided that giving up Wishtan was a mistake. So they refurbished the old base. Then to make it more secure without so many foot patrols, they used armored bulldozers to flatten walls and compounds on either side of Pharmacy Road without seeking permission from local people. One of the buildings they demolished was a mosque across the road from the base. After anxious pleading the two men who said they owned it were allowed to remove some copies of the Qur'an, a gas heater and a rug before the building was reduced to rubble.

The marines' commanding officer, Captain Matt Peterson, was asked if this tactic risked pushing the locals into the arms of the Taliban. "Short term there is a sacrifice of convenience to an extreme degree, and that's not something that's lost on us. But I think what people understand is that in order to increase security on that route and in order to prevent the enemy from putting any IEDs there, these types of drastic steps are necessary." According to the BBC reporter, a local mullah disagreed. "Can democracy be brought by a cannon?" he asked. "Is that what the meaning of democracy is in the world? We don't want this democracy. We don't want this law of the infidel, we want the rule of Islam."

In February 2010, U.S. troops in Helmand mounted Operation Mushtarak, a large-scale offensive in the district of Marjah a few miles west of Lashkar Gah. U.S. troop strength in the province had just increased as part of Obama's decision in December 2009 to send 33,000 more troops to Afghanistan, his second surge. Arriving in waves of helicopters, marines raced to set up a series of new patrol bases. In line with their usual tactics, the Taliban offered minimal resistance, having disappeared well in advance. The major losers were the estimated 25,000 civilians who fled to Lashkar Gah and other towns to avoid being caught in crossfire. Before the offensive, U.S. spokespersons built up Marjah's importance, describing it as a key strategic center. They trumpeted their success in capturing it and making it possible for a district governor and other officials to start work. But civilian advisers who took part in opening schools after the raid described the place as a series of isolated farms, "like rural Michigan," according to one I spoke with, or "not much more than a crossroads," as another put it. Neither wanted his name used.

A few months later, reporters found security in Marjah was patchy. Hit-and-run attacks on U.S. bases occurred almost daily. The Taliban threatened anyone associated with the government. Foreign officials lived in the fortified district center and rarely went out. "There's no safe location in Marjah where you can say, one hundred percent, I'm not going to get shot at," said Lieutenant Colonel Kyle Ellison, commander of the Second Battalion, Sixth Marine Regiment. A year after Operation Mushtarak, ISAF claimed that "there has been real progress in Marjah. Today, Marjah, now a distinct district, has a governor, schools, health clinics and half a dozen markets that continue to grow." What ISAF did not say was that the district governor is based in Lashkar Gah and travels to his work in a convoy with six U.S. mine-resistant vehicles or Afghan police vehicles armed with mounted machine guns. The district prosecutor is believed to have obtained clearance from the Taliban before taking up his appointment.

Similar complexities prevail in Kandahar, where U.S. forces mounted a huge operation in the summer of 2010. Once again the Taliban melted away before marines swept through districts to the south and west of the city, setting up small bases. The Taliban replied by stepping up their intimidation of local officials. Kandahar's deputy mayor was assassinated, and when he was replaced, his successor was promptly murdered too. Taliban fighters on motorbikes were said to swarm roads in the heart of the city at night, checking motorists' documents and warning them against collaborating with the government. As a result, some two-thirds of the 119 budgeted government jobs in the city remained unfilled, as municipal workers were assassinated or quit despite generous U.S.-funded salaries. "Nobody wants to work with me—they're all afraid," Kandahar's Mayor Hamid Haidari told reporters. "Everyone wants to stay alive." On April 15, 2011, General Khan Mohammad Mujahid, Kandahar's police chief, was killed in the main police compound when a man, dressed in police uniform, approached him and detonated himself. The general's murder came four days after he had told reporters, "I am hopeful that we will have a safe and secure environment in our city. We have destroyed and eradicated [the insurgents'] safe havens, so they don't have bases to plan their attacks and operations."

This floundering war is now in its eleventh year with no clear end in sight. The United States has set December 2014 as a target date for handing all security work to Afghan troops and police, but there is no guarantee that the date will not slip. In Iraq, when Barack Obama took office, he inherited a "status of forces agreement," which the Bush administration had signed with the government of Iraq. This regulated what U.S. troops could and could not do. In Afghanistan, by contrast, U.S. forces are unconstrained by any legal contract with the government in Kabul. Unlike Iraq, where the Iraqi Government managed to negotiate an exit date for all U.S. forces, U.S. forces in Afghanistan can stay as long as the U.S. president decides. Obama campaigned on a pledge to end the war in Iraq but repeats Bush's claim that the war in Afghanistan is one of necessity, not choice.

In June 2011 Obama announced that the 33,000 extra troops he had ordered to Afghanistan in his second surge in December 2009 would be withdrawn by the end of September 2012. This would still leave more American troops in the country than when he became president. The target of further withdrawals by December 2014 only covered U.S. combat troops, and Obama was seeking to persuade the Afghan Government to accept a "strategic partnership agreement" for tens of thousands of U.S. troops, described as trainers, advisers and logistics experts, to remain in Afghanistan indefinitely after 2014.

How have we come to this? Why is it that a president who inherited a war in Afghanistan that most members of his party had stopped supporting by the time of his inauguration doubled the number of American troops there within his first two years of office? How has he allowed it to become the longest war in U.S. history and kept open the option that U.S. troops might still be in harm's way in Afghanistan in 2017 at the end of his second White House term, for which he is vigorously campaigning?

Obama's war is uncomfortably similar to the one the Russians fought in the 1980s. At its heart it is a long-running civil war among Afghans into which foreigners have unwisely intervened. In the 1980s the backdrop to the internal Afghan struggle was the ideological contest for global influence between the West and the Soviet Union. Each side supported and armed local Afghan proxies. Thirty years later the civil war continues but the international context has changed. Today the American goal, as set by George W. Bush and continued by Obama, is to destroy al Qaeda and other terrorist groups while maintaining a capacity to project U.S. military power into a region that borders a still-powerful Russia and a China that is emerging as a major global player. But the real contest in Afghanistan is among Afghans—between forces of modernization and those of tradition or, as the Soviets put it, of counterrevolution, as I discuss in more detail in Chapter Two.

Both then and now, non-Muslim foreigners prop up a government in Kabul as it tries to create a state that can command national loyalty, exert control over its territory, collect taxes and bring development to some of the world's poorest and most conservative people. Both then and now the Kabul modernizers' endeavor runs into armed resistance. Both then and now the insurgents have the safe haven of the lawless tribal areas of northwest Pakistan to escape to and emerge from as well as a government in Islamabad that aids them, openly or secretly.

With its large component of private-sector security contractors and aid consultants, today's contingent of foreign civilians in Afghanistan is more varied than the narrow corps of Soviet diplomats and government officials in the 1980s. But a similar mixture of motives can be found. There are gleam-in-the-eye idealists who are shocked by Afghanistan's backwardness and take on a personal mission to change it, pragmatists who do what they can with no great conviction that significant improvement is possible and careerists and adventurers with varying degrees of greed and cynicism who are attracted by the high pay and hardship allowances and mainly seek to survive until their lucrative contracts end.

Mikhail Gorbachev also found himself saddled with an unpopular war in Afghanistan when he became the Soviet Union's leader in March 1985, but, unlike Barack Obama, he immediately told his senior Soviet colleagues he wanted to end it. Beyond the Kremlin walls his policy shift was divulged only to Babrak Karmal, the Afghan leader, and in a society without a free press it was easy to keep the decision secret. Gorbachev went public a year later, though it took a further three years to complete the withdrawal. When the last Soviet infantryman finally left Afghanistan, in February 1989, nine years and eight weeks had elapsed since the day the invasion began. The U.S. war in Afghanistan has gone beyond that time span, and the contingent of around 142,000 foreign troops far exceeds the maximum of 118,000 that the Soviets ever had there. In early 2011 the United States had 90,000 troops attached to ISAF and another 10,000 operating independently in eastern Afghanistan in the hunt for al Qaeda.

Gorbachev's decision to withdraw was in some ways easier to reach than a comparable step would be for Obama. The Soviet leader's predecessors had sent troops to Afghanistan to keep an allied socialist party in power and forestall the risk of the country becoming a U.S. ally and a site for hostile U.S. bases on the Soviet Union's southern flank. By the late 1980s, when the Kremlin announced its withdrawal timetable, the context had changed dramatically. Gorbachev wanted to make peace with Washington, curb the superpower arms race and end the Cold War. Afghanistan had lost its strategic significance. The nature of its government was no longer of interest to Moscow. All that the Kremlin wanted was to pull out with dignity.

Initially, the Soviets thought this could best be done if Afghanistan had a coalition government in which the socialists and the mujahedin, as the resistance groups called themselves, shared power, perhaps under the aegis of the former king. When this proved impossible and the mujahedin remained intransigent, with the backing of Washington and Pakistan, Gorbachev resolved to pull his troops out regardless.

Bush's Afghan legacy to Obama contained two wars: one against al Qaeda, the other against the Taliban. The two movements' leaders had come together briefly in the late 1990s, but since 9/11, al Qaeda had fragmented into separate franchises with militants and training arrangements in Pakistan, Somalia, Yemen and other countries. Al Qaeda did not need Afghanistan. They did not need a single headquarters or camps in one particular country. They were dispersed and decentralized. None of the nineteen men who mounted the quadruple hijacking on 9/11 were Afghans (fifteen were from Saudi Arabia), and they had trained in Germany and the United States. Long before Obama took office most counterterrorist experts were sure Osama bin

Laden, al Qaeda's founder, had left Afghanistan and moved to Pakistan. In the weeks following the U.S. attack, which began on October 7, 2001, the Americans had tried to capture bin Laden in the Tora Bora mountain caves in eastern Afghanistan, but they sent barely a hundred special forces alongside various anti-Taliban militias. In December they seized the cave complex, but by then bin Laden had escaped.

The experts assumed the al Qaeda leader had moved to south Waziristan or one of the other wild, semi-autonomous tribal regions of northwest Pakistan. They did not realize that around 2005 he had moved on to a comfortable compound in Abbottabad, a quiet town near the Pakistani capital. Wherever bin Laden was in Pakistan, his departure from Afghanistan had removed the original rationale for the war there. However much of an icon he was for his followers, by early 2002 he had become an isolated figure who relied for his communications on a cumbersome premodern system of couriers and had little connection to any operational decision making. In April 2011, General David Petraeus said al Qaeda numbers in Afghanistan were "generally assessed at less than 100 or so." A month later, bin Laden's killing in Pakistan by a team of U.S. Navy SEALs offered a dramatic opportunity for reexamining the reasons for maintaining a huge U.S. troop presence in Afghanistan.

At times Obama seemed to recognize that Afghanistan was not strategically significant in the fight against al Qaeda. On March 27, 2009, in his first speech on the region's issues as president, he said, "Multiple intelligence estimates have warned that al Qaeda is actively planning attacks on the US homeland from its safe-haven in Pakistan." He spent more time in the speech talking about Pakistan than Afghanistan.

This was Obama's chance to de-escalate the rhetoric on the Taliban, and make it clear to the American people that the Taliban had much narrower goals than al Qaeda. They were not global jihadis. They had no agenda beyond Afghanistan's borders. Yet when he turned to Afghanistan's internal politics in the March 2009 speech, Obama continued the language of the Bush administration. The Taliban "must be met with force, and they must be defeated," he declared, thereby trapping himself in a policy which it would be hard to reverse.

As a candidate for the presidency, Obama had campaigned on sending more troops to Afghanistan, arguing that Bush's attack on Iraq had diverted military resources from the more important struggle. In February 2009, within weeks of his inauguration, the White House announced that 17,000 extra U.S. troops would be deployed there. In his March 2009 speech Obama said a further 4,000 would go there to train the Afghan army. The escalation contrasted sharply with Gorbachev's first pronouncements on withdrawing from the Soviet war in Afghanistan.

In his book *Obama's Wars,* Bob Woodward reveals the discussions on Afghanistan that went on inside the administration throughout 2009. Although they show a president who was cautious about the U.S. military's demands, he accepted their premise that extra troops were needed. General David McKiernan, the senior U.S. commander in Afghanistan, had put in a request for an extra 30,000 troops in the final weeks of the Bush presidency. General David Petraeus, the head of U.S. Central Command, approved the plan. When the request was put to the new president in February 2009, Richard Holbrooke, Obama's special envoy for Afghanistan and Pakistan who had worked for the State Department during the Vietnam War, pointed out that Lyndon Johnson had faced similar requests from his military commanders for troop surges and given in to them, with disastrous consequences. "Ghosts," Obama whispered. In spite of that reminder, the new president agreed to let the military have more troops, though only 17,000 and not the 30,000 McKiernan wanted. He accepted their argument that without an increase the Afghan presidential elections planned for August 2009 might be too insecure to go ahead.

After August, however, there were more requests for extra troops. This time Obama took longer to review his strategy before giving the military another 30,000 in December 2009. As the Woodward account makes clear, the framework of the administration's discussions continued to be narrow and only consisted of security proposals. No ideas were offered by Obama's National Security Council advisers, the State Department or the intelligence agencies for ending the war by negotiation with the Taliban and other resistance groups or by encouraging Afghans to end their civil war through a political agreement on power-sharing. The existing strategy of treating the Taliban as umbilically linked with al Qaeda and seeking to defeat them was maintained without challenge. Plans for withdrawing U.S. troops remained dependent, as they had been under Bush, on training Afghan forces to be able to replace the Americans to do the same job. Afghans would take over U.S. garrisons against the Taliban, but war would continue.

A striking revelation in Woodward's account was the virtual unanimity of the U.S. top brass in wanting more troops. Only General Karl Eikenberry, the former U.S. commander in Afghanistan who had become the ambassador in Kabul, opposed a troop surge. The contrast with the Soviets is remarkable. Not one of the field commanders nor the defense and security ministers who made fact-finding trips to Afghanistan asked Gorbachev for an increase in the number of Soviet troops. On the contrary, several senior military figures told him the war could not be won and political negotiations were the only way to leave with honor. Ironically, the Soviet official who was most hesitant to withdraw troops was a civilian. As noted in Chapter Three, Eduard Shevardnadze, the foreign minister, was concerned that the Soviet Union's international image would suffer if it appeared to be abandoning its friends.

Perhaps the most remarkable feature of the White House arguments over Afghan policy is the power of the men in uniform not only to dominate the debate but to get their way on most points. Compared to the Kremlin meetings on Afghanistan in the 1980s, the difference is stunning. One might have thought that in a closed society where top politicians, let alone ordinary citizens, are deprived of alternative sources of information, it would be easier than it is in a democracy for generals to control discussions on military issues with their political masters. In practice, it turns out that the military face less challenge from politicians in the U.S. system, where right-wing radio and TV stations exert a dominant influence, the arms industry is a major job provider and all but a handful of politicians succumb to pressure to look strong on defense.

The international context of the Soviet and American wars in Afghanistan also contains ironies. The Soviet invasion was condemned by almost every United Nations member state. Throughout the nine years of its intervention, the Kremlin remained isolated. It did not even ask its Warsaw Pact allies to take part, no doubt realizing that they would be far from enthusiastic or useful. The war was unpopular enough among the Soviet population.

The war's lack of support became one of the main factors that convinced Gorbachev to withdraw. Muslim countries as well as many others in the Third World would not accept that Moscow had progressive global intentions as long as it was embroiled in Afghanistan. This clearly undermined the Kremlin's position in the superpower rivalry of the Cold War. By contrast, the United States has UN backing for its war in Afghanistan and has enlisted some forty-seven countries to join its coalition through appeals to their loyalty and offers of aid. Very few governments dare to break ranks, even though the war is unpopular in almost all the countries that supply troops or train the Afghan police. Even when governments do end their commitment of troops, as Canada and the Netherlands have done, they decline to criticize the United States openly or declare, like the child and the unclothed emperor, that the war cannot be won.

A key problem that faced the Russians was that the Afghan Government they invaded the country to defend was perceived by conservative rural Afghans as radical, un-Islamic and brutal. In the cities its reputation was considerably better, which is partly why it survived long after Moscow withdrew its troops. But hearts and minds in the Afghan countryside could never be won by the Russians thanks to their own military tactics and their Afghan socialist allies' image as traitors and nonbelievers.

The United States has a similar problem since it is perceived as having installed Hamid Karzai. In spite of two elections, he is considered by most Afghans to be America's man. Although he is a Pashtun, his reputation in Pashtun areas is further sullied by his record of appointing massively corrupt officials. The Tajiks, who form Afghanistan's second largest ethnic group, have always been uneasy about Karzai, and many voted for the former foreign minister, Abdullah Abdullah, a fellow Tajik, who ran against Karzai in the August 2009 election.

Regularly repeated statements by NATO officials that hardly any Afghan remembers Taliban rule as positive may impress people in the United States and Britain. It is less convincing in Helmand and Kandahar, where many people feel security was better under the Taliban, commerce flourished and officials were more honest, even if they delivered fewer services than are available today.

There are many foreign myths about Afghanistan. Throughout this book, we will examine thirteen in detail. It is entirely appropriate that the first centers on the Taliban.

The key requirement in any war is "Know your enemy." Getting that basic point wrong leads to mistake after mistake.

MYTH NUMBER ONE:
The Taliban have little popular support.

To fill the knowledge gap caused by the lack of contact British officials in Helmand had with Afghans, Britain's Department for International Development commissioned an Afghan NGO to conduct opinion surveys on how people compared the Taliban to the Afghan government. The results, published in 2010, were strikingly unfavorable to the coalition. They suggested that NATO's long campaign to demonize the Taliban was no more effective than the Soviet effort to demonize their opponents, the mujahedin, had been in the 1980s.

One DFID-sponsored survey reported on Helmandis' attitudes to the province's mix of justice systems. When disputes arise, the first port of call is the committee of village elders and mullahs. If they fail to solve them, cases go to district governors or in Taliban areas to local commanders. According to the survey, many people were satisfied with the security and justice that the Taliban provide. More than half the male respondents called them "completely trustworthy and fair." The Taliban took money through taxes on farm crops, road tolls and *zakat* (donations for the poor), but people said the important thing was that they did not demand bribes.

Women respondents were more critical, with only a quarter saying they trusted the Taliban. But even this low figure contrasted with the minimal faith that both sexes had in the government justice system because of the bribery and favoritism that went with it. Only 7 percent of men and women said they trusted it. At the national level they felt the government discriminated against Pashtuns, the main ethnic group in southern and eastern Afghanistan, and in favor of northern Tajiks and Uzbeks. The Taliban, like most Helmandis, are mainly Pashtun. According to the survey report, "Most ordinary people associate the government with practices and behaviors they dislike: the inability to provide security, dependence on foreign military, eradication of a basic livelihood crop (poppy), and as having a history of partisanship (the perceived preferential treatment of Northerners)."

DFID officials had the unfavorable survey results taken off the Web soon after they were first published, but members of the PRT appeared to agree with the findings. "Justice is an area where the Taliban are able to compete in providing fast, cheap, cost-effective and accessible punishment for serious criminal offenses," one British official in Lashkar Gah told me.

Sherard Cowper-Coles, Britain's special representative for Afghanistan and Pakistan in 2009 and 2010, put it bluntly shortly after leaving government service and taking a job in the private sector. Speaking of the Taliban, he told a British parliamentary select committee in November 2010, "They are violent. They are unpleasant. But, in my view, for many southern Pashtuns they represent a less bad alternative—a fairer, more predictable alternative than a corrupt and predatory Government."

When he took office, President Obama stepped up U.S. aid and development as part of COIN, the military's counterinsurgency strategy. Since January 2009, the number of U.S. civilians on the ground in Afghanistan has tripled to more than a thousand. But can the aid program make a difference by giving the Afghan Government legitimacy and weakening the Taliban?

First of all, it must be said that aid has come very late in Helmand. According to Nick Abbott, the British official who headed DFID's Afghanistan team, "The key moment was the summer of 2008 with the decision to develop the districts outside Lashkar Gah." Why wasn't this done in the spring of 2002 immediately after the Taliban were toppled? Remember Bush and British Prime Minister Tony Blair's promise that the West would not walk away from Afghanistan? In the rush to topple Saddam Hussein in Iraq, they promptly did.

This walking away by Bush and Blair allowed the Taliban to recover and reemerge with the argument that, like the Soviets before them, the latest set of foreign occupiers had brought no benefit to ordinary people in the Pashtun heartlands. The Taliban could also argue that like the mujahedin when they took power in the 1990s after the Soviets had gone, the new government of Hamid Karzai was betraying Islam by its nepotism and corruption.

Second, the aid program is proceeding at a snail's pace and will take years to deliver comprehensive results. Schools and health clinics can be built and staffed relatively quickly, but giving people justice, honest police and officials who observe the rule of law—the issues on which the Taliban are seen as strong —will need much more time.

Third comes the question of the high cost of delivering aid in a war zone, given the massive danger facing foreigners who provide and try to monitor it. Without the vast expense that goes to building and maintaining Western fortresses in southern Afghanistan and flying staff between them, the same amount of money would go much further in needy developing countries that are at peace. Aid could return to Afghanistan once Afghans have settled their conflicts. Alternatively, instead of sending 70 percent of their Afghan aid money to Helmand and Kandahar, the Americans and British could send most of it to more peaceful provinces. Yet Washington and London are going in the opposite direction by planning to increase their spending in Afghanistan's two most dangerous places.

Fourth, aid as COIN endangers the work—and lives—of independent NGOs by linking them with foreign forces in Afghan minds and turning them into insurgents' targets, a point frequently made by Afghan NGOs as well as international charities like Oxfam and Doctors Without Borders. As a result, while foreign government aid goes up, charitable aid diminishes.

There were 225 aid workers killed, kidnapped or injured in violent attacks in 2010, compared to 85 in 2002. The increase results in part from the higher number of them operating in violent places. But there is also an increase in apparently politically motivated attacks, rising from 29 percent of the total number of attacks where motives could be determined in 2003, to 49 percent in 2008.

Five Doctors Without Borders staff were executed in northwest Afghanistan in July 2004, but, although the Taliban quickly claimed responsibility, senior officials from Doctors Without Borders said they felt that this was an opportunistic statement designed to warn foreign aid workers and that others were behind the murders. The organization repeatedly urged the Afghan Government to make a serious hunt for the killers.

Since mid-2008, the risks for NGOs have lessened. Doctors Without Borders returned to Helmand in 2009 after getting written commitments to respect its neutrality from NATO, the Afghan Government and the Taliban high command. Laurent Saillard, director of the Agency Coordinating Body for Afghan Relief, an umbrella organization of 106 foreign and local NGOs, reported in 2010 that the Taliban had become more careful in targeting NGOs. "It's a very thin line to walk—you're taking money from countries with a very clear political agenda, and yet pretending to be impartial and neutral," he said. "But it's feasible because the Taliban have learned to be pragmatic. If a project is supported by the community, they let the NGO keep working as long as it doesn't conduct any political activity." The Taliban now say they make a clear distinction between independent NGOs and those who are coalition partners in delivering aid. They view the latter as legitimate military targets.

Fifth, does aid really enhance the legitimacy of Afghan Government representatives in Helmand? Under COIN, what PRT officials call "government-in-a-box" is supposed to drop in as soon as ISAF floods an area with troops and pushes the Taliban underground. The difficulty is that ISAF does not choose the officials who arrive to fly the government flag, since the Karzai regime makes the appointments and is supposed to be sovereign.

Much of the American and British effort in Helmand in 2009 and 2010 went to preventing a shady former provincial governor, Sher Mohammed Akhundzada, and a shady former police chief, Abdul Rahman Jan, from continuing to exert influence locally. They had been appointed by Karzai after the Taliban withdrew. U.S. diplomatic cables released by WikiLeaks in November 2010 show that the British persuaded Karzai to remove them in 2005 on suspicion of corruption. The British were furious when a delegation of Kabul ministers brought both men to a meeting of local elders in Nad Ali in February 2010. The cables quote U.S. diplomats as complaining that Akhundzada, now a senator in Kabul, and Jan "still enjoy direct access to Karzai and have significant ties to the narcotics industry."

Less senior officials also appear to have their hands in the till. According to other leaked cables, PRT advisers believed that several members of the staff of the current Helmand governor, Gulab Mangal, diverted British funds from a program to get farmers to plant crops other than poppy. They bought low-quality wheat seeds and fertilizer in place of what they were supposed to give farmers and pocketed the difference. The lists of beneficiaries were also said to have been rigged in favor of friends of Mangal's staff. When the British complained, the governor mobilized the National Directorate of Security, and several staff members were arrested.

I have focused on Helmand because it has had so much attention from the Americans and British. The deployment of extra troops had had some military effect in the province in pushing the Taliban to take cover and enabling officials in the Karzai government to open more bazaars and local offices. In July 2011, amid much public relations fanfare, ISAF transferred security in Lashkar Gah to Afghan forces while US and British troops remained in large numbers as essential back-up. But these tactical gains do not amount to a strategy that can end resentment of foreign occupation or eliminate resistance to it. Nor can they be replicated and sustained all over Afghanistan. Not even the fiercest of war hawks expects a similar deployment to be possible in each of Afghanistan's thirty-four provinces. It would require a million and a quarter troops. The Russians never had more than 118,000.

The picture from the whole country suggests that whatever small advances the United States and Britain are achieving in Helmand, the conflict is widening and deepening elsewhere in Afghanistan. The aim of building up Afghan security forces to have them fight the Taliban in place of ISAF is problematic. Around $11 billion of the $100 billion that the United States planned to spend on Afghanistan in 2011 was due to go on training Afghan security forces, the largest yearly sum to date. But the new Afghan National Army was still 90 percent staffed by non-Pashtuns, making it seem almost as much of a foreign occupying force to Afghans in the Taliban heartlands as the United States and its allies.

Even if the Afghan army were acceptable to local civilians, the poor educational level of its members means it is decades away from being a credible fighting force. Illiteracy rates are almost 85 percent for enlisted service members and only slightly better for noncommissioned officers. "It's a matter of life and death," according to Lieutenant General William Caldwell, the head of the U.S. training mission. "If they can't read a number and a letter, they can't read a map. If they can't read a map, they can't call in artillery fire, helicopter support, aircraft support."

COIN's key test is whether Taliban members are giving up. General David Petraeus, the commander of U.S. forces in Afghanistan from June 2010 to July 2011, stepped up the use of drones and nighttime raids by Special Forces to assassinate Taliban field commanders in the hope of deterring others. With 339 reportedly killed between August and October 2010, he claimed substantial success. The new strategy, however, has echoes of the discredited Phoenix assassination program, the equally faulty "body count" policy from the Vietnam War, and, as the Pentagon's report to Congress admitted, the supply of new Taliban is inexhaustible. Critics point to two further problems. The new commanders may be more ruthless than those they replace. By killing the more experienced and better-connected local commanders, the United States is undermining the group of people with whom it will one day have to negotiate.

If the assassination program is designed to frighten Taliban into dropping their guns, the carrot is the Afghan Government's reintegration policy. Rolled out in 2010, it offers benefits to Taliban who return to civilian life. PRT advisers in Helmand declined to give me figures on how many had come forward but suggested it was only dozens.

Six months later, Petraeus told Congress in March 2011 that 700 had reintegrated and another 2,000 were "in the early stages of the process." These are small numbers, which will scarcely dent the Taliban's strength, given their ability to recruit replacements. Indeed, in testimony to the U.S. Senate only five days before the notoriously optimistic General Petraeus's remarks, General Ronald Burgess, the director of the Defense Intelligence Agency, said, "Reintegration efforts have not yet notably degraded insurgent capability, [or] forced insurgents to alter their strategy or goals." Major General Phil Jones, the director of a unit that is monitoring the program, told reporters in June 2011 that only a handful of the 1,700 people who had enrolled in the program were mid-level commanders rather than simple fighters, and two-thirds were from the north, where the insurgency was weaker than in the south. In Helmand, officials admitted that another problem with the reintegration program was that it provided "perverse incentives" by offering former Taliban jobs or vocational training while other Afghans in Helmand or more peaceful provinces received no rewards.

Amnesty is also a difficult issue. Should a Taliban member who has killed other Afghans or foreign troops be able to escape retribution? If not, what of the anomaly that the Afghan Government and Parliament are full of men with blood on their hands from earlier phases in the country's three decades of war and who have never faced a court? And why would Taliban commanders give up if they know they're going straight to jail?

In Lashkar Gah, they showed us the new Afghan prison. A year earlier the old building was in chaos, controlled by its own inmates. The new one has carpeted cells where inmates sleep on two-tiered bunks or the floor. The Afghan governor, a jovial figure in vest and track suit, put his arms around inmates in avuncular style. One wing housed former Taliban, I was told. I was allowed to select four to interview on why they had switched sides. All denied any link with the movement. If this was proof of success in getting Taliban to defect, it seemed rather thin.

Does the United States understand why Afghans join the Taliban? Do Afghans understand why the United States is in their country? Without clear answers, no COIN has any chance of success. A 2009 survey commissioned by DFID asked what led people to join the Taliban and another insurgent group, Hezb-i Islami, which operates south of Kabul. It also examined how much support local people gave the two groups. The survey interviewed 192 people in Kandahar, Wardak and around Kabul, but for security reasons not in Helmand. Only ten supported the government. The rest saw it as corrupt and partisan. Most supported the Taliban, at least what they called the "good Taliban," defined as those who showed religious piety, attacked foreign forces but not Afghans and delivered justice quickly and fairly. They did not like Pakistani Taliban and Taliban linked to narcotics.

Afghans do not like al Qaeda, but they do not equate the Taliban with this Arab-led movement. Suspicion of the Arab volunteers was already strong during the resistance to the Soviets when every mujahedin wanted to be a *ghazi* (hero) while every Arab jihadi wanted to be a *shahid* (martyr). "So we let them go in the front line," as some mujahedin joked.

Few respondents in the DFID survey said they understood why foreign forces were in Afghanistan. Most thought foreigners had their own motives, and most wanted UN sanctions and travel bans on senior Taliban to be lifted so that they would be free to return to Afghan political life.

A key point was made by older respondents who lived through the tragedies of the last thirty years. To them the ghosts of Afghanistan's past are ever present, even if foreigners overlook them. The withdrawal of U.S. troops should be linked to a negotiated settlement, they said. Otherwise the country would suffer another flare-up in the civil war, as happened when Soviet forces left.

The next three chapters describe how Soviet and U.S. mistakes helped to create that earlier disaster.

[2] THE SOVIET INVASION

"We have carefully studied all aspects of this action and come to the conclusion that if our troops were introduced, the situation in your country would not only not improve, but would worsen."

—SOVIET PRIME MINISTER ALEXEI KOSYGIN
TO AFGHAN PRESIDENT, MARCH 20, 1979

"EXPLOSION? WHAT EXPLOSION?" Afghanistan's Foreign Minister Shah Mohammed Dost inquired with an elegant raising of his eyebrows when I interrupted our interview to ask whether the sudden noise I had just heard was an explosion.

It was November 1981, almost two years since Soviet troops had invaded, and the official spin from Moscow and its allies in Kabul was that everything was under control.

"Ah yes, the dynamiting," Dost said as another boom sounded in the distance. He looked relieved, but eager to assure me I was mistaken if I thought I could hear the sound of war from his office in central Kabul, a stone's thrown from the presidential palace. "They do it almost every day, sometimes twice a day, for producing stones for construction, you know."

A tall, slim man with a neatly clipped mustache, Dost had started his diplomatic career under King Zahir Shah and was now the most prominent face of Afghanistan's Moscow-installed regime. He wanted me to understand that the explosions could not be military since the war was virtually over: "We've destroyed the main hideouts of the bandits and mercenaries. Now they can't act in a group form. It's only a few individuals who indulge in terrorist activities and sabotage, which is common all over the world. We hope to eliminate that also."

In the first weeks after the December 1979 invasion, Soviet officials had been so confident of quick victory that they gave Western reporters astonishing access, even allowing them to ride on tanks or drive rented cars and taxis alongside Soviet convoys. By the spring of 1980 the mood had changed as the Kremlin saw it was in for a long war of attrition. The press was no longer welcome. There were no embeds for reporters to accompany a fighting unit, even for trusted Soviet correspondents. The war became a taboo in the Soviet media, while Western journalists who applied for visas for Afghanistan were routinely refused. The only way to cover the conflict was to endure days and nights of walking along precarious mountain paths with guerrilla fighters from mujahedin safe havens in Pakistan. A few stories that appeared in Western papers via this route were careful and low-key, but many were romantic, self-promoting accounts of heroic exploits by reporters who donned a *shalwar kameez,* the long-tailed shirt, and a *pakol,* the pie-shaped Afghan woolen hat, to slip into Afghanistan alongside the men with the guns. Some saw a chance to make a name for themselves by witnessing or claiming to have witnessed the latest Soviet atrocity. Mujahedin groups encouraged this adventure journalism, uncritical, exaggerating and occasionally dishonest. Some film and TV teams later admitted that the "action" recorded on their treks into Afghanistan had been staged for their cameras. Footage of mujahedin crouching behind rocks and firing weapons was often artificial since there were no Soviet or Afghan Government troops nearby. But it helped to bring support and funding from Western governments and sympathetic aid groups.

By 1981, the Soviets were realizing the no-visa policy was a mistake. Their case was not being heard. So a handful of Western journalists were let in for short trips in small groups or occasionally on their own. The Soviets preferred to take Moscow-based correspondents in the hope they had a greater awareness of Soviet attitudes and aims. Afghanistan was theoretically a sovereign country, but visas were clearly under Soviet control. One morning in the autumn of 1981, the press attaché at the Soviet embassy in London gave in to my repeated requests and told me that a visa would be granted if I went to the Afghan consulate. For cost-saving reasons, the *Guardian* had no Moscow-based correspondent in those years, but the paper had sent me as a Russian-speaker on various assignments to the USSR since 1970.

I was mildly surprised to get the visa, since I had clashed with Soviet officials in the emotion-filled days after the invasion at a crowded public meeting at the London School of Economics. A senior Soviet diplomat and I shared the platform along with other speakers. He insisted that the intervention (his preferred word) was justified since the Afghan Government had asked Moscow to send troops to aid it in its struggle against rebels. I countered that the invasion was illegal since the United Nations had not authorized it (the same argument that was to recur over the U.S. invasion of Iraq in 2003). What particularly embarrassed the diplomat was my remark that it was odd that Hafizullah Amin, the Afghan leader who had invited the Soviet troops, was murdered by his guests on their first day in Kabul. This smelled more like regime change than fraternal help.

The point produced a joke that circulated in Moscow some months later: Question: Why are we still in Afghanistan? Answer: We're still looking for the people who invited us.

By 1981 passions had cooled, and with the precious visa in my passport I landed in Kabul on a bright autumn morning after changing

planes and an overnight stay in Delhi. After the heat of India's capital
I was struck by the extraordinary clarity of Kabul's air and the sky's
deep blue, a color that almost matched the country's most famous
mineral stone, lapis lazuli. The city sits on a high plateau surrounded
by a ring of khaki mountains and beyond them glittering in the distance the snowcapped peaks of the Hindu Kush. In the dozen trips
I've made to Kabul its magnificent setting never ceases to amaze me.
The country's poverty is overwhelming and the stories a reporter
hears or sees are often tragic, but you can always lift your eyes to
the hills and feel a restorative surge of nature's beauty to revive your
energy. Even the pollution of Kabul's current traffic cannot entirely
take the thrill away.

On that first trip, the city itself, and not just its majestic surroundings, exuded a sense of calm. It was totally unexpected. Where was
the war? And where were the Russians? Whatever was going on in the
Afghan countryside where most journalists trying to cover the war
were tramping and camping, there was little sign of war or preparation
for it in Kabul.

In the two weeks I spent in the city I saw hardly any Soviet troops.
On the few occasions I spotted some, they were acting as tourists rather
than enforcers. As though the war was far away, they wore floppy khaki
hats and no helmets and would drive in open-sided jeeps to Chicken
Street, known by its English name to Afghans and foreigners alike as the
city's best market for souvenirs. In the days before their tours of duty
ended they would wander up and down, peering through the windows
at jewelry, carpets and brass water jugs and hunting for a few cheap
gifts. Their soldiers' allowance was low and not paid in cash so they
found it hard to scrape any Afghan money together at all. "All they want
is one sheepskin jacket," a carpet merchant muttered to me in English
after a young Soviet sergeant, with an armband that identified him as
a patrol leader, burst hurriedly into the shop, looked around and disappeared next door.

The Soviets preferred to leave as many military duties as possible to Afghans. In Kabul the effort was successful, and security was in Afghan army and police hands. The Afghan army was made up largely of conscripts, and there were no reliable figures on its size. A document published by the U.S. State Department in 1981 claimed the army shrank from 100,000 in 1979 to 25,000 by the end of 1980 as a result of massive desertions, but this may have been propaganda aimed at weakening Soviet morale. It was certainly true that many senior officers from the royal period fled into exile after the king was deposed in 1973, but the Russians paid for hundreds of young men to come to the Soviet Union for short military courses in the 1970s. In this way they quickly built a new corps of officers who were eager to modernize and develop their country and felt sympathetic to the Soviet Union.

From what I could see in Kabul, the Soviets were able to depend on Afghans for urban law and order, if not for war fighting. Car bombs and suicide attacks, which have become a permanent threat in today's Kabul, were unknown during the Soviet period, and Afghans went about their daily business without fear of sudden mass slaughter. Unlike Kabul today, where no diplomats or foreign contractors have their partners or children with them, many Soviet diplomats came with their families, and the embassy had a flourishing kindergarten, grade school and high school. At the city's two university campuses most young women were unveiled, as were most of the female staff in banks, stores, schools, factories and government offices. A few wore a loose head-scarf over their hair. Only in the bazaar where poorer people shopped was the all-embracing burqa common, usually blue, pink or a light shade of brown.

The Afghan Government wanted to develop the country, but they accepted the burqa as a product of tradition that had to be handled carefully. They did not condemn it or invest the issue of women's dress with the politically charged, almost totemic significance it acquired when the Taliban took power in 1996 and enforced the burqa on every woman, an enforcement reversed by the Bush administration when it toppled the Taliban and hailed the lifting of the obligatory burqa rule as the complete emancipation of Afghan women.

Officials at the Afghan embassy in London had told me I must register with the press department of the Foreign Ministry as soon as I arrived. Luckily, no one was sent to meet me at the airport from where I would undoubtedly have been escorted to a government hotel. A colleague who had stayed briefly in Kabul on a transit visa without revealing he was a reporter had given me the name of a family-run hotel. He chose it for fear that the major hotels would be watched and his identity discovered. Although I was in Kabul officially, I decided to try the same hotel, if only to have less chance my room would be bugged—not that this meant much since I had no contacts, would not be making many phone calls and could speak no Dari, Afghanistan's main language, which is close to Farsi, spoken in neighboring Iran. A battered taxi deposited me at a two-story villa with a pleasant garden full of roses. The unexpected bonus was that the small hotel was virtually opposite the main Soviet military hospital. From the window of my room I could see Soviet troops haggling with small Afghan boys for a skewer of kebab from one of the stalls down the road. Unlike U.S. bases in today's Afghanistan with their razor wire and tiers of Hesco barriers, the Soviet hospital was easily approached. Occasionally I spotted an ambulance delivering wounded men to a row of olive-green tents in the grounds, which had been added to relieve pressure on the overflowing wards. The soldiers had sustained their injuries in mujahedin ambushes on the supply routes to Kabul or when their vehicles struck mines or in failed tank-led assaults on mujahedin-held villages. Thanks to my view of the hospital I did get a glimpse of the war, although I did not stay up on watch all night or try to calculate the number of Russian casualties.

British and American diplomats were involved in this kind of intelligence work, as I discovered when I called in at the British embassy. Having little official business to do with a government they regarded as Moscow's puppet, Western diplomats spent much of their time assessing the fortunes of war. The U.S. chargé's residence was on the road that Soviet oil tanker trucks took on their long overland journey from the then Soviet Republic of Uzbekistan to Kabul. He enjoyed counting trucks going past his windows, I was told, and eagerly noted how many had been damaged.

When I registered with the Afghan Foreign Ministry, they assigned me—as I had expected—a minder who was to act as interpreter and accompany me on all my interviews. Unlike the British military minder I was required to have in Helmand in 2010, he was unarmed. Called Naqib, he told me he was an engineer whose wife was studying in the Soviet Union, like many of the brighter high school graduates. He and his superiors accepted most of my requests to meet Afghan ministers and other officials. Their key objective was to challenge the stories being written by reporters traveling with the mujahedin and convince me that opposition claims that Kabul was surrounded and close to collapse were wildly untrue.

Without a knowledge of Dari and shadowed by my minder, I realized it was impossible to meet many Afghans independently and hear their views, though I found a few shopkeepers who spoke some English. But from the evidence of my own eyes the mujahedin claims of a city under siege certainly seemed false. The dozens of little kebab stalls in the street had as much lamb from the countryside as they needed. Pomegranates, watermelons and grapes spilled out of the bazaar.

I never discovered a definitive explanation for the explosions I had heard during my interview with Foreign Minister Dost, but his point that Kabul was unaffected by the destruction of war was valid. I persuaded my minder to take me up to Qargha Lake, about ten miles northwest of the city center. It was one of the few excursion spots permitted to the diplomatic corps, and indeed any foreigners in Kabul at the time. A patchy golf course with a bumpy fairway and greens that contained more dust than grass had been laid out just below a dam. Visitors could drive up to the dam and from the road along the top of the retaining wall could look across to the mountains of Paghman, where fighting had been intense that summer. On the day we went the golden leaves of birch trees glinted in the sun at the far end of the lake some two miles away. Soviet tanks could be seen maneuvering, and there was the rumble of artillery fire and puffs of smoke from low-flying MiG-24 helicopter gunships. Here at last was war but far enough from the city not to change the basic truth that the Afghan capital was safe.

The countryside was another story. At the United Nations guesthouse in Kabul—a favorite place for foreigners to meet during weekends—aid workers told me of their frustration at the restrictions they faced. The UN had dozens of consultants involved in rural development, but they were not allowed out of Kabul to supervise the projects they were supposed to be running. Afghan Government officials admitted that because of the mujahedin's activity, land reform was operating in only a quarter of the country's districts, and half the schools were closed.

I asked to travel to other cities. Naqib explained that Herat and Kandahar had security problems, but he promised to try to take me to Jalalabad and Mazar-i Sharif. To protect me, he said, we would go by air. I suspected it was really for his safety rather than mine. If we were caught at an impromptu mujahedin checkpoint on the road, it was a reasonable bet that as a British citizen my life would have been spared. A government official might be shot or have his throat slit.

A few days later, Naqib and I flew in a rickety two-engine highwinged Soviet Antonov to Jalalabad, the capital of Nangahar province, which borders Pakistan. The mujahedin were nearby, and our movement in the town was limited. Between interviews with officials we spent most of the time in our hotel. At least I was not cooped up in a fortified garrison, as I would be three decades later with the British in Helmand, but it was almost as frustrating.

Our next trip was from Kabul to Mazar-i Sharif, the main city on the plains of northern Afghanistan, where dust seemed to blow in uncontrollably. The plane found a gap in the Hindu Kush, and our wing-tips were on a level with the highest peaks before we emerged over the semi-desert that stretches up to the Amu Darya, the fabled river Oxus.

The small airport in Mazar was guarded by Afghan rather than Soviet troops. As Naqib went off to check on our baggage, a policeman at the terminal whispered that the mujahedin controlled the hills we could see on the far side of the runway. His flicker of a smile suggested he approved of the fact.

The interviews that Naqib organized took place in offices close to the center, but we could walk around and sit in teahouses. As we stood in the grounds of the fifteenth-century shrine of Ali bin Talib, the Fourth Caliph of Islam, admiring its light blue and turquoise tiles, three MiG-24s swooped low over the minarets, scattering the white pigeons that waddled among the beggars. In my almost empty hotel, small-arms fire could be heard nearby during the night. Next morning in answer to my inquiries, Naqib insisted the sound came from wedding parties with jubilant family members firing rifles into the air. He was right about the custom. What was suspicious was the timing. I had been told the city had a curfew from ten p.m. to dawn, so did people really carry on celebrating in their gardens until three a.m. on cold November nights?

Before we left for Mazar I had moved out of my family-run hotel in Kabul. As soon as Naqib had learned where I was staying, he pleaded with me to shift to a bigger hotel. I initially argued, correctly, that the *Guardian* was not a wealthy paper, but after three days I agreed to move. I took a room in the Kabul Hotel, which was only a short walk from the central bazaar and almost opposite the Arg, the citadel built toward the end of the nineteenth century by Abdur Rahman, the king who got the British to leave Afghanistan after the Second Anglo-Afghan war. Now it housed Babrak Karmal, the Soviet-installed Afghan leader.

As well as being more central than my first hotel, the Kabul had a res-taurant, but there was something creepy about the building. In February 1979, four militants from Settam-i Melli, a small Maoist-influenced party, had seized Adolph Dubs, the American ambassador, and taken refuge upstairs in Room 117. They wanted to swap him for three of their imprisoned colleagues. Afghan troops and Soviet advisers rushed to the building and negotiations were held. There was an exchange of fire and the ambassador was killed. Although the United States made a formal protest to Moscow, American diplomats did not believe the Russians or the Afghan authorities wanted to see the ambassador dead. They treated his death as the result of a misguided and premature rescue effort that went wrong. When I checked into the hotel, the receptionist assigned me to a room on the first floor. Although I made sure it was not Room 117, I could not help casting a wary glance at its door every time I walked down the dimly lit corridor.

One advantage of the Kabul Hotel was that it was a favorite place for better-off families to hold wedding parties. They were lively affairs, and I would often peep in at the open door of the banqueting room, where I would be spotted and immediately invited to join in the fun. This consisted of a lavish buffet, music and dancing, one gender at a time. Men danced with men, then left the floor for women to dance with women, while the bride and groom sat on ornate chairs on a raised platform, invariably looking less relaxed and cheerful than everyone else. Naqib had gone home by then, so the weddings provided a brief chance to talk to Afghans in the person of the male guests, some of whom spoke English. None dissented from the official view that the mujahedin did not have the capacity to attack Kabul other than through an occasional short-range rocket that landed somewhere in the outskirts and rarely caused any serious damage. I also noted that the weddings always ended by ten p.m., unlike Mazar's purported all-night festivities.

The Russians had been in Afghanistan for two years by the time I came, but they made no effort to switch the country's economy to the Soviet model in which every business was state-owned, even down to the level of hairdressers, tailors and cobblers. Private enterprise and family-owned businesses continued to thrive in Kabul. The country's borders were wide open for trade. Laden with freight, brightly painted trucks with ornate wooden prows that towered over the driver's cab like the front of an eighteenth-century galleon drove up and down from Pakistan, regardless of the fact they were traveling through a war zone. Commerce was king. Just as it must have been before the Soviet invasion, the bazaar was a cosmopolitan Aladdin's cave with a richness of choice to stun any Russian. Soviets lived with an economy where almost everything was Soviet-made and imported goods were scarce. Yet here, in a poor Third World country which they were supposed to be helping to develop, they were confronted with shops stacked with toiletries and razor blades from Britain, perfumes from France, cigarettes from the United States, cans of beer from West Germany, toothpaste from China and TV sets from Japan. One benefit of a posting in Afghanistan for Soviet officers was the chance to buy these foreign goods, particularly cameras, cassette players and other electrical items. At home friends would think them stupid or unusually mean if they did not seize the opportunity. Artyom Borovik, one of the first Soviet journalists who was allowed to travel to wartime Afghanistan, recorded a satirical ditty he heard from a Soviet army major: "Kabul, thank goodness, I was there, you gave me clothes and shoes to wear."

MYTH NUMBER TWO:
The Soviet invasion was an unprovoked attack designed to capture new territory.

When the Soviets ordered troops into Afghanistan, Western governments saw it in strategic terms as a dangerous precedent and an international threat. They pointed out that it was the first time since World War II that Moscow had dared take military action beyond the area of the Warsaw Pact. The Soviet invasions of Hungary in 1956 and Czechoslovakia in 1968 were widely criticized, but Western governments took no retaliatory action, having long accepted that those two countries were part of the Soviet-led communist bloc. Afghanistan never had been. Some analysts claimed Moscow's invasion was an ominous first step on a road through Pakistan to the sea, designed to satisfy a long-standing Kremlin desire for warm-water ports. Jimmy Carter, the U.S. president, thought it was aimed at the oil fields of the Gulf and called it the most serious threat to world peace since World War II.

In fact, the invasion's primary aim was to protect the Soviet Union's southern border and save a revolutionary government that was meeting armed resistance. If the Afghan Government fell, Soviet leaders feared Afghanistan might come under American control. They made the decision to invade with great reluctance.

The People's Democratic Party of Afghanistan (PDPA) had come to power in April 1978 in a military coup against President Daoud Khan. Not officially a communist party, it espoused a form of socialist modernization that was common in the Third World in the 1960s and 1970s. In the ideological split between Moscow and Beijing, it supported the USSR rather than China. Many of its leaders had studied in Moscow or one of the Soviet Union's Central Asian republics.

Moscow had a long history of engagement with left-wing groups and movements in Afghanistan. The country's strategic position on the Soviet Union's southern flank and as the northern gateway to India had made it a prime recipient of both sides' assistance in the Cold War. U.S. projects tended to be in the south of the country. In the 1950s, the Americans sought to gain influence by building the Kandahar-to-Kabul highway and irrigation projects in the Helmand valley. The Soviets concentrated more on Kabul and the north. They developed the gas fields of Shibergan, built a fertilizer plant in Balkh and dug out the economically and strategically important Salang road tunnel under the Hindu Kush to link the capital and the northern plains. The Soviets built and largely staffed Kabul's Polytechnic University and paid for hundreds of young Afghans to study engineering, physics and agronomy at Soviet universities. They equipped the Afghan army and air force and invited over three thousand officers for training in the Soviet Union.

Zahir Shah, who became king at age nineteen in 1933, was happy to keep a balance between Moscow and Washington, partly as a way of maximizing foreign aid but also because he knew that foreign interference would increase if he tilted too far toward one of the superpowers. His first cousin Daoud Khan, whom he appointed prime minister, was a fervent supporter of Pashtun nationalism and the creation of a nation of Pashtunistan. He advocated regaining the city of Peshawar and other parts of Afghanistan that the British had added to their empire in British India in the nineteenth century. Mainly populated by fellow Pashtuns (called Pathans in Pakistan), they are now located in the northwest of Pakistan in the Federally Administered Tribal Areas (FATAs). Daoud's obsession with the Pashtunistan issue created tensions with Pakistan, and Zahir Shah sacked him in 1963.

Out of power, Daoud developed close ties with the PDPA, which had been founded in 1965. He became known as the Red Prince because of his interest in social reform. When Daoud got his revenge on Zahir by deposing him in 1973, while the king was abroad having medical treatment, he turned the country into a republic and called himself president. Many Afghans assumed the Russians were behind the coup. After all, several army officers who had trained in the Soviet Union had helped him seize power, and the USSR was the first country to recognize the new government.

Daoud saw himself as a modernizing nationalist in the image of Egypt's Gamal Abdel Nasser or Yugoslavia's Marshal Tito. Although Afghanistan was officially non-aligned between both sides in the Cold War, Daoud initially took its foreign policy in a direction that was closer to the USSR than the United States. He changed tack, however, after a stormy meeting with Leonid Brezhnev, the Soviet leader, in the Kremlin in 1977. American advisers were working on aid projects in northern Afghanistan, and Brezhnev urged Daoud to get them to leave. Daoud felt his independence was under threat, stood up and made to leave the room. His officials calmed him down, but the damage was done. From then on, Daoud changed course. He sent his brother to China and the United States to promote better relations with their governments. He dropped his overt interest in the Pashtunistan issue and patched up his relations with Pakistan. He traveled to Saudi Arabia and Iran and was promised aid from both countries.

On domestic issues Daoud became arrogant and unapproachable and dismissed some of the more left-wing members of the cabinet. Shortly before his Moscow trip, he had already promulgated a new constitution, which banned all parties other than his own National Revolutionary Party. The Islamists also opposed these moves, and some started armed resistance.

The coup that toppled him in April 1978 was a hastily improvised affair. It was prompted by the assassination of Mir Akbar Khyber, a popular senior PDPA official. "To this day no one knows who killed him," Abdul Karim Misaq, a member of the PDPA's Politburo and one of the men who organized the funeral, told me in London in March 2011. Like several former PDPA leaders, he received political asylum in Britain in the 1990s. Frail and in his seventies but still with a lock of strong white hair that flops over his forehead, Misaq recounted the events that followed Khyber's death. "We wanted to confront Daoud and we decided to exploit Khyber's assassination to make ourselves more popular and come out of our shells," he said.

Khyber lived in Mikrorayon (the Russian word for "subdistrict"), a suburb near the airport which had been built like a modern housing project in the Soviet Union with five-story buildings, supermarkets and schools on wide boulevards. It stood out from the big houses behind high walls where Kabul's upper-middle class traditionally lived but was eagerly sought out by officials from poorer backgrounds who were proud to have government jobs. It had become a kind of PDPA stronghold and would later house many Soviet civilian advisers.

"We intended to take Khyber's corpse from the morgue in the hospital near the university and carry it on foot across town to his home in

Mikrorayon. This would bring out students who were members of the PDPA as well as other people and show that the party was alive. But the police were cleverer than we were. We found they had moved his body that night to his home."

The funeral committee had to devise a new plan. They hit on something that might later, in the manner of Eastern Europe's "color revolutions," have been called the Tulip Revolution. "It was April and tulips were out," Misaq recalled, "so everyone, young, old, women, men brought bunches of tulips. We took the body over the bridge, past the U.S. embassy, and the Arg to the Pul-i Khisti mosque. It was one of the largest demonstrations Kabul has ever seen, about forty to fifty thousand people."

Alarmed by the size of the crowd, Daoud ordered his police to detain the top PDPA men, Nur Mohammed Taraki and Babrak Karmal. Hafizullah Amin, Taraki's deputy as party leader, was still at large. He sent messages to two key members of the PDPA, the commander of the Fourth Armored Brigade and an air force colonel at Bagram air base, north of Kabul, urging them to topple Daoud. They sent tanks and aircraft against the presidential palace in the Arg. A lengthy battle culminated in Daoud's murder and the death of eighteen members of his family. It was a bloody precursor to thirty years of war, chaos and violent regime change that continue to the present.

Though the PDPA was Moscow's natural ally, the trouble was that it contained two wings, a Dari-speaking one called Parcham (Banner) and another known as Khalq (Nation). Khalq was mainly made up of Pashtuns, Afghanistan's largest ethnic group. It attracted many Afghans from poor rural families who had moved to the cities in the hope of finding work. Taraki and Amin were members of the Ghilzai tribe of Pashtuns who are spread across southern and eastern Afghanistan, the most feudal and conservative part of the country. Both men were impatient to change its ancient social and economic structures. Taraki came from a peasant family in Ghazni province but got a job as a clerk in

Bombay before moving to Kabul. He fancied himself a poet. Amin was the son of an office worker who had moved to Paghman near Kabul. His father died young, and Amin was brought up by his elder brother, who had a clerical job in a cotton factory. Obviously bright, he went to Kabul University and went on to get a master's degree in education in the United States.

The Parcham wing of the party was smaller in number and tended to attract men and women with a social conscience from middle-class and even royalist families. Babrak Karmal, its leader and a cofounder of the PDPA, came from the old Pashtun aristocracy. His father was an army general. A powerful orator, he had been a popular student leader at Kabul University and was imprisoned for five years for political agitation. On release he returned to full-time politics and was elected to Parliament under Zahir Shah.

The party's two wings were at odds for most of the 1970s. Although they patched things up at a unification conference in 1977, Parcham and Khalq continued to command separate loyalties and work against each other. Based on ethnic, linguistic and class differences, this dissension was never resolved and only became worse once the party was in power. It was one of the many tragedies of recent Afghan history.

The PDPA began as the first modern nonreligious party in Afghanistan. It had an ideological program representing secular values of inclusiveness and gender equality that aimed to develop the country. Many of Afghanistan's best-educated young people joined it at university or soon after. It also captured the allegiance of a generation of young Soviet-trained army officers.

A typical Parcham member was Ahmad Sarwar, whom I got to know when he was the senior Afghan diplomat in London from 1986 to 1989. A dedicated and idealistic nationalist, he attended the elite U.S.-financed Habibia school in Kabul, where his best friend was King Zahir Shah's son Daoud. His wife, Laila, was a granddaughter of Abdur Rahman, who built the Arg in Kabul. Her sister was married to

Mohammed Najib, a Parcham member and medical doctor who later became Afghan president (and changed his name to Najibullah to give it an Islamic flavor).

Islamist parties were also gaining strength at Kabul's universities in the 1960s and 1970s, angry at the elite's Western ways. They had one thing in common with the PDPA. Unlike the parties of the past, which accepted the country's traditional social and political system, the PDPA and the Islamists represented programmatic movements for change. Their members were impatient and radical. But while the Islamists splintered into a series of small parties, each dominated by a single powerful leader, the PDPA grew to become a mass party with tens of thousands of members, albeit informally divided between the Parcham and Khalq wings.

The April 1978 coup took the Parcham wing by surprise. Many were trying to escape from Daoud's crackdown on opposition politicians after the funeral demonstrations for Mir Akbar Khyber. "During the night Najib, who was head of the Kabul city branch of the PDPA, was in hiding with other top party people. They were afraid Daoud would arrest them too," Ahmad Sarwar recalled. "When they heard explosions, they sent a friend into central Kabul to find out what it was. He came back and told them, 'It might be a coup and it seems to be our friends.'" Babrak Karmal, the Parcham leader, later said he had opposed the coup. With the benefit of hindsight he told a Russian reporter many years afterwards, "It was the greatest crime against the people of Afghanistan. Parcham's leaders were against armed action because the country was not ready for a revolution. . . . I knew that people would not support us if we decided to seize power and that we would be unable to keep power without such support." The Russians were also caught off guard, according to Aleksandr Puzanov, the Soviet ambassador in Kabul. In a telegram to Moscow he complained about the ultra-left rhetoric of Taraki and Amin and warned with some prescience that there would be factional fighting between Khalq and Parcham, though he promised to "take steps to overcome the differences in the Afghan leadership."

The most important thing for Moscow was that compared to the Daoud government, the new one's ideology was likely to be, as Puzanov noted, "more sympathetic to the Soviet Union, further consolidating and strengthening our position in Afghanistan." The PDPA coup removed the looming threat that Daoud would move Afghanistan from the Soviet sphere of influence. It seemed bound to strengthen the Soviet-led socialist camp around the world. By the same token the United States denounced it. I was the *Guardian*'s correspondent in Washington at the time, having been posted there in 1975. By chance the coup happened on the day of one of the occasional lunches that Zbigniew Brzezinski, Jimmy Carter's national security adviser, hosted for European correspondents to brief them off the record on U.S. policy. Brzezinski was visibly angry. When one of us suggested that the PDPA might not automatically be Soviet puppets and could be nationalists like the Vietnamese or Yugoslav communists, he snorted. "They are like Bulgarians," he said, picking the country widely considered to be more subservient to Moscow than any other member of the Warsaw Pact.

In Kabul the April coup was widely welcomed even in non-PDPA political circles. Before it happened, Ahmad Sarwar recalled, "the mood was becoming more and more revolutionary. People were complaining that a family was running the country and had done so for decades. There was a shortage of jobs, low salaries, poor health services and too few experts." People put flowers in the muzzles of soldiers' rifles and Amin was considered a hero. "If the coup hadn't happened," Sarwar added, "Daoud would have killed all the top PDPA people, Parcham and Khalq."

Taraki, the general secretary of the PDPA, became chairman of a newly appointed revolutionary council, in effect the country's president. He also became prime minister. Hafizullah Amin was his deputy. Misaq, who had helped to organize Mir Akbar Khyber's funeral, became minister of finance. The PDPA's Khalq wing was in the ascendancy. They promulgated a series of reforms designed to help the weakest members of Afghan society. They forbade child marriages, making it illegal for girls under sixteen and boys under eighteen to wed. They launched adult literacy campaigns, with classes for women as well as men. Although they were in separate rooms, the very idea of educating women angered village mullahs and the ulema—the religious scholars— as well as upsetting many rural males who ruled their families like patri- archs. The PDPA's Khalq wing codified the dowry system, effectively reducing the amount the bride had to bring with her almost to nothing. They canceled the debts of peasants who had taken mortgages on small plots of land, usually at exorbitant rates of interest. No one was allowed to own more than three acres of the best agricultural land; any surplus would be expropriated and given to landless peasants. The reform alien- ated traditional maliks, the tribal chiefs who were often large landown- ers. Many turned to armed resistance, linking up with militant Islamists who had gone to Pakistan to get help from the Pakistani authorities.

To understand the mood of the men who ran the land reform pro- gram I tracked down another political refugee in London. In a small apartment in a public housing complex in the suburb of Hounslow amid the engine whine from planes landing at nearby Heathrow Airport, I found Saleh Mohammed Zeary. Living alone at the age of seventy-six, he is one of the thousands of Afghans who over the last thirty-five years of civil war have been forced to flee their country for asylum abroad. His wife and two of their children were murdered in Kabul by thugs working for one of the mujahedin leaders two years after the PDPA lost power in 1992. At the time he was on a trip to Pakistan to try to arrange the family's permanent departure from Afghanistan.

Zeary is short and slim, with a trim white mustache. His easy smile reveals a slight gap in his front teeth as well as a surprisingly mellow lack of bitterness. Born and educated in Kandahar, Zeary went on to study medicine at Kabul University. What prompted him to become a

founding member of the PDPA in 1965, he told me, was shock at realizing the country's lack of development. "After more than forty years
of freedom since 1919 [Afghanistan's independence from Britain] there
were only 700 doctors in the whole country, and 500 of them worked in
Kabul." He and student friends got Marxist literature from the Tudeh
Party, Iran's communist party, and copied it out by hand so that their
comrades could read it too. They were also impressed, he told me, by
Account of the Kingdom of Cabul and Its Dependencies in Persia and India,
published in 1815 by the British imperialist Mountstuart Elphinstone,
with its detailed description of the country's tribal customs.

In Western books and the media, King Zahir Shah's four decades
in power are often referred to as a golden age in part because of a relatively liberal constitution and the eventual creation of a parliament. But
rules for running as a candidate were restrictive and the parliament's
powers were limited. The truth is that the monarchy was a time of
repression and lack of development for all but a narrow upper class.
Zeary spent six years in prison in the 1960s for giving a speech criticiz-
ing Zahir Shah's regime. Undeterred, he remained politically active on
his release and joined the PDPA's leadership. A Pashtun, he was a member of the party's Khalq wing. When the April 1978 coup happened, he
was as surprised as the Parchamis, he told me: "There was no program,
no decision of the leadership, nothing. The party had good contacts in
the military. Amin organized it after the leadership was put in jail."

Zeary knew the coup was not a revolution, "not like that one," he
laughed, pointing to the television set in the corner of the room. It was
February 2011. The sound was turned down, but the screen showed the
huge crowd in Cairo's Tahrir Square demanding Hosni Mubarak's res-
ignation. "We were not against democracy," he said. "We had expected
to take power through Parliament."

Zeary asked Taraki to appoint him minister of agriculture so he
could bring in land reform. Taraki agreed, even though Zeary had studied medicine and had no agrarian expertise. For a time there was no

resistance to the reforms, Zeary insisted. "Peasants were happy at first, but when they heard we were communists, they changed. The whole world was against us. They said we don't believe in Islam, and they weren't wrong. They could see we didn't pray. We liberated women from having to pay dowry and they said we believed in free love." People felt the land reform was theft and that God would punish them for accepting stolen goods. He paused, searching for a modern image to describe the social conservatism that most Pashtuns accept without thinking: "The Taliban are wild people. The place I was brought up in, long before the Taliban, was a kind of volunteer Taliban society."

Leaders of the PDPA's Parcham wing felt Taraki and Amin and the other ministers were going too far too fast. When they objected during party meetings, Taraki and Amin decided to remove them. Karmal and several other senior figures were sent abroad as ambassadors in August 1978. Sultan Ali Keshtmand, a leading Parchami who was serving as minister of planning, was treated more harshly than any of the others, perhaps because he was a member of the Hazara minority, who practice Shia Islam and mainly live in central Afghanistan in the valleys of the Hindu Kush and the Baba mountains. Keshtmand was arrested, tortured into making a confession and sentenced to death on a charge of having tried to mount a coup—a sentence later commuted to twenty years in prison. After the Soviet invasion he was released along with all other political prisoners and appointed deputy prime minister under Karmal, the man the Russians chose as Afghanistan's new leader. Keshtmand became prime minister in 1981 and served in that post for the next seven years.

Today Sultan Ali Keshtmand also lives in London, where he was given political asylum after the mujahedin took power. Few of his neighbors in the high-rise block where he and his wife, Karima, live know that this polite elderly couple were once key players in the 1980s, he as prime minister and she as general secretary of the Democratic Organization of Afghan Women.

As I tramped up the stairs to see them in a London suburb as unfashionable as the ones where Misaq and Zeary live, I could not help comparing their modest lifestyles with those of Hamid Karzai's government today. Here were three former ministers who must have had access to huge sums of public money. Yet there was no hint of wealth, luxury goods and secret bank accounts about them, unlike the men currently in power in Afghanistan, which, under the new post-Soviet and post-Taliban dispensation, is named by Transparency International in its 2010 report as the world's third most corrupt state, exceeded only by Myanmar and Somalia.

"In the first three months after the April 1978 coup, my brothers were in hiding. There was a strong Parchami underground organization which we had set up. But we were not planning a coup. We did not like coups and had actually opposed the idea of mounting the April one," Keshtmand told me. "In power Amin and Taraki wanted to eradicate literacy within five years. It was ridiculous. The land reforms were unpopular. They were promulgating these so-called revolutionary decrees which they wanted to implement by force. Society wasn't ready. People hadn't been consulted. But Amin and Taraki thought that the peasants would accept them as being in their interest."

After expelling the Parchamis, the Khalqi faction accelerated their radical reforms. They changed the national flag from Islamic green to communist red. Armed resistance spread to more regions of the country. Taraki and Amin sent in the army, but when units started to desert, Soviet military advisers were asked to come to strengthen it. Fearing this was not enough, the Kabul regime's Khalqi leaders appealed thirteen times for full-scale Soviet military support through 1978 and 1979, even as Soviet diplomats (as we now know from Soviet archives and memoirs of former Soviet officials) sent the Kremlin alarmist reports on the developing counterrevolutionary crisis.

The Soviet leaders were uncertain how to react. Their advice to Kabul to abandon or delay the reforms had gone unheeded. Taraki and

Amin preferred to deal with dissent and resistance through repression and imprisonment. Their victims included hundreds of Parchamis in spite of appeals from the Kremlin. Summoned to Moscow in March 1979, Taraki was told by Alexei Kosygin, the Soviet prime minister, that the Kremlin would send arms and other supplies to help him put down the counterrevolution but no Soviet troops since this would only help the rebels as well as the Americans. "Our mutual enemies are just waiting for the moment when Soviet forces appear on Afghan territory. This would give them an excuse to deploy military forma-tions hostile to you on Afghan territory," Kosygin insisted. "We have carefully studied all aspects of this action and come to the conclu-sion that if our troops were introduced, the situation in your country would not only not improve, but would worsen." Moscow considered President Taraki the softer and saner of the two Khalqi leaders, and in September 1979 during a stopover on his return from a summit meet-ing of the Non-Aligned Movement in Havana, Taraki was urged by the Soviet leader Leonid Brezhnev to sack Amin. But when Taraki got home, it was Amin who emerged with the upper hand. He was invited by Taraki to a meeting. While he was being greeted on the stairs by one of Taraki's aides, shooting erupted. Amin ran off with blood on his clothes, but no one was sure what had prompted the violence. Amin took refuge in the Defense Ministry and instructed his troops to arrest Taraki and hold him in a small building in the Arg, the presiden-tial palace complex. The revolutionary council, the country's highest governing body, sacked Taraki as its chairman and elected Amin in his place. A few days later Taraki was suffocated when a pillow was pressed over his face.

Taraki's murder infuriated Brezhnev, who felt personally betrayed. He wanted to punish Amin. The Afghan leader was thought to have killed over 10,000 people by then, and Ghulam Faruq Yaqubi, Karmal's minister for state security, would later publish a list of 12,000 victims of the Khalqi period. Karima Keshtmand, the wife of the arrested Parcham minister of planning, told me in London in April 2011 how she used to walk before dawn every two weeks to Pul-i Charkhi, the main prison on the outskirts of Kabul, to bring her husband food on the few days when visitors were allowed to approach. The authorities claimed they had no knowledge of him and refused to take the food, but Karima Keshtmand recalled that thousands of other desperate women turned up every fortnight in the hope of access to their own imprisoned loved ones.

The crisis in the ruling party's Khalq faction and the growing strength of the mujahedin plunged the Soviet leadership into a deeper quandary. The KGB felt Amin had to be replaced by Babrak Karmal, the leader of the PDPA's more moderate Parcham wing. The Soviet military were wary of the change. They had good contacts with the Afghan generals, who were mostly Khalqis. Both groups agreed that some way had to be found to remove Amin from power and find another, more reliable leader.

Khalqi ministers were worried about what Amin might do next. "We couldn't say anything," Zeary told me. "If he could kill Taraki, he could kill us too. We were frightened." Misaq, by contrast, remained loyal to Amin, even after being approached by a Soviet diplomat to defect. "The official invited me to change sides, but I refused. It wasn't done obviously. They just said, 'Amin may kill you. You can come with us. We will save you.' I think they were already preparing Babrak to take over."

Misaq reported the Soviet diplomat's approach to Amin during a meeting of PDPA Politburo members with a Soviet general who was about to return to Moscow. "Amin was angry," Misaq recalled. "He started writing a letter to Brezhnev in Pashto, saying Puzanov [the Soviet ambassador] is a Parcham agent and is trying to kidnap a member of our government. He asked an interpreter to translate it into Russian. I told Amin this looks like a very unofficial letter. It ought to be typed. Amin laughed and said, 'Brezhnev and I are friends.'" Soon afterward, Puzanov was summoned back to Moscow and replaced.

Soviet leaders had few cards left to play. They wanted to preserve détente and their relatively good relations with the West. These would be jeopardized by invading Afghanistan. But they also feared the collapse of an allied regime in a neighboring country. With the toppling of the Shah of Iran in February 1979 and the onset of an Islamic revolution, the Americans had recently lost their main strategic foothold in the region. The Kremlin assumed Washington would be looking for an alternative country to project U.S. interests on the Soviet Union's southern flank. Afghanistan seemed an obvious choice. Yuri Andropov, head of the KGB, even argued that the United States might deploy nuclear missiles in Afghanistan if the PDPA regime was toppled.

Rumors about Amin's loyalty had begun to circulate. The new Afghan president had studied at Columbia University in New York in the late 1950s and received an MA in education. In 1962 he went back there to enroll in a PhD program. Although he was later expelled from the United States for left-wing activities as head of the Afghan students' association, allegations that he was a CIA agent who wanted to turn Afghanistan into a U.S. ally were taken seriously by the KGB in 1979. They had in their possession the transcript of a party meeting from 1977 in which colleagues accused him of links with the CIA while he was studying in New York. Amin did not deny it but said he was only stringing the CIA along because he needed money. Andropov passed the evidence on to the Politburo, the main Soviet decision-making body.

On December 12, the Politburo, with at least ten of its fourteen full members present, decided to reverse the previous policy of non-intervention. Prime Minister Kosygin, who had been so firmly against intervention earlier in the year, was not present. The rest of the Politburo took the fateful step of ordering a large contingent of troops to prepare to cross the border in order to effect regime change in Kabul. Soviet troops were to topple Amin and replace him with Karmal's team, which would soften the revolution in order to save it. On December 25 the Fortieth Soviet Army moved in.

Like the U.S. decision to attack Afghanistan in 2001, the Soviet invasion was based on a short-term assessment of national security. In contrast to the Americans, who allowed no more than four weeks to pass after 9/11 before taking action, the Russians went through months of top-level discussions and hesitation about the wisdom of going in. What finally tipped them into invading were feelings of anger at Amin, a sense that they were losing control and a desire for revenge for the killing of Taraki. As was to be the case with Bush's decision in 2001, the views of experts were not sought. Little thought was given to the "Day Two problem": what to do after the primary mission of toppling the government was completed. No account was taken of the risk that the attack might recruit more people to take up terrorism or armed resistance and thereby create new and greater threats to national security. Neither government considered the danger that they might be dragged into a long conflict with no easy exit. In both Moscow and Washington, leaders expected their forces would be able to withdraw within weeks or, at most, months.

MYTH NUMBER THREE:
The Soviet invasion led to a civil war and Western aid for the Afghan resistance.

What provoked civil war was not the arrival of Soviet troops. Every one of the Pakistan-based Afghan mujahedin leaders who became famous during the 1980s as the Peshawar Seven went into exile and supported armed resistance to the Afghan Government before December 1979, many of them several years earlier.

Yunis Khalis, a fundamentalist who founded Hezb-i Islami (the Party of Islam), left Kabul as early as 1973 soon after Daoud Khan came to power. He was unhappy with Daoud's modernizing tendencies.

Abdul Rasul Sayyaf, a well-educated preacher and Arabic speaker who was close to the Saudi royal family and is believed to be the man who invited Osama bin Laden to Afghanistan to help the Afghan resistance after the Soviets invaded, also left Kabul in 1973 after mounting a failed coup against Daoud. In Pakistan they organized supplies of arms to their supporters back in Afghanistan to fight the government several years before the PDPA's 1978 coup and the subsequent Soviet invasion.

Burhanuddin Rabbani, a Tajik, was an Islamist scholar who founded Jamiyat-i Islami (the Society of Islam). Wanted by Daoud's police, he fled to the countryside in 1974 and from there to Saudi Arabia and Pakistan.

Gulbuddin Hekmatyar was and still is the eternal rebel, acting today as one of the main armed opponents of the U.S.-led occupation. In his early career a supporter of the pro-Soviet PDPA, he was jailed for two years by Daoud Khan's regime. On release he became an Islamist, established his own political party and mounted an armed uprising in 1975 with support from Pakistan's Inter-Service Intelligence (ISI) directorate. When it failed, he escaped to Peshawar.

Imprisoned for four years during the monarchy in the 1960s, the Islamic Pashtun intellectual Sibghatullah Mojadeddi, known for a more moderate approach than Hekmatyar and Sayyaf, was in Denmark when the coup against Zahir Shah took place in 1973. He left soon afterward for Saudi Arabia and founded the Afghan National Liberation Front.

Pir Sayyid Ahmed Gailani, a friend of the deposed royal family, was one of only two of the mujahedin leaders who stayed in Kabul at least until the PDPA coup of April 1978. But even he left Afghanistan before the Soviet invasion.

Mohammad Nabi Mohammadi also left before the invasion. A lifelong anticommunist, he was elected to the Afghan Parliament during the monarchy. His puritanical style would inspire many Taliban leaders.

So the notion that the Soviet invasion sparked a civil war and armed resistance is wrong. Fighting was already under way against the Daoud regime in the mid-1970s and intensified against Taraki and Amin. The Russians sent military advisers and some special forces at various points in 1979 but saw the task of their full-scale invasion as ending resistance once and for all and making it possible for the more moderate Parchami wing of the ruling party to gain control of the country.

Western backing for the mujahedin had also begun before the Soviet troops arrived. It served Western propaganda to say the Russians had no justification for entering Afghanistan and that their move was essentially an aggressive land grab that the West should resist. In fact, U.S. officials had seen a potential advantage for themselves in the mujahedin resistance. It would create problems for a key Soviet ally and perhaps trap the Soviets into a major blunder. In his memoirs, Robert Gates, then a senior CIA official and later the defense secretary under George W. Bush and Barack Obama, recounts a staff meeting in March 1979 where CIA officials asked whether they should keep the mujahedin going, thereby "sucking the Soviets into a Vietnamese quagmire." The meeting agreed to fund them to buy weapons. By July 1979 Zbigniew Brzezinski, Jimmy Carter's national security adviser, had persuaded Carter to sign a directive for CIA support for the anti-PDPA mujahedin. This was several months before Soviet tanks rolled in. The aid consisted of nonmilitary supplies and cash, which the Americans knew would be used to buy arms. Brzezinski remains pleased to have done so, saying in an interview with TheRealNews that was uploaded in January 2010 that on the day of the Soviet invasion in December, he sent Carter a memo with the comment "We have a chance to give the Soviets their Vietnam." Brzezinski denies having said this to Carter before the invasion. The timing is less important than Brzezinski's satisfaction in having intensified and prolonged a civil war that took almost a million lives and led to the creation of the Taliban movement and ten years of U.S. occupation.

U.S. officials have always ridiculed any CIA link with Amin, but during his 1981 interview with me, Mohammed Dost, the foreign minister, insisted there was one. "I believe he was tied up somehow and had connections with the CIA. As we analyze it, no sane person could do what he did unless there was something," he said. "He was trying either to destroy the country or split it. He used language which was unfamiliar to the Afghan people, talking about Marxism-Leninism and the international proletariat, and so on. He adopted very extreme slogans which they might probably use in some very advanced socialist countries. But you know the situation in Afghanistan and what stage of social development we are at. He was trying to dissociate people from the revolution." Dost's comments made it clear that two years after the Soviet invasion, senior Afghan officials still saw their project as a revolution. They also thought its aims were bound to be popular now that they had moderated the Khalqi excesses.

Dr. Abdul Ghafar Lakanwal, president of the Agricultural Cooperative Union, was typical of the new generation of social engineers, not all of them trained in the Soviet Union. Aged thirty-seven, he had a PhD from a university in West Germany. "The April revolution was the starting point for vital socio-economic changes," he explained during an interview on my visit to Kabul in 1981. "Ninety-five per cent of the Afghan people were illiterate. Eighty-five per cent lived on the land. Four-fifths of them had an average of five acres from which to feed a typical family of twelve people. Many were landless, while others had to work for landlords without any right to an agreed reward for their labor."

I found Lakanwal's next point especially interesting. It highlighted the Achilles' heel of the 1978 revolution. Bad though Afghanistan's land system was, the country never had the extreme land-hunger of pre-revolutionary Mexico or China that had erupted in squatters' movements or peasant uprisings. Afghan peasants did not see issues primarily in class terms. They were linked to their landlord by ties of religion, clan and family and were unready to flout his authority. This, Lakanwal argued, was a key reason why the 1978 land reform decrees had not been greeted with open arms. There were also what he called "technical mistakes." The decrees took away land but left water rights with the landlord. They gave peasants no tools or credit to buy seeds. The aims of the reform were not explained. As a result, opponents were able to argue that the changes were un-Islamic. "The counterrevolution gained more from the reforms than we did," Lakanwal concluded sadly.

As happens with every revolution, the Afghan changes split families. Boz Mohammed, a Foreign Ministry official from Patiya province on the border with Pakistan, told me how his uncle was the richest family head in a village of twenty-five households. As a result, he was the only one to have several wives. His father, by contrast, was poor. Boz Mohammed's political revolt began long before the 1978 revolution when he urged his father not to pay the customary one-third of his crop to the village mullah. Because he was unusually bright, Boz had been the only boy in the village to get a decent education and go on to university. No more than thirty others had done so in a district of 10,000 people.

Now, because of the revolution and the widespread opposition to it, Boz's uncle had fled with his wives and children over the mountains to Pakistan. Boz used a courier to send several letters urging him to come home. He tried to explain to him that the word "socialism" was out. The government's new program described the country as being in "an evolutionary phase of the national democratic revolution." A consultative committee had been set up known as the National Fatherland Front, which included tribal leaders and mullahs. Babrak Karmal regularly attended Friday prayers and could be seen on TV emerging from the mosque. Above all, the land reform decrees had been modified. Three acres of first-class land were still the maximum permitted for every farmer, but exceptions were being made for religious schools and mosques, as well as for landowners who agreed to mechanize production and sell their crops to the state. Boz's arguments were not convincing enough. His uncle stayed in Pakistan.

Lakanwal found the phenomenon infuriating. Whole villages were being enticed to flee to Pakistan. Peer pressure made it impossible for individuals to hold out. "The counterrevolution is psychologically terrorizing the peasants against us with religious slogans," he insisted.

Karmal's government focused on social reform in Kabul and the cities of the north where security was good. Sultan Ali Keshtmand, the former planning minister, became prime minister in 1981. His wife, Karima, who had been a teacher during King Zahir Shah's rule until she was sacked for her political activity as a member of the PDPA, ran the Democratic Organization of Afghan Women, where she presided over a huge expansion in jobs for women, made possible by the provision of free day nurseries and kindergartens. During Zahir Shah's time, Afghanistan had only four such institutions, mainly used by upper-middle-class mothers. In the 1980s, places for 18,000 preschool children were created in residential areas in Kabul, Jalalabad and Mazar-i Sharif. Following the model of communist East Germany, state-owned factories were instructed to set up day nurseries and kindergartens for their workers. Some 22,000 places were organized, according to Karima Keshtmand.

Karima Keshtmand remembers with pride how she showed Valentina Tereshkova, the Soviet cosmonaut who became the first woman in space, around kindergartens in Kabul. The Russian star had just come from an official visit to India and Pakistan. When she saw all the women carers and teachers, unveiled and wearing Western dress, she commented, "But this is like Europe."

I sought out the Soviet civilian contingent in Kabul, diplomats and advisers at the embassy and journalists who lived mainly in villas nearby. They admitted that armed resistance was greater than it had been before their troops arrived. But, like American and British officials in Afghanistan today, they were reluctant to concede that the presence of foreign forces had sparked resistance on nationalistic or patriotic lines. They preferred to see the war as a struggle between a progressive Afghan Government and a fanatical insurgency.

"You can't just say Afghans feel national pride and oppose the government because it's identified with the Soviet Union," said one Russian diplomat, who preferred not to be named. "The situation is more complicated. People look at things in more detail. Who is killing my son? Who is destroying schools? Who is taking my crops? A struggle is going on now in every village. The bandits threaten one family because a son is in the army. Maybe they kill his father or brother, but people in the villages are beginning to ask the government for protection. Things are balanced at the moment. Many people are neutral. If they swing one way, the Karmal government is finished, however many troops we have here. If they swing to the government, the bandits are finished."

The diplomat's analysis touched the essence of every insurgency against a government that lacks full legitimacy. Change the word Karmal to Karzai and you can hear the same refrain today.

Soviet officials acknowledged that the Afghan countryside in the regions close to the Pakistani border was not safe, but they believed that holding Kabul, the other main cities and the roads connecting them was enough to keep the mujahedin at bay and prevent Afghanistan from going over to the Western side. The war was one of attrition, and the Russians felt that as they represented the forces of modernity, time was on their side. "You can't expect quick results in a country which is still in many ways in the fifteenth or sixteenth century," Vasily Safronchuk, the top Soviet adviser in Afghanistan, told me. Although he was the deputy ambassador, he had years of Afghan experience and was often described as Moscow's proconsul, the real political power in the country. He compared the situation to the Bolsheviks' victory in Russia's civil war. "Here in embryo is the history of our own revolution. It took us at least five years to consolidate our power and win through in Russia, and ten years in Central Asia," he said.

In the company of other Europeans and away from Afghan ears, Russian diplomats and journalists in Kabul talked in classic colonial terms. The job of bringing civilization to backward nations was arduous, they said, but necessary to make the world a better place. They complained about the local people as Europeans and Americans often do in any developing country. They were unreliable, ungrateful, unpunctual, inefficient and unnecessarily suspicious of foreigners. "The first two words we learn here," one Russian diplomat said, "are 'tomorrow' and 'the day after tomorrow.' The third phrase is 'parwa nes,' which means 'No problem.' You know, you get a new suit made, and when you collect it, you notice a button is missing. You complain to the tailor and what does he answer?—'parwa nes.' Some of us call this place 'Parwanesistan'." A quarter of a century later his comments find their echo in the sneers, complaints and accusations of ingratitude that waft through the dining rooms and bars of every guesthouse for foreign contractors and development consultants in Kabul today.

Then as now, the Afghan war was a classic example of asymmetric conflict. The mujahedin could not confront the Soviets head-on on the battlefield, and certainly not in the air, but they could use classic resistance techniques: burning schools and other government buildings in rural areas, denouncing people who worked with the Soviet-backed regime as traitors and assassinating them. Kabul might be safe from open warfare, allowing people to walk the streets and go about their daily business without anxiety or fear. But government officials and Soviet staff were not safe from intimidation.

One afternoon in November 1981, I sat in the garden of his news agency's large house with Yuri Volkov, a lanky journalist who first worked in Afghanistan in 1958 and had had several assignments under his belt since then. Winter had not yet set in, and the air of the high plateau where Kabul sits was crisp and warm as long as the sun was up. "There's a bandit over that wall right now," Volkov announced as he handed me a glass of hot tea. Startled, I sat upright. "You won't recognize him," Volkov went on. "Who knows who is a bandit here? He may be carrying a machine gun under his robes. Sometimes they even veil themselves to look like women."

Only that morning one of his staff had told him that a night letter had been slipped under her front door, warning her not to continue

working for the Soviets. This was constantly happening to people on
the Soviet staff, he confided. One of the woman's friends had recently
been murdered with her sister for being collaborators. His views were
borne out by Afghan officials. The head of the ruling party's branch at
Kabul University told me five of his colleagues had been assassinated
in the last two years. Mullahs who worked with the government under
its new policy of financing the building of dozens of new mosques, in
a bid to show the revolution was not against Islam, were prime targets.

"Are you afraid of being assassinated?" I asked Abdul Aziz Sadiq,
a mullah who worked closely with the government as vice president
of the Islamic Affairs Council of Afghanistan. With his loosely bound
turban, a blanket slung over his shoulders and his feet in embroidered
slippers with a curling-back toe, he was the only official I met who still
wore traditional dress. Sometimes the revolution seemed to have produced a kind of sartorial, almost suicidal, apartheid, with suits for party
members while men in the bazaar and the countryside still wore turbans and the shalwar kameez. "I am a religious figure. I cannot think
about the future. The Qur'an does not instruct us to think about the
future," he replied. "Besides, I'm not a member of the party, so there
is no danger of being killed for that." I asked if his serenity meant he
took no precautions. He hesitated for a moment. Then his hand went to
the top right-hand drawer in his desk. Out came a small pistol. "I carry
this," he said, smiling.

Soviet officials tried hard to heal the split between Khalqis and
Parchamis in the PDPA, which they found infuriating and frustrating.
They urged Karmal to appoint Khalqis to top jobs and not behave like
Taraki and Amin, who had expelled, imprisoned and killed hundreds of
Parchamis. Saleh Mohammed Zeary, who had overseen the land reform
before the invasion, was imprisoned when Soviet troops arrived. "I was
put in Pul-i Charkhi prison with all the Khalqi leadership. We stayed
there for a month and were then let out. They couldn't do without us.
Karmal asked me to come back to work. I couldn't support the invasion

but we believed in the USSR as our ideological leader with the same objectives as ours," Zeary told me in London in 2011.

Abdul Karim Misaq, who felt a strong sense of nationalism, refused. As finance minister, he had become disillusioned with Soviet aid several months before the invasion. "They bought our natural gas at a very low price and sold it abroad at a high price," he recalled when I interviewed him in London in March 2011. "They made us buy oil, sugar, and wheat from them at high prices." He could not agree with the invasion. "Babrak invited me to join the government, but we had to sign a document supporting him and saying he had become President legally. I refused to sign because I knew the people of Afghanistan and the world would stand against the Soviet invasion. Babrak told me I'd be out of work and have to stay at home if I didn't sign." For the next nine years he was under virtual house arrest in Mikrorayon with an armed guard at the foot of his staircase, checking all visitors' names and how long they stayed. After the Soviet withdrawal, Najibullah invited him to take a government job. This time Misaq relented, confident that Najibullah was a nationalist. He was appointed mayor of Kabul.

During their time there, Soviet advisers were embedded in every ministry, but as was to happen again after the Americans arrived in Kabul in 2001, the presence of foreigners increased the Afghan Government's sense of dependence. The aim was to help Afghans make their decisions, but it tended to make them feel impotent. As Yuli Vorontsov, Soviet ambassador to Afghanistan, told the Soviet Politburo on November 13, 1986, "Many PDPA leaders take no initiatives. They are used to waiting for our advisers' recommendations and they become somehow helpless. Apparently, at the beginning the advisers would often 'slap their wrists'."

Soviet diplomats' perceptions that the struggle in Afghanistan was about modernization versus tradition and that their social policies represented progress were correct as far as they went. What the Russians found hard to admit was the additional factor that their invasion had transformed and expanded a civil war into a war of national liberation. Tens of thousands of Afghans who had been unmoved by the PDPA's reforms were easily mobilized by the mujahedin argument that it was their patriotic duty to fight against atheistic foreign invaders.

In 1981 the Russians refused to accept the possibility of defeat or even of compromise with the insurgents. They continued to see the war in class, rather than national, terms. "These are people who lost a lot of feudal privileges," Safronchuk, the Soviet proconsul, told me. "It's natural they should oppose the revolution. I don't see anything abnormal in that. But you cannot negotiate with outright counter-revolutionaries."

Surrender was the rebels' only option, he insisted. They could then join the consultative organs that the Afghan Government had set up and make their views known that way. "The National Fatherland Front is there for people who support the revolution or are neutral. If people repent and recognize the revolution's goal, of course they can be brought in, but to expect anything else is rather naive politically," he added. His position was identical to the one the Americans and the Afghan Government were to take for a decade after the fall of the Taliban. The Taliban were urged to lay down their arms, accept the Afghan constitution and be "reconciled" to the prevailing political system. Any suggestion that there could be negotiations with the Taliban was condemned out of hand.

Safronchuk subscribed to the notion that history was on the march and revolutions were irreversible, even in countries as undeveloped as Afghanistan. "The peasant population here is overwhelming and Muslim influence is very strong. That is the negative side," he said. "The positive side is that the Afghan party with seventeen years of struggle, much of it underground—they can never be defeated. A process is underway which is the same as in Vietnam, Nicaragua, Angola and Ethiopia."

ON MY NEXT reporting visit to Kabul, for three weeks in February 1986, I found the war had changed subtly. Each side, the mujahedin and the government, could point to some successes. The mujahedin were now able to cause more fear in Kabul thanks to the long-range 122mm Grad rockets they had acquired, some captured from Soviet forces but most supplied from China via the CIA. Lobbed into the capital on an almost daily basis, the weapons were untargeted. At least three times they landed in the U.S. embassy compound. Although they produced minimal damage and few casualties, the rockets were an irritant that people in Kabul had not had to face before. In this sense the mujahedin could claim to have made tactical progress.

Soviet forces were also performing better than in the first two years of the war. Several ground assaults with tanks into the Panjshir valley northeast of Kabul, where the legendary mujahedin leader Ahmad Shah Massoud had his headquarters, had failed to quash resistance. But the Soviets had kept Massoud from moving his men in large numbers onto the plains north of Kabul. Thus, the Russians could keep open their crucial supply lines through the nearby Salang tunnel to Kabul and the south. By 1986 they had also enlarged their security perimeter around several key cities (although Herat in the west and Kandahar in the south remained unsafe). With a minder but no military escort I was taken to villages around Jalalabad, Mazar-i Sharif and Kabul, something that had not been possible on my first visit in 1981. In Jalalabad they took me forty miles south of the city to within five miles of the Pakistani border to see destruction they said was caused by long-range mujahedin rockets. Wearing ordinary clothes rather than army uniforms, peasants with AK-47s stood guard in their villages or went through simple drills for my benefit. The aim was to show the effectiveness of transferring some of the security burden from the regular army to "people's militias"—a tactic that Obama would later copy.

They also claimed that many rebels were giving up and joining the government side. In a village some six miles to the east of Mazar-i Sharif, I met Mohammad Feroz, who said his three sons had been with

the mujahedin two years earlier. Occasionally they would slip into the
village to see him and get food, but their visits were always short and
unannounced. Now two were back for good and had joined the newly
formed village militia. The third son had joined the Afghan National
Army. Their role in having fought for the rebels was forgiven. This policy too has its echoes in Karzai's U.S.-backed program of reintegration
under which Taliban fighters are urged to drop their weapons and join
the government side.

The Soviet advances were significant. Although they were not
enough to suggest the Soviet Union and its Afghan allies could win the
war, they did indicate that the Russians could not lose it. The Russians
had abandoned any hopes of controlling the Afghan countryside, and
the war was essentially a strategic stalemate in which the Kremlin's goal
of keeping the Afghan government flag flying in the major cities and
protecting the supply lines between them could be prolonged indefinitely, albeit at a high cost in soldiers' lives.

In private, U.S. officials had come to the same conclusion about the
Soviet war although they only admitted it publicly many years later. As
Morton Abramowitz, who directed the State Department's Bureau of
Intelligence and Research at the time, said in 1997, "In 1985 there was
a real concern that the [mujahedin] were losing, that they were sort of
being diminished, falling apart. Losses were high and their impact on
the Soviets was not great." For a Western reporter to write in a major
newspaper that the Soviets were making advances was a guarantee of
unpopularity, and I was fiercely denounced by the mujahedin's cote-
rie of supporters on the Pakistani side of the border. They considered
it unacceptable for anyone to travel to Kabul to report what the war
looked like from that vantage point. Suggesting that the mujahedin
were not winning was an unpardonable offense. Doris Lessing, the brilliant novelist who had once supported communism but later turned
against Moscow, attacked me in an enthusiastic book she wrote about
the fundamentalists she met on a short stay in Pakistan. Radek Sikorski,

then a young anti-Soviet crusader and later Poland's foreign minister, called me the most unpopular man in Peshawar.

My rogue status was given a further boost when Babrak Karmal, the Afghan leader, agreed to let me interview him. He had not met a Western correspondent for several years. On my first visit in 1981, officials declined my request to see him, but this time they let me into the Arg, the fortress compound in central Kabul that houses the presidential palace.

Derided in the West for having been put into power by the Soviet invasion, Karmal had been acknowledged in Afghanistan as an undoubted leader since his time as a passionate orator and left-wing student activist at Kabul University. He had denounced Afghanistan's feudal system in numerous fiery speeches.

By the time I met him, Karmal was fifty-seven and in apparent good health in spite of smoking one cigarette after the other throughout the ninety-minute interview. It was held in a gloomy room, paneled in dark wood and with the curtains drawn so that it felt like a bunker even though it was aboveground. The Afghan president and PDPA leader wore a suit and a black polo-neck sweater. His heavy black-framed glasses made it hard to see his eyes but there was a nervous energy in his movements as he spoke boastfully about his own position and that of the country. Leaks in Washington had just revealed that President Ronald Reagan had persuaded Congress to approve $300 million in covert military aid to the mujahedin over the next two years, more than ten times what was going to the Nicaraguan Contras, the other big U.S. commitment to subversion at the time. Would the Afghan president request more Soviet troops to deal with the increased threat? I asked Karmal. On no account, he replied. Afghan defense forces could handle things on their own. Extra aid to the mujahedin "will never be able to disturb our people's determination to defend their aspirations or deflect them from the path of revolution," he insisted, as though the increase in U.S. help was a minor matter.

Security around the country was almost total, he claimed, as he invited me to come back in a year's time and travel all over Afghanistan "on horseback." "Then you will see how the government controls everything," he said.

Little did I know that this bombastic performance would turn out to be his last media interview as ruling party leader. A few days later the Kremlin told him his time was up.

[3] THE GORBACHEV EFFECT

"Our people don't understand what we are doing there."

—NIKOLAI RYZHKOV,
SOVIET PRIME MINISTER, JANUARY 1987

FIVE YEARS AFTER Soviet forces went into Afghanistan, the reins of power in Moscow were taken by a new leader, who wanted to find an orderly and dignified way out. Unlike Barack Obama, who inherited a war in Afghanistan and chose to regard it as justified, necessary and winnable, Mikhail Gorbachev felt the original aims of the invasion had been wrongly conceived and the war had become a stalemate in which military victory was impossible. The Soviet Union's Fortieth Army had made progress on the battlefield along with allied Afghan forces and their newly created militias, but he realized this would never be enough to defeat the mujahedin.

Gorbachev decided that the exit strategy had to be based on politics—by pursuing negotiations seriously with a view to reaching agreement with Pakistan, Iran and the mujahedin's backers in Saudi Arabia and the United States. The objective should be for all sides to recognize Afghanistan as a neutral country. This would take Afghanistan out of Cold War competition and eliminate any risk of it becoming a site for U.S. bases. As for its form of government, it should be based on compromise between the PDPA and the mujahedin. The Kabul regime must broaden its support.

Karmal had made a few reluctant moves in this direction, but Gorbachev felt they were insufficient. Karmal should be replaced. At the international level Gorbachev saw that the war was undermining Soviet prestige and distracting attention from his efforts to curb the nuclear arms race by fostering better relations with the West. The Kremlin's claim that its troops were legally in Afghanistan because they had been invited by a legitimate Afghan government to help put down a rebel movement initiated by the CIA and other outside forces was accepted only by its allies. Moscow had had no success in winning more international support, least of all from Muslim states. In November 1980, by an overwhelming margin, the UN General Assembly had called for all Soviet forces to withdraw from Afghanistan. The resolution was renewed every year.

The war was taking a high toll in young Soviet lives. Total Soviet losses by the end of the fighting amounted to 15,051 dead. Because of the intensity of the fighting in the first part of the war, when the Russians mounted several futile offensives, they probably exceeded 9,000 by the time Gorbachev came to power. It was a huge toll, roughly equivalent, proportionally, to U.S. losses in Vietnam. With a force in Afghanistan that never exceeded 118,000 throughout its nine-year engagement, the Soviet casualty rate was comparable to the U.S. loss of 58,260 from an army averaging around 400,000 over eight years in Vietnam.

The political impact of soldiers' deaths differed in the two countries. The Soviet Union's tightly controlled system prevented dissent over the war from emerging in politicians' speeches or the media. There were no street or campus protests in the USSR, as there were in the United States over Vietnam. But the Communist Party's Central Committee was receiving countless letters from Soviet parents and other citizens over the cost in young lives and the apparent pointlessness of the mission. Their anxiety reached the ears of Soviet leaders.

In the early Gorbachev period, it was still hard for foreign journalists to get unguarded views on the Afghan war from ordinary Russians.
It was too sensitive an issue to discuss. But in 1989 after political conditions in the USSR had loosened dramatically, I met a group of veterans
of the Afghan war in a gloomy housing complex on the eastern edge of
Moscow and listened to their complaints. Known as Afgantsy, they were
trying to collect money to build a monument to fallen comrades since
it was clear the authorities were not going to erect one. They were conscripts, unlike U.S. and British troops in Afghanistan today, so perhaps
they had a heightened sense of anger. "You remember that mother who
lost her son," said Igor. (Like his friends, he asked not to have to give
his surname.) "She kept repeating, 'He fulfilled his duty. He fulfilled his
duty to the end.' That's the most tragic thing. What duty? I suppose
that's what saves her, her notion of duty. She hasn't yet realized it was
all a ridiculous mistake. I'm putting it mildly. If she opened her eyes to
our whole Afghan thing, she'd probably find it hard to hold out."

Yuri told me he only began to think seriously about the politics
of the war after he got back to Moscow. "Slowly, very slowly, after the
war you begin to think, to imagine, to remember what happened—
the ruined villages, the expressions on people's faces," he said. His first
glimmerings of the war's futility came when he realized how little contact he and his comrades had with Afghans, the people they were supposed to be helping. "Mainly our contact was with kids in the villages
we went through. They were always running some kind of little business. Swapping stuff, selling stuff. Sometimes drugs. It was very cheap.
You felt the aim was to get us hooked. There was not much contact
with Afghan adults except the sarandoy, the police."

The cultural awareness training given to NATO troops in today's
Afghanistan sounds like a throwback to Soviet times. "They gave us a
small piece of paper telling us what not to do and a little dictionary,"
Igor said. "That was it. Don't fraternize. Don't look at women. Don't go
into cemeteries. Don't go into mosques." While Soviet officials called

the enemy bandits and rebels, Soviet soldiers preferred the term *dukhi*, ghosts. The mujahedin were an invisible force, who disappeared into the shadows or merged into the civilian population when you tried to chase them. Igor was contemptuous of the Afghan army when compared to the "ghosts": "Many are cowards. If the ghosts shoot, the army runs away." Igor recalled asking one Afghan soldier what he would do when his conscript service ended. "He said he'd join the ghosts. They pay better."

The Afgantsy felt angry with their fellow citizens as well as their government. Unlike the veterans of the Great Patriotic War, as Russians call World War II, they were treated with indifference or contempt. In theory, families with sons in Afghanistan were supposed to jump up the line in the wait for a state-supplied apartment, but bureaucrats often did not obey the rule. Wounded veterans experienced problems in getting artificial limbs from Soviet hospitals. I had first run into Yuri, Igor and their friends some months earlier at an extraordinary reception in central Moscow offered by a group of American veterans of the Vietnam War. Motivated by curiosity and solidarity with what they felt were similar victims of a disastrous superpower intervention in a Third World country, the Americans had financed the trip to Moscow out of their own pockets. They were a generation ahead, grayer, balder and fatter than the Russian vets, but both sides found an easy rapport as they swapped stories about the difficulties of readjusting to civilian life and the poor treatment they got from fellow citizens. With the Cold War winding down, it was the high point of U.S.-Soviet friendship. The Americans promised to raise money to send the Russian vets the most modern prosthetics.

In a Moscow bookshop two years later I found an anthology of letters and poems sent to their families by soldiers serving in Afghanistan. Called *My Darlings* and edited by Pyotr Tkachenko, an author with Defense Ministry connections, the book explicitly challenged negative Russian attitudes to the Afgantsy. It praised their sacrifice and selflessness and said they had fought as bravely as veterans of World War II. They may not have been directly defending their homeland, but they were doing their "internationalist duty" by risking their lives to help Afghans.

All soldiers' letters were censored, as is usual in most armies during wartime, and many of the young conscripts had only a basic education. So the letters were inevitably laconic and direct, full of simple pleas to family, wives and girlfriends not to worry. They described the primitive *kishlaks* or villages with mud-brick homes and walled compounds where Afghans lived, and when their letters touched cautiously on hardships, they were usually concerned with the deep cold of winter or the loneliness of being garrisoned in outposts in the mountains.

Every so often I came across a phrase that showed that soldiers wondered about the point of their mission in Afghanistan. First Lieutenant Sergei Ivankovich, who was later killed, wrote: "I'm so fed up. You don't know what you're fighting for or whether the Afghan people really need us. . . . They're obscure and completely illiterate. They don't even know they've had a revolution and there's a new government in the country. So there's a lot that's incomprehensible and puzzling in this place and in people's awareness. . . . we have to hunt the rebels and protect these people. It's all very strange." Private Sergei Bolotnikov, a farmworker from Kazakhstan, told his wife and small daughter in May 1980:

> One can't help thinking, thank God I'm still alive. I miss you so much, Marinochka, and little Svetlana. I'm so lonely. It's unbearable. Sometimes I just want to fall on a pile of hay and cry and cry. Then you remember the fighting, how you jump across rocks, slide downhill and look for a place to hide from the bullets and then shoot. How you crawl up to a house from where they're shooting at you, toss a grenade and then from behind a wall shoot the people who were in the house. You look at the corpses and you're pleased you've been lucky. You were smarter than they were. How often I've been in these exchanges. It's

awful even to think about it, still alive and without a scratch. I've
never hidden behind my mates. 'Cos when fighting starts you forget
everything, you put all thoughts aside, and remember one thing only:
run up there, crawl up there, and kill. Otherwise they will kill you.

In June 1980 he was telling his wife that "at prayers the mullahs tell
people that the Russians have come to kill them and take their wives
and snatch their children, so pick up your guns, go into the mountains,
and then the Russians will leave. It's such a pity they don't understand
us or we them. If only we could explain to them why we've come." His
opinion of the Afghan army was low. "Afghan soldiers aged between
17 and 35 are serving with us. They go out with us on operations. It's
much quieter without them. At least when they go ahead it's not bad.
You know they won't shoot you in the back. They're all Muslims and
forcibly pressed into the army. More than once whole units have gone
over to the rebels."

Three months later, Sergei was dead. His wife, Marina, managed to
track down a member of his unit. She got an answer relatively quickly.
"Dear Marina and daughter Svetlana, I got your first letter and am sending you an immediate reply. You ask how your husband and our friend
Sergei Bolotnikov died. It happened on September 24 in the village of
Bach in Kunar province. There was an exchange of fire and Private
Sergei Bolotnikov was wounded in the arm. He carried on firing but
got a second serious and fatal wound. An enemy bullet went through
his head and came out through the cheek. He died in the arms of a
comrade, saying 'Marina' and 'Svetlana'. Your husband died a hero."

AT THE TIME he was selected to lead the country in March 1985, Mikhail
Gorbachev already sensed the futility of seeking a military victory. He
had chaired a Politburo meeting shortly before the death of his predecessor, Konstantin Chernenko, at which the defense minister and the KGB
chief reported on a trip to Kabul. They said the Afghan officer corps

was still torn by the Khalq/Parcham split, almost half the border with Pakistan was a "hole" and 80 percent of the territory was controlled by the "bandits." After Chernenko's funeral, Gorbachev received Babrak Karmal in the Kremlin. The meeting was expected to be no more than a courtesy call, but the transcript shows they discussed the situation in detail. Gorbachev used standard phrases about the Afghan revolution's "irreversibility," but his central message to Karmal was that he must broaden the base of his power in order to save it. "Comrade Karmal," he said, "you naturally understand, as other members of the Afghan leadership obviously do, that Soviet troops cannot stay in Afghanistan forever."

A month later, in his private diary, Gorbachev's closest foreign policy adviser, Anatoly Chernyayev, discussed the letters being sent to the Central Committee and *Pravda*, the main Communist Party paper. Chernyayev wrote, "The main message: why do we need this, and when will it end?! Women are writing, pitying the young men who are dying and suffering mentally there. They are writing that if 'this is so necessary,' then send volunteers, at least soldiers with commissions, and not conscripts. . . . Officers, and even one general who signed his name are saying they are unable to explain to their soldiers and subordinates 'why they are here'." Reinforcing the point that Afghans were less interested in defending the regime than the Soviet Army was, he mentioned two letters from the crews of a tank and a helicopter. They accused *Pravda* of falsely describing a battle in which Afghan troops supposedly fought heroically. In reality, they wrote, "we were the ones fighting and everything was completely different [from your report]." Their complaints sounded like those from today's Afghanistan where U.S. and U.K. troops blame the Afghan National Army for a lack of motivation.

There were arguments against withdrawal. The most important was that any perception of retreat or that Moscow was abandoning a foreign ally could undermine Soviet prestige within the communist world and among national liberation movements. In the spring of 1985

Gorbachev asked a commission of key ministers to look into the "consequences, pluses and minuses of a withdrawal." Separately, in June, he received a damning report from General Valentin Varennikov, the head of the Defense Ministry's Operational Group in Afghanistan. Varennikov, who had opposed the invasion before it happened, noted that Soviet military successes had no long-term effect on the opposition, which continued to grow. In comments that sounded uncannily like the problems facing U.S. forces today, he said the Afghan Government failed in the key counterinsurgency strategy of holding territory cleared of guerrillas. As a result, "combat actions for stabilizing the situation in the country can have only a temporary character. With time the insurgents in these districts are capable of re-establishing lost positions."

Also that summer, General Mikhail Zaitsev, Soviet commander in East Germany, was appointed as the new military chief in Afghanistan and was asked to evaluate the army's options. Zaitsev reported that the only way to achieve military success would be to seal the country's borders with Pakistan, and this would require at least a quarter of a million troops. He recognized this was unrealistic.

The two generals' analyses highlighted the problems that had dogged the Soviet invasion from the start. In December 1979, troops seized Kabul in a blitzkrieg, bringing thousands of troops into the capital in waves of aircraft while others rumbled down from Soviet Uzbekistan in tanks, armored personnel carriers and trucks. This was an easy success. What was harder was to dislodge the mujahedin, who had taken over parts of the countryside while Taraki and Amin were in power.

The first major Soviet offensive took place in the Kunar valley at the end of February 1980. A fertile sixty-mile-long valley, inhabited mainly by Pashtuns, it connects the Hindu Kush with the Pakistani border and was a crucial corridor for mujahedin supplies to Nuristan, Badakhshan and other northern provinces. The area had fallen to the mujahedin in the summer of 1979 before the Soviet invasion. The Russians deployed

5,000 troops. After two days of bombardment by aircraft and artillery, helicopters dropped soldiers on mountain ridges while tanks and armored personnel carriers rumbled into the villages. Perhaps as many as 150,000 people fled to Pakistan. Edward Girardet of the *Christian Science Monitor*, one of the few Western reporters who traveled with the mujahedin and wrote careful, evidence-based reports, described the onslaught as a painful setback for the guerrillas, who were still basking in the glory of having pushed the government's representatives out a year earlier. But guerrilla losses were low since many slipped away in the face of the Soviet advance. The pool of angry refugees created hundreds of new mujahedin recruits, ready to infiltrate back when the Soviet forces withdrew.

In 1981 and 1982, Soviet operations focused on the Panjshir valley northeast of Kabul, mounting as many as six offensives against Ahmad Shah Massoud, a charismatic Tajik commander. In the biggest operation in May 1982, the Russians led 15,000 Soviet and Afghan army troops into the valley. But the mujahedin—well supplied from Pakistan with mortars, rocket-propelled grenades and anti-aircraft guns, and with a good knowledge of the local terrain—beat them back after six weeks.

From then on, the Russians concentrated on smaller operations, and on both sides the war became one of targeting the other side's logistics rather than seizing territory. The Russians wanted to keep control of the main cities and the supply lines between them, in particular the road from Uzbekistan across the northern semi-desert to Kabul through the Salang tunnel. The mujahedin did their best to mine and ambush it. Meanwhile, the Russians went after mujahedin logistics by trying to stem the flow of arms and men across the border from Pakistan. Unlike the Americans, who subjected Laos and Cambodia to heavy and sustained bombing during the Vietnam War to try to interdict enemy supply trails, the Russians did not attack mujahedin in Pakistan. Instead, they bombed houses and irrigation systems and dropped mines in villages throughout the Afghan border provinces, forcing agriculture to come to a halt and leaving thousands of people without livelihoods. Many crossed the border into Pakistan.

Mujahedin supporters claimed the Soviet strategy was intended to create a depopulated *cordon sanitaire* that would deny support to the mujahedin when they came in from Pakistan and make it hard for them to find food and shelter. PDPA officials denied this. As Ahmad Sarwar, the former Afghan chargé in London who had served in the Kabul Foreign Ministry from 1982 to 1986, told me in 2011, "I don't believe the Russians pushed people out. [The strategy] made it easier for the enemy to recruit volunteers. The Afghan Government tried to control the border to stop people leaving Afghanistan." Whether they were encouraged to go by the mujahedin or the Soviets or whether they left for Pakistan under peer pressure as other tribal members crossed the border to safety, by the end of 1988 there were 3.3 million Afghans in Pakistan, and another million were in Iran.

The massive hardship their tactics were causing Afghan villagers did not mean the Russians had given up on trying to win hearts and minds. They used to make occasional forays into rural areas to contact local elders, offer medical aid and free food and urge people to support the Afghan Government. The Soviet news agency TASS reported that in the nine years of the occupation, Soviet troops built and restored more than eighty schools, twenty-five hospitals, twenty-six kindergartens, thirty-five mosques and 325 residential houses. Hundreds of miles of ditches and canals were dug and boreholes were drilled to supply freshwater. These figures do not include aid for infrastructure projects paid by Moscow but completed with Afghan labor.

Indeed, the Soviet agenda included the full range of nation-building objectives that the Americans were to set themselves a quarter century later: political reforms, economic development, infrastructure improvements and education. But, again, as is true with the Americans and their ISAF allies, spending on these projects was far outweighed by the money used for military purposes.

The military absorbed about 94 percent of Soviet spending in Afghanistan, while nonmilitary aid accounted for only 6 percent. Meanwhile, according to the Congressional Research Service, the war in Afghanistan cost the United States $187.9 billion between 2001 and 2009, of which $175 billion went to the Department of Defense and only $12.9 billion to diplomacy and aid, giving a ratio of military to non-military spending of 94:6, the same proportion as the Soviets reached.

The war involved appalling brutality on all sides. Vitaly Krivenko, an officer in a motor-rifle regiment, was manning a roadblock near Herat sometime after being dispatched from the Soviet Union in 1985. On one side was a village where people were friendly. The deserted village opposite was thought to harbor mujahedin preparing an ambush. The troops called in close air support, but the helicopter gunships that arrived destroyed the wrong village. "So what?" Krivenko wrote, "how many other villages got wiped out, for good reason or simply for fun?" In the autumn of 1989 Andrei Greshnov interviewed Mohamed Hamid, a mujahedin detainee, in Kabul's interrogation prison. Greshnov asked about popular attitudes to Soviet soldiers. Hamid replied, "It varied. In general nobody was happy with the arrival of foreign forces or with the government they had put in place. I personally saw what the shuravi [Soviets] got up to in the provinces. They would wipe out whole villages in retaliation for one rifle shot. . . . I thought a great deal about what was going on in my country and wrote to my brother who was studying in the USSR. He and I have taken a different path in life. Part of the population of course supports the present regime. But those who do that are already infidels and they will have to pay for the blood they have shed."

Asked if he had ever killed Soviet soldiers or tortured prisoners, Hamid said, "People who wanted to cut off heads went ahead and did it. People who didn't want to didn't do it. Incidentally, torture and the cutting off of heads are not some kind of special regime thought up especially for Soviet soldiers. Any infidel can end up without his head, including an Afghan. . . . I prefer to sell my enemy for cash to people who are willing to buy rather than torture him. I saw that in Logar province. In the region of Sorkhab we destroyed a column and took several Soviet prisoners. They cut the heads off the soldiers but sold [ransomed] the officers." How common this kind of incident was is impossible to say. It is equally difficult to say how many people were killed by Soviet attacks. The number of civilian deaths during the war has never been calculated with accuracy. Estimates of civilians killed by both sides over the nine years of fighting range widely, from 600,000 to 1.5 million.

It is to Gorbachev's immense credit that he made a firm decision to withdraw Soviet troops after receiving his skeptical generals' reports about the chances of success and the cost of prolonging the fighting. Never an enthusiast for the war, he now had the considered views of his military experts. Though generals in most armies have a professional bias toward optimism, the Soviet high command made no effort to disguise the reality as they saw it. Fortified by their analysis, Gorbachev summoned Karmal to Moscow. He had already warned the Afghan leader in March that Soviet troops could not stay in Afghanistan forever. Now he went further. As Chernyayev put it in his diary entry for October 17, 1985, "I was at the Politburo today. There was a historic statement about Afghanistan. Gorbachev has finally made up his mind to put an end to it." The Soviet leader told his Politburo colleagues that in his meeting with Karmal a few hours earlier, he had warned the Afghan leader to start compromising with the regime's opponents so that Soviet troops could leave. Gorbachev reported that the Afghan leader was dumbfounded. He tried to argue that the Russians needed Afghanistan more than he did. Gorbachev replied that the USSR would continue to provide weaponry, equipment and aircraft, but its troops would be leaving. He urged Karmal, "If you want to survive you have to broaden the regime's social base, forget about socialism, share real power with the people who have real authority, including the leaders of bands and organizations that are now hostile towards you. Restore Islam to its rights, [restore] people's customs, lean on the traditional authorities, find a way to make the people see what they are getting from the revolution." Impatiently, he also warned the Afghan leader to stop the squabbles between Parchamis and Khalqis and "turn the army into an army."

Karmal tried to dissuade Gorbachev from withdrawing by arguing that Islamic fundamentalists would take over, threatening the stability of the Soviet Union's Central Asian republics. The Karmal case was a forerunner of what became the central plank of U.S. policy under Bush and Obama. Allowing the Karzai government to fall, it was claimed, would lead to a victory for al Qaeda and a dramatic boost to the popularity of jihadi movements everywhere.

Karmal's argument was hollow. In the mid-1980s, the Kremlin had little reason to feel anxiety about the appeal of fundamentalism in Central Asia or worry that it would become an anti-Soviet force. Even when the Soviet Union started to wobble in 1989, the Central Asian republics with their nominally Muslim populations were conspicuous by their quiescence. Unlike the Baltics or the three republics of the Caucasus, Central Asia spawned no grassroots popular fronts demanding freedom for political and religious activity and national sovereignty. At the elite level, the region's communist leaders declined to follow the example of party secretaries in the other Soviet republics who called for economic autonomy and later moved to ask for full independence. Even after the failure of the August 1991 coup against Gorbachev, men like Nursultan Nazarbayev, the Communist Party leader of Kazakhstan, became Gorbachev's main ally against Boris Yeltsin in trying to retain some sort of federal structure for the USSR instead of opting for what actually emerged—fifteen republics without any Soviet center at all. So Soviet Central Asia's leaders had independence thrust upon them. It was only after the USSR had broken apart that they gradually started on the long road to nation building.

During their meeting in October 1985, Gorbachev issued no threat to remove Karmal, but the thought that the Afghan leader might have to be replaced was already in the Soviet leader's mind. Chernyayev reports Gorbachev as telling the Politburo later: "With or without Karmal we will follow this line firmly, which must in a minimally short amount of time lead to our withdrawal from Afghanistan."

Gorbachev had two things in his favor. First, an international negotiating track already existed, and this could be exploited to provide a dignified cover for a Soviet retreat. The USSR and the United States had been negotiating with the Afghan and Pakistani governments under a UN mediator at Geneva since 1982. Even though neither the United States nor Pakistan recognized the Kabul regime, they were prepared to consider its views and talk to it through the UN mediator and Soviet officials. In general terms the framework for a deal had long been agreed. This was that the Russians would withdraw once "interference" from outside had ended, a formula that supported Moscow's argument that the USSR had only intervened in Afghanistan as a response to other countries' interventions. The obstacle to finalizing a deal was that until Gorbachev came to power, the Kremlin had been refusing to offer any timetable for the start of the Soviet withdrawal or how long it would take to complete.

This refusal prevented the Geneva talks from making progress. Once Gorbachev was installed as the Kremlin's new leader, the talks accelerated. All sides accepted that a peace deal would involve four separate agreements: mutual diplomatic recognition between Afghanistan and Pakistan and promises of non-interference and respect for sovereignty, acceptance of the right of refugees to return, international guarantees of the deal from the USSR and the United States, and an agreement on the "interrelationships" among the first three points. This would specify how many months the Soviet pullout would take, and when it would start.

The second factor that eased the process for Gorbachev was that most of his senior military men, and not just Zaitsev and Varennikov, felt the war was not worth fighting. There was no mismatch between the civilians and the military. This was very different from the political context that faced Obama a quarter of a century later (as the Woodward book *Obama's Wars* makes clear). If he tried to reject his top generals' demands for tens of thousands of extra troops to be sent to Afghanistan, the American president could face serious opposition from powerful men who could go public and influence opinion in their favor. In Britain, similarly, Prime Minister Gordon Brown and his successor, David Cameron, came under pressure from the top brass not to set a firm timeline for withdrawal.

In 1980s Moscow things were different. Gorbachev found his plans for withdrawal had broad support from the top brass. "We have lost this battle. The majority of the Afghan people support the counter-revolution now," Marshal Sergei Akhromeyev, the chief of the general staff, told the Politburo in November 1986. He pointed out, just as the defense minister and the KGB chief had done two years earlier, that while Soviet forces could clear an area, they could not hold it for long. "After seven years in Afghanistan, there is not one square kilometer left untouched by a boot of a Soviet soldier. But as soon as they leave a place, the enemy returns and restores it all back the way it used to be. . . . We lost the peasantry, who has not benefited from the revolution at all. 80% of the country is in the hands of the counterrevolution, and the peasant's situation is better there than in the government-controlled areas." When the Politburo met again the following January, it was Marshal Sergei Sokolov's turn to sound a note of despair. "The military situation has deteriorated recently," the defense minister told his colleagues. "The amount of shelling of our garrisons has doubled. They mainly shoot from villages, calculating that we would not fire at settlements in response. . . . This war cannot be won militarily." Conspicuously absent from all the internal Soviet discussions is any recommendation for the Afghan army to be built up in order to fill the gap left by Soviet troops. The Obama administration has pinned its exit strategy on training and equipping enough Afghan troops and police to allow for a U.S. pull-out by 2014. The assumption is that any solution in Afghanistan must be military, however much U.S. decision makers pay lip service to the importance of a political settlement.

The Soviet leadership refused to trap itself into a similar position. While they intended to keep sending supplies and equipment to the Afghan army, their troop withdrawal was not dependent on this. The Kremlin's preferred option was for a political agreement with the muja-hedin, but it was prepared to leave even without one.

In the gamut of problems that faced Moscow then and Washington today, one factor was identical—the role of Pakistan. As long as Pakistan offered the mujahedin a safe haven and kept the border open for weapons and fighters to cross into Afghanistan, Gorbachev and his colleagues realized the war could never be won. Obama had to wrestle with the same uncomfortable truth, made worse in his case because Pakistan was ostensibly Washington's friend and client while in reality being beyond control.

MYTH NUMBER FOUR:
The USSR suffered a massive military defeat in Afghanistan at the hands of the mujahedin.

This is one of the most persistent myths of Afghan history. It has been regularly trumpeted by every former mujahedin leader, from Osama bin Laden and Taliban commanders to the warlords in the current Afghan Government. It is also accepted unthinkingly as part of the Western narrative of the war, repeated by politicians in Europe and the United States as well as analysts like Zbigniew Brzezinski.

Some Western politicians go so far as to say that the alleged Soviet defeat in Afghanistan helped to cause the collapse of the Soviet Union itself. On this they agree with bin Laden and al Qaeda's other leaders, who have claimed they destroyed one superpower and are on their way to destroying another.

The reality is that the Afghan mujahedin did not defeat the Soviets on the battlefield. They won some important encounters, notably in the Panjshir valley, but lost others, for example in April 1986, when the Soviets captured a major cave complex at Zhawar in Paktiya province and drove out Jalaluddin Haqqani, a mujahedin commander who was later to ally himself with the Taliban and still remains a major threat to the Americans.

Even after the Russians withdrew, the mujahedin failed to inflict a military defeat on the Najibullah regime and its army and militias, as we will see in the next chapter. What is true is that neither side defeated the other. Just as the mujahedin failed to beat the Soviets, the Soviets did not defeat the mujahedin. The Soviets left Afghanistan when they calculated that the war had become a stalemate and was no longer worth the high price in money, men and international prestige that they were having to pay to keep it going.

MYTH NUMBER FIVE:
Afghans have always beaten foreign armies, from Alexander the Great to modern times.

Afghan history is certainly littered with occasions when foreign invaders were humiliated on the battlefield. But there have also been many cases when foreign armies penetrated the country and inflicted major defeats. In 330 BC, Alexander the Great marched his troops successfully through the area of Central Asia that is now Afghanistan, meeting little serious opposition. On his way he founded the city of Kandahar, naming the new settlement after himself. He then moved on to the Indus valley in the north of the subcontinent. In the winter of 327 to 326 BC, he returned and fought the powerful clans of the Kunar and Swat valleys in what are eastern Afghanistan and northwestern Pakistan today. Although he suffered wounds in the shoulder and ankle, he and his troops overcame all resistance and sacked the enemies' forts. More than a millennium later, the Mongol leader Genghis Khan, another great conqueror and empire builder, also moved his army through the area, brushing resistance aside.

Since Afghanistan emerged as a modern state in the eighteenth century, there have been three wars with Britain, which further dented the myth of the invincible Afghan. The British invasion of 1839, which led to the so-called First Anglo-Afghan War, was a prime example of the up-and-down fortunes of war—initial victory for the intruders followed by stunning defeat followed by a second victory. The politics of the war had several echoes with the Soviet invasion of 1979. Tsarist Russia and the British Empire were competing for influence over Central Asia and Afghanistan, the region that lay between them, in what became known as the Great Game. The Afghan ruler Mohammed Dost had aroused British suspicions by starting negotiations with Russia. To preempt any more such contacts, the British marched up from India to effect regime change. Like the Kremlin in 1979, they claimed they had only come to Afghanistan by invitation to suppress foreign interference and rebel opposition. Once in Kabul, the British installed a new ruler and sent Mohammed Dost into exile in India. When resistance developed, they first tried to quell it, but in 1842 they decided to withdraw. On the way back to India their army of 4,500 men was ambushed and massacred north of Jalalabad. One survivor, an army chaplain, Reverend G. R. Gleig, described the First Anglo-Afghan War as "a war begun for no wise purpose, carried on with a strange mixture of rashness and timidity, brought to a close after suffering and disaster, without much glory attached either to the government which directed, or the great body of troops which waged it. Not one benefit, political or military, has Britain acquired with this war. Our eventual evacuation of the country resembled the retreat of an army defeated."

Disaster it was—though it was overtaken by victory three years later when British forces captured Kandahar and Kabul again. They put Mohammed Dost, the previous Afghan emir, back in power on condition he resist any advances by Russia. Having made the point that they were interested not in occupation but only in control over the country's foreign policy, they wisely withdrew a month later.

In 1878 the British invaded again after a new Afghan ruler, Sher Ali, appeared to be favoring the Russians. His offense was nothing more threatening to British power than to allow a Russian ambassador to take up residence in Kabul. Though the British suffered a major defeat at the battle of Maiwand near Kandahar in 1880, their main army marched down from Kabul and beat the Afghans. The British then moved the frontier of British India up to the Khyber Pass, and Afghanistan had to cede various frontier areas as well as the city of Quetta to Britain. Britain again insisted on taking charge of Afghanistan's foreign policy in return for "protecting" the Afghan emir. A year later, they withdrew, satisfied that they had a buffer against Russian expansion. The areas they had seized, along with the city of Peshawar, which Sikh rulers from south Asia had wrested from Afghanistan in 1834, remain a bone of contention between Afghanistan and Pakistan today, as Chapter Two's discussion of the Pashtunistan issue explained.

The Third Anglo-Afghan War was different from the earlier two in origin though not in outcome. This time the fighting was launched by the Afghans. Amanullah Khan, who had just become the country's ruler after his father's assassination, sent troops across the border into British India in May 1919 in an attempt to capture Peshawar and other towns that many Afghans considered theirs. Within a month they were forced to retreat, in part because British planes bombed Kabul and other cities in one of the first displays of airpower in Central Asia. While the war ended in tactical victory for the British, the fact that their troop losses were twice those of the Afghans suggested it was a strategic defeat. They forced the Afghans to accept the so-called Durand line as the de facto frontier between Afghanistan and British India, though to this day no Afghan government has acknowledged it as their country's southern border in international law. In return the British abandoned control of

Afghan foreign policy at last. Afghanistan was recognized as an independent state with the right to conduct its own affairs.

The varied results of the three Anglo-Afghan wars undermine the simple claim that Afghans always defeat foreigners. What is true is that foreigners have always had a hard time occupying the country for a long period. The British came to understand that. From bitter experience they kept their interventions in Afghanistan relatively short, preferring domination over its foreign affairs to the option of long-term settlement and internal control, which they adopted in India and managed to maintain for more than a century.

The notion of the invincible Afghan runs into another area of contradictory evidence. Without doubt Afghans have a proud history of tenacious, resourceful and fierce guerrilla warfare, but the record shows they have spent as much time fighting each other as they have spent fighting foreigners. That point will be discussed at greater length in the next chapter.

MYTH NUMBER SIX:

The CIA's supply of Stinger missiles to the mujahedin forced the Soviets out of Afghanistan.

This is one of the most frequently repeated myths of the Soviet period in Afghanistan. It was given new life by George Crile's 2003 book *Charlie Wilson's War* and the 2007 film of the same name, starring Tom Hanks as the loud-mouthed congressman from Texas. Book and movie claim that Wilson turned the tide of the war by persuading President Reagan to supply the mujahedin with shoulder-fired missiles that could shoot down helicopters. The Stingers certainly forced a shift in Soviet tactics. Helicopter crews switched their operations to night raids since the mujahedin had no night-vision equipment. Pilots of assault helicopters and fixed-wing aircraft made their bombing runs at greater height, thereby diminishing the accuracy of the attacks, but the rate of aircraft losses did not change significantly. According to one

U.S. Government estimate, quoted by the veteran Washington-based analyst Selig Harrison, roughly a thousand Soviet and Afghan aircraft were destroyed in the seven years of war to the end of 1986 (a rate of around 143 a year), mainly by Chinese heavy machine guns and other less sophisticated anti-aircraft weaponry, whereas during 1987, when Stingers were widely used, Soviet and Afghan aircraft losses numbered between 150 and 200.

The best study of the Stingers issue was done by Alan J. Kuperman of the University of Texas. He argues that the Stinger myth has been distorted on both sides of the old Cold War debate. Hawks assert that the Stingers hastened the Soviet retreat from Afghanistan and the eventual collapse of Soviet communism, thereby vindicating their hard-line stance that military pressure won the Cold War for the West. Doves claim the Stingers prolonged the war by provoking the Soviets to delay withdrawal in order to save face. The evidence for both claims is questionable.

Kuperman points out that the Soviet decision to prepare to withdraw from Afghanistan was made by the Politburo in October 1985. Gorbachev signaled it for the first time publicly when he told the Twenty-seventh Communist Party Congress in February 1986 that Afghanistan was a "bleeding wound" and "we would like to withdraw Soviet troops in the nearest future." The undisclosed decision and the public announcement came several months before Stinger missiles entered Afghanistan in significant quantities in the autumn of 1986. None of the secret Politburo discussions that have since been declassified mentioned the Stingers or any other shift in mujahedin equipment as the reason for the policy change from indefinite occupation to preparations for retreat. The Soviet leadership's assessment of the need to withdraw was based almost entirely on the political stalemate in Afghanistan and their view that the Afghan regime had to accept "national reconciliation" in place of one-party rule maintained by force while Moscow must abandon its initial objectives. The Kremlin's new aim was to preserve a neutral but friendly government in Kabul rather than insist that the Afghan "revolution" continue.

The defeat the Soviet Union suffered in Afghanistan was political, not military. Moscow's attempt to safeguard the PDPA program of radical reform in one of the world's poorest and most conservative countries had run into the sand. Eduard Shevardnadze, the Soviet foreign minister, summed it up starkly during a Politburo meeting in January 1987: "We went into Afghanistan in total ignorance of the psychology of the people." Gorbachev was equally blunt: "We were tied in by ideology. We assumed it was possible to jump three stages at once—from feudalism to socialism. Now we can look at the situation openly." It took another year before an article in the Moscow weekly *Literaturnaya Gazeta* in February 1988 offered the first public admission of failure in the Soviet media:

> *Since those December days when the USSR's troops went into Afghanistan, the Kabul government's political course has changed many times. State meetings are preceded by a mullah saying prayers. The flag is no longer red and has a green Islamic stripe. The party has stopped talking about building socialism. It has renounced the monopoly of power and proclaimed pluralism. All this makes it possible to say the goals which the PDPA originally announced have not been achieved and the revolutionary government themselves have abandoned them. As a result, the presence of Soviet troops in the country loses its point. Withdrawal is as inevitable as it is logical.*

It was the second failure of modernization in Afghanistan in the twentieth century. The first effort, under Amanullah Khan in the 1920s, also ran into armed resistance and came to nothing. Acclaimed as a hero after winning the country's formal independence at the end of the Third Afghan War, Amanullah developed an ambition to change Afghanistan's ancient social customs. He was influenced by the secular reforms that Kemal Ataturk was introducing in Turkey as well as by the way of life he saw during a long tour of Europe in 1927. He inaugurated obligatory military service, in part to promote a sense of nationhood in place of traditional tribal loyalties. He drew up a new constitution, which removed the divine authority of the country's rulers while keeping the hereditary monarchy. The constitution called for education at primary school level to be compulsory. He pressed for girls to be educated and set up coeducational schools. Women were ordered to abandon the traditional veil. He himself wore Western dress and insisted his ministers and government officials do likewise.

The reforms aroused immediate opposition from tribal and clerical leaders who argued that Amanullah had fallen prey to foreign un-Islamic ideas. A small urban elite was imposing alien practices on the majority, they claimed. Armed revolts broke out in several parts of the country (helped in some places by the British, who were, as usual, worried by growing influence on Afghanistan from Russia, now under Soviet rule). In January 1929 Amanullah was forced to abdicate and go into exile.

The failure of his reform strategy presaged what was to happen to the PDPA two generations later. It also contains a lesson for the current U.S.-led occupation. Hamid Karzai and the program of modernization that the United States and its allies are financing may also come to grief. The armed insurgency in the Pashtun heartlands of southern Afghanistan is in part a revolt against what is seen as the imposition of alien customs.

Like the Stinger myth, which has blossomed in recent years as part of a right-wing propaganda attempt to manipulate history, a massive Western propaganda and disinformation campaign went on during the war itself. The U.S. and British embassies in New Delhi, Islamabad and Kabul played a key role in it, as I discovered on my February 1986 visit to Afghanistan. Western diplomats in Kabul told me the Soviets could not operate in Paghman, the royal family's former summer resort outside the city. Whether they genuinely thought it was true I had no way of knowing, but I challenged Brigadier-General Abdul Haq Ulomi, head of the PDPA Central Committee's armed forces department, to let me see if the diplomats were right. He hesitated at first, but three days later officials took me to the town in an ordinary unarmored car. Paghman sits on a hillside below a wall of mountains, making it cooler than the capital. Large houses on the upper slopes showed signs of extensive damage, and ruined telegraph and power lines lay on the ground beside the main road. But the town clearly had a few inhabitants and shops were open.

The Arch of Independence, which Amanullah had built as an Afghan replica of the Arc de Triomphe that he had admired in Paris, was scarred with bullet holes but still stood erect. (It would be destroyed in the fighting between rival mujahedin factions a decade later.) As signs of a government presence in the town, I saw armed Afghan police and troops standing guard at fortified posts and on nearby hilltops. There were no Soviet troops in sight. Party officials acknowledged that mujahedin operated from the mountains above the town and occasionally entered at night in small groups, but said they had not mounted a major assault for almost a year. A week later, I attended a briefing at the U.S. embassy in the Pakistani capital of Islamabad. There the spokesman asserted that "Paghman appears to remain firmly in the hands of the resistance despite repeated regime and Soviet efforts to assert military control." At the British embassy in Islamabad, briefers balanced their list of alleged mujahedin successes by reporting a few "regime claims" of success, but the general thrust of the British propaganda was the same as the Americans'. The mujahedin were winning, and government morale was in decline. A situation report that a British diplomat showed me claimed that "all villages within 40 kilometers of Jalalabad have been destroyed." This described an area where I had been with my Afghan Government minder two weeks earlier, touring villages that were thriving and unscathed.

The wire service reporters at the embassy briefings hurried back to their offices to put out these tendentious stories. They sourced them to "travelers from Kabul," a formula stipulated by the briefers to create a sense that these were independent witnesses. From the speed with which these officially inspired reports appeared on the wires, it was clear that no checking was done, nor could journalists have checked without going to the places mentioned. For Western governments it was a case of propaganda made easy.

While the situation on the ground in Afghanistan remained dead-locked in spite of Western efforts to portray it as imminent Soviet defeat, the talks in Geneva began to move ahead. The UN's tireless negotiator, Diego Cordovez, was increasingly optimistic about a positive result. In Kabul major changes were afoot.

Shortly after Gorbachev's "bleeding wound" speech, Vladimir Kryuchkov, the deputy head of the KGB in charge of foreign operations, flew to Kabul to tell Babrak Karmal he should quit for reasons of health. In a wide-ranging interview, a few days earlier, I had asked Karmal about his health. He laughed and said he was fine. Kryuchkov was having none of this. According to the version Karmal gave a Soviet newspaper several years later, Kryuchkov "came to see me to recommend that I go to the Soviet Union to rest and get well. 'When you want to go back, we will bring you back here,' he said." In case Karmal had not got the message, Kryuchkov reminded him delicately of the fate of his predecessor, Hafizullah Amin. "Now, comrade Karmal, you should be very careful. Your enemies may kill you," he warned. To which Karmal retorted with a flash of wit: "No. Only my friends can kill me now."

Though angry and disappointed, the Afghan leader had no choice. He left for Moscow, where he was hospitalized and treated for a kidney disorder. He returned to Kabul, showing amazing defiance and still refusing to resign. It required a further arm-twisting visit to Kabul by Kryuchkov to get him to agree. Reluctantly, Karmal summoned his Afghan party colleagues and told them he had become too ill to continue as leader of the PDPA, the country's most powerful post. He was allowed to keep the presidency, a largely ceremonial post, as a face-saver and to preserve party unity since some senior PDPA officials still supported him.

Karmal's nonviolent loss of power made history. It was the first time since the powerful King Abdur Rahman had died in office in 1901 that an Afghan leader had resigned and been treated with dignity rather than been killed or forced to go abroad. Six of Karmal's ten predecessors were assassinated or executed, one was ousted by force and imprisoned, one was deposed while out of the country, and two were bundled into exile.

Karmal's place as party leader was taken by Mohammed Najibullah, a member of the Parcham wing who had been serving as the intelligence chief. A Pashtun from the Ghilzai tribe, which has its roots in Paktiya province on the border with Pakistan, Najibullah was born in Kabul. At university he was one of the hundreds of students who gravitated toward the PDPA because they liked its agenda of development and reform. He joined the party at the age of eighteen a few months after it was formed. Four years later he showed his leadership powers by organizing a large Parcham demonstration against the U.S. vice president, Spiro Agnew, who was visiting Kabul. A few eggs were thrown at Agnew's car and Najibullah was jailed for nine months. On release he rose rapidly within party ranks and was head of the party's Kabul branch at the age of 31 when the coup was mounted against President Daoud in April 1978.

With Karmal out of power the Russians aimed at maintaining a government in Kabul that would be at best friendly to the Soviet Union and at worst neutral between the superpowers, and therefore not become an American ally that might allow the United States to operate military facilities on its territory as Pakistan did. Gorbachev asked Najibullah to accelerate the pace of national reconciliation, bring noncommunists into his government and open contacts with the mujahedin. It was hoped that as a Pashtun, he would be more acceptable to the mujahedin leaders, most of whom, with the exception of Ahmad Shah Massoud, were Pashtun.

Soviet thinking was evolving fast. Even Andrei Gromyko, who as foreign minister in 1979 was one of the men who decided on the invasion to protect the PDPA, changed his mind. He told the Politburo in January 1987 that some form of coalition government was needed in Kabul. Prime Minister Nikolai Ryzhkov said the Afghan army should stop using conscripts and become a professional army with attractive salaries for officers and men so as to discourage desertions. But whatever tactical changes the Russians recommended the new Afghan leader adopt, Ryzhkov said the Kremlin's strategy had to be to bring Soviet troops home by 1989. "We have to take a firm line to withdraw from there within two years," Ryzhkov said. "It is better to pay in cash, in kerosene, not in men. Our people do not understand what we are doing there or why are we sitting there for seven years."

To support the new strategy, the Kremlin urged Najibullah to end the socialist decrees of the PDPA's first years in power. To reduce opposition from landlords, the government raised the maximum holding from three to fifty acres. Property owners who had fled abroad were invited to come home and reclaim their expropriated assets. A new constitution was adopted that enshrined a multiparty system and a mixed economy. The Democratic Republic of Afghanistan, the country's official name, had the word "Democratic" dropped on the grounds that "Democratic Republic" was a phrase only used by socialist states. A clause was added to the constitution that "no law shall run counter to the sacred principles of Islam." The country's first Islamic university was opened.

On New Year's Day 1987 Najibullah made a dramatic announcement that was designed to accelerate the process of national reconciliation. He declared a cease-fire that he would continue indefinitely as long as the mujahedin reciprocated. He was willing to negotiate with anyone, including representatives of the exiled King Zahir Shah. "We don't want to exclude different political groups, moderates, monarchists, and the heads of armed anti-government bands active abroad," Najibullah said. The mujahedin leaders were all based in Peshawar in Pakistan, but Najibullah's phrasing did not satisfy them as it downplayed their status as a nationwide resistance movement rather than a minor group of insurgents. On his side many of Najibullah's PDPA colleagues were wary of "national reconciliation," fearing too many concessions were being offered. This may explain why he spoke only vaguely of being open to talks and did not say clearly that he was ready to form a coalition government or explain what the PDPA's role in such a government might be. Would the PDPA insist on leading the government or would it take a minority role? The mujahedin promptly rejected the cease-fire offer.

Soviet decision makers were also split. Marshal Sergei Akhromeyev, the chief of the general staff, took a pessimistic line. He feared Najibullah could not last long in power. Moscow should therefore persuade the Americans to support a mujahedin-led coalition government in which the PDPA would be junior partners. Kryuchkov, the KGB chief, took a more robust position. He felt Moscow should maximize PDPA control within any coalition. Foreign Minister Shevardnadze supported a softer variation of the KGB line, arguing that Najibullah could head the coalition government as long as he first resigned from the PDPA so as to make it easier for the mujahedin to join the new government. Shevardnadze feared that Akhromeyev's option would lead to mujahedin dominance and an eventual bloodbath of Moscow's friends.

Disputes over national reconciliation and coalition government simmered throughout 1987. The Soviets and Diego Cordovez, the UN mediator, continued to press for an agreement with the mujahedin although Cordovez knew his mandate did not include any responsibility for organizing talks among Afghans. Moscow persuaded Najibullah to make more overtures to opposition parties such as allowing them to open offices and publish newspapers in Kabul. Arrangements were made to adopt a new constitution and name a head of state (Karmal had been made to resign the presidency in November 1986) via a Loya Jirga ("grand council" in the Pashto language), a traditional mechanism started by the Pashtun emirs under which tribal and clan leaders are invited to the capital for a nationwide consultation. Ex-king Zahir Shah was the obvious candidate.

Najibullah went along with Moscow part of the way but showed his defiance of the Kremlin and his impatience with the mujahedin by having himself named as the new president in September 1987.

The American view varied. At times Washington expressed concern that the Russians were linking the need for agreement on a coalition government to the timetable for withdrawal. The United States feared this could delay a Russian retreat for years and might be a deliberate ploy to put everything off. Cordovez complained that Western governments considered national reconciliation as nothing but a "Communist slogan." At other times the Americans seemed uninterested in the issue, believing coalition politics were irrelevant since Najibullah and the PDPA would inevitably collapse as soon as the Russians pulled their forces out.

Pakistan also wavered, occasionally showing support for the idea of a transitional coalition government while the Russians withdrew, but more often taking the position that the priority was a fast Soviet departure. The mujahedin showed little interest in a coalition, particularly after Najibullah declared himself president. They preferred to apply more political and psychological pressure by announcing the formation of an alternative government that would take over once the Russians left Afghanistan. The United States supported the move and persuaded the Peshawar Seven, the leading mujahedin parties, to publish the names of their government's ministers in February 1988. The Peshawar Seven was itself a coalition of moderates—who supported a return to the old pre-communist system and the restoration of the king—and Islamic fundamentalists, who wanted to rewrite the constitution in line with Sharia law. The fundamentalists won out. They announced that their proposed new government would be headed by Yunis Khalis, an Islamist. It would have twenty-eight seats with seven posts reserved for "good Muslims" from Kabul. This term appeared to mean anyone from the Afghan regime who was not a member of the PDPA. It was not so much a compromise as a slap in Najibullah's face. As Khalis put it, "If we accepted a coalition with the Communists after nine years of fighting, what was the purpose of our jihad?"

Pakistan had long supported the mujahedin against the regime in Kabul, but at the last minute appeared to come around to the idea of a coalition with the PDPA. The *Guardian* sent me to Geneva to cover the UN-mediated talks among the Soviet Union, the United States, Pakistan and the Afghan Government as they reached their climax in March 1988. Zain Noorani, the Pakistani foreign minister, said during a press conference there: "We should take up with Mr. Cordovez the idea of a second track, leading to the formation of an interim government. Without it there is no earthly possibility of the refugees returning and peace being restored." Whether this statement signified serious support for talks between the mujahedin and the Najibullah regime or was only meant to give an image of flexibility is hard to say. For years Pakistan's position had been full support for the Peshawar Seven, and particularly the group's Islamist members.

To independent analysts, the benefit of a coalition government was obvious. If one accepted the fact that the Afghan tragedy was primarily a civil war into which the Russians had unwisely inserted themselves by sending an invasion force, then it was clear that the removal of the Russians would not automatically end the war. Without agreement among the Afghan factions, fighting would continue.

The same dilemma would emerge two decades later when ISAF increased its presence to the point where the U.S.-led alliance had more troops in Afghanistan than the Russians ever had. The complicating factor of a foreign army on Afghan soil did not alter the fact that the current war is still a civil war between a government and a nationwide insurgency. Since victory by one side is impossible, compromise and negotiations provide a better, though not an easy, option. The withdrawal of foreign forces would not necessarily lead to peace.

By the end of 1987 Gorbachev had lost patience with the lack of progress on national reconciliation. He was anxious to leave Afghanistan as soon as it could be done with dignity. At a meeting with President Reagan in Washington in December, he announced that a Soviet withdrawal could be carried out "in twelve months, maybe less." With the Geneva talks advancing toward their climax, the Reagan administration and the U.S. Congress suddenly became worried that the Najibullah regime might survive in power. Far from being humiliated as the United States had been in Vietnam, the Soviet Union might emerge from Afghanistan with its honor intact. It could plausibly even declare victory.

To prevent this grim option Washington raised objections to the "non-interference" clauses in the proposed Geneva accords, which specified that foreign aid to the mujahedin must end when the Soviet Union withdrew its troops but said nothing about Soviet aid to the Kabul government having to end. Under such an agreement, Moscow could continue giving the Afghan army weapons and equipment as well as supplying the government with economic help, even as the mujahedin were left on their own.

Shevardnadze was shocked when his U.S. counterpart, Secretary of State George Shultz, flew to Moscow in February 1988 to tell him that Washington wanted "symmetry" in connection with the non-interference agreement. Either it would be "negative symmetry" in which the Soviet Union stopped its aid to the Kabul government while the United States and its friends stopped their aid to the mujahedin or it would be "positive symmetry" in which both sides could continue their supply of arms. By any standard, the latter term was an outrageous Orwellian euphemism, comparable to "collateral damage" as a

way of masking the reality that bombing and missile strikes cause civilian deaths. "Positive symmetry" meant "war goes on."

The Russians felt Washington was moving the goalposts. They had
long known the mujahedin gained much of their strength from cross-
border supplies. It was not the Stingers that caused them the major
problems. It was the daily drip-drip of rifles, ammunition and new
jihadi volunteers coming up through Pakistan that kept the mujahedin struggle going. Instead of forcing Pakistan to stop the flow, "positive symmetry" in the Geneva accords would allow it to continue or
even increase. The war had also attracted a massive influx of Arab and
other Muslim jihadis, financed by the CIA and the Saudis, who eagerly
crossed into Afghanistan from Pakistan. Osama bin Laden, a wealthy
Saudi businessman who arrived in Pakistan in the mid-1980s to fight
the Russians, was one of them, along with other fundamentalists who
would go on to found al Qaeda in August 1988 while the Russians were
leaving Afghanistan. This was the international network bin Laden and
his Arab colleagues decided they needed in order to continue the struggle against infidel influence in the Muslim world.

The Soviets had banked on the Geneva accords to close down mujahedin activity in Pakistan. Now they were being asked to accept it would
continue, thereby seriously weakening the chances of the Najibullah
regime's survival after a Soviet pullout. The new U.S. proposal meant,
in effect, that the Soviets would be unilaterally withdrawing their forces
without any concession from the Americans or the mujahedin. Shultz
later admitted that Shevardnadze felt betrayed. "He was very upset. He
kept accusing us of changing our position at the last minute, of upping
the ante, of reneging on earlier understandings. And of course he had
a point," Shultz told an interviewer. Washington knew the Russians
had become desperate to leave Afghanistan. The Americans' hard bargaining worked. Within weeks Moscow accepted the notion of positive symmetry and announced that their troop withdrawal would start
on May 15 provided the Geneva agreement was signed by then. Their

initial proposal had called for a four-year withdrawal. Now they said it would take no more than nine months to complete and half the forces would go within the first three months.

It had become clear that a coalition government was not going to emerge in Kabul. For Moscow the best option was to trust that Najibullah and the PDPA would somehow survive. Cordovez also realized there was no chance of agreement among the Afghan groups. Zahir Shah, the exiled king, whom he had seen as the key figure around whom most Afghans could rally, wanted other people to arrange everything for him. In his residence in Rome, the king, a vain and weak man, was unwilling to take any initiative himself. "Zahir Shah simply failed to gather the physical and intellectual strength that was needed," Cordovez said. "Had he only traveled to Peshawar, he would have instantly emerged as the leader of a mass of refugees eager to return to their homeland. No resistance leader would have been able to demonstrate the political support required to challenge the former monarch."

The deal on positive symmetry infuriated Najibullah. On the eve of the planned signature of the Geneva agreements Shevardnadze flew to Kabul and was told the Afghan foreign minister was not ready to take part in the signing ceremony. In a last-minute bid to get Najibullah to instruct his minister to sign, Gorbachev rushed to meet him. No Soviet leader had been to Afghanistan throughout the eight-year war. Even at this stage it was considered too risky to go. So both men traveled to Tashkent, the capital of Soviet Uzbekistan, where Gorbachev told Najibullah there was no alternative to positive symmetry. The mujahedin would continue to get new supplies but so would he. The only concession, a trivial diplomatic nicety, was that the U.S.-Soviet agreement on symmetry would not be written into the accords but would form part of an exchange of letters between Moscow and Washington.

The failure of what were admittedly only halfhearted efforts to create a coalition government in Kabul meant that hopes for a cease-fire were clearly futile. In some conflicts the guns fall silent during the course of peace talks or even when the various sides first sit down to talk. Other conflicts only produce a cease-fire on the day the peace agreement is signed. The Geneva accords on Afghanistan were unusual. They were a peace deal that did not bring peace.

When I flew to Kabul two weeks later, just as ministers arrived in Geneva to sign the accords, I found a mood of uncertainty. By now the U.S.-supplied Stinger missiles affected civilian flights, even if their impact on the air war was not decisive. Instead of losing altitude as it reached the Kabul plateau, my Ariana Afghan Airlines plane arrived above the city at its cruising height of 30,000 feet. The mud-brick houses on the lower slopes of the hills below us looked like toys. The river was little more than a distant glint in the sun. Then the plane swooped down in a gut-wrenching series of corkscrew turns, firing flares, just in case any heat-seeking missile was on its way to hit us.

In the Kabul Hotel, as so often, a wedding was under way. Just before seven p.m. the male guests left the couple on their ceremonial dais and swarmed out of the hall into the lobby where a TV screen was about to show a bigger event—the completion of the Geneva accords. In a semicircle around the TV men fiddled with worry beads as they waited for the historic signatures that would mean Soviet troops would start withdrawing in a month's time and be gone fully within less than a year. After eight years of foreign occupation it seemed hard to believe.

Will there be peace? I asked a wedding guest who had come down from Baghlan, north of the Hindu Kush. "Maybe," he said, "but the main thing is to have the Russians leave." A thirty-nine-year-old university teacher was more doubtful. He was eagerly waiting for his next birthday when he would be exempt from military service. He feared the demand for conscripts would go up and exemptions would be cut after the Russians went. He was also worried about a mujahedin victory and how they would treat people who had not left Kabul and joined the resistance. "Now it's time for the mujahedin to settle," he said. "Are they going to say that everyone who stayed in Kabul is a Communist?"

Officially, the Afghan Government welcomed the accords. Najibullah described them as "the happiest and most brilliant event in Afghanistan's history." He called for a public rally to celebrate them. But there were clear signs of anxiety. The tenth anniversary of the PDPA's April 1978 coup was approaching, and Najibullah exploited it to send a complicated set of messages. On the one hand, the Geneva accords restored Afghanistan's independence by ending foreign interference and paving the way for the Russians to leave. Najibullah even had a huge poster of Amanullah Khan, the ruler who secured Afghanistan's independence from the British, erected at a traffic circle in the center of Kabul. On the other hand, if the mujahedin refused to discuss the formation of a coalition government, then let them not think the PDPA was weak. A huge military parade was organized on the anniversary to show off the Afghan army's strength. A reviewing stand was placed opposite the Eid Gah mosque, the country's most important mosque, which had been renovated three years earlier to demonstrate the regime's Islamic credentials. From the stand, Najibullah and his Politburo colleagues watched Soviet T-62 tanks and ground-to-ground rockets on olive-green launchers rumble by. Low-flying MiG-24 helicopter gunships clattered past, the sound of their rotors echoing against the brown hillsides.

The most striking element was the infantry. Along with thousands of soldiers carrying regimental banners, a company of women, dressed in tribal costume, came marching through. They carried AK-47s but looked more like a theater troupe than a genuine combat unit. Once they had gone past, fifty thousand civilians joined the march. Some carried the national flag. Others sported banners showing three clasped hands, the logo of the government's national reconciliation policy.

It was a fascinating and spectacular production, at least as propaganda. But one of the more remarkable features of the day was the way the Soviet Union chose to be represented at the historic event. An allied party, the PDPA, was celebrating ten years in power. A peace deal had just been signed in Geneva. Yet the top Soviet official sent to attend the parade was an elderly bureaucrat in a gray suit, Igor Orlov, who was not even a member of the Politburo or a government minister in Moscow. He was nothing more senior than a vice president of Russia's Supreme Soviet, a rubber-stamp parliament, and somewhat less influential than the lieutenant governor of an American state. If this was a calculated insult intended to express Moscow's dismay that Najibullah had not thanked them sufficiently in public for the years of Soviet sacrifice in Afghanistan, it was impressive. As Obama was to discover with Hamid Karzai, leaders of occupied countries rarely show gratitude.

Within the diplomatic community in Kabul, I found opinion divided about the regime's chances of survival. Some thought it was doomed. In the days after the Geneva signing, the Afghan army had pulled back from a number of border villages in the face of mujahedin attack. Najibullah had presented this move as a gesture to the refugees in Pakistan, and the first step in the creation of a series of demilitarized zones along the border, but from any angle it was a retreat. Other diplomats thought the Soviet withdrawal would weaken the mujahedin. How many peasants would want to carry on fighting to liberate distant Kabul rather than slip back to their villages, which the infidel PDPA had never bothered to enter anyway? The regime's main aim was to hold the capital and a few strategic towns. Although the Soviets were leaving, the government had 70,000 well-trained police and troops to defend itself plus modern weaponry and an air force.

The Americans claimed that they were sure of victory for their side. As Robert Peck, the deputy assistant secretary of state who monitored the Geneva talks, told Congress: "We are confident that a PDPA-dominated regime cannot survive a Soviet withdrawal. Our estimate is that the government could splinter and fall even before the final Soviet pullout. Once the Soviet protectors are gone, the regime will be unable to project power into the countryside, and its early demise will be inevitable."

Did Peck really believe this, or was it part of the psychological campaign that had long accompanied the shooting war?

[4] RECONCILIATION FAILS

"The only thing I question is whether we should have continued on this momentum, this inertia of aiding the mujahedin after the Soviets had left. I think that was probably in retrospect a mistake."

—CHARLES COGAN, CIA DIRECTOR OF OPERATIONS
FOR THE MIDDLE EAST AND SOUTH ASIA,
1979–84 (INTERVIEWED IN 1997)

"The Soviet-backed government of Najibullah is remembered today as the last strong and relatively benign leader."

—STRATEGIC CONFLICT ASSESSMENT REPORT
FOR THE BRITISH GOVERNMENT, 2008

IT WAS FEBRUARY 15, 1989. Stiff and unsmiling, General Boris Gromov stood in the armored personnel carrier that served as his command vehicle as it rumbled toward the TV cameras that waited on the bridge over the river Oxus. It was the end of Gromov's third tour of duty in Afghanistan, culminating in his promotion to command the Soviet Union's Fortieth Army. As his vehicle moved behind long columns of troops and armor, he cut a proud figure, no doubt hoping that as the last combat officer to leave Afghanistan, his dignified bearing would reinforce the image of a difficult job completed with honor. Officially known as the Friendship Bridge, its name encapsulated what Russian propaganda wanted to project as the core principle of the Soviet Union's historic relationship with Afghanistan. Now, after nine years of doing their "internationalist duty" to protect an allied neighbor, the troops were going home and the Kremlin's armed intervention was over. All that was missing was a banner proclaiming "Mission Accomplished."

In Kabul at almost the same moment, an Ariana Afghan Airlines flight was bringing me in from Moscow, where I had recently moved to be the *Guardian*'s correspondent in the Soviet Union. Most of my Western and Russian friends thought I was crazy to volunteer to fly there. They were convinced the mujahedin would quickly take power, prompting a bloodbath in which foreigners would be an easy target. Those known to have reported from Kabul during the Soviet occupation would be especially vulnerable.

I was not so sure. Under their nine-month withdrawal plan, most Russians had already left Kabul and the areas between the capital and the Pakistani border in the autumn and winter of 1988. The mujahedin had not managed to capture any city abandoned by the Russians. They were chaotically disunited, and commanders from rival factions sometimes fought each other. The Afghan army was holding up, and the thousands of bureaucrats in government offices as well as most of Kabul's secular middle class were terrified of what a mujahedin victory would bring. The notion of a popular uprising in the city on their behalf seemed fanciful. Continued resistance by government forces was more likely, I felt.

Western governments were doing as much as they could to develop a sense of panic. They ordered their diplomats to pack their bags and go, citing the risk of a collapse in law and order. The British chargé managed to get himself filmed by a British TV crew pulling the flag down in the embassy compound and telling the reporter he was not sure whether he would get to the airport safely before the storm broke.

Staffan de Mistura, who was working for the United Nations coordinator for Afghanistan (and became the secretary-general's special representative in Afghanistan in early 2010), was urged by the U.S. chargé to join him on what the American called "the last flight" to Islamabad. He was told he had to be ready to go in forty minutes. De Mistura refused, citing his need to continue the UN's humanitarian responsibilities, as he told me in 2010. He felt the Western diplomats' hasty departure was psychological warfare against the Najibullah regime.

The mujahedin were also doing their best to undermine morale in Kabul. They mounted a siege to prevent food and grain from coming into the city, and people were lining up before dawn at bakeries to get the few loaves available. Najibullah was taking no chances. He went on television and in a speech full of quotations from the Qur'an announced a state of emergency, which banned public gatherings and permitted house searches without warrants. He positioned tanks and armored personnel carriers at key intersections in Kabul and ordered troops to patrol the bazaars. Some 30,000 PDPA members were given rifles. Others were supplied with military uniforms and ordered to wear them to give the impression of defiant readiness.

To beat the blockade the Russians pumped in fuel and food by air and road. Sultan Ali Keshtmand, one of the most experienced administrators, was reappointed prime minister to stiffen the government response to the crisis. "Huge convoys of trucks were coming in from Soviet Uzbekistan," he recalled later. "Troops helped to secure the roads. PDPA branches and trade unions helped to distribute the food. About a million people were entitled to free rations of flour, sugar, cooking oil and tea. Thousands of mullahs were on the government payroll. In three months we managed to rebuild our grain and fuel stocks."

Not everyone had access to the supplies. The UN was using stocks from the World Food Programme to help 32,000 women and children who had fled to Kabul from villages believed to be under mujahedin control. According to de Mistura, they had been denied government rations because longtime Kabul residents had priority in the sharing of scarce supplies. He chose to stay behind to help them and managed to organize an Ethiopian Airlines plane to bring some food in. One morning I visited a three-room mother-and-child clinic in the city's muddy outskirts where UN food was arriving. Outside the doors a sea of women, veiled from head to toe in blue or yellow burqas, frantically pushed forward. Many of the children who clutched at their hands had runny noses and watery eyes. Subzero temperatures, no heating, contaminated water and lack of food were combining to spread bronchitis and other infections. "Fifty children have died of malnutrition here in the last month," said Momina Qayyumi, the clinic's midwife, as bags of flour and cans of powdered milk were unloaded from a United Nations truck. Her figures were much higher than those given by government ministers, who tended to deny that the rebel food blockade had caused starvation.

The supplies were part of the only emergency planeload of UN food relief to reach Kabul. The UN had prepared 390 tons of food in Pakistan and were hoping to organize a shuttle of a dozen flights. An Egyptian plane, which was due to fly in from Islamabad, never took off, and the Ethiopian plane chartered by the UN made only one trip even though there had been no rocket attacks at Kabul airport for weeks, with the official Ariana Afghan Airlines making regular flights. UN officials did not believe the reason for the lack of flights was concern over security. They were convinced Western governments were putting pressure on smaller countries to end the airlift. "Once again due to Cold War logic, both sides [the Afghan Government and the West] did not really worry about civilians being cornered by their conflict," de Mistura told me in 2010.

With the Russians gone from Afghanistan, Najibullah made a virtue out of necessity. He sought to present himself as a nationalist leader who had won independence and was less reliant on foreign help than the mujahedin in spite of all their patriotic claims. "We only took help from one infidel. The other side has taken help from several infidels," he told a group of tribal elders. He did not spell out that the mujahedin had been aided by the United States, Britain, China and other non-Muslim countries while he had only needed the Russians, but this was his message. Shown on TV as they listened to his speech, the elders remained impassive and inscrutable.

Najibullah received me in the modern building that housed the headquarters of the PDPA on February 27. It was within the secure perimeter of the Arg, but he preferred it to the ornate and rather dark presidential palace, where I had interviewed Karmal three years earlier. From his window you could look down on an elevated concrete plinth on top of which was the first Soviet T-62 tank that had forced its way into the presidential compound in 1978 to spearhead the coup that brought the PDPA to power.

At forty-three, Najibullah was a strong, broad-shouldered man who lived up to his nickname, the Ox, except that he had soft hands and long fingers more suited to a pianist. His jet-black hair and mustache were showing the first hints of gray. He knew some English from time spent in Peshawar, the Pakistani frontier city where his father was Afghanistan's trade representative during the monarchy. It was ironic that the city had become the headquarters of the mujahedin, the enemies with whom he now wanted to make peace.

Najibullah used the interview to appeal to the West to reconsider its hostility and take account of the human cost of continuing to arm the mujahedin, now that the Russians had left Afghanistan. He described himself as a nationalist who wanted good relations with East and West. At one point he even described the Soviet military presence in his country, which had just ended, as a diktat. It was a remarkable choice of phrase since he was still relying heavily on Moscow's help, but the aim was to project himself to his compatriots as a man who stood up to foreigners if they tried to bully Afghanistan.

Geoffrey Howe, Britain's foreign secretary under Margaret Thatcher, had recently publicly urged him to step down. I asked Najibullah for his reaction. "We make decisions on democratic principles, not on the basis of proposals from [President George H. W.] Bush or Howe. If Howe made such a proposal and I resigned, wouldn't that be interference in Afghanistan's internal affairs?" Then came his unexpected reference to the Soviet military presence. "We've released ourselves with so much difficulty from one diktat, and now you're trying to impose another one on us." It made him sound as though he were some kind of liberator.

Najibullah's presentation of himself as a patriot was clever politics. Although he still asked for and wanted Soviet economic help, the fact that Afghanistan was free of foreign troops helped to strengthen his regime. Many Afghans accepted his nationalism as genuine.

MYTH NUMBER SEVEN:
After the Soviets withdrew, the West walked away.

One of the commonest promises Western politicians made after they toppled the Taliban in 2001 was that "this time" the West would not walk away, as it had done after the Russians pulled out. On the contrary, "this time" they would stay and help rebuild the country. Afghans were surprised to hear these promises. They remembered history in rather a different way. Far from forgetting about Afghanistan in February 1989, the United States showed no letup in its close involvement with the mujahedin, first by arming them in the hope they would quickly overthrow the Najibullah regime and then by blocking moves toward negotiations. The overall effect of these policies was to prolong and deepen Afghanistan's destruction, as the comment by Charles Cogan, CIA director of operations for the Middle East and South Asia, 1979–1984, at the head of this chapter suggests. Had Washington indeed walked away after 1989, the country might have had a better chance of resolving its conflicts and starting on reconstruction.

Once the first U.S. effort to destabilize the Najibullah regime through psychological warfare had failed, the next test was to be on the battlefield. The city of Jalalabad was chosen by the mujahedin as the target for a major offensive. It was only forty miles from the Pakistani border along a reasonably flat and easy road, and the Russians had pulled out in May of the previous year. The idea was to install a provisional mujahedin government in the city to undermine the Najibullah regime's morale and provide a magnet to attract new recruits to the jihad.

The Americans and the government of Benazir Bhutto in Pakistan as well as Pakistan's Inter-Service Intelligence (ISI) directorate favored Gulbuddin Hekmatyar as the best leader for the provisional Afghan Government. The Saudis liked Abdul Rasul Sayyaf. In early March, forces loyal to each of the two mujahedin leaders, numbering up to 10,000 men, including many Arabs, captured the village of Samarkhel on the outskirts of Jalalabad after its commander took a bribe to abandon it. Their next target was Jalalabad airfield, which lies south of the city. Seventy government troops who surrendered were tortured and killed. Their bodies were then mutilated, a blunder by the mujahedin, which only made the remaining government troops fight harder. The Eleventh Division of the Afghan army tried to hold a defense line while the Afghan air force, which had total command of the skies, bombed the mujahedin positions from high altitude, too far for Stinger missiles to reach them. The army also used heavy Soviet Scud missiles fired from long range.

Aware that the battle of Jalalabad was a crucial show of strength and vital for his regime's survival, Najibullah took personal charge of its defense, according to Ahmad Sarwar, the diplomat whom I had gotten to know in London when he was Afghan chargé. Sarwar was a close relative to Najibullah by marriage. The two men's wives were sisters. This meant Sarwar could phone the president at any time, a privilege other Afghan diplomats did not enjoy. Sarwar was later transferred to India as ambassador, but after the PDPA regime collapsed he was forced to leave New Delhi. He received political asylum in Germany with his family, joining the vast diaspora of educated Afghans already in Europe.

"I thought they were going to lose Jalalabad," he admitted during
a day of reminiscence in January 2011 in his apartment in Wesseling, a
small town on the banks of the Rhine. "On March 21, 1989, I'd arranged
for the BBC Persian service in London to do a telephone interview with
Najib [Sarwar continued to call his brother-in-law by his original name
before it was Islamicized]. When they asked him how the mujahedin
attack on Jalalabad was going, he used the phrase 'If pressure from outside becomes stronger, they might win'." Sarwar was alarmed by the
pessimistic tone of Najibullah's answer. He took it as a hint the Afghan
leader was preparing an explanation for the city's imminent collapse.

"But Jalalabad didn't fall. Najib showed great discipline, control and
energy. For fourteen days he didn't come home but slept on a small
bed in his Kabul office, giving instructions," Sarwar told me. The president ordered 400 elite paratroopers to drop into the city to help with
its defense. The tide of battle turned, and the mujahedin advance was
halted. By July Afghan Government troops had regained Samarkhel,
and the mujahedin retreated. Their failure came under strong criticism
from Ahmad Shah Massoud, the Tajik mujahedin commander, and
Abdul Haq, a Pashtun leader who had mounted various guerrilla operations against Soviet forces around Kabul. They blamed Hekmatyar and
Sayyaf for turning to conventional warfare, at which the government
had more experience.

Victory in Jalalabad gave the government a huge lift in confidence.
It showed that the Afghan army could fight well even without Soviet
assistance. The contrast with Obama's war is glaring. By the summer
of 2011, U.S. commanders were not yet willing to let the new Afghan
National Army take on the Taliban unaided. The much-trumpeted
"transition" of various districts to control by Afghan security forces
kept NATO forces in a position of "overwatch" with the ability to react
rapidly in support of the Afghan army.

The departure of Soviet forces eliminated a key element in many
Afghans' motivation for supporting jihad. Najibullah took advantage of

the new situation to try to negotiate local cease-fires, hoping to peck away at the mujahedin's fragile unity. The issue of whether to agree to a cease-fire widened a long-standing split between field commanders and the mujahedin's political leadership in Peshawar who never risked their own lives on the front line. In Kandahar, for example, Nur ul Haq Ulomi, the city's governor, gave mujahedin commanders money and permission to come into town to visit their families, provided they did so without carrying weapons. North of Kabul there were reports that the government had made deals to secure the crucial highway from the Salang tunnel through which vital Soviet supplies were brought. Local mujahedin commanders would stop their fighting in exchange for being allowed to run their own affairs and have a share of the goods, food and gasoline that came down by convoy.

Increasingly confident that the mujahedin could not win a pitched battle, Sarwar and his brother-in-law discussed alternative scenarios. Sarwar remembered a conversation he had with Najibullah in Kabul, where he spent a few days while moving from London to take up his post as ambassador in New Delhi in September 1989. Najibullah asked him how people in Britain thought the mujahedin would seek to topple him. "I told him they had three options. One was the capture of Jalalabad, but that had failed. The others were a coup or the undermining of the [PDPA] party from inside," Sarwar told me. If there was to be a coup, the party's Khalqi members were the main threat. Their loyalty could never be guaranteed. But a new threat was emerging from within the party's Parcham wing, where there was increasing dissent among people who still felt loyal to Babrak Karmal, the former president who had left Kabul and was living in Moscow.

It was the Khalqis—or least one of them—who struck first. Najibullah had been wary of the Khalqis for some time before the Soviet withdrawal, and in 1988 he sacked several. But he retained, and promoted, Shahnawaz Tanai, the Khalqi wing's chairman, to the key post of defense minister. Tanai opposed national reconciliation, the centerpiece of Najibullah's political strategy, but Najibullah felt it was better to have Tanai on his team than to let him plot from the sidelines. His calculation failed. On March 6, 1990, from his base at Bagram airfield Tanai ordered aircraft to attack government buildings in Kabul and urged the army to mutiny. It was a partial repetition of the coup that had brought the PDPA to power in April 1978. Tanai claimed he had to take action because the president was undermining the national army by giving too many weapons to tribal militias and creating a presidential security guard. In reality, Tanai was fulfilling his own narrow version of national reconciliation. He had forged secret contacts with Hekmatyar, a fellow Pashtun nationalist. Tanai hoped to seize power in alliance with Hekmatyar whose fundamentalist views would give Tanai Islamic credibility.

The coup failed. The army did not rebel and the provincial governors remained loyal. Tanai fled the next day by helicopter to Pakistan, where Hekmatyar had his headquarters.

Najibullah responded by launching a purge of most senior Khalqis. Some were dismissed from their party and government positions. Others were arrested. The purge made sense at one level, but it had the effect of removing a counterweight to the party's pro-Karmal faction, who believed Najibullah was playing excessively on his Pashtun origins, even though his first language was Dari. Ominously, tribal thinking, never far from the surface in Afghan politics, was becoming important again.

The political role of militias—which Tanai had criticized—was also growing, a development that would play a part in Najibullah's eventual collapse. Karmal had been the first leader to put heavy reliance on militias in the early 1980s, as Antonio Giustozzi, a leading analyst of Afghanistan, has detailed in his book, *Empires of Mud*. The local forces my Afghan minder had taken me to see in Jalalabad and Mazar in 1986 were typical of the new units. The aim was to use rural people who had refused to serve in the regular army. They received salaries in the hope this would prevent them from joining the mujahedin. Their job was to police village paths and roads and obstruct passage for the mujahedin. The government asked tribal elders to supply men for the new militias, though it recognized the danger that they could become private armies loyal to their tribe or village rather than to Kabul, especially when their duties became more military rather than merely policing. In order to forestall this danger, the authorities took the names of volunteers from the elders but let the Defense Ministry select the commanders. Officers of the regular army based in the area would be in charge of military training while political commissars would transform them into "soldiers of the revolution."

Change the political vocabulary and the idea was similar to what General David Petraeus, the overall U.S. commander in Afghanistan, would try to do from 2010 onward in Helmand and Kandahar. He turned to tribal leaders and asked them to form the Afghan Local Police, a set of district militias that was separate from the National Police.

Babrak Karmal had started the practice during his regime, but under his scheme each militia commander selected his own junior officers, with the result that their primary loyalty was to him rather than the government. Under Najibullah the system expanded. Militiamen were paid twice the salary of an army recruit. If they joined a militia, they were exempt from conscription. Enlisted soldiers could even leave the army and transfer to a militia in their home village. Communities that offered men or a complete local self-defense unit were rewarded with access to electricity and television sets.

Once the Soviets started withdrawing, Najibullah went a step further. The new emphasis was on getting mujahedin units to defect to the government side, in much the same way as U.S. counterinsurgency strategy tries to reintegrate local Taliban commanders and their units, also by offering community incentives and cash. Najibullah was remarkably successful (much more so than the Americans), and by early 1990, some 100,000 former mujahedin were in various pro-government militias. This played a large role in weakening the jihad.

The expansion of the militias created an unpredictable dynamic. They began to outstrip the army. In Herat province in 1990, the Seventeenth Infantry Division numbered 3,400 regular troops while the militias totaled four times that many. In nearby Shindand, militias out-numbered the Twenty-first Division eight to one. The consequences were far-reaching. In historical terms, the effect on Afghanistan's politi-cal economy was massive and long-lasting. Coupled with the hundreds of pro-jihad commanders who had been fighting the Soviets for almost a decade, the emergence of dozens of new pro-government militias cre-ated a vast cadre of full-time men of the gun. This turned the endemic and age-old danger of village warlordism in Afghan society into a much larger and potentially nationwide phenomenon. Militia commanders became the "new khans," replacing tribal elders and the ulema, the reli-gious leadership, as the dominant players.

In addition to the phenomenon of the new khans, three more problems arose. First, Najibullah's reliance on militias enhanced the danger of minor revolts turning into major threats to the regime, as their commanders developed links to each other and not just to the Defense Ministry. They were sometimes called on to fight outside their own areas, further increasing their status. Second, the priority given to building up the militias undermined recruiting for the army, which in turn led to greater recourse to militias. Finally, their increasing strength encouraged lack of discipline. Most militiamen wore no official uni-forms. Their autonomy led to rivalries and armed clashes between mili-tias over who should guard the roads—always a good source of revenue to be exacted from travelers. As a result, banditry in the countryside now seemed to have official sanction, further undermining people's trust in Najibullah's government.

The most powerful pro-government militia leader in northern Afghanistan was Abdul Rashid Dostum. He was an Uzbek, Afghanistan's third largest ethnic group. Born to a peasant family near Shibergan in Jowzjan province, he joined the PDPA's Parcham wing and became a paratrooper. By the time of the April 1978 coup he commanded an armored unit in the regular army. When the Khalqis moved against the Parchamis a few months later, Dostum went to Pakistan. But as a secular modernizer he was alienated by the anti-Soviet and Islamic fundamentalist atmosphere of Peshawar and after the Soviet invasion returned to Afghanistan to rejoin the government army. Put in charge of one of the new militias, he built it into a formidable force by using government cash to recruit new troops and persuade mujahedin commanders to defect.

By 1988 he headed an army division, which operated around his home area of Shibergan. His next promotion was to the command of the Seventh Army Corps in charge of 25,000 troops covering the whole of northern Afghanistan. Although the corps was part of the regular army, Dostum controlled recruitment, and his troops remained loyal to him. The corps was essentially Dostum's militia. This was to become unmistakably clear in 1992, when he became a key figure in toppling Najibullah and paving the way for the mujahedin to enter Kabul.

MYTH NUMBER EIGHT:

In 1992 the mujahedin overthrew Kabul's regime and won a major victory over Moscow.

The key factor that undermined Najibullah was an announcement made in Moscow in August 1991 shortly after a coup mounted against Gorbachev by Soviet hard-liners collapsed. Although he survived the attempted putsch, Gorbachev's power base virtually disappeared. Huge splits had emerged within both the Communist Party and the KGB, seriously undermining their political authority. The economy was in desperate straits, heavily dependent on Western loans. Gorbachev's longtime rival, Boris Yeltsin, who headed the Russian government, emerged in a dominant position. He was determined to cut back on the country's international commitments and focus on introducing market reforms, if necessary by abolishing the Soviet Union and letting its constituent republics go their own way. In September the Russian Government announced that from January 1, 1992, no more arms would be delivered to Kabul. Gasoline, food and all other forms of aid would also come to a halt.

The decision was catastrophic for the morale of Najibullah's supporters as well as for the PDPA. It took away one of the main guarantees for their survival. The Afghan air force would be grounded for lack of fuel. The army would run out of ammunition and weaponry. The regime had survived the departure of Soviet troops but now would truly be on its own.

Ironically, the men in Moscow who were setting the stage for the Afghan regime's demise were the political heirs of the very men who had brought the regime into being. It was not the mujahedin who overthrew Najibullah but Russian decision makers in the Kremlin, once they lost interest in supporting expensive foreign allies. In one of the great ironies of history, it was Moscow that toppled the government that Moscow had sacrificed so many lives in order to put and keep in place. It was not just Afghanistan that was told to go it alone. The same message went out to Cuba, Angola and other onetime allies. The mood for global retrenchment had begun under Gorbachev but accelerated dramatically under Yeltsin. It was strongly shared by his vice president, Alexander Rutskoi, a former commander of an air assault regiment in Afghanistan who had been made a Hero of the Soviet Union in 1988 for his bravery there. Like many other Russian officers who had served in Afghanistan, he felt the regime in Kabul had become too costly to defend.

The dramatic switch in Kremlin policy became publicly evident when Professor Burhanuddin Rabbani, head of the Tajik Jamiyat-i Islami, one of the seven main mujahedin groups, was invited to Moscow in November 1991 in his capacity as foreign minister of the Afghan Interim Government that had been proclaimed by the mujahedin. In a statement after the meeting, Boris Pankin, the Soviet foreign minister, "confirmed the necessity for a complete transfer of state power to an interim Islamic government." The declaration amounted to the abandonment of Najibullah and official recognition of his rivals. In today's Afghan context, the Kremlin announcement could be compared to an invitation by Hillary Clinton to Mullah Mohammed Omar to come to Washington and a declaration that the United States now wanted power transferred from Hamid Karzai to the Taliban.

Russia's dumping of Najibullah and the news that Russian aid was coming to an end transformed Afghanistan's internal political dynamic. Army officers, militia commanders and party leaders hurried to calculate their chances of survival in the new environment. It was not just that Najibullah was denied fuel and food aid. He no longer had cash to pay the militias, his own troops or commanders like Dostum.

The Russian decision also had a powerful effect on Afghanistan's neighbors. The link between Kabul and Moscow that had lasted for a decade and a half was about to break and decision makers in the region looked for ways to gain influence in the post-Soviet dispensation. The Uzbeks are a Turkic ethnic group and their language is close to Turkish. Turkey and Uzbekistan, which was about to declare its independence as the Soviet Union broke up, were especially interested in Dostum, the most powerful Uzbek in Afghanistan. Iran wanted to protect its eastern borders. India had good relations with Ahmad Shah Massoud, the Tajik mujahedin leader who controlled the northeast, and his political mentor, Professor Rabbani. Pakistan had close connections with the Pashtun jihadi fundamentalists, Hekmatyar, Sayyaf and Khalis, and wanted to be sure they filled the vacuum that might soon open up in Kabul.

In northern Afghanistan Dostum was the key player. In the autumn of 1991 he put out feelers to Massoud about forming an alliance to replace Najibullah. In early 1992 he contacted Hezb-i Wahdat, the mujahedin party that represented Hazaras in the center of the country below the ridge of the Hindu Kush. As Shias, Hezb-i Wahdat was backed by Iran. Their common concern was that the post-Najibullah regime in Kabul might fall into Pashtun hands.

While Dostum plotted, the first government commander to defect was General Abdul Momin, a Tajik in charge of the garrison at Hayratan, the frontier town on the river Oxus, the main gateway to the newly independent state of Uzbekistan. His refusal to obey government orders started a chain reaction within the armed forces. In mid-March Dostum announced that the garrison in Mazar-i Sharif, the major town in the north, was also breaking from Najibullah. Making it clear that he had wider political ambitions, Dostum declared that he had formed the Junbesh-i Melli, the National Movement, and he was its leader.

Dostum's move galvanized Massoud, who began to advance toward Kabul in mid-April. His forces moved out of the Panjshir valley and took control of Jabal us Saraj, the town that commands the road toward the southern entrance to the Salang tunnel. There was no resistance, and Massoud's forces rapidly moved on to Charikar, little more than thirty miles north of the capital. The nearby Bagram air base also fell.

Within the PDPA, which Najibullah had renamed Hezb-i Watan (the Fatherland Party), the Russian aid cutoff and the mass departure of all the Russian advisers caused panic. Sarwar's assessment that Najibullah's enemies would try one or all three methods to oust him was beginning to come true. Efforts to mount a coup and capture Jalalabad had failed, but the third scheme—a revolt within the party—was becoming a reality.

For reasons that are unclear, Najibullah decided to invite Babrak Karmal in November to return from Moscow, where he had been given security protection by the Soviet authorities. For reasons that are equally obscure Karmal accepted. If Najibullah's purpose was to suppress complaints from the pro-Karmal faction, it had the opposite effect. Karmal's Kabul apartment became a new center of plotting and political intrigue. Before he returned, the former Afghan leader appears to have made contact with Rabbani and Massoud's group. When they marched into Kabul a few months later, Karmal, instead of being arrested, remained at liberty.

The crucial issue in the dying months of Najibullah's regime was whether there would be a transition to a government of national unity or at least a government in which the mujahedin groups would share power among themselves on a stable basis. Alternatively, with the prospect of taking control in Kabul becoming real at last after almost two decades of war, would each mujahedin leader try to grab whatever he could?

The UN wanted to negotiate an interim government acceptable to all Afghans that would rule until elections could be held under UN auspices. Benon Sevan, the UN mediator, proposed the classic Afghan method, a Loya Jirga, or national consultative meeting, in this case made up of mujahedin, tribal and political leaders, to agree on the framework. The United States backed the plan, but in a sign of dissension ahead Hekmatyar accused the United States of "trying to impose a coalition government with communists, Westernized Afghans and Zahir Shah [the former king] at its head." In a sentence, he had mentioned all the fundamentalists' enemies—left-wing modernizers as well as traditional monarchists, all united by a secular rather than an Islamist approach to the way Afghanistan should be governed.

With the writing on the wall and at Sevan's suggestion, Najibullah announced on March 18 that he was prepared to resign and transfer power to an interim government. Far from stabilizing the situation and making it easier for his colleagues from the renamed PDPA to reach a collective deal with the mujahedin, his surrender prompted more of the Parchamis to run for the exits individually. The army, which had already been hollowed out by the rise of the militias over the previous two years, imploded as units split on ethnic lines. Scores of Pashtun officers fled south to link up with Hekmatyar's Hezb-i Islami. Tajik army officers made their new loyalties apparent by abandoning Kabul and moving to the Panjshir to transfer their allegiance to Massoud, whom they assumed to be the future victor. General Mohammed Nabi Azimi, a Tajik who commanded the Kabul garrison, opened contacts with

Massoud, as did Abdul Wakil, the foreign minister who had signed the
Geneva accords in April 1988.

Najibullah's wife and three daughters had left Kabul for India
a short time earlier to stay at the Afghan embassy with the Sarwars.
Sevan promised the Afghan president safe conduct, and on April 16
after midnight a UN plane arrived at Kabul airport to take him into
exile. A convoy of UN vehicles fetched Najibullah from the presidential
palace under cover of darkness, but troops loyal to Dostum were at
the airport and blocked him from reaching the aircraft. In coordination
with Massoud, the Uzbek commander had flown several hundred of
his troops to Kabul airport from the Bagram air base. Their aim was to
help to forestall a takeover by Hekmatyar, but now they were holding
a different catch.

Why Dostum would not let Najibullah leave the country has never
been explained. He probably wanted to demonstrate to his new ally,
Massoud, that he had broken all links with his PDPA past. Najibullah
was allowed to be driven back into town and take refuge in a UN compound, where he was to all intents and purposes under house arrest.
If Dostum and his new mujahedin allies had intended to put him on
trial, they never went ahead. During the four years of mujahedin rule
in Kabul, the UN was not asked to hand Najibullah over. Sevan later
claimed he asked Massoud, after they had taken full power in Kabul, to
allow Najibullah to leave Afghanistan, but they turned him down.

SEVERAL LESSONS CAN be drawn from the three years of Najibullah's
regime, particularly in light of the tragic upheavals that the arrival of
the mujahedin in Kabul would bring for Afghans. In today's Afghanistan,
many Afghans in their late thirties or older look back on the Najibullah
period with nostalgia and his picture is occasionally seen on wind-
shields or bumper stickers in Kabul. People remember it as a time of
genuine national sovereignty in which a secular and apparently uncor-
rupt regime was in charge. The Russians were no longer around, nor,

at least in the capital, were the fundamentalists. Life proceeded calmly in conditions of reasonable security, unlike the Kabul of today with its suicide attacks and the overwhelming presence of arrogant-looking foreign contractors and convoys of NATO armored vehicles that demand precedence on the roads, warning local drivers to stay well clear or risk being shot.

Some older Afghans even hark back favorably to the Soviet period, when millions of rubles of aid flowed into the country and did not disappear into ministers' or other corrupt pockets in the way it has done more recently under U.S. occupation.

Two decades after Najibullah's fall, the future of Hamid Karzai's regime may depend in large part on whether the lessons of the early 1990s are absorbed. Afghan governments can implode very rapidly in situations of civil war. An army can be weakened by reliance on militias, especially when they are based on a single ethnicity.

But the overriding conclusion of the Najibullah period is that peace talks must begin early and be sustained with determination. They should focus not just on withdrawing all U.S. and other foreign troops and ensuring international recognition of Afghan neutrality. They must include all Afghan stakeholders, including the Taliban and the other resistance groups, in working out a new constitution, probably with substantial devolution of power to the provinces, as well as guarantees of human rights. Afghanistan has never had a strong central government which rural people respect and it is better to leave as much power in local hands as possible rather than impose an authority which many will see as alien.

While Afghans will have to make the key decisions, an outside mediator, preferably with a UN mandate, is in the best position to start the process by bringing the parties to the table or shuttling between them if they are unwilling to meet face-to-face. Talks must be comprehensive in the sense that they include not only the main Afghan political players and their military commanders but also the governments of the regional states. Afghanistan's neighbors have legitimate interests in the country, the main one being that it should not come under the exclusive influence of a rival state. After the Great Game of the nineteenth century and the Cold War in the twentieth, neutrality or non-alignment for Afghanistan is the only basis for a lasting solution.

[5] MUJAHEDIN DISASTER

"The key problem was the failure of the resistance to coalesce into a single movement led by a person confident to run the country and be accepted throughout Afghanistan."

—CHARLES DUNBAR, CHARGÉ D'AFFAIRES,
U.S. EMBASSY, KABUL, 1981–83

SHIRAZUDDIN SIDDIQI REMEMBERS well the doubts he felt when he watched the first mujahedin walking into Kabul in April 1992. He had never seen guerrilla fighters before, but having recently graduated from Kabul University's drama faculty he knew that appearances are telling. "With their sandals and beards they left me uneasy. I wondered if they had the capacity to govern," he told me over dinner in 2010 in Kabul, where he was working for the BBC.

"I expressed my concern to my uncle. 'I didn't support the communists but I'm worried about these people,' I said. 'Don't worry. They read the Qur'an. They respect the ulema,' he replied." Siddiqi was not entirely reassured but felt he should suspend judgment until he could see what sort of government the mujahedin put in place. The very next day one of his cousins was killed by a rocket, fired by Ahmad Shah

Massoud's forces. He had been sitting under a tree in a Kabul suburb when the lethal device roared in without warning and exploded nearby.

His sudden death was one of the first casualties of mujahedin rule. For the next four years, shelling and gunfire were to cast a pall of terror over the city, taking the lives of tens of thousands of civilians and destroying countless homes. In almost fifteen years of war no Afghan city had suffered such destruction. There was little of the governance that Siddiqi was expecting to see from the mujahedin in the hopes that it would dispel his doubts. Fear and insecurity dominated everything. Each evening people thanked God that they were still alive and able to go to bed in the expectation of facing a new day, although there was no guarantee that rockets would not come in the hours of darkness too.

Siddiqi got into the habit of rising early and leaving home at three a.m. to walk to a shop for cigarettes. He and his family lived near Bala Hissar, an ancient fort that the British used in the nineteenth century that had become a stronghold of Massoud's forces. "The streets were riddled with bodies, left over from the previous hours of shelling," he recalled with a shudder. "As the dawn broke you began to spot them."

The fighting that tore Kabul apart stemmed from long years of rivalry between mujahedin leaders during the jihad against the Soviet occupation. Although they made various attempts to create a united front, the agreements were never translated into reality. There were tensions between Tajiks and Pashtuns, and among the Pashtuns between traditional monarchists and the Islamic fundamentalists. The fundamentalists themselves were divided among followers of Hekmatyar, Sayyaf and Khalis.

The slow implosion of Najibullah's regime should have created a sense of urgency to resolve these tensions so that Afghanistan's new rulers could enter the capital together. But the imminence of power had the opposite effect. Mujahedin rivalries only became worse once the prize was within their grasp. Massoud and Hekmatyar both wanted supreme power.

Massoud's troops had reached Kabul well before Dostum's forces blocked Najibullah from leaving. Flush with the huge quantities of weapons they had seized from captured government garrisons at Charikar, Massoud also had possession of an arsenal surrendered to him by officers from the army and air force, including Soviet tanks, Scud missiles and MiG-21 fighters. Along with his ally Dostum's army of Uzbeks, Massoud had mastery of the capital. Hekmatyar, strongly backed by Pakistan, was still several miles away to the south.

Hekmatyar sent his men forward with the aim of infiltrating Kabul in small groups. But Kabul's key buildings, including the presidential palace, the prime minister's office and the Defense Ministry as well as the airport, were already in Massoud's hands. Hekmatyar's forces only managed to get to the gates of the Ministry of Justice and the Ministry of Interior before being driven back after the air force was brought in to bomb and strafe them. Hundreds of Hekmatyar fighters were killed or taken prisoner. In the western sector of the city, the Hekmatyar forces crossed the Kabul river and were about to seize control of Kabul University when they were attacked by Sayyaf's forces whom they had expected to be their allies. The Hekmatyar forces were cut into two groups and suffered more heavy casualties. Only a few managed to escape to the headquarters Hekmatyar had set up in Chahar Asyab in the southern outskirts of Kabul.

The Afghan capital was firmly under Massoud's control. But Hekmatyar's failure to seize any part of it did not mean it was safe. The city was within artillery range of Hekmatyar's forces, which soon started launching long-range rockets, supplied by Pakistan, in daily and nightly volleys.

A last-ditch effort was made to reach a power-sharing agreement between the mujahedin groups and their various political parties, and on April 25 it appeared to succeed. In Peshawar in Pakistan they formed an interim government for Afghanistan and a Supreme Leadership Council. There would be a rotating presidency that would go to

Sibghatullah Mojadeddi, a Pashtun traditionalist, for two months, after which he would be succeeded by Rabbani, head of the Tajik Jamiyat-i Islami and foreign minister of the mujahedin's former interim government who had been received in Moscow before Najibullah fell. Their main job was to prepare a provisional constitution for an Islamic republic, which was to be ratified by a Loya Jirga later in the year. In the hope of persuading him to make peace, Hekmatyar was invited to take up the post of prime minister.

In the *Guardian's* Moscow office, my two colleagues and I were busy covering Boris Yeltsin's hectic efforts to reform the Russian economy in the first months after the Soviet Union collapsed. But toward the end of June 1992 I was able to persuade the paper's foreign news desk to let me travel to Kabul to cover developments. There I found the already terrified residents of the city in a heightened state of alarm.

The Peshawar agreement had failed. Hekmatyar had rejected the offer of becoming prime minister, and new fault lines had appeared in the ranks of the mujahedin. Hotels in the city center were considered unsafe because of the risk of fighting, and the BBC bureau chief let me share a room in its house in the suburb of Wazir Akbar Khan, an area of medium-sized homes that was close to several embassies and considered less likely to be a scene of armed clashes. Western diplomats and civilians were not targets, as was to be the case a decade or so later. Nothing like the 1979 abduction and murder of the U.S. ambassador, Adolph Dubs, had been repeated.

One advantage of the mujahedin takeover was that visas were easily available, and journalists did not have to have government minders. You could hire a translator and driver independently of the government. One morning fighting broke out in the heart of downtown Kabul outside the Interior Ministry, a massive Soviet-built structure close to the Indian embassy and virtually next door to the former residence of the U.S. ambassador. It turned out that another mujahedin alliance had snapped. Men from Hezb-i Wahdat, the party representing Hazaras, had clashed with some of Massoud's Tajiks, their former friends. They were running around the city using heavy machine guns and rocket-propelled grenades.

For some hours it was too dangerous to go anywhere near, and police cordoned off several city blocks. But later that day I could visit the Jamhuriyat hospital behind the Interior Ministry where windows had been blown out by the exchanges of fire. Doctors and nurses had fled the building, leaving about fifteen seriously ill patients unattended. A few members of the patients' families were huddling with them in terror while the sounds of new gunfire echoed through the streets outside.

The fighting appeared to be an inflated hunt for revenge after a minor incident. Eyewitnesses told us that a car full of armed men from Hezb-i Wahdat had failed to stop when challenged by two young men from Jamiyat-i Islami outside a hotel, which Jamiyat was using as a dormitory. In the ensuing argument the car was shot at and some of its passengers were injured. Wahdat forces arrived to avenge their wounded colleagues and fired rockets at the four-story hotel, destroying the front. It looked as though the already fragile mujahedin alliance was degenerating into gang warfare.

In Paghman, the old summer resort of Afghan kings on Kabul's outskirts, there were similar tensions. Massoud's forces controlled the lower part of the town and let us through their checkpoints. Our taxi driver came from the area but had moved to Kabul fourteen years earlier and had not been back up the road since, he told us with some excitement. He drove slowly so that he could point out landmarks on the way and spot whose houses had been destroyed and whose still stood. A great shout greeted him as a man picking up firewood and tying it into bundles suddenly dropped his work and rushed to the car. He smothered the driver with kisses. He was a schoolteacher and the driver's old neighbor. After several minutes of eager conversation they told me they hoped peace would gradually take hold at last but admitted they were far from sure. Even in Paghman, new demarcations of territory had sprung up. The schoolteacher warned us not to go further up the road since the next checkpoint was controlled by gunmen loyal to Sayyaf. They were tough and unpredictable, he said.

The one town that seemed calm was Jalalabad. In contrast to the Soviet period, it was no longer necessary to get there by air. Soon after one leaves Kabul the narrow road winds and plunges down through a thirty-mile gorge with tall cliffs on either side, a prime site for ambushes during the Soviet occupation. A second gorge, equally magnificent with its series of small waterfalls tumbling down walls of colored rock, leads to the vale of Jalalabad, where orange groves were full of new fruit when we reached there.

Set in a fertile plain in eastern Afghanistan close to the Pakistani border, Jalalabad and the surrounding province of Nangarhar were under the control of a coalition of fundamentalist Pashtun groups, led by Yunis Khalis. There were no Hazara, Tajik or Uzbek politicians to contend with. Apparently confident that peace had been restored, the city's new rulers were busy repairing ex-king Zahir Shah's palace. The blood-red bougainvillea had been pruned, the gravel alleys were free of weeds and the swimming pool had water in it. Even the tennis court looked playable. The net posts were vertical, and all they lacked was the net itself.

The palace had been taken over by Abdul Qadir, the new governor of Nangarhar. During the PDPA time the governor lived in a modest building in a side street off the main road to Pakistan and the royal palace was used as a guesthouse for foreign dignitaries. The mujahedin clearly had other ideas. I could see new scaffolding at the back of the building where restoration of the dining room was under way.

While security in Jalalabad was good, people had other issues to worry about. Fundamentalist pressures were affecting every aspect of public life. Nangarhar always was Afghanistan's lushest and green-est province, and the Kabul river is at its widest there, swollen by the waters of several other rivers before it tips across Afghanistan's eastern edge and joins the valley of the Indus. I found Jalalabad's bazaar still full of what locals loved to describe as the best fruit and vegetables in the country, just as they had when I visited the city during the Soviet occupation. But the narrow streets and alleys were strangely quiet. Something was missing. Three-wheeled tuc-tucs and horse-drawn carts trundled up and down, but the jangle of cassette players which used to blare out from the shops had disappeared. All singing, except of pro-mujahedin and other jihadi themes, was banned. Across town, Jalalabad's only cinema stood in ruins, looted and wrecked a few days after the mujahedin entered the city. They considered it a temple of decadence.

Fewer women were in the street than in Kabul, apparently anxious about emerging in public. The handful bold enough to defy self-imposed or husband-imposed purdah put on the full-length burqa before they ventured out. Schools were still closed while the authorities decided what to do about girls and the old textbooks. The medical college had not reopened, and parents feared that women might be excluded.

I went to see Mohammed Akbar, the town's new deputy mayor. He told me the college would be split so that women and men studied apart in future. Coeducation of the kind he saw during his exile in Pakistan was not what he wanted. "Pakistan is not an Islamic state. Foreigners control it. The United States drives Pakistan," he insisted. "Here in Afghanistan we want no outside driver."

On the way back to Kabul, our taxi broke down and my translator and I had to flag down a bus laden with returning refugees. We stumbled down an aisle piled with sacks and bags and squeezed into the seats. Like our driver to Paghman who had not been home for fourteen years, fellow passengers listed the number of years they had been away from Afghanistan. Most were uncertain whether they were making the right move in coming back, but with the collapse of the Najibullah's regime, Pakistan was pressing refugees to leave. The mujahedin factions were also encouraging people to resume their old lives. The refugees had heard there was fighting in Kabul, but everyone wanted to believe the insecurity would not last for long.

Back in Kabul I found that political tension had risen still further. President Mojadeddi's two-month term was nearly over, but he had announced he would not hand power to Rabbani. He was annoyed that Rabbani had allegedly violated the Peshawar agreement by holding meetings of the Leadership Council of mujahedin groups without consulting him. He was also upset that Massoud, the new defense minister and Rabbani's close ally, was blocking his access to radio and TV.

A wider group known as the Resistance Council on which Dostum and the Hazara groups were represented went into emergency session to discuss the crisis. Rabbani contacted Hekmatyar, who was still sulking in his base at Chahar Asyab south of Kabul, and urged him to reconsider his boycott of the government and the offer of the prime ministership, which was still open. The two men appeared to reach agreement. Although Hekmatyar said he would not take the prime minister's post himself, he would send a nominee to fill it now that Rabbani, a fellow fundamentalist, was about to become president. The deal suggested that the battles among the biggest two mujahedin groups and the danger of all-out civil war were over. Mojadeddi could not afford to block it.

The official transfer of power from Mojadeddi to Rabbani was a chaotic affair. On a blisteringly hot Kabul day, along with a crowd of bearded officials, most of them in Islamic dress, I pushed into a small palace in the presidential compound. Several members of the Russian embassy were on hand, sweating in Western suits and outnumbering the rest of the tiny diplomatic corps. Theirs was still the biggest embassy in Kabul. One offered me his business card. It had "USSR" crossed out and "Russia" written in by hand.

The outgoing president and his successor sat with their supporters in the front row. A solemn recitation from the Qur'an could not hide the fact that we were witnessing the bitter climax of a long battle between two professorial egos. The protagonists were both academics. Mojadeddi, by fourteen years the older man, was a tall, thin and frail-looking figure. He came from an illustrious Pashtun religious family. His grandfather had helped to organize jihad against the British at the end of World War I but also fought the secularizing reforms of Amanullah Khan.

Mojadeddi did his undergraduate and graduate studies at Cairo's prestigious al-Azhar University. In Kabul he lectured at several high schools and the university, but his anti-reformist politics irritated King Zahir Shah's regime. In 1959, when the Soviet leader, Nikita Khrushchev, visited Kabul, Mojadeddi was accused of plotting to assassinate him. He spent four years in prison without trial and on release was exiled to Egypt and Saudi Arabia for a year. By the time he came back, left-wing ideas had gained ground on Kabul's campuses thanks to the general upsurge in anticolonial and socialist thinking throughout the Third World promoted by Nasser, Sukarno and the Algerian and Cuban revolutions. On his official website, Mojadeddi's biographers put it more grandly: "In the course of over five years of Professor Mojadeddi's absence from the political and educational scene in Afghanistan, communism spread at an unprecedented pace in the country, affecting the innocent minds of thousands of Afghan youth who no longer had the opportunity to be exposed to the meaningful and decent ideological and political alternative that Professor Mojadeddi's school of thought provided. This, in itself could be construed as one of the main causes of the tragic turn of political events in Afghanistan."

When Daoud ousted the king in 1973, Mojadeddi was out of the country. He remained abroad, first in Saudi Arabia and then in Denmark, where he set up the Islamic Cultural Center of Scandinavia and stayed for four years. After the 1978 coup, which brought the PDPA to power, Mojadeddi decided the best response was armed struggle. He left Denmark for Saudi Arabia and Pakistan to get promises of finance and weapons, and set up the Afghan National Liberation Front, a name modeled, ironically, on those of movements usually associated with the left. Mojadeddi became the front's spiritual leader.

Next to this austere bespectacled figure, Rabbani resembled a ban-tamweight fighter, short, pugnacious and broad-shouldered. He too first became known through powerful lectures at Kabul University. But there the similarities ended. A Tajik from Badakhshan in northern Afghanistan, he studied Islamic law and theology at Kabul University before getting a lectureship upon graduating in 1963. He became known for firebrand political speeches attacking the communists and other left-ists on campus before he departed to Cairo three years later for further Islamic study at al-Azhar University, which Mojadeddi had also attended. On his return to Kabul he took charge of getting students into orga-nized politics and was elected head of Jamiyat-i Islami, the Society of Islam. Shortly after Daoud Khan took power in the 1973 coup, Rabbani was threatened with arrest but escaped to Pakistan from where he also helped to inspire armed attacks against Daoud's modernization project.

By 1992 Rabbani's authority far outweighed Mojadeddi's, thanks mainly to his closeness to his fellow Tajik, Massoud. By contrast, the commanders loyal to Mojadeddi played only a minor role on the battle-field against the Russians and the Afghan army.

Mojadeddi's discomfort at the transfer of power was plain to see. He was reluctant to resign but had been warned by Massoud that he would be forced out if he tried to cling to the presidency. In a petty gesture of defiance Mojadeddi insisted he would not hand power at the ceremony directly to Rabbani but would return it to the Leadership Council. The council's spokesman then rose. Without further consultation he declared that the council was ready to offer Professor Rabbani the post, as set out in the Peshawar accords. Wearing his favorite black turban with white stripes, a broadly smiling Rabbani consented. Mojadeddi shuffled forward to embrace him, stiffly and with no warmth.

Rabbani's arrival in power brought the imposition of codes of behavior, which most Kabulis had never experienced. They took the capital back to the early 1950s. Harsh codes of conduct are usually asso-ciated in most foreigners' minds outside with the emergence of the Taliban. In fact, the mujahedin started the curbs on liberty. The Taliban merely extended them. From 1992 there were restrictions on women appearing in public, a ban on alcohol and censorship of entertain-ment. Movie theaters were closed and TV films were shortened so as to remove any scene in which women and men walked or talked together, let alone touched each other. Women announcers were banned from TV. The burqa was not compulsory, as it was to become under the Taliban, but all women had to wear the head-scarf, or hijab. Rabbani refused to allow women to attend the United Nations' Fourth World Conference on Women in Beijing in 1995. Crime was met with the harshest punishment. A wooden gallows was erected in a park near the main bazaar in downtown Kabul where convicts were hanged in public.

A key issue for the new administration was the fate of the large number of people who had worked for the PDPA government under the Russians and during the Najibullah years. During his time in power Mojadeddi had announced that officials could carry on working. Rabbani's position was less clear, and, as often happens when regimes change, the struggle for survival produced a variety of inconsistent outcomes.

Many government employees went underground or fled. If they were lucky they reached Europe. If not, they moved to Iran and Pakistan. Asef Omar was relatively fortunate. He had left Kabul in 1985 on a Soviet scholarship to study engineering in Odessa. "I graduated in 1991 but decided to stay on. Ukraine had become independent but I got an extension to my visa by saying I wanted to go on to further educa-tion and I would pay my own way," he told me in Kabul in 2010. "My real aim was to stay outside Afghanistan as I thought the mujahedin might soon come to power."

In Ukraine Omar found prejudice against Afghans was starting to become open, along with bias against Chechens and anyone with a

darker skin. The police constantly stopped young men with black hair
and demanded to see their papers. Like many young men in the chaos
of the collapse of the Soviet state economy, he was working as a small
trader, buying and selling imported goods. Omar decided to return to
Kabul and says he was one of the few graduates with a Soviet degree
who managed to get a job, more by luck than design. "People were
accused of being 'infidels' and sacked or not hired. I wrote an article
about the difficulties and it was spotted by the BBC Pashto service. They
interviewed me and after the interview was aired I got a job in a government office because they wanted to prove me wrong," he said, smiling.

Ahmad Farid was one of those who lost their jobs. He had spent six
years studying computers and information technology in Georgia and
Tajikistan while they were still part of the USSR. He returned to Kabul
in 1990 and secured a government post. When the mujahedin took
over, he was fired. Roshan Zakia and her husband were police officers
in Kabul during the Soviet and Najibullah regimes. With the arrival of
the mujahedin they had to pack their bags and move to Pakistan. They
felt safe to return only when the Taliban were toppled.

Senior officers from the old army were an exception. Several PDPA
generals had defected in the months before Najibullah's regime collapsed and Rabbani felt he needed to reward them. He also wanted their
experience as he and Massoud embarked on the difficult task of creating
a professional army out of the competing mujahedin groups. Rabbani's
top priority was security, and he had come to power with expectations
that he could avert a new civil war. His first policy announcements on
military issues were encouraging. The militias and tribal regiments
would be disbanded, though it was made clear this did not apply to
Dostum's men who had helped to prevent Najibullah's escape. They
were considered to be part of the regular army, and Dostum had already
been named a four-star general by Mojadeddi.

Only groups authorized by the Defense and Interior ministries
would be allowed to stay in Kabul. To enforce the new arrangements,

hundreds of Afghan troops began an operation to rid the city of the thousands of armed men who had brought random fighting to the streets of the capital over the previous two months. At least two were killed as government forces, backed by armored personnel carriers and tanks, arrived at public buildings and private residences occupied by the armed men and ordered them to leave. In plain clothes and nominally attached to various factions, the gunmen appeared to be under no command. They took over houses, stole cars and looted property. The United Nations lost nine of its vehicles. UN officials saw them being driven brazenly around Kabul with their UN plates still visible. On one occasion a mujahedin group even brought a car back and asked for it to be repaired, a UN official told me. A warehouse belonging to the UN's Children's Fund was seized and the UN Development Programme lost valuable water supply equipment. Food aid frequently went missing, and the World Food Programme had lost sixty of the one hundred trucks sent in from Pakistan in the first eight weeks of mujahedin rule.

The hopes invested in Rabbani's deal for one of Hekmatyar's people to take the post of prime minister soon came to nothing. Hekmatyar refused to send a representative and stayed aloof on the edge of Kabul. For four years there was a bewildering array of switching sides, temporary alliances and fighting between the former mujahedin commanders and their various political parties. Hekmatyar took up the prime ministership only in June 1996, when the Taliban were already at the city's gates.

The ethnic factor played a major role in the fighting. Rabbani and Massoud, as Tajiks, had the upper hand because of their superior weaponry and troop numbers. Because they represented small minorities, neither Dostum as an Uzbek nor Abdul Ali Mazari as a Hazara Shia could hope for power. Dostum was more interested in being the supreme leader in northwestern Afghanistan. Mazari's position was more ambiguous, since he wanted to protect the Hazara heartland in

the Hindu Kush but also to defend the considerable Hazara community in Kabul. Along with Rabbani and Massoud, they had a common
interest in blocking Hekmatyar, who, they feared, wanted to establish
Pashtun control over Kabul and the rest of the country.

Rabbani's vanity and ambition were an important sub-theme in
the growing chaos. He used various mechanisms to delay resigning
from the presidency after four months as agreed, first by claiming more
time was needed to draft a new constitution and then by persuading a
meeting of elders that the general instability meant it was impossible
to change horses. Dostum, Mazari, Mojadeddi and Hekmatyar claimed
the vote at the elders' meeting was rigged.

Another sub-theme was the behavior of Mazari's Hezb-i Wahdat,
whose men were running western suburbs of Kabul with a heavy
hand. In February 1993 Massoud's people joined with Sayyaf's to attack
Hezb-i Wahdat's headquarters, even though two members of the party
were ministers in the government. The assault started a tit-for-tat series
of mutual attacks between Hezb-i Wahdat and government forces that
left hundreds dead and laid waste to large sections of western Kabul.
By 1995 almost the entire area was rubble. The attacks were accompanied by kidnapping and rape—deliberate acts of violence that Afghan
women had rarely suffered in modern times and which led many to
commit suicide because of the dishonor it brought.

Every armed group was responsible for some destruction. The
worst was caused by Hekmatyar and Massoud. As a result of their
repeated exchanges of rockets and artillery fire, most of southern Kabul
was razed to the ground. The devastation was even more extensive than
what the western districts had suffered.

In the final year of mujahedin rule, it was the Taliban's turn to terrorize the people of Kabul. Launching rockets from positions on the
capital city's southern outskirts in November 1995, they killed scores
of civilians and destroyed what was left of several urban districts.
Massoud's forces had stopped them capturing the city several months

earlier, but the next time the Taliban advanced in September 1996 they found no resistance. Kabul was exhausted.

MYTH NUMBER NINE:
Soviet shelling destroyed Kabul.

When Western forces, diplomats, aid workers and journalists arrived in Kabul in 2002 after the fall of the Taliban, most were coming to the Afghan capital for the first time. They were staggered to see huge swaths of the city in ruins. Roads were lined with the empty shells of buildings. Houses stood roofless and with gaping holes where windows used to be. People drew parallels with Dresden and Hiroshima.

Newspaper articles and TV broadcasts routinely described the devastation as the work of Soviet forces. Because Cold War attitudes are still wired into most older people's minds and get passed on to the next generation unchallenged, new visitors to Kabul tend to assume that only the Russians could have acted so wantonly. An image of Russian cruelty was easily reinforced by the fact that Kabul's destruction took place over the same period that Russian forces were devastating the Chechen capital, Grozny, with artillery and rocket fire, the later atrocities all well covered by Western TV and newspaper reporting at the time. But the truth is that Kabul's ruin happened more than three years after the Russians had left Afghanistan. The sad and shameful truth is that the Afghan capital was destroyed by Afghans.

The mujahedin's behavior was one of the many causes that led to the rise of the Taliban. It also explains why the billboards that salute the mujahedin leaders as heroes and liberators anger many Kabulis to this day.

[6] TALIBAN TAKEOVER

"It is not in the interests of Afghanistan or any of us here that the Taliban be isolated."

—ROBIN RAPHEL, SENIOR U.S. DIPLOMAT,
IN A CLOSED-DOOR SPEECH AT THE
UNITED NATIONS, NOVEMBER 1996

KABUL HAD JUST fallen to the Taliban, and up at the Intercontinental Hotel, perched on a ridge above the city, excited young gunmen were dragging crates of whisky and brandy out of the cellars and piling them into the road. A tank cranked itself into position and with a heave of its steel treads rolled up and down, crushing the sinful booty. What was meant to be a ceremony of fundamentalist solemnity rapidly became farcical as the driver, succumbing to the fumes that rose from the broken bottles, took his tank on an increasingly erratic orbit. No matter. In the New Afghanistan all alcohol had to be eradicated and the tank driver's commander ordered him to continue until no crate remained intact.

It was late September 1996, and along with other journalists I had flown in, this time via Peshawar, to report on yet another violent shift of power in Afghanistan. After six years as the *Guardian*'s bureau chief

in Moscow I had returned to the paper's London office in 1994 to be a
roving foreign correspondent and columnist.

The bottle-crushing was only one of many extraordinary scenes
in the Taliban's first days of power in Kabul. We saw wide-eyed
young Islamists, like peasant boys parachuted into Gomorrah, waving
Kalashnikovs at cars and ordering their drivers out. They ripped music
cassettes from the dashboard and hung the tapes from lampposts where
they fluttered in the breeze like brown streamers. Television sets were
confiscated and destroyed. Satellite dishes were shot at, as though for
target practice.

In government offices people were rapidly switching sides. The
Bakhtar News Agency, which produced a daily bulletin in stilted English
for embassies and the media, went overnight from denouncing the
advancing Taliban to denouncing the retreating mujahedin. I went to
the press department of the Foreign Ministry to get the reaction of the
official whose job it was to provide foreign reporters with an accreditation card. I found him in a bizarre position, standing on a chair and
removing a picture of the mountains of Nuristan from his office wall.
The Taliban frowned on any portrayal of living creatures, animal or
human. The landscape on the wall contained a tiny image of a deer, he
pointed out, and he feared the Taliban would consider it, and perhaps
him, unacceptable.

The Taliban march on Kabul was so rapid that it caught the
mujahedin government as unprepared as everyone else. Ahmad Shah
Massoud, the defense minister who was dubbed the Lion of Panjshir
when he resisted the Soviets, adopted his favorite tactic of retreating
into the mountains in the hope of counter-attacking later. He ordered
his men to leave the city without firing a shot and go back north to
their home territory in the Panjshir. In March 1995, when the Taliban
first tried to capture Kabul, Massoud's forces were waiting on the
outskirts and drove them back. The sudden shift in September 1996
stunned Kabulis, but the crowds that came out to watch the Taliban's

pickup trucks roaring around the streets of Kabul were mainly support-ive. The bearded young Islamists with their promise of social justice and a clampdown on corruption seemed to offer an end to the battles between rival mujahedin leaders that had ravaged the capital.

Like the early Protestants in medieval Europe, the Taliban rep-resented a younger generation of believers dismayed and shocked by the greed and incompetence of their onetime heroes. The mujahedin had carried the flag of Islamist resistance to the Soviet invaders in the 1980s, but once in power they became a selfish new establishment that betrayed people's hopes. Instead of providing honest government they fought each other.

MOST TALIBAN HAD spent the years of the Soviet occupation as chil-dren in madrassas (religious schools) in the refugee camps of Pakistan. But those who became Taliban leaders were ones who had been old enough to fight the Russians and the Afghan communists. They never expected they would one day form a second wave of warriors, this time purifying their country from compatriots and fellow Muslims rather than foreign infidels and their homegrown communist lackeys.

The spark was lit by Mohammed Omar Akhund, a senior mullah from Kandahar, who was in his late thirties. Unlike the political lead-ers of the anti-Soviet jihad, who had spent most of the war in homes in Pakistan's northwestern city of Peshawar, Mullah Omar went into battle against the Russians as a field commander. He was wounded four times and in 1992, fighting the Najibullah regime's forces, took the blast of an explosion on his face. He had to have his right eye removed at the Red Cross Hospital in Quetta. His unit was originally a subgroup of the mujahedin, but in 1994, two years after the mujahedin had taken power in Kabul, he revived his unit and called it the Taliban, which means "the students" in Arabic. He summoned them to a new war and called for volunteers from the hundreds of demobilized mujahedin foot soldiers as well as from teenagers from the madrassas. Most were still in refugee camps in Pakistan. A few had returned to Pashtun villages in southern Afghanistan.

Pakistan's Inter-Service Intelligence directorate, the country's main intelligence agency, played a large part in building up the Taliban. The ISI was as dismayed by the constant warfare between the mujahedin groups as Mullah Omar and his young colleagues were. The ISI wanted a strong Afghan government that it could influence, if not control. During the war against the Russians, the ISI's favorite commander was Gulbuddin Hekmatyar, but it lost faith in him because of his intransigence and his battles with Massoud in Kabul.

Turning their attention to the Taliban, the ISI trained and armed them. In the spring of 1994 it tested them out on the front line, helping them to mount an attack on Spin Boldak, the main Pakistani-Afghan frontier crossing between Quetta and Kandahar. The Taliban captured the town and soon won the support of local businessmen by eliminating the chain of roadblocks along the main trunk road where drivers used to have to pay tolls to local mujahedin commanders, who had become little more than bandits.

In those early days, the Kabul government of President Burhanuddin Rabbani, the Tajik Islamist, saw the Taliban as potential allies, since their advance mainly threatened the government's rival, Hekmatyar. In November 1994 the Taliban entered Kandahar with the help of its pro-Rabbani commander, Naqibullah, and then pushed into Helmand and Zabul provinces. Moving north, they captured Hekmatyar's headquarters at Chahar Asyab on Kabul's southern outskirts in February 1995 but were unable to go further.

Their capture of Kabul in 1996 was initially seen as positive, not just by Pakistan but by a wide range of foreign governments, including the U.S. The Taliban, being mostly Sunni, were fiercely hostile to Iran's Shia government, and Washington, still obsessed with Ayatollah Khomeini's anti-Western line, saw the Taliban as a useful source of pressure on Tehran.

After fifteen years of civil war, the United States also seemed to welcome the fact that Afghanistan had a government with a good chance of controlling the whole country. U.S. diplomats in Islamabad advised American reporters in Kabul that Robin Raphel, the assistant secretary of state for south Asian affairs, was planning to fly in to meet Taliban officials. Her trip would have amounted to the first step toward full diplomatic recognition. With other journalists I set off for the airport, but the trip was canceled, apparently because First Lady Hillary Clinton and other leading feminists told the administration it would send a terrible signal in view of the Taliban's medieval attitudes to women.

Splits in Washington's Afghan policy had emerged earlier over a lucrative deal to build a pipeline through western Afghanistan to take natural gas from Turkmenistan to Pakistan. Helped by its eminent consultant, Henry Kissinger, the former U.S. secretary of state, the U.S. oil company Unocal signed an outline agreement with the Turkmen Government in October 1995. Although the Taliban were not yet in control of Kabul, the pipeline would have to go through southwestern Afghanistan, where they were dominant. This inclined Unocal as well as some top U.S. officials to look favorably on the Taliban in the hope they could end Afghanistan's decades of instability. It was clear that international financing for the pipeline project would not be forthcoming until one group was in charge of both Kabul and Kandahar. A rival Argentinian company, Bridas, also planned to build a pipeline, but the Taliban preferred Unocal. They thought a deal with Unocal would bring U.S. recognition.

That objective became more remote when, within days of the Taliban's arrival in Kabul, evidence of grotesque repression developed in full view of Western reporters. Destroying crates of alcohol and festooning lampposts with cassette tapes were more comic than tragic. But there was no reason to smile when Taliban gunmen went into hospitals, ordering female doctors and other women workers to go home. The ban on women working spelled near-disaster for Kabul's thousands of war widows, who had to feed their families without male support. I checked the situation at Kabul's Jamhuriyat hospital. It was a depressing place that was already short of medicine, drugs and water, but the Taliban takeover had left it seriously short of staff. The deputy director and several other male doctors had disappeared. Their colleagues assumed they had fled north along with thousands of Tajiks who wanted to escape the Taliban. No female nurses or doctors were at work. I was told they were putting their faith in a Taliban promise of three months' pay to stay at home while new regulations were formulated.

In defiance of the Taliban, two women were cleaning the corridor. One said she was a widow with eight children. Paid partly by the state and partly by Doctors Without Borders, she could not afford to stay at home. Her fourteen-year-old daughter was looking after her younger children.

In his office, Dr. Hashmat, a young male doctor, revealed that the hospital director was given a handwritten leaflet from the Taliban that morning, saying no woman could talk to a man inside the building. As we spoke, the door opened and two turbaned young men with long black beards strode in. One carried a Kalashnikov. They had the grace to smile and shake hands, then started to fire questions. About 90 percent of Kabul's population speaks Dari, a variant of Persian. The Taliban invaders were Pashtun, so linguistic complications added to the feeling that Kabul was under foreign occupation again, as in Soviet times. Ferozan, my interpreter who was a university lecturer, found himself translating for the Taliban, although they assumed he was another doctor. "Have you got any patients here who were soldiers or officials in the Rabbani regime [the mujahedin regime that had collapsed]?" one of the Taliban asked. One could guess why they wanted to know. "We don't ask where people come from," said Dr. Hashmat. "We are doctors. It is not our business."

The two Taliban repeated the question a number of times before taking an interest in Dr. Hashmat's naked chin. "Why haven't you gotten a beard? You had better grow one from now on," one of the Taliban threatened. Under their rules beards had to be long enough to be held in a fist. Anything less was forbidden.

The Taliban asked Ferozan if he was a Pashtun, then gave him a hearty embrace on hearing he was. They asked if I was a Western reporter, though my appearance with notebook in hand should have given it away already. There were scores of us in Kabul, and the Taliban showed no hostility. I seized the moment of slight relaxation to ask if they had been to Kabul before. "No," they said. "Do you like it?" I asked. "Very nice," the older of the two replied. "But Islamic rule has not yet been implemented." With that ambiguous comment, they left the room and set off cruising again.

Similar scenes were enacted throughout the capital. Girls' schools were ordered shut. Boys' schools and the city's two universities were also closed until a new "Islamic" curriculum could be prepared. Burqas, once worn mainly by poorer women in the bazaar, became compulsory for all women. Taliban enforcers flayed the ankles of any woman who showed even an inch of bare skin below the regulation new hemlines.

But even as repression grew, men and women could still be heard saying that their family's newfound safety from the civil war's shells and rocket fire made it worth it. In the calculus of security-versus-rights, the absence of fighting and destruction meant more than the loss of some personal freedoms.

One step the Taliban took on their first day in Kabul left an especially chilling impression. A hit squad burst into the United Nations compound, where Najibullah had lived for more than four years after his regime collapsed. They took him away to the Arg, the presidential palace where he had ruled for six years, and tortured and shot him. His bloodstained corpse, along with that of his brother, was then hanged from a gantry at a traffic roundabout for passersby to see. Members of his tribe were allowed to take it down after forty-eight hours, and shortly before I reached the city, but the horrendous spectacle was the talk of Kabul for weeks.

During their time in power the mujahedin had respected Najibullah's sanctuary in spite of their long years of previous hostility toward him. Indeed, shortly before withdrawing from Kabul as the Taliban advanced, Ahmad Shah Massoud offered to take the deposed PDPA leader with them. Najibullah refused, apparently under the illusion that as a fellow Pashtun he could work with the incoming Taliban and even modify their hard-line policies. Elders from his tribe, the Ahmadzai, in the southern province of Gardez, had already endorsed the Taliban during their advance on the capital.

I visited the onetime UN safe house on one of Kabul's downtown avenues to talk to its staff. It was clearly marked with high wooden gates painted in deep blue, the UN's trademark color. Najibullah's exercise bicycle stood in the hall of the main house, which was defended by sandbags and metal window screens. In the garden shaded by pine and fir trees I saw parallel bars where he, his brother, an aide and a bodyguard took turns at gymnastics.

Najibullah had left the compound with the Taliban without offering any resistance, according to a member of the kitchen staff who overheard the gunmen. "We need you. We want to ask you about the situation. We will let you come back," they told Najibullah. The former president took them at their word.

A doctor who examined his body after it was taken down from the traffic gantry saw marks of heavy beating on the torso, as if from rifle butts or other blunt objects. What happened after the beating is not clear. Terry Pitzner, an American who headed the office of the United Nations High Commission for Refugees in Afghanistan, followed Najibullah's fate more closely than any other foreigner. As the designated link man between the ex-president and the international community, he regularly visited the compound. Pitzner told me he heard from unnamed sources that once he was in the presidential palace Najibullah was told he was to be hanged. "He wanted to make a final statement to sum up his life," Pitzner said. "In Islam that is important. He may have insisted and started yelling. That's when they shot him."

Pitzner was shocked by Najibullah's execution. "We became friends. It was a pleasure to see each other," Pitzner recalled. On each visit he used to bring a satellite phone so that Najibullah could call his wife and family in New Delhi. The ex-president spoke good English and was teaching himself more of the language by listening to the BBC. Pitzner also brought books and other English reading matter. "I took him *The Great Game* by Peter Hopkirk, a history of Afghanistan in the last century," he recalled. "It had a profound effect on him and he started to translate it into Pashto. 'Afghans keep making the same mistakes. They ought to learn,' he told me."

Years of house arrest had given Najibullah plenty of time to reflect on the global shifts of power since the Soviet Union imploded. "He felt he was a victim of the Cold War," Pitzner said. "The Russians and Americans were arm-in-arm, and he was still sitting there. He was a man who wanted to walk out vindicated and leave with honor."

Could the UN have done more to save him? The guards outside the compound were provided by the Afghan Government, and when they disappeared as the Taliban captured Kabul, Najibullah was left unprotected. He apparently saw no need to flee. UN officials elsewhere in Kabul heard the guards had gone and made anxious calls throughout the evening, but none was senior enough to act without political clearance from UN authorities in Islamabad or New York. The last UN plane had left for Pakistan before the Afghan guards abandoned the ex-president's safe house. The only options were to hide him somewhere else or have another UN plane brought in, but this would have required help from special forces. "Ultimately the UN relies on its member governments," one official told me. "The Security Council had long ago chosen not to offer him protection." Najibullah was marooned, like a guest without transport who finds his hosts have gone upstairs to bed. He just sat and waited.

Whatever they thought of his politics, many Afghans found his summary execution and the subsequent mutilation of his body a violation of Islam. Even some Taliban leaders appeared to be embarrassed. Sher Mohammed Stanekzai, a Taliban deputy foreign minister, told reporters in Kabul that the Taliban wanted good relations with every country and would not export fundamentalism or terrorism. Lynching was not Taliban policy, he declared. Najibullah's punishment was exceptional because he had hanged so many people. "Under his leadership our country was destroyed. It was the anger of our people which killed him," he said, as though some outside agency had done the deed.

There were other cases of summary justice. Mohammad Zalmai, the newly appointed Taliban deputy commander of Kabul's Police District Two, agreed to an interview three weeks after his movement captured the city. The area, one of the oldest and poorest in Kabul, is known as Murad Khani. Close to the city's central bazaar and packed with roadside stalls, teeming alleys and hundreds of shoppers, it used to be a favorite haunt of pickpockets. The police commander invited a Taliban patrolman to join me and my translator. To the approval of his boss, the patrolman described an incident he had witnessed in Logar province south of Kabul. Incensed by a theft, a group of Taliban took a tin of cooking oil a man had allegedly stolen from a shop, poured some into a saucepan and heated it to boiling point. Then they dipped his right hand into the bubbling liquid, took it out and severed it at the wrist with an axe. To make sure the message was widely received, the alleged thief was paraded around the street with the stump of his mutilated arm held up for all to see.

Public punishments such as this had helped to reduce crime dramatically in Kabul since the Taliban took power in Kabul, Zalmai boasted. Shopkeepers were so pleased at the change that they were getting rid of their night watchmen and security guards. "You can walk around the streets with large sums of money, and you will be perfectly safe," he said. Aged thirty-four and a mullah, he was vague about what qualifications impressed the Taliban leadership enough to give him responsibility for several hundred thousand Kabul citizens. He had never been involved in police work before. He did not attend secondary school but studied Islam in a madrassa, he said. During the Soviet occupation he was a mujahedin commander. The Taliban ordered Kabul's traffic police to stay with their jobs. The rest of the police were dismissed, except for "the few who had not committed crimes," Zalmai said. The new fundamentalist police had no rank structure and received no salary. "We work for God," he said.

Ten days after securing the capital, Taliban forces moved north toward the Salang tunnel with the aim of capturing the rest of the country. But Massoud's retreat to his native stronghold, the Panjshir valley, was a tactical withdrawal designed to give him time to prepare to block the Salang's southern approaches. Meanwhile, General Abdul Rashid Dostum, the powerful Uzbek commander, urged the Taliban to join forces with him and Massoud in a broadly based national Islamic government. Dostum made clear that if the Taliban insisted on fighting, he had forces that could block the Salang from the north.

I drove up to the Salang approaches. There was no sign that the Taliban were ready for compromise with the leaders whom their movement had come into existence to overthrow. Taliban sappers were blasting rocks that Massoud's forces had placed to block the road. "We plan to go forward," said Fazil Bary, who commanded thirty men, as he sat in his Toyota LandCruiser pickup drinking tea, with a large black kettle resting on an ammunition box in front of him. Three other bearded men in loose brown robes were squashed in alongside. Asked if he knew the Panjshir valley was the graveyard for hundreds of Soviet troops from several abortive campaigns to seize it, he laughed: "We have the power of the Qur'an behind us." An hour later some of his men started to climb the path above the river, which emerged from the mouth of the gorge. They were needed to reinforce other Taliban who had moved up a few days earlier. Mortars and tank rounds were fired over the hills toward Massoud positions.

Bary, who was thirty-five, said he had spent all his young adulthood as a mujahed, "a warrior of God," resisting the Soviet occupation of his country. But when the mujahedin leaders took over the government four years before, they "deviated from Islam," he said. Disappointed and betrayed, he had no choice but to go back to the struggle, he explained. His younger companions nodded sagely. With the earflaps of his Russian soldier's hat flopping as he talked ("my turban's inside the car," he said, smiling), the scene had comic touches: the glasses of tea, the tin of snuff in his hand, his name scrawled on the hood of the LandCruiser just to remind potential rivals that he was the one who had "liberated" it. Yet this was no bunch of amiable ruffians, affable though they might be to foreign reporters. They were the front line of a group of minimally educated men who were imposing on Afghanistan a version of Islam that had no parallel in the world.

Like every Talib in a position of authority, however lowly, Bary called himself a mullah. He had a wife and a five-year-old daughter, he told us. "I don't want her to go to school," he declared. "I will give her whatever rights are bestowed by the Qur'an, but no more. The only knowledge which is compulsory for women as much as men is knowledge of the Qur'an." Hundreds of spent cartridges from the Soviet anti-aircraft cannon he and his comrades were using as long-range artillery lay on the ground nearby. They did not know their ammunition came to them courtesy of women's work. A slip of paper in every tin contained the name of the packer, and the quality controller. All were Russian female names. I thought better of pointing this out. It was not the occasion to start an argument that might go out of control.

With John Burns of the *New York Times,* I decided to drive through the Salang under the Hindu Kush to see what resistance Dostum was preparing to offer the Taliban. We were in a battered old yellow Toyota, a typical Kabul taxi, but our trusted driver, Amir Shah, who later became an Associated Press reporter in Kabul, was confident we could cover any distance, however long. Winding up a series of hairpin bends the road was covered in the steepest places by wooden roofs to protect it from avalanches. We took a last look at the spectacular valley below before entering the 1.6-mile-long tunnel, a black void in front of us. The tunnel had no lights, and we trusted it would be open at the far end. In 1982 two Soviet convoys collided, causing traffic to stop. Some 64 Soviet troops and 112 Afghan civilians died from the exhaust fumes of idling engines in what may have been the world's deadliest road accident. There was no blockage on the mid-October day we traveled, though we found the first snows of winter were falling at the tunnel's northern exit. Severe weather can also close the Salang.

Three hours later we had wound our way down the foothills of the Hindu Kush and were in the arid plains of northern Afghanistan. A few sheep grazed, but the roads were virtually empty until we sighted an ancient black Cadillac approaching from the other direction. Behind it came several LandCruisers, trucks mounted with anti-aircraft cannon and half a dozen Soviet-made jeeps full of troops. We wondered who the passengers could be. Suddenly it struck us that this might be General Dostum, perhaps on his way to meet Massoud. We turned our car and followed at a discreet distance.

They stopped in Khinjan, a small town on the northern slopes of the Salang, and went into an old guesthouse where the Russian engineers who supervised the building of the tunnel in the early 1960s had lived. A helicopter clattered into a field shortly afterward. We learned that it was bringing Massoud from his headquarters in the Panjshir. He and Dostum had not met for three years.

John Burns and I were the only journalists in Khinjan, but after their ninety-minute meeting, which they had originally meant to keep secret until they had safely left, they agreed to be interviewed. It was a historic encounter, the birth of what became known as the Northern

Alliance. Massoud and Dostum preferred to call it the United Front since the phrase "Northern Alliance" sounded limiting in their bid to recover the whole country, but the Northern Alliance label stuck. Five years later, after 9/11, its troops would march triumphantly into Kabul with the help of U.S. airpower.

When we entered the dimly lit guesthouse, we found the two men sitting with Abdul Karim Khalili, the head of Hezb-i Wahdat, an armed movement that represented the Shia community of Hazara people. The Shia are deeply suspicious of the Taliban's Sunni fundamentalism. Khalili had arrived in Khinjan before Dostum.

We watched the three leaders shake hands and sign a statement inviting every leader of the mujahedin movement to unite to form a new government. They set up a "supreme defense council," but, in a clear overture to the Taliban to call a cease-fire and join them, they said its composition would be announced later. But they would jointly resist "anyone who continues to fight against one of the signatories of this statement," they warned.

Their ultimatum to sue for peace or face a united military front was a serious blow to the Taliban, which had hoped the opposition would remain divided, allowing them to pick off each one separately in a light-ning campaign to conquer the country after seizing Kabul.

The creation of the Northern Alliance meant that Afghanistan was effectively partitioned on ethnic lines, with the Tajiks and Uzbeks of the northern provinces combining with the Hazara against the largely Pashtun Taliban in the east and south.

As we waited for the leaders' meeting to finish, we noticed another European pacing up and down in the street. We went up to him, and he identified himself as Oleg Nevelyayev, the Russian vice-consul in Mazar. He was delighted with developments since Russia and the for-mer Soviet states of Central Asia had made no secret of their alarm at the rise of the Taliban. The formation of the Northern Alliance in the north gave them the buffer zone for which they had hoped. The historic irony was stunning. Moscow was backing the very people who had fought its occupation in the 1980s.

We filed our exclusive story, but next day our plan to return to Kabul was thwarted. We heard that heavy fighting had broken out between the Taliban and Massoud's forces at the Salang's southern gateway, a sign that the Taliban would not accept the Northern Alliance's cease-fire ultimatum. We seemed to be stuck, but the map showed a road that crossed the Hindu Kush further to the west. Amir Shah, our driver, who was a Hazara, told us it was the old royal road that used to connect northern Afghanistan with the Hazara homeland of Bamiyan before the Salang tunnel was built in 1964. It would take at least three days to cross, if at all, since he was sure it had not been repaired for thirty years. He doubted whether his banger of a taxi could make the trip, but, spurred on by our impatience to get back to Kabul plus the promise of a handsome reward, he agreed to try. He had never traveled the road before but may also have been seduced by the fact that we would descend into Hazara country, if he managed to get his ancient car up to the pass through the Hindu Kush.

The trip met his worst fears. After two hours the car was still bumping along on the valley floor when the stony road became a river. Water lapped under the sides of the doors and formed itself into a handsome wake behind us. Having crossed that obstacle without stalling we climbed into a gorge between vertical granite walls. A pontoon bridge over white-water rapids had several holes that we had to stop and fill. It took half an hour of lugging and heaving to find stones big enough to cover the gaps.

The villages we passed were preparing for a new round of fighting. The Taliban capture of Kabul and the determination of non-Pashtuns to resist any further advance meant that even the remotest parts of Afghanistan were back at war for the first time since the Soviets had withdrawn. Roadblocks were set up and looted Soviet hardware was pressed back into service. The pattern was the same in every settlement

we drove through. Two or three young men—often no more than sixteen years old—with Kalashnikov rifles would run out and wave to
the car to stop. In their stone or mud-brick headquarters a dozen others lounged over tea. The term "BBC" was usually enough to get us
through, though sometimes we had to explain whom we worked for
and why journalists were their friends. Down went the rope or chain
that blocked the road, and we were on our way.

At Doshi, a middle-aged man in a camouflage jacket said with
unconcealed pride: "I run a kind of university here. Every day I graduate a new fighter." His thirty students, probably illiterate in everything
but gun types, stood around him listening intently, their eyes searching ours for confirmation that we approved. The group we had stumbled upon had three armored personnel carriers, one artillery piece
and a truck with an anti-aircraft gun, as well as an automatic rifle for
every man.

A decade of war after 1978 had corrupted one generation of young
men, and now the next generation was about to go the same way. In
most Afghan mountain villages nothing seemed to change except the
enemies. Local armed groups made and broke military alliances with
promiscuity. The one constant was that no one disarmed. They just
stashed their weapons away for the next round.

In Kabul and other cities you met the "commanders," men who
had sizable groups of fighters at their beck and call. When you took the
back roads into the mountains, you found the walk-on parts, what an
Afghan Shakespeare might have called "Third Mujahed," a creature in a
dusty turban and blanket, wearing sneakers that had lost their laces, and
possessing nothing of any significance except his gun.

Most countries' politics are an alphabet soup of initials for parties'
names. Afghan politics is more like a series of family trees, with a main
group giving birth to factions that in turn split. Third Mujahed is on the
bottom branch, barely knowing who the opponents are or why his local
leaders are fighting them. He has never been to school, because the

village has no school. His mother and sisters never leave home because this is not accepted in the backcountry. The Taliban militia's ban on professional women has shocked Kabul and the outside world. But it is fully in line with rural traditions, regardless of whether the village is Sunni or Shia, Pashtun or Tajik. Field- and housework are all that women are allowed to do, even in small towns. During an hour's stop in Ghorband, while a puncture was fixed, we did not see one woman in the main street.

"Fighting and shopping are all that Afghans ever do," a Kabul resident had told us. "If you can keep them shopping, there's some hope." By shopping, he did not necessarily mean exchanging money for goods, so much as sitting with the shopkeeper over endless cups of tea. It is a male affair.

People often switch sides, running up a new flag when they hear a bigger group has taken power over the hill. At Khatarhaq we saw a row of thirty shops, which had been smashed and emptied the previous year by groups loyal to Massoud. At the time his main enemy was not the Taliban but a section of the Hazara people. Now Abdul Karim Khalili, their leader, was in alliance with Massoud, as we had just witnessed. Victory is often bought rather than won. In Pul-i-Khumri, the provincial governor, Said Jaffer Nadiri, told us he had captured six Taliban agents who had come to find commanders to bribe. "It is the common pattern all over Afghanistan," he said.

In Do Ab, on the last stretch of our journey back to Kabul, we heard of a group whom the locals called "Fake Taliban." When the real Taliban were moving apparently unstoppably toward northern Afghanistan after capturing Kabul, these men entered the town to take charge. When the tide turned and the real Taliban fell back, they hastily left. They did not even loot, though they would have found precious little to take.

We sat with Do Ab's newest guerrillas in their unfurnished living room. Supper consisted of bread and rice. At bedtime they simply moved from a cross-legged position on the floor to a recumbent one. Their one distraction was a shortwave radio. Their favorite station was Radio Tehran, with the BBC Persian service a close second. Every time they tuned in, a foreign voice brought news of the latest fighting. Third Mujahed cocked an ear and wondered what it changed.

We reached Bamiyan and found it still in anti-Taliban hands. Khalili's second-in-command let us sit and write our stories in his guesthouse. A young boy led us to a ladder. We followed him up to a flat roof. He brought two chairs and a table where we put our laptops while he went down again to bring us tea. Never had I worked in front of such an amazing vista. The descending sun was sending near-horizontal rays onto the face of a wide sandstone cliff a hundred yards away. Its lower part was pockmarked with caves, scooped out of the soft surface, looking from a distance as though a volley of cannonballs had been fired into the wall. At each end and brightly illuminated by the sun as though made of gold were tall niches containing the two vast Buddha statues that the Taliban would destroy a few years later. It was hard to concentrate. My eyes kept straying from the screen until the statues slowly darkened and disappeared.

On the ancient Silk Road across Central Asia, Bamiyan was once part of the Gandhara kingdom whose craftsmen developed the art of making sinuous Buddha statues, now on display in most of the world's great museums. The two at Bamiyan were the tallest in the world at 180 and 121 feet high respectively. They were made in the sixth and seventh centuries AD. Their immense size and their position in narrow niches cut into a wall of sandstone inevitably made them more rigid in appearance than the small Gandhara Buddhas, but what they lost in delicacy was more than made up in monumentality and strength. For centuries pilgrims came from far and wide to see them. During the British Raj no collection of snapshots was complete without one of a fellow squinting into the sun from under a pith helmet with one of the Buddhas looming behind him. In the hippie years of the 1960s and early 1970s before civil war erupted in Afghanistan, the more adventurous trekkers on the overland trip from Europe to India always made the detour to Bamiyan. Now they were ours to enjoy. Next morning we visited them at close hand, taking a rough staircase inside the cliff that went from the base of each statue to the side of the head. In the cave behind the legs of the taller of the two statues we saw boxes of ammunition and other explosives, which Khalili's group, Hezb-i Wahdat, were storing, no doubt to keep them dry. It seemed highly risky and meant that when the Taliban later captured the area and decided to destroy the statues, they had much of the wherewithal to hand.

The caves beside the colossal Buddhas were once home to pilgrims. Now around a hundred Hazara families were camping in them. The richer ones had bricked up the front, and put in doors, windows and stoves to make a home. The poorer made do with a screen of sacking. "Life in the Stone Age is better than none at all," a young woman with a baby and two other small children in one of the better caves told us. She had escaped from the mujahedin shelling of Kabul the year before. Her mother came up, and although she held a veil over the lower part of her face, we saw tears fall as her daughter explained how the family kept going. In the morning they climbed down the cliff-face to fetch water. Then they would wash clothes and spread them on the ground to dry, and bake bread in a small homemade oven.

BACK IN KABUL, we found the atmosphere had become tenser. Massoud's forces had pushed the Taliban back to a line only a few miles north of the capital. Half of the fertile Tajik-populated Shomali plain was in Massoud's hands. On the city's outskirts, Taliban fighters were using multiple-rocket launchers to fire at villages suspected of sheltering Tajik troops.

The Taliban moved into some villages on foot, taking a terrible toll. In the hamlet of Sarchesma they torched houses in full view of their victims. "Everything is gone," screamed Nazwar, a middle-aged woman, when we visited the hamlet the next day. "My grain is burning. My house is burning. My life is burning. Please, please tell them not to attack civilian areas."

The smell of charred wood hung in the air. Several doors in the tall mud-brick walls along the winding village street showed signs of having been kicked in. Within the once-intimate family compounds, blackened roof beams lay amid dust and rubble. A cold-blooded atrocity of collective punishment had been inflicted on the hamlet. Only four of its 120 homes were unscathed. Half a dozen trucks piled high with the remains of people's lives lurched along the dirt road in the opposite direction as we drove in. Women and children perched on top, men hung from the sides. The fire released a huge cloud of smoke, which drifted over the front lines separating the Taliban and Massoud's troops.

It was only thanks to a brief lull in the fighting that we had been able to reach Sarchesma. At first we thought the village was deserted. But our car quickly attracted a crowd of wailing and hysterical people. All begged us to see what was left of their homes. The most desperate was Khairuddin, a man of fifty-five. He had lost his daughter and all three grandsons when a Taliban fighter fired a rocket from a hill above the village shortly before the troops moved in. Khairuddin brought the veil his daughter was wearing when she died. He held up the blood-stained blue garment and a pair of green plastic shoes. "I buried them all yesterday," he said, half shouting, half weeping.

In the atmosphere of grief, shock, despair and anger, it was hard at first to piece together what had happened. As people slowly calmed down, the story began to emerge. It was a classic case of helpless civilians caught in the crossfire. The Taliban had entered the village, summoned everyone to the central square and ordered them to hand in their weapons. In almost every rural Afghan home a gun is treated as an heirloom and a necessity. "People said it was dangerous to give up their weapons," Khairuddin said. "The Taliban said: 'Don't worry. We are your security. We are your bodyguards.'"

After the guns were handed over, the Taliban warned the villagers to report any sign of Massoud's forces trying to infiltrate Sarchesma. The villagers were Tajiks, and it was highly likely that Massoud would try to move in to get support from people of his own ethnicity. Moving south from the Salang, his forces had been spreading through the Tajik-populated towns and villages west of the main road.

Having issued their warning, the Taliban returned to their base on a hill outside Sarchesma. Early next morning the villagers, now without their guns, woke to find Massoud people had sneaked in during the night. From the shelter of the village the Massoud troops fired on the Taliban. The Taliban responded with the rocket attack that killed Khairuddin's family. After a day of intermittent exchanges, the Massoud forces withdrew. Now it was time for retribution. It was assumed that Sarchesma had welcomed Massoud's people even though they had no way to expel them, any more than they could expel the Taliban. Between twenty and thirty Taliban entered the village the next morning. Systematically, they poured gasoline on the houses and set them ablaze. Nizamuddin, a middle-aged farmer, showed the pile of scarred and blackened grain in his storehouse. Recently harvested, it represented a large part of his income for the year.

"Who's to blame for this?" we asked. There was a long silence before a woman said: "We're poor. How can we know?" "If we say the Taliban, they will kill us," Nizamuddin chipped in. "Are these good Muslims?" he said sarcastically. "They are the best Muslims in the world, and they burn our homes." A younger neighbor produced a metal bowl containing a pile of ash. "This is the Qur'an," he exclaimed, his voice rising with outrage. One could just make out the edges of charred pages. "This is the book of God. Why are you doing this? You can kill us, but don't burn our book. We pay honor to the ashes of the Qur'an.

The Qur'an is the book of God." Nizamuddin said Sarchesma had been
a mujahedin stronghold during the Soviet occupation and was repeatedly bombed and rocketed by the Russians. "You know," he said, "we
killed more than forty Russian soldiers here, but they never burned our
village down."

IT WAS THREE weeks since the Taliban had conquered Kabul, and
their mullahs and other officials we had encountered were all relatively
junior. To meet the ideologues who had launched this fierce and obscu-
rantist movement we knew we would have to get to their Kandahar
heartland. Amir Shah, our Hazara driver, was exhausted by the trip
through the Hindu Kush, so John Burns and I hired another driver who
owned a minivan.

The road from Kabul to Kandahar was once known as the
Eisenhower Highway. Built in the 1950s when the United States and
the Soviet Union competed peacefully for Afghan friendship, this U.S.-
funded 300-mile ribbon of tarmac was plied for two decades by gar-
ishly painted trucks and buses with no concern for security. Then came
civil war and the Soviet invasion. Ambushes turned the highway into
a deathtrap until the victorious Taliban swept into the Afghan capital,
eliminating all security problems once again. For us the only threat was
colossal discomfort. Years of neglect had brought the road close to collapse. Long stretches rippled like a corrugated roof, making travel in
our vehicle unbearable even at five miles an hour. What should have
been a six-hour journey took twenty-three.

Mullah Nur Agha Hashim, head of the Taliban's liaison office
in Kandahar, set the scene for our inquiry into the movement's style
of government when we asked about the Taliban budget and how
they decided their spending priorities. He looked blank. It was clear
the Taliban had nothing resembling normal state administration, let
alone service delivery. What role did the government play in connection with the foreign aid that the United Nations and a few Western

nongovernmental organizations were still providing? The official relaxed visibly. "We identify projects. We assist them in assisting us," he answered, as though the Taliban were doing foreigners a great favor.

Mullah Mohammad Hassan Rahmani, the governor of Kandahar and a close associate of Mullah Omar, the Taliban leader, was happy to receive us for two hours as soon as our translator contacted his office. An unhurried and genial figure, Mullah Hassan seemed relaxed in his black turban and long, gray shirt hanging loosely over pajama-style trousers. He lolled in an armchair, with his bare left foot on a side table. His other leg had been pulped by shrapnel. In its place was a metal rod and plastic foot, which he planted toward us in what seemed a practiced gesture. He clearly saw it as a badge of honor and a useful talking point, knowing we would inquire into his record in the jihad. He lost his knee in combat against the Russians, he proudly told us.

The governor strongly denied that he and his colleagues were motivated by anger at the sacrifices they had made in war. To illustrate the point, he described how a mujahedin doctor gave him emergency treatment for the shrapnel wound to his leg. He was taken out of the city on a donkey, then transferred to a camel for a two-day journey to the border with Pakistan, from where he was taken to the hospital. "I felt no pain because I believed I was injured on behalf of Islam," he said. He went on to recount a separate incident where a mullah was struck by a car. Screaming with pain, the man was picked up by another driver, who was already taking three wounded mujahedin to hospital. "Why do you make so much noise?" the driver asked. "These men do not shriek. They were wounded in the jihad."

Like the liaison office head, the governor was vague on economic issues and preferred to discuss the Taliban's social policy. Television was banned under Taliban rule, and the governor explained why: "Worshipping statues was forbidden by the Prophet and watching television is the same as seeing statues. Drawing pictures or looking at them is sinful. . . . People have a right to entertainment," he conceded, "but instead of going to the cinema, they can go to the gardens and see the flowers. Then they will see the essence of Islam."

Large weddings with male and female guests and music and dancing were also forbidden, the governor said. But there was no ban on education for girls or work for women as a matter of religious law. The problems were practical. Girls had to be taught in a separate building from boys, and the Taliban had not had the funds to build any new schools in the two years they had held power in Kandahar. Women would be allowed to work outside the home once the war was over.

Stoning was the right punishment for adultery, the governor contended, with the man put into a sack and the woman wearing her burqa placed in a pit up to her waist before the crowd pitched in. It was an effective deterrent, the governor said, since he recalled only three cases in Kandahar in the last two years. "I was busy and couldn't see it. In fact I've never seen it," he added, as if to reject any suspicion that people might enjoy watching such things.

On the crucial issue of whether the Taliban wanted to spread their views beyond Afghanistan's borders, including to Islamic neighbors like Iran, Pakistan and the Central Asian states, Mullah Hassan was adamant that this was "enemy propaganda," Afghanistan wanted good relations with every country and would not interfere abroad. He admitted being annoyed that no foreign countries had yet recognized the Taliban, but it would carry on regardless. As for foreign loans, they had no wish to take any if it meant paying interest.

The governor's position on every issue sounded firm, if not principled, but we had noticed some contradictions in Taliban behavior. Young militiamen loved having their pictures taken by foreign photographers, whatever the Qur'an said. The Taliban employed former officials from the old Soviet-backed regime, which they considered atheist and communist. They were happy to take foreign aid from non-Muslim humanitarian agencies such as the International Committee of the Red Cross and the World Food Programme.

Were there other areas in which contradictions lurked? Among Afghans, Kandahar, the Pashtun capital, had a reputation for plentiful homosexuality long before the Taliban seized power. A culture that hides young women from all but their closest family's gaze must offer alternative attractions to physically active men. In Kabul we had seen young Taliban militiamen, their eyes decorated with kohl, holding hands and touching each other with obvious affection. Our interview had already lasted more than an hour, but it seemed feeble not to ask the governor of Kandahar for his attitude to gay men.

"We have a dilemma on this," he replied unexpectedly. Was he wavering between tolerance and censure? "There are two schools of thought here. One group of scholars believes you should take these people to the top of the highest building in the city, and hurl them to their deaths," the governor explained. We asked him about the other school of thought. "They believe in a different approach. They recommend you dig a pit near a wall somewhere, put these people in it, then topple the wall so that they are buried alive," he replied.

He must have noticed the effect his answer had on our expressions. In apparent mitigation he explained that a third group of scholars argued that homosexuals should merely be put on public display for a few hours with blackened faces. This was the Taliban's favored solution. "We have punished people in this way in Kandahar," he said. "Homosexuality is a very big crime."

The interview over, we decided to find the spot where the most recent stoning had taken place two months earlier. Mullah Hassan had said it was beside the Eid Gah mosque. A common case of adultery had turned into a cruel tragedy with Nur Bibi, a housewife and mother, waist-deep in a pit, and Turiolay, a motorcycle salesman bound hand and foot abut two yards away while a crowd of strangers hurled stones until both were bruised, bloodstained and dead.

Our appearance as foreigners quickly attracted a crowd. They willingly pointed to the pile of stones, which still lay close to where Turiolay

had died and the slight indentation in the ground where Nur Bibi's pit
was dug. "He wasn't blindfolded. His hands were tied behind his back,"
recalled Rahmatullah, a young man who witnessed the execution. "A
mullah pronounced some words which we couldn't hear. Then the
Taliban threw the first stones. After that ordinary people joined in." A
crowd of several thousand stood in the blazing sun to watch or take part.

Another young man, who gave his name as Mohammad Karim,
seemed proud to tell us that he was one of the people who threw stones.
With evident gusto he reenacted the scene for us, picking a stone from
the ground and hurling it down again with force. "We aimed below the
face," he said, "but, no, I didn't feel sorry for them. I was happy to see
Sharia law being implemented. We have to punish this sort of thing."
Other witnesses said it took seven stones to finish the man off, but Nur
Bibi lasted longer.

Adding to the cruelty, members of Nur Bibi's family were ordered
to attend her killing. After several stones had crushed her deep into
the pit, her seventeen-year-old son was asked to come forward, lift her
bloodstained veil and check if she was dead. Witnesses said he cried as
he obeyed the order and reported that his mother was still alive. At that
point one of the Taliban finished off the judicial proceedings by lifting
a boulder and dropping it on the woman's head.

Since no one seemed sure of the details of the crime, we resolved
to find the dead couple's homes. In a poor area of central Kandahar a
small boy led us between mud-brick walls along a winding path beside
an open sewer. The path opened up to a wide area of ruins, the results
of carpet bombing by the Russians in 1986, residents said.

On the edge of this wasteland, the child pointed to a wooden
door. We knocked, and an elderly woman came out. She was starting to answer our questions when two Taliban appeared, attracted by
the chattering crowd of curious neighbors and children. They ordered
her inside and told us to leave. "Pick up stones," our interpreter heard
one of the Taliban tell the crowd. The incident might have become

ugly if we had not decided to counter-attack. We warned the young Talib that the governor of Kandahar had advised us of the case. This impressed him, and he never gave an order for the crowd to throw their stones, though as we beat our retreat a few children let fly regardless. Fortunately, their aim was poor.

Next morning we sent our interpreter back. Unaccompanied by foreigners and in typical Kandahari clothes, he was able to uncover the pathetic background to the execution. Turiolay was about thirty-eight when he died. He spent his life selling motorcycles in a roadside market less than fifty yards from the stoning-ground. Nur Bibi was his step-mother. His father had married her some fifteen years earlier after his first wife died. He died himself a few years later, and Nur Bibi, now a widow in her twenties, carried on living in the family home.

Turiolay's wife, Nazaneen, told the interpreter that she saw her husband and Nur Bibi developing an intimate relationship, though it took time for her to realize it was physical. She blamed the other woman for the betrayal. "Turiolay was not in love," she insisted, "but something inside them forced them together." A cousin described Turiolay as "a good Muslim" who prayed in the mosque five times a day and observed the fasts. "Unfortunately," he said, "Satan cheated him and made him resort to this relationship."

The affair lasted a number of years and might have gone on longer if the Taliban had not come to power. By then the two sons Nur Bibi had had by Turiolay's father were in their teens. Influenced by Taliban thinking, they resolved to denounce their mother.

Under Islamic law, four witnesses are needed to prove adultery, a requirement that is almost impossible to fulfill. The teenagers suggested to the Taliban that they hide on a neighbor's roof. From this vantage point one summer night they watched Turiolay and Nur Bibi on their own flat roof coupling under the stars. Caught in flagrante, the adulterous pair had no defense. After a month in prison they were taken out to die.

Gulolai, the motorcycle salesman's twelve-year-old daughter and the oldest of the eight children he had with Nazaneen, said she saw her father being stoned. "I was sitting on top of a parked truck. All I did was cry," she told the interpreter before bursting into tears and running into the house. How the injured wife felt once Turiolay was dead was not entirely clear, though her laconic tone hinted she regretted his execution. She had stayed away from the stoning, and she could not give the interpreter any photo of her dead husband. "The only one I possess is a tiny one on an identity card he had during the mujahedin struggle against the Russians." She produced the photo. "The children often look at it," she said softly. As for the boys who denounced their mother, the interpreter could not locate them.

LIKE ALL OTHER reporters, we wanted to interview Mullah Omar, the Taliban leader in charge of this harsh regime. But he had never yet met with a non-Muslim. He received no foreign delegations or any representative of the international agencies that delivered food and medicine. Norbert Hull, a UN envoy who had been trying to organize peace talks between the Taliban and representatives of the former government, was given only underlings to meet. Yet the mullah who had changed the political face of Afghanistan and sent tremors of anxiety through Iran, Uzbekistan and other neighboring states because of his extreme form of Islamic fundamentalism was not immersed in prayer all day, we learned.

Every morning from his modest office in the center of Kandahar, Mullah Omar used a satellite telephone to give instructions on how Afghanistan should be run. "He is busy with the affairs of Kabul in the mornings," said Mullah Hashim, the liaison office head. "In the afternoons he receives governors from different provinces. He is in charge of all military matters." Although the Taliban had a six-person *shura* (council), Mullah Omar, who chaired it, was more than just the first among equals. He appointed all governors, ministers and other top officials, according to Hashim.

The supreme leader had been compared to Ayatollah Khomeini, who ran Iran with an iron hand from the provincial city of Qom. But Mullah Omar was seen by his followers as a military and political chief rather than a spiritual leader. An unusually tall man of roughly six and a half feet, Mullah Omar acquired his reputation as a brilliant commander during the ten-year struggle against Soviet occupation.

With no sense of awe, Mullah Hassan, the governor of Kandahar, had described Mullah Omar to us as a political leader more than a fount of wisdom. "He has not too much religious knowledge. He was involved in fighting for years and did not have the time to acquire it. A lot of scholars know more than he does," he said. His remarks were far from the adulation that surrounded the Iranian ayatollah. "He was one of the less powerful people among the mujahedin at the beginning, and had few fighters with him. No one expected this."

In spite of his reputation as no scholar, Mullah Omar claims to have learned the Qur'an by heart, according to an Iranian journalist who met him in 1995. Mullah Omar is a Pashtun from southwest Afghanistan, but he spoke to the journalist in fluent Dari (the Persian language spoken by educated Afghans in Kabul and northern Afghanistan) and appeared well-read.

In the early years of the anti-Soviet struggle, Mullah Omar was a follower of Mohammed Nabi, one of the less extreme among the Peshawar Seven group of mujahedin leaders. Nabi's movement, known as Harakat-i-Inqilab-i-Islami, was a clerical association more than a party. It stood between the fundamentalists who wanted an Islamic state and the secular royalists. It agreed with the Islamists on the need to apply Sharia law strictly and with the royalists on the compatibility of Islam and the monarchy. Kandahar was the seat of the Pashtun tribal kings.

As a sign of his followers' devotion, Mullah Omar was given the rare title Prince of All Believers (Amir-ul-Momineen) in 1995. "Whatever our rank, when we come before him we consider ourselves as just a simple soldier of God (mujahed)," said Mullah Hashim. "He has many qualities. He is very pious, has charisma, is kind to everyone and believes in justice." The supreme leader was said to go home to his wife and children on Thursdays. The rest of the time he worked and slept in a small office near Kandahar's holiest place, the Mosque of the Cloak, a garment once worn, it is believed, by the Prophet Mohammed and brought to the city in 1761. At times of military stress the cloak is taken out and shown to worshippers. Mullah Omar displayed it in 1995 to a crowd of followers packed into the courtyard of the shrine after the Taliban's first attempt to storm into Kabul was blocked.

Despite taking Kabul in 1996, the Taliban decided not to move their headquarters from Kandahar. Kabul was not yet immune from a mujahedin counterattack, and Mullah Omar and his colleagues appeared to feel happier close to the Cloak of the Prophet and the ancient royal throne than in the confusion of a Kabul that largely rejected their ultra-fundamentalist style of life.

A YEAR LATER, in November 1997, I was in Kandahar again. This time I hitched a ride with Pino Arlacchi, a former Italian anti-Mafia law enforcement specialist who had just become the new head of the United Nations Office for Drug Control and Crime Prevention and invited a few journalists to cover his trip to the Taliban capital.

Poppy production in Afghanistan had soared in the 1980s. The civil war and Soviet invasion undermined traditional agriculture, and farmers turned to poppy as an easy way of making a living. The mujahedin used profits from opium poppy farming to buy weapons. By 1994 Afghanistan was the world's major source of illicit opium. Arlacchi wanted to work out a deal to cut poppy production in both Afghanistan and Pakistan. He pointed out that like a balloon that is squeezed in one place only to expand in another, eradication measures in Pakistan had led to an increase in Afghanistan in the 1980s and 1990s, so it was pointless to press for a reduction in Afghanistan now without doing the same across the border. He would go on from Kandahar to Islamabad.

In Kandahar, Arlacchi's host was the one-legged governor Mullah Mohammed Hassan, whom John Burns of the *New York Times* and I had interviewed the previous October. In his private meeting with Arlacchi, Hassan announced that Mullah Omar promised to end all opium poppy production in Taliban-controlled territory the following year if the UN and foreign governments provided farmers with money to plant alternative crops. Arlacchi found himself in the unexpected position of urging caution. Money could not be found so fast. But he reached agreement with Hassan on funding a pilot program in which poppy would be banned in three districts where farmers would get seeds and fertilizer for alternative crops. If the scheme worked, it would be extended every year until after five years the area would be completely without poppies. There would also be an immediate ban on cultivating poppy in areas where it was not already growing. UN monitors on the ground and U.S. satellite photography from space would check for violations. "The Taliban have agreed that if any extra hectares are detected by us . . . the poppies will be destroyed," Arlacchi told me after the meeting. UN inspectors would also supervise the immediate destruction of heroin laboratories.

The Taliban's readiness to cooperate with international officials seemed to be connected with problems they were facing on the battlefield as well as with annoyance that their government was still not recognized internationally. In May they had captured the northern stronghold of Mazar-i Sharif, thanks in part to a deal with a local Uzbek leader, Abdul Malik Palahwan. He betrayed them a few weeks later and retook the town, capturing and massacring 3,000 Taliban troops. It was a serious reversal, which once again dashed their hopes of securing the whole of Afghanistan. Their chance of moving north through the Salang tunnel had disappeared earlier when Massoud and Dostum destroyed the entrances so that it could only be crossed on foot.

Another element of Arlacchi's agreement was that an old Kandahar wool factory, destroyed in the civil war, would be rehabilitated at foreign expense on condition that half its workers were women. Preference would go to farmers' wives as a way of making up for lost income from poppies, and the UN would subsidize a bus to transport them to and from work. This was a breakthrough since the Taliban usually banned women from working except as nurses, midwives and doctors (in self-employed clinics or all-women hospital wards). In the wool factory they would be separated from men by a large curtain. "I told them, you have a unique opportunity to improve your image," Arlacchi said. "You have two problems: women and drugs. The press distrusts you, so employ a number of women—of course, in line with your Sharia law."

In an interview after Arlacchi's meeting, Governor Hassan was as affable as he had been on my visit the previous year, though he took a tough line on what he saw as foreign governments' double standards. He insisted Mullah Omar's promise to stop poppy production was serious even though, he said, it was not banned by the Qur'an. The Qur'an only banned its use for drugs just as alcohol and any other mind-altering substances were banned. In the corner of his office Hassan had several sacks of confiscated cannabis resin, opium gum and heroin, which he had shown Arlacchi earlier as a sign of their intent. "We've already destroyed several heroin labs along the Pakistani border. Whenever we catch a drug trafficker or a man running a heroin factory, we arrest them," he said. As for punishment, he went on, "first we try to get a commitment from the person not to do it in future, or someone else [a tribal leader] will make the commitment for him. Generally we sentence them to physical lashes. It's worse than prison."

Hassan portrayed the Taliban as victims of international hypocrisy. He was certainly correct in seeing contradictions in U.S. policy. The United States had just given visas for a Taliban team to visit the Texas headquarters of the oil company Unocal. A Unocal mission was already training some two hundred Afghans in Kandahar to work on the natural gas pipeline project. On the other hand Madeleine Albright, the new secretary of state, missed no opportunity to speak vehemently against the Taliban's human rights practices. Yet, Hassan argued, what the former mujahedin were doing was overlooked. Abdul Malik Palahwan's treatment of Taliban prisoners of war in Mazar earlier in the year was an outrageous violation of human rights. "We have evidence that two hundred prisoners were put into freight containers every night and taken to the desert and shot. One prisoner escaped and told the tale. It goes beyond all international norms," Hassan said. As for Massoud and Dostum and the prospect for agreement with them on a power-sharing government, Governor Hassan said,

> *These people don't stick by their word. If you invite them into government, they will want all the power. They don't respect their fellow Afghans or human or property rights. When they were running the country there were two hundred roadblocks on the way from Jalalabad to Herat where traders had to pay bribes. Most factories in Kabul were destroyed and their looted machinery was sold in Pakistan.*
>
> *When Rabbani [the last mujahedin-backed Afghan president] was in power, he didn't have control. No schools were open. UN food aid was seized by the prime minister [Hekmatyar]. Dostum, Malik and Rabbani's supporters looted all the international agencies' buildings in Mazar, the International Committee of the Red Cross, the UN and everything. The UN and Western countries are not fair. They should study what went on before the Taliban came and see the changes the Taliban have brought. We control eighty per cent of the country. We have brought peace, and disarmed the illegal armed groups. Now people know no one will harm their property or their dignity. There's only one murder every six months now because everyone knows he will be punished according to Islamic law. Before the Taliban, hundreds were killed and there was no law.*

AFTER ARLACCHI'S MISSION in Kandahar was over, I flew on a small
UN aircraft from Islamabad to Kabul. It was the only safe way to travel
and was used by NGO workers and journalists as well as UN staff. The
Guardian wanted me to report on how life for Kabulis had changed
in the year since the Taliban consolidated their rule after their turbulent takeover in 1996. One shift, I soon discovered, was a tightening of
restrictions on the media. When I checked in at the Foreign Ministry
to get my accreditation card they insisted I stay at the Intercontinental
Hotel. It had a splendid location on a ridge with superb views in two
directions across the Kabul plateau but was a long way from the center.
There was nowhere to walk to with any ease.

The hotel looked decrepit, like a beached whale waiting to die. It
had not been managed or owned by the chain of the same name for
twenty years. The Taliban management kept up appearances with a
fully manned reception desk and bellboys, but I soon discovered I was
the only guest. The hot water and heating were not working and I had
to ask the reception desk to lend me a small electric heater.

The next morning I resolved to escape. I paid for three more nights
and moved to the main UN guesthouse in the center of town. It was a
good place to meet the aid community and hear their take on the Taliban.
The management at the Intercontinental saw me leave with my suitcase
but did not ask where I was going or why I had paid for extra nights. My
departure was a benefit since it canceled their need to provide any service at all. Insisting I go to the hotel must have been a Taliban scheme to
extract foreign currency rather than put me under surveillance.

MYTH NUMBER TEN:

The Taliban were by far the harshest government Afghanistan has ever had.
Aid workers and UN staff had mixed views on Taliban rule after one
year. On the plus side was a softening of the ban on girls' education.
The notion that the Taliban were ideological fanatics was too simple.
They could be pragmatic when they wanted to be.

I was invited to attend a meeting of NGO education staff, where the main agenda item was an expansion of home schools. To get around the closing of girls' schools, dozens of parents (mainly women) were running classes in their houses or apartments. Women teachers, fired from their previous jobs, were working in these home schools. Their salaries and the children's writing books and pencils came from NGOs or the UN children's agency, UNICEF. No one had exact figures for the number of pupils attending these private but free classes in Kabul, but as each agency recounted how many places it was subsidizing the total clearly ran into thousands. Did the Taliban know this was going on? I asked. "Of course," one aid official said. "The Ministry of Education allows it to continue. They're getting a lot of pressure from parents who want their daughters to be educated." The official Taliban line against girls' education was that it had to be curtailed for security reasons and a shortage of resources. If the home schools could guarantee security and did not ask for government funding, they were acceptable. A UNICEF official said his organization preferred to call them "community schools." "The feeling is that if we can get the informal sector going, it may eventually lead to the revival of the formal sector," he said.

Naturally I asked if I could visit a home school. Some people at the meeting were against the idea for fear the Taliban would feel obliged to close them if the media publicized them. Others thought it would be possible provided the school was not identified in the article and the existence of home schooling for girls was not presented in triumphant terms as a Taliban climbdown. Next morning I was taken to a large rambling private house where six hundred children were taught in three daily shifts. The class sizes were large, but boys and girls sat in the same crowded rooms. The head teacher told me with a smile that 6 percent of the children had parents who were Taliban.

There were home schools in other cities, too. Anders Fänge of the Swedish Committee for Afghanistan, a large independent aid agency, later told me how the Taliban governor of Ghazni province had said to him in 1998, "We know you have these girls' schools, but just don't tell me about them." On another occasion a Taliban minister said to Fänge, "I have two daughters. Can you get them in?"

University education for young women in Kabul had stopped, but a representative from the NGO Save the Children reported that Taliban officials were talking of reopening the medical faculty for female students so as to train midwives, nurses and doctors since women patients should not be treated by men. The concession was granted shortly afterward, as I discovered when I met Arsala Rahmani several years later. He was deputy minister of higher education and later minister of Islamic affairs in the Taliban government. After the Taliban's collapse, he fled Afghanistan but was invited back to Kabul and appointed to the Senate in 2006. In an interview in March 2010 he conceded that the Taliban made a string of mistakes when they were in power. "They didn't have good management, they were young, they had no experts and couldn't run ministries. My boss was a boy of twenty-five, who couldn't even sign an official letter," he said. He described reports of religious bans on girls' education and women being denied the chance to work as false: "That wasn't their idea, then or now. We didn't let girls go to school because of lack of security. There was a war on. But now in Pakistan, Taliban girls go to school and university. My son is a doctor and I want him to marry a lady doctor. I've got three daughters. During the Taliban time they were in Pakistan and all studied there.

"When I was deputy minister of higher education," Rahmani continued, "people came to me and said they had girls who had finished school and wanted to study medicine. I consulted Mullah Omar and he authorized us to set up rooms in a central Kabul hospital, now called Daoud Khan hospital, where women could study to become doctors. Around 1,200 graduated, and if you track them down you'll see my signature on their degree certificates."

The Taliban also softened their initial ban on work outside the home for war widows and other needy women. Some 370,000 people in Kabul depended on World Food Programme supplies, which included bread sold at subsidized prices. Women were making shawls and carpets in WFP food-for-work programs. The programs pre-dated the Taliban and stopped when the Taliban seized the capital. After two weeks they resumed.

Aid workers at the UN guesthouse in Kabul in 1997 had positive things to say about personal security under the Taliban compared to the previous chaos. "In the first mujahedin period children were kidnapped. There was a real problem with extortion then," one said. Others said extortion still happened but on a lesser scale. "The Taliban will go into a house on a raid to search for weapons, and when the owner says he has none, they'll say a rifle costs a million Afghanis ($40), so give us a million," another aid worker said. "As any political movement gets bigger, the initial 'purity' is bound to be diluted or polluted. People become corrupt and take advantage of their power."

The Taliban's fear of hidden enemies was causing problems at the university and in government service. Seventy of the university's 200-strong teaching staff had just been fired. Some were blacklisted because they had been members of the PDPA or its militias or had studied in the Soviet Union and other communist countries. Civil servants were also being purged for similar reasons.

One of the biggest issues the aid workers complained of was the rise of Pashtun racism and a new focus on ethnicity. In hospitals and other government-run public facilities, people were urged to speak Pashto instead of Dari, the language traditionally used in Kabul and by the elite. People who had always spoken Dari were suddenly switching. The Hazaras, the Shia minority that had always faced discrimination, were becoming increasingly fearful and many had already left Kabul to return to Bamiyan.

The picture of life in Kabul under the Taliban that the aid officials painted was by no means cheerful, but it was not as starkly black-and-white as most politicians in the West liked to make it. Nor was the difference between their rule and that of the mujahedin very great. For most people in Kabul the biggest problems were not human rights but the collapse in the economy and homelessness. There was no money or materials to rebuild the huge swaths of the city's houses and shops that were destroyed by shelling during mujahedin rule.

MYTH NUMBER ELEVEN:

The Taliban invited Osama bin Laden to use Afghanistan as a safe haven.

In 1997, the name of Osama bin Laden was only just beginning to appear in the international media. A rich Saudi entrepreneur, he had gotten to know the mujahedin leaders during the anti-Soviet jihad after first traveling to Peshawar in 1980. Two years later he settled there, using his construction company to build roads and storage facilities as well as the network of tunnels in the mountains of eastern Afghanistan near Khost that the CIA had helped him to finance and which he was later to use after 9/11 to escape U.S. bombing.

In 1988 he founded al Qaeda with the aim of spreading jihad to other countries. He returned to Saudi Arabia as a hero of the anti-Soviet resistance but was disillusioned with the royal family for collaborating with the United States in the first Gulf War against Saddam Hussein in 1990–1991. In Afghanistan there was cause for disappointment too. The mujahedin's incompetence and constant squabbling were preventing them from toppling Najibullah. Bin Laden turned his attention to jihad against the West as well as to helping Arab militants with terrorist actions against Arab rulers in Yemen, Algeria and his native Saudi Arabia. It was a disgrace, he thought, that the land of Mecca and Medina, the holiest places for Islam, should be hosting U.S. bases. He moved to Sudan in 1992 and set up his new headquarters there. But after Sudan came under Saudi pressure to deport him, he had to find somewhere else to live. The communists had finally lost power in Afghanistan, and bin Laden decided it might be the best place after all.

Bin Laden's return to Afghanistan in May 1996 was prompted less by a revival of interest in Afghan politics than by his need for a safe haven. His return was sponsored by the mujahedin leaders with whom he had become friendly during the anti-Soviet struggle. He flew to Jalalabad on a plane chartered by Rabbani's government that also carried scores of bin Laden's Arab fighters as well as a large family contingent. He probably chose Jalalabad rather than Kabul because of its closeness to Peshawar by road as well as to the mountains that he knew well. They contained the tunnels he had used in the jihad against the Russians and could provide a good setting for al Qaeda to train new volunteers for its global war. Jalalabad was also the headquarters of several Pashtun mujahedin who were willing to protect him and were negotiating with Rabbani in Kabul about forming an anti-Taliban front.

It is unlikely that bin Laden came to help in the fight against the Taliban. On the other hand, he certainly did not come back to Afghanistan at the Taliban's invitation, as is often asserted. It was only months later, after the Taliban captured Jalalabad from the mujahedin, that he was obliged to switch his allegiance or leave Afghanistan again. He chose the first option and in 1997 moved himself and his large entourage to Kandahar, in the Taliban heartland. From here he organized the setting-up of jihadi training bases in eastern Afghanistan, the area he knew well from the 1980s and which had come under secure Taliban control.

Although bin Laden's name was high on a U.S. watch list and cropped up occasionally in specialist articles on international terrorism, he had not yet delivered the fatwa calling on Muslims to fulfill their "duty" of killing Americans and their allies that made him notorious later. Beyond the circle of professional security experts, few people in the West knew his name.

That changed on November 17, 1997, when six gunmen killed fifty-eight British, Japanese, Spanish and Swiss tourists shortly after they got off their bus at an ancient Pharaonic site at Luxor on the Nile. Some victims were stabbed to death as they lay bleeding on the ground. Four Egyptians also died. It was the biggest attack on Western civilians by jihadis and had a catastrophic effect on Egypt's tourist industry. The finger of suspicion immediately pointed to Ayman al-Zawahiri, an Egyptian and close colleague of bin Laden, as the organizer of the crime, along with bin Laden himself. Bin Laden was known to be living in Kandahar, and the first international demands began to be made for his arrest and surrender for trial.

"Bin Laden's activities have been stopped and he is under close watch as a guest and a refugee," Kandahar's Governor Hassan told me when I raised his case during Pino Arlacchi's visit. It happened to be a week after the Luxor massacre. "He has been told he's not allowed to do anything against any country in the world. He will not do anything against any country, including the United States." Asked if the Taliban would extradite him, Hassan gave a firm "No."

For over a year, the Taliban had secretly been making similar points to American officials when they raised questions about bin Laden on Saudi Arabia's behalf. State Department cables released after 9/11 reveal that at a meeting on September 18 very shortly before the Taliban captured Kabul, a U.S. diplomat in the Islamabad embassy had urged the Taliban to hand bin Laden over. He was told the Taliban did not support terrorism and would not give bin Laden refuge.

In December 1996, U.S. Secretary of State Warren Christopher wrote to the Taliban warning them that harboring bin Laden and allowing him to conduct uncontrolled activities "greatly hurt prospects for Afghanistan rejoining the world community." The letter was delivered by Robin Raphel, the assistant secretary of state for south Asian affairs, to the Taliban's designated UN representative. His name was Hamid Karzai, and he would of course become the country's president after

the fall of the Taliban five years later. It was one of the odder ironies
for two countries, Afghanistan and the United States, whose history
is riddled with alliances and personal connections that shift according
to the interests of the moment. During the struggle against the Soviet
occupation, Osama bin Laden was getting support from the CIA. At
the peak of the Taliban's power, Hamid Karzai was on the Taliban side.

Like many Pashtuns, Karzai was angered and disappointed by the
mujahedin performance once they took power in Kabul. He had welcomed the Taliban victory. His official links with them did not last long,
however, and he refused to take up his post as their man at the UN.
(The post was an unofficial liaison office since the UN did not recognize the Taliban as a government and Afghanistan's UN seat was still
occupied by the Northern Alliance, the official name of the mujahedin,
even though they had lost power in Kabul.) Karzai's reason for refusal
was not that he abhorred the Taliban's social policies or their friendship
with bin Laden but because he did not like the Taliban's closeness to
Pakistan's ISI, which, he felt, was manipulating the movement.

By the beginning of 1997, U.S. policy toward the Taliban was dominated by the bin Laden issue. The Unocal rivalry with Bridas over the
gas pipeline had spawned complex lawsuits, and the chances of seeing
the pipeline built anytime soon had vanished. Taliban hostility to Iran
was no longer considered so valuable. The U.S./Taliban axis revolved
around one single question: using the Taliban to arrest bin Laden and
weaken al Qaeda.

In early 1997, the Americans asked to visit the militants' training
camps in eastern Afghanistan and were told there was no objection in
principle. It was only a matter of arranging a schedule. But in April,
after the United States had demanded bin Laden's expulsion from
Afghanistan, the Taliban withdrew their acceptance of a U.S. visit to
the training camps. In December they told American diplomats that
bin Laden was "being kept under restriction." The cat-and-mouse game
continued throughout the early part of 1998. Governor Hassan told

a team of visiting U.S. diplomats in Kandahar that bin Laden had not issued an anti-American fatwa and was under control and not allowed to organize anti-U.S. activities.

After jihadis detonated explosives at the U.S. embassies in Nairobi, Kenya, and Dar es Salaam, Tanzania, in August 1998, killing over 200 and wounding 4,000, the U.S. tone sharpened. President Bill Clinton launched Operation Infinite Reach: U.S. warships fired cruise missiles at three of bin Laden's camps near Khost close to the Pakistani border. The camps had been built in the 1980s with CIA help so their location was well-known to the Pentagon. It was unclear whether anyone was killed.

Mullah Omar's initial reaction was astonishing in several ways. Two days after the missile attack, the Taliban leader took the unprecedented step of coming on the line after one of his staff called the home phone number of Michael Malinowski, the director of the Office of Pakistan, Afghanistan and Bangladesh Affairs at the State Department. Omar warned him that the missile strikes would spread bin Laden's anti-American message even wider by uniting the fundamentalist Islamic world and would cause further jihadi attacks. He asked for proof that bin Laden was involved in the Africa bombings and said he saw no evidence implicating bin Laden in terrorist activities since being given sanctuary in Afghanistan (the same line he was to take in 2001 after the attacks on the World Trade Center and the Pentagon on 9/11). He suggested that in view of Bill Clinton's domestic problems (the Monica Lewinsky scandal), Congress should force the president to resign in order to restore U.S. popularity in the Islamic world.

Malinowski described the unexpected call and the tone of Omar's remarks as neither blustering nor threatening. Omar suggested the dialogue should continue via the Taliban and U.S. embassies in Islamabad. Malinowski's reply, repeated regularly thereafter by other U.S. officials, was that unless bin Laden was handed over, the Taliban would be considered accomplices in his crimes. The Taliban responded that expelling bin Laden would violate the rules of hospitality but he could be tried by the Taliban. They accused the United States of coercing suspects in the African bombings to admit to links with bin Laden.

Coincidentally, the United Nations had resumed its involvement in the Afghan issue again, though its primary focus was the civil war between the Taliban and the Northern Alliance rather than bin Laden. Lakhdar Brahimi, a former Algerian foreign minister with long experience as a UN special envoy, had been making periodic visits to the region since July 1997 to try to get the Taliban and the Northern Alliance to talk to each other. The Taliban were initially more interested in getting recognition from the United Nations and taking the seat that the Northern Alliance still held. During the summer of 1998 they recaptured Mazar and took Dostum's headquarters at Shibergan as well as the Hazara capital, Bamiyan. Taliban fighters killed as many as 4,000 Hazaras.

Seemingly at the apex of the Talibans' power, Mullah Omar agreed to meet Brahimi in Kandahar in October. It was his first encounter with a foreign diplomat. International officials were intrigued. How would the reclusive Taliban leader behave? "I had been told the normal procedure was that you go in and have your say," Brahimi told me later. "Mullah Omar listens and merely says his shura [council] will discuss it. Then he goes out while you wait. Someone else eventually comes in and gives the response. But it was not like that at all. We had a real conversation for three hours, though we were sitting on the floor the whole time. Mullah Omar takes himself very seriously. He thinks he is the Amir-ul-Momineen—Commander of the Faithful. He prides himself on being frank and sincere."

Brahimi found Omar, who was at that stage thought to be forty-one years old, shy and apparently embarrassed by the absence of his right eye. "It's very hard to get eye contact even with his good left eye," the UN envoy said. "He keeps his head down a lot and often keeps his hand over the place where the right eye was."

Before the meeting there had been reports that the Taliban leader would never meet an infidel. Brahimi is a Muslim but found this not to be true: "I had non-Muslims in my small team of about five people, and there was no objection." Brahimi raised the issue of bin Laden and the U.S. demand for his extradition. The Taliban leader repeated his refusal. "Mullah Omar told me categorically that bin Laden was not involved in the embassy attacks," Brahimi said. "He saw the issue purely in terms of Afghan traditions of hospitality and the Islamic duty of solidarity among people who had taken up arms against the Soviet invaders."

Brahimi concluded that the Taliban leader was "cut-off, entirely surrounded by people like himself, very suspicious of intellectuals and the elite." At a second meeting in March 1999, Omar agreed to send a Taliban team for talks with the Northern Alliance in Ashkhabad in Turkmenistan. The encounter went well, and the two sides issued a declaration promising a cease-fire and agreeing to meet again. A few weeks later the Taliban called it off, claiming the Northern Alliance had broken the cease-fire. Soon afterward, the Taliban launched a new offensive and Brahimi told the UN secretary general, Kofi Annan, he was resigning as he saw little hope that the two sides would reach agreement.

The Taliban deal with the UN on cutting poppy production had also collapsed, and planting increased sharply. Tired of what it saw as Taliban prevarication on the bin Laden issue, the United States imposed economic sanctions. Armed and aided by Russia and Iran, the Northern Alliance began to recapture ground. In a final blow to the Taliban's position, in October 1999 the UN Security Council gave way to U.S. pressure and imposed sanctions on senior Taliban officials, bin Laden and several of his al Qaeda associates. The Security Council froze Taliban assets, denied the right of commercial aircraft to fly in and out of Taliban territory and described the Taliban's failure to surrender bin Laden as a threat to international peace and security. This last phrase was ominous, since it is often used as a platform from which to authorize international military action.

The United States followed the resolution by sending a top diplomat, Karl Inderfurth, to meet the Taliban's unofficial representative in New York and remind him that bin Laden must be handed over. The Taliban made two counteroffers. Bin Laden could be "confined" in Afghanistan under UN "supervision," or a panel of Islamic scholars, one from Afghanistan, one from Saudi Arabia and one from a third country, could decide his future. Inderfurth rejected the first proposal and said the United States would not be bound by the scholars' decisions although he hoped they would lead to bin Laden's extradition.

In May 2000 the Clinton administration gave the Taliban an outline of the evidence linking bin Laden to the embassy bombings, but not the full dossier. The Taliban rejected it as insufficient. From then on, contacts between the United States and the Taliban were increasingly strained. In February 2001, the Bush administration told Abdul Mujahid, the Taliban's New York representative, to leave the United States.

As the political climate worsened, the thankless task of liaising with the Taliban on behalf of the United Nations was given to Francesc Vendrell, a dapper British-educated Catalan with long experience of working as a UN envoy in countries in crisis. Vendrell has the cautious optimism and precise diction of the natural diplomat. As the UN secretary general's new special envoy to Afghanistan, he had to be based in Islamabad rather than Kabul or Kandahar since the Northern Alliance and not the Taliban had UN recognition. Vendrell had two missions. The first was to set up UN offices in the main cities under Taliban control as well as one in Northern Alliance territory with the aim of fact-finding and keeping contact with the two sides. The second was to pick up the baton of trying to negotiate a cease-fire.

Vendrell's lot was not an easy one. As he told me in London in 2010, "I was supposed to bring about a political settlement between the Taliban and the Northern Alliance, which was unlikely. One constant in Afghan politics is that whenever serious mediation is tried, one party is in control of most of the territory and is not ready for compromise." It was an elegant understatement for decades of civil war.

Undaunted, Vendrell talked to the Taliban, flew to Tajikistan, where Ahmad Shah Massoud had offices, and traveled to Rome to meet the king's people, who put forward their time-honored suggestion of a Loya Jirga, a national conference representing the various Afghan tribes. Vendrell's main Taliban interlocutor was Mullah Wakil Ahmad Muttawakil, whom he found "decent, agreeable and relatively moderate." (In 2002, the Americans detained Muttawakil, and he was kept in their custody and under house arrest in Kabul for a total of three years.)

Vendrell also met Governor Hassan of Kandahar, whom he called "quite a jolly man." This tallied with my impression of him during interviews in 1996 and 1997. It was in Hassan's house that Vendrell had the opportunity to talk to Mullah Omar in the autumn of 2000. Vendrell is not a Muslim, and before he went into the room he and his team wondered whether they would be expected not to shake hands. "I put out my hand and we did. His handshake was very limp. I don't know whether he always does it like that, but his arm was hanging down," Vendrell recalled. He mimicked the soft loose movement for me. "Omar was very tall, about six foot three," said Vendrell, "with an enormous beard almost reaching up to his eyes. He had an empty socket where the right eye was, and wore no patch. He wore a Kandahari robe that reached just below his knees. He had bare legs and feet."

Unlike Brahimi, Vendrell was given a sofa to sit on. Omar sat on another sofa squeezed between his interpreter and another official. Speaking almost in a whisper, he asked the UN envoy why the world hated the Taliban. "I thought what to say," Vendrell told me. "Then I said, 'You have a tendency to execute people in public and some of your methods are strange'—I put it as 'unusual.' I also pointed out that Afghanistan was the main exporter of opium. That went down badly, I saw. I also said he had someone as a guest who was the United States' main enemy, and that the Taliban treatment of women goes down badly." Although his staff had bristled at Vendrell's complaints, Omar himself remained impassive. "He didn't try to explain Taliban policy. He didn't look angry. He didn't react." Three months earlier Omar had issued a fatwa banning poppy cultivation and opium production so he may well not have appreciated the references to opium.

Nevertheless, on the substance of Vendrell's visit, the Taliban leader was as non-confrontational as he had been in his extraordinary phone call with the State Department's Michael Malinowski in 1998. Vendrell did not propose that the Taliban meet the Northern Alliance again for talks, since he felt this raised excessive expectations. Instead, he suggested the Taliban write him a letter requesting the UN to use its good offices to mediate. He would ask the Northern Alliance for the same letter. Omar agreed to have his people write the letter. It even said the Taliban were committed to reaching agreement for a political solution to the country's war.

In December 2000, the UN Security Council passed a new and tougher resolution on sanctions. In addition to reaffirming the earlier call for bin Laden's extradition it imposed an arms embargo, banned Ariana Afghan Airlines from landing anywhere beyond the borders of Afghanistan, called for all terrorist training camps to be closed and demanded an end to illicit drug production.

The move tipped the balance within the Taliban leadership in favor of the hard-liners. They were insulted that Mullah Omar's fatwa on opium had been ignored rather than followed up with international aid for Afghan farmers. When rumors developed that the Taliban were planning to destroy the Bamiyan Buddhas, Vendrell met Muttawakil to tell him of the international outrage that would surely follow. "He told me it wouldn't happen, but it did," Vendrell recalled. When the Buddhas went down, it was a clear sign to Vendrell that the hard-liners—including the defense, interior and justice ministers—were in charge.

In the ensuing months Vendrell continued his contacts with the Northern Alliance and the king. They were gearing up for a renewed military push against the Taliban. Two former senior mujahedin commanders, Abdul Haq and Abdul Rahim Wardak (who later became Karzai's defense minister), wanted to open a Pashtun-led front in eastern Afghanistan to work with Ahmad Shah Massoud.

But on September 9, Massoud, the Lion of Panjshir, was assassinated by two al Qaeda suicide bombers posing as journalists.

Two days later, suicide pilots flew hijacked aircraft into the World Trade Center in New York and the Pentagon in Washington, with a fourth plane crashing in a field in rural Pennsylvania.

Everything changed.

[7] TALIBAN TOPPLED

"America has never sought to occupy any nation in the world. We are a good people."

—Karl Eikenberry,
former U.S. Ambassador to Afghanistan

"Even the nomads don't know where to go these days."

—A refugee from Kandahar

Abdul Salam Zaeef was as stunned as any American when a neighbor rushed into his home in Islamabad on September 11, 2001, and told him that amazing scenes were unfolding on television. The Taliban ambassador to Pakistan, Zaeef had no TV set, so he quickly crossed the road to a friend's house where a crowd was already gathered around the screen.

In New York the World Trade Center was ablaze. People were throwing themselves from the twin towers and falling to the street. "The scene was horrific, and I stared at the pictures in disbelief," he recalled in his autobiography. Zaeef's mind raced to the likely repercussions of the unfolding tragedy. He was sure Osama bin Laden would claim responsibility for the attack whether he was involved or not since "his mouth is not easily controlled," as the ambassador put it. "I knew that Afghanistan and its poverty-stricken people would ultimately suffer for what had just taken place in America. The United States would seek revenge and they would turn to our troubled country."

As they watched what was happening in New York, Zaeef's excited Taliban colleagues were shaking each other's hands. He wondered how their reaction could be so shortsighted and superficial. Back home, he was unable to sleep. At one a.m. the phone rang. It was Mullah Omar, calling from Kandahar to consult on what kind of official response to make. The next morning the ambassador called a press conference in Islamabad, where he read out a statement condemning the 9/11 attacks: "We strongly condemn the events that happened in the United States at the World Trade Center and the Pentagon. We share the grief of all those who have lost their nearest and dearest in these incidents. All those responsible must be brought to justice. We want them to be brought to justice and we want America to be patient and careful in their actions."

In Washington, President Bush was declaring that those who harbored terrorists were as guilty as those who committed terrorism. He called on the Taliban to hand bin Laden over. Mullah Omar replied that he needed evidence that bin Laden was responsible for the attacks. Afghanistan would then try bin Laden in an Islamic court. For his part, Zaeef wrote a long letter to Bush, which he sent to the U.S. embassy in Islamabad to pass on to Washington. In it he pleaded for American restraint, arguing that "we don't want to fight anymore nor do we have the power to do so."

As the United States stepped up its preparations for war, Zaeef drove to Kandahar, where he found Mullah Omar blindly confident that the United States was unlikely to attack. Zaeef tried to warn the Taliban leader, telling him the authorities in Pakistan were no longer allies. They had switched their allegiance from the Taliban, were urging the United States to launch air strikes on Afghanistan and had started talking to the Northern Alliance of mujahedin groups, assuming they would be part of the country's next government.

Flying in the face of these warnings, Omar continued to claim that America could not attack Afghanistan without valid reason. He had asked Washington for hard evidence incriminating bin Laden and said the Taliban would take no further action until they were shown proof of his guilt.

Given that the Taliban made no preparations to resist any impending attack, Zaeef's account seems plausible. Omar's passivity was one more sign of how out of touch the Taliban leader had become. The destruction of the historic Buddha statues at Bamiyan earlier in the year in the face of appeals from the United Nations and many foreign governments already suggested he was living in an air of unreality and isolation about the way the outside world perceived the Taliban. His response to 9/11 confirmed it.

History gets telescoped in people's minds, and it is easy to forget that almost four weeks passed after the 9/11 attacks before the United States launched its air strikes on Afghanistan. The path to war was methodical. First, a fourteen-ship battle group was sent to the Persian Gulf. A hundred combat aircraft were readied. Targets for missile raids were prepared.

Clinton had acted more quickly after al Qaeda blew up the U.S. embassies in Dar es Salaam, Tanzania, and Nairobi, Kenya, in August 1998. But his response—seventy-five cruise missiles fired at four training camps for militants in Afghanistan, an offensive that caused minimal casualties and had little effect—was a relative pinprick compared to what Bush was preparing to do against Afghanistan. Bush wanted nothing less than regime change.

Afghanistan's religious leaders met in Kabul on September 20 and asked bin Laden to leave the country. Bin Laden ignored them. Had he not done so and had the Taliban offered proof he was gone from Afghanistan, Bush's reprisals might conceivably have been averted. An American attack might also not have occurred if the Taliban had detained bin Laden and handed him over, as Bush demanded. But this

option was unlikely since Bush did nothing to make the Taliban position easier by sending proof or addressing them in calm diplomatic
language rather than with threats. With the White House, many senators and representatives and much of the media clamoring for revenge,
the administration feared that to comply with Taliban requests for evidence of bin Laden's role would look weak. Bush's initial nervous reaction to being told of the attacks on the World Trade Center while he
was visiting a primary school in Florida had already raised doubts over
his leadership qualities. Rather than make a serious proposal for talks,
Bush preferred to issue an ultimatum. It would be easier to justify a U.S.
attack once it was rejected.

Was it ever likely the Taliban would abandon their guest? Much
depended on what drove the Taliban relationship with bin Laden. The al
Qaeda leader had earned Omar's support by giving the Taliban substantial financing. In return Omar had helped bin Laden by providing him
with a political base in Kandahar and the chance to use the old training
camps near Tora Bora in the mountains of eastern Afghanistan. So both
men were in each other's debt.

Two other intriguing questions arise. If Mullah Omar had tried to
force bin Laden to leave Afghanistan, could he have done so? I put the
question to Francesc Vendrell, the UN envoy who had met Omar a year
before 9/11 and negotiated on several occasions with other Taliban leaders. "If he had asked him to go before 9/11 happened, I think bin Laden
would have left. After 9/11 he wouldn't have had anywhere to go," he
replied. "Omar fell under bin Laden's spell, I suspect. He was charismatic.
He had traveled the world. Omar and bin Laden were joined like the lip
and teeth. He lived nearby, about ten miles out of Kandahar. He probably only left for Tora Bora in October." Could the Taliban have arrested
him in Kandahar? "They had the power to do so. Bin Laden had his Arab
militia, but not more than a thousand people, and the Taliban could have
whipped up a popular frenzy to arrest him." Once bin Laden had gone
into hiding in Tora Bora, they would have had a much harder task.

For Bush, the Taliban were an easy target, since they had been international pariahs long before 9/11. Although they ruled most of the country after capturing the capital in 1996, Afghanistan's UN seat remained in the hands of the Northern Alliance, as the defeated muja-hedin government was known. It was a legal and political nonsense, as cynical in its origins as the treatment of Cambodia in 1979 after Vietnamese troops toppled the genocidal regime of Pol Pot's Khmer Rouge. Vietnam was a Soviet ally so in the spirit of the Cold War, China and the Western states on the UN Security Council kept the country's UN seat in Khmer Rouge hands rather than let it go to Cambodia's new Soviet-supported government.

Even in the Muslim world, the Taliban's brand of fundamental-ism, with its eccentric attitudes to women's clothes, music, sports, kite-flying and all symbols of modernity like television, made them pariahs. Only three countries—Pakistan, Saudi Arabia and the United Arab Emirates—recognized the Taliban as Afghanistan's legitimate rul-ers after they captured Kabul in 1996. Countries that might have been tempted to deal with the Taliban were also intimidated, long before 9/11, by Washington's campaign against any state that hosted al Qaeda.

Indeed, evidence emerged a few days after 9/11 that the Bush administration had warned the Taliban two months earlier that it might take military action to topple the regime unless they handed bin Laden over. The revelation came from Niaz Naik, a former foreign minister of Pakistan who attended a four-day meeting in mid-July 2001 of former senior U.S., Russian, Pakistani and Iranian officials as well as UN dip-lomats in a Berlin hotel. The conference, the third in a series dubbed "Brainstorming on Afghanistan," provided an opportunity for a classic device known as track-two diplomacy. As opposed to "track one," the standard practice whereby countries' diplomats and other official rep-resentatives discuss issues, "track two" is designed to offer a forum for governments to pass messages and sound out each other's thinking by means of independent experts. The experts are often former officials who still have close links with their governments although they present themselves as not expressing official views. The Americans were Tom Simons, a former U.S. ambassador to Pakistan, Karl Inderfurth, a former assistant secretary of state for south Asian affairs who had negotiated with the Taliban two years earlier, and Lee Coldren, who had headed the Office of Pakistan, Afghan and Bangladesh Affairs in the State Department until 1997.

As Naik told me in a phone interview from Islamabad in September 2001, "The Americans indicated to us that in case the Taliban does not behave and in case Pakistan also doesn't help us to influence the Taliban, then the United States would be left with no option but to take an overt action against Afghanistan. I told the Pakistani government, who informed the Taliban via our foreign office and the Taliban ambassador here."

Coldren confirmed the broad outline of the American position at the Berlin meeting. "I think there was some discussion of the fact that the United States was so disgusted with the Taliban that they might be considering some military action," he told the *Guardian*. The three former U.S. diplomats "based our discussion on hearsay from U.S. officials," he said. It was not an agenda item at the meeting "but was mentioned just in passing."

Apparently embarrassed by the disclosure, Simons downplayed the suggestion that anything was imminent. "We were clear that feeling in Washington was strong, and that military action was one of the options down the road. But details, I don't know where they came from." But Simons conceded that the Bush administration, still less than six months in office, was reassessing U.S. policy toward Afghanistan and taking the role of the Taliban and al Qaeda more seriously than Clinton had. "It was clear the trend of U.S. government policy was widening. People should worry, Taliban, bin Laden ought to worry—the drift of U.S. policy was to get away from single issue, from concentrating on bin Laden as under Clinton, and get broader."

The administration was ready with its new strategy, by coincidence, on the day before the attacks in New York and Washington. On March 23, 2004, at a session of the 9/11 Commission, the National Commission on Terrorist Attacks Upon the United States, which started public hearings in New York City in 2003, Secretary of State Colin Powell said that on September 10, 2001, national security officials had agreed on a three-phase plan toward the Taliban. They would be presented with a final ultimatum to hand over bin Laden. Failing that, covert military aid would be channeled to anti-Taliban groups. If both those options failed, the United States would seek to overthrow the Taliban regime "through more direct action." The three-step strategy did not represent an immediate plan to attack the Taliban. The process was expected to take up to three years. But it meant that after 9/11 Bush had all the necessary measures available on his desk and could easily accelerate the process by running them together. U.S. Special Forces would move into Afghanistan to aid the Northern Alliance with advanced communications and other logistical help while U.S. air strikes would hit Taliban assets in Kabul and Kandahar. Other units of Special Forces would raid al Qaeda bases around Tora Bora.

In Europe, 9/11 had produced almost as great a shock as it did in the United States. Politicians and the media rushed to express solidarity and sympathy. The French newspaper *Le Monde* printed a fulsome headline, "We Are All Americans." For the first time in its history NATO invoked Article 5 of its founding treaty, which describes an attack on one allied member state as an attack on all. Russia's president, Vladimir Putin, was the first foreign leader to offer public condolences.

9/11 also led to a sudden upsurge of international interest in Afghanistan. Governments realized they had to do some research at last. Jonathan Powell, Tony Blair's chief of staff, later joked that he became the government's Afghan specialist overnight. His qualifications? After the attacks he had rushed out of 10 Downing Street to the nearest store and bought every book on the country he could find.

But, as the initial shock diminished around the world, if not in the United States, calls for caution began to make themselves heard. It was not just the Taliban that pleaded for U.S. restraint. UN officials did their best to remind the world that Afghanistan was in the midst of a devastating drought that had forced hundreds of thousands to flee to camps to get humanitarian aid and required massive convoys of trucks to deliver food. The World Food Programme warned that an estimated 3.8 million Afghans were completely dependent on outside aid and had only enough food stocks for two to three weeks. Ruud Lubbers, the UN High Commissioner for Refugees (UNHCR), traveled to Washington to tell the State Department that millions of Afghans already faced starvation and homelessness, and U.S. attacks might hit many more. Private aid agencies like Oxfam and Care International warned that war would make the plight of drought victims worse. It was pointed out that the Taliban were not obstructing aid deliveries nor could they be blamed for the drought. The fact that insufficient food aid was coming in was the fault of foreign governments, which had not provided enough funding in response to the UN's numerous appeals.

Sibghatullah Mojadeddi, the head of one of the former anti-Taliban groups of mujahedin who served as the first president of Afghanistan after Najibullah was toppled, also urged the United States to exercise restraint. In Europe officials were torn between the desire to maintain solidarity with the United States and anxiety that they might be giving Washington a blank check for any action that the United States could designate as necessary under the "war on terror," which Bush had declared in a speech to Congress on September 20. Tens of thousands of protesters marched in various cities, including Amsterdam, Athens, London and Madrid. In Amsterdam they carried banners saying "Justice, not Revenge." Over 20,000 rallied in New York and Washington on September 29. Some carried placards saying "Our Grief Is Not a Cry for War."

In newspaper offices, opinion was divided. Tense discussions took place at the *Guardian*'s regular morning conference as reporters, columnists and editors argued over the impending attack on Afghanistan. It was known that Britain intended to take military action alongside the United States (just as it would do against Iraq seventeen months later). The *Guardian* had supported the NATO attack on Kosovo two years earlier on the grounds that the province's Albanian majority was facing an immediate humanitarian catastrophe at the hands of Serbian forces under Slobodan Milosevic's command. Action had to be taken to eliminate the threat, even if in the short term the situation might worsen, the paper's editorials argued. The paper was to oppose the attack on Iraq in 2003 on the grounds that Saddam Hussein posed no imminent threat and the UN had not authorized an end to the work of its weapons inspectors, let alone a war to remove him from power.

The Afghan crisis was different. Debate in the editorial conference revolved round two main issues: whether the United States was justified in using military force in response to 9/11 and whether toppling the Taliban was a necessary element in the hunt for bin Laden and al Qaeda. If al Qaeda was perceived as the exclusive danger, some argued that raids by Special Forces should first be tried in a limited area of the border between Afghanistan and Pakistan. It would not be necessary to bring war to Afghanistan's main population centers in Kabul and Kandahar, thereby risking civilian casualties. Supporters of the U.S. and British attack on Afghanistan argued that the two countries had no alternative but to take military action. The Taliban were a vicious regime with an appalling record of violating human rights. They deserved to be removed from power. Opponents countered that if the Taliban were toppled, the successor regime would be dominated by fundamentalist warlords whose attitude to human rights was only marginally better than the Taliban's. The change was not sufficient to justify the risks of all-out war.

With the support of two leading columnists, one of whom high-lighted the Taliban's medieval attitude to women, the argument for inva-sion carried the day. In its main editorial on October 8, 2001, the morning after the United States and Britain launched their attacks on Afghanistan (with British submarines in the Arabian Sea firing cruise missiles), the *Guardian* expressed no doubt about their legitimacy: "At a time of such seriousness, it needs to be said as clearly and as unemotively as possible at the outset that the United States was entitled to launch a military response." The Taliban had ignored pleas to surrender bin Laden and his associates. "There is no question, therefore, but that a monstrous injus-tice against America remains unassuaged," it said. "As long as that kind of danger—that scale of evil—remains loose in the world, then military action can be justified not just as an act of justice but as an act of legiti-mate self-defense to protect our nations from further attack and further casualties." Finally, the editorial praised Bush for taking into account the issue of the Afghan drought. "As the attacks began," it concluded, "he also promised drops of food, medicine and other supplies to Afghan civilians. . . . Words are the easy part. It is now for the U.S. military and their allies to put those words into action. Nothing in the world is more important right now than that they succeed."

The war's opponents (myself included) argued that attacking Afghanistan would provoke anger in many parts of the Muslim world and increase the terrorist risk. The "war" against terrorism was not a job for troops or missiles. It should not really be a war at all. Dealing with terrorism had to be a combination of politics and the police. Countries needed to improve their security measures against hijacking, intensify their intelligence sharing and put political pressure on states that shielded terrorists. Some advocates of military action had drawn an analogy between Pearl Harbor and the 9/11 attacks. But Pearl Harbor was accompanied by simultaneous strikes against British positions in Southeast Asia and was the opening shot by the Japanese Government in a campaign of imperial expansion across Asia. The war's critics in the

Guardian office argued that bin Laden was not interested in territory. His was a war of ideas that targeted the corruption of Islamic rulers as much as the U.S. strategy of maintaining bases and repeatedly intervening militarily in Muslim countries. Confronting ideas was a long and complex struggle with no shortcuts based on military action, especially when that action risked creating more support for bin Laden's complaints about U.S. interventionism.

Some opponents of the attack on Afghanistan felt Bush had made regime change one of his war aims so as to give himself a fail-safe option. Toppling the Taliban would be relatively simple, and certainly easier than catching or killing the elusive bin Laden. Instead of having to hit the bull's eye, any strike on the dartboard would be trumpeted as proof that Bush had scored. It would also get widespread praise from women in Western countries where the Taliban were so detested. This would be a kind of "collateral benefit." A similar human rights case would be made by Bush and Blair over Iraq. For Iraqis and the world to be rid of Saddam Hussein's regime would be an undeniable bonus whether or not weapons of mass destruction were found.

Other critics of the attack on Afghanistan raised the issue of international law and argued that the UN Security Council had not authorized it. Resolution 1368, passed the day after the 9/11 atrocities, called on all member states to bring the perpetrators of terrorism to justice. It did not authorize the use of force to do it or as punishment for a government that failed to comply. Resolution 1373, passed by the Security Council on September 28, just over a week before Bush's air strikes on Afghanistan, went further by outlining an extensive range of actions for members to adopt to curb terrorism. But they consisted entirely of police measures, such as closing down bank accounts and fund-raising activities that financed terrorism as well as moves to prevent recruitment and arms supplies to terrorist groups. Resolution 1373 said nothing about the use of military force. Indeed, neither resolution even mentioned Afghanistan by name.

Under international law, war cannot be justified in terms of revenge or retaliation, yet the U.S. response to 9/11 was clearly punitive and vindictive. Polls showed that most Americans were happy with that. In his autobiography, *Decision Points,* published in November 2010, Bush acknowledged his primary motive was revenge: "My blood was boiling. We were going to find out who did this, and kick their ass." In his public statements at the time Bush had to rely on another justification, the right of self-defense under imminent threat of attack. Al Qaeda had attacked the United States and was known to have training bases in Afghanistan that could be used for more attacks, he argued. The fact that the nineteen 9/11 attackers were not Afghans and had trained in Germany and the United States was ignored. The International Court of Justice, which was set up by the United Nations in 1945, had rejected a similar self-defense argument when the Reagan administration used it in the 1980s to justify bombing and mining harbors in Nicaragua that were allegedly being used for training guerrillas fighting the U.S.-supported government of El Salvador. The court said this was stretching the concept of self-defense too far. The United States refused to be bound by its judgment and announced that in future it would only accept the ICJ's jurisdiction on a case-by-case basis. No doubt it would have repeated its refusal if the ICJ had ever adjudicated on the attack on Afghanistan and come out against the United States.

The matter of "imminence" was also open to serious doubt. The 9/11 attacks had taken years to prepare. To suggest that bin Laden and al Qaeda were in a position to mount further attacks so soon after 9/11 stretched credibility. There was ample time for the United States to try to reduce its capabilities by a variety of means short of war.

A final point in the arguments made against going to war was that Article 51 of the UN Charter, which permits self-defense, talks of it in the context of armed attacks by another country. Under Washington's own definition, the 9/11 attacks were "criminal attacks" by a non-state actor. The armed forces of Afghanistan had not attacked the United States.

In spite of these criticisms, the overwhelming majority of Americans and most Europeans supported Bush's war. In the United States both main parties united behind it. Only one member of Congress dared to oppose Bush. Representative Barbara Lee, of California's ninth congressional district, said to the House of Representatives on September 14: "We are not dealing with a conventional war." "We cannot respond in a conventional manner. . . . If we rush to launch a counterattack, we run too great a risk that women, children, and other non-combatants will be caught in the crossfire. . . . we must be careful not to embark on an open-ended war with neither an exit strategy nor a focused target. We cannot repeat past mistakes." After her speech she received death threats. But when we read her words today, her prescience is chilling.

Once Bush launched his war on October 7, the arguments over legality faded, but as TV viewers around the world saw wave after wave of missiles striking targets in and around Kabul and Kandahar, a few senior figures raised doubts. Ten days into the air campaign, the UN Human Rights Commissioner, Mary Robinson, a former president of Ireland, called for a bombing pause to allow relief supplies to reach refugees. Erugrul Ciragan, a senior adviser in the Turkish prime minister's office, told me and other reporters who accompanied Jack Straw, the British foreign secretary, on a trip on October 18 to Ankara: "How long can bombing go on? It's a poor country. It can create a negative attitude in Iran and Pakistan, where there is instability." The Turkish government favored the insertion of foreign ground troops in the hope of ending the war more quickly.

Bush rejected any halt in the bombing campaign, but Western governments had begun to focus on what sort of regime would take over in Kabul. They also needed to work out who would handle security once the Taliban were toppled. At that stage the Bush administration was not as hostile to giving the UN a role as it became a few months later when Bush switched his attention to toppling Saddam Hussein in Iraq. Provided the United States had a major, if not the decisive, say, it was happy to see the UN negotiate a new Afghan government. Washington urged Kofi Annan to reappoint Lakhdar Brahimi, who had served as the UN secretary general's special envoy for Afghanistan from July 1997 until October 1999.

There was concern in many quarters that the Northern Alliance might win too quick and easy a victory. Such a victory was vehemently opposed by Pakistan, Washington's main U.S. ally in the region, which did not want to see a crushing Taliban defeat and a takeover by Tajik and Uzbek warlords. Pakistan argued for a strong role in the new Afghan government to be given to the Pashtun, on their own or as the leading partners in coalition with representatives of the other ethnic groups. With Northern Alliance fighters and armored vehicles impatiently chafing at Taliban defense lines north of Kabul, observers began to note that the United States was not using its B-52 bombers to hit them even though it was targeting other Taliban assets in central Kabul and elsewhere in the country. At a breakfast meeting with reporters in October in London, Brahimi, the new UN special envoy Afghanistan, told us: "If anyone is less popular than the Taliban, it's the Northern Alliance. The Americans are holding back. They haven't bombed Taliban positions north of Kabul for fear of the Northern Alliance taking revenge on civilians and looting. They're a very unruly bunch." It was a significant, if belated, switch in policy. After a decade and a half of help to the mujahedin during the Soviet occupation and Najibullah's three years of power, the Americans were drawing back from the people they had once armed and financed.

Who could replace Northern Alliance troops in Kabul when the city fell? One idea was to use a UN peacekeeping force, possibly consisting of troops from Muslim nations such as Turkey and Bangladesh. This was initially seen as preferable to having Western forces on the ground. Straw raised the idea with the Turks in his talks in Ankara in mid-October.

Ensuring representation for Pashtuns in any future government was tricky. Without a satisfactory answer, the risk was that a largely

Pashtun ruling group (the Taliban) would be replaced by a largely Tajik and Uzbek group (the Northern Alliance). This could be a recipe for a renewed civil war. Could a role be given to some Taliban in a power-sharing government? On a trip to Pakistan, Secretary of State Powell talked of finding Taliban moderates who would break from Mullah Omar and join a broad-based government provided they repudiated al Qaeda. It was not clear whether this was a serious proposal or, more probably, a device to create dissension in Taliban ranks.

There was also talk of bringing King Zahir Shah back as a unifying figure who stood above tribal politics—the same formula that the Soviets had toyed with more than a decade earlier. The king, who was by then eighty-six years old, was flattered and interested, though he annoyed Western governments by receiving a Northern Alliance delegation at his villa in Rome and agreeing with them on a proposed governing council. Under the plan, the king's representatives would have sixty seats, the Northern Alliance would have fifty and there would only be ten for other Afghans. Western officials applauded the general sentiment of a coalition between Pashtun monarchists and Tajik and Uzbek leaders, but they felt he was being too specific about seat numbers and had jumped the gun. Previously considered weak and hesitant, the king was now seen as demanding too much for himself too soon. Washington abandoned any idea that he could play an executive role in post-Taliban Afghanistan or chair a conference of Afghans that could select a provisional government.

On November 8, aided by ferocious U.S. bombing, the Northern Alliance captured Mazar-i Sharif, the city on the plains north of the Hindu Kush that the Taliban had held since 1998. Many Taliban escaped, and a few defected, but between four hundred and six hundred people were estimated to have died in the city, although it was not possible to separate the toll of dead civilians from that of combatants. There were reports of summary executions of Taliban prisoners by Northern Alliance troops.

Fear that similar atrocities would happen on a larger scale in Kabul became a major theme in Western discussions. Officials suggested the city should be demilitarized after the Taliban were driven out, so as to prevent the warlords of the Northern Alliance taking over. People remembered the carnage and destruction they had caused in the capital when they were in power in the mid-1990s. "We'll encourage our friends [the Northern Alliance] to head south but not into Kabul itself," Bush told reporters after meeting Pakistan's president, Pervez Musharraf, on November 10. A few hours earlier, Secretary of State Powell said, "It might be better to let Kabul become an open city," meaning that it should be demilitarized.

Their idea did not last long. After seizing Mazar, the Northern Alliance were eager to capture the capital. The United States felt it could not delay them much longer and launched strikes by B-52 bombers on the Taliban lines. On November 12, the Taliban retreated in disarray, leaving the way open for the Northern Alliance to march into Kabul, just over five years since they themselves had retreated with scarcely a shot fired.

After the Taliban left the capital, the focus switched to Kandahar, the Taliban heartland, which was expected to resist longer. Anticipating the impending battle, the *Guardian* had already sent me to Quetta, the capital of the desert province of Baluchistan and the Pakistani city closest to Kandahar. Here for the first time my fellow reporters and I heard mention of a Pashtun tribal leader called Hamid Karzai who was expected to play a big role in post-Taliban Afghanistan. For all but a few diplomats, his brief period on the Taliban side and his designation as their UN representative in 1996, which he never took up, had escaped public notice.

Hamid Karzai's half-brother Ahmed Wali Karzai lived in a new suburb on the outskirts of Quetta. Reporters would drive from the city's bustling downtown full of rickety three-wheelers and honking buses to an area of dusty empty lots and half-built homes. A few two-story

houses were complete, and we would sit for hours in the marble courtyard of one of them, waiting to interview Ahmed Wali Karzai. After
fleeing from Afghanistan during the Soviet occupation, he had run a
restaurant in Chicago until 1992 and spoke excellent English. Little did
we know that a few months later he would become a key player in
southern Afghanistan and eventually be known by the Americans as the
Godfather of Kandahar, the linchpin of an empire built on corruption.

In November 2001, we knew Ahmed Wali Karzai only as the half-
brother of a shadowy figure who had high-level U.S. backing and was
operating somewhere across the Afghan border. Ahmed would speak to
Hamid by satellite phone at least once a day, he told us, to get regular
updates on the progress of the Pashtun uprising against the Taliban.
One day he would claim that Hamid had taken control of the province of Uruzgan, the home area of Mullah Omar. Another day the
story would be that morale among the Taliban was low and only the
extremists who were close to the Arab jihadi volunteers wanted to
go on fighting. The rest would like to make a deal with independent
Pashtun tribal leaders to prevent a Northern Alliance takeover. Finally
on December 6 Ahmed said that Hamid and his people were negotiating with village elders and local Taliban commanders, but Ahmed
denied that his brother was offering money. "If the commanders agree,
then our forces move in," he explained. It sounded like a classic Afghan
arrangement, but we had no way of verifying whether any of Ahmed's
reports were true. By then what we did know was that Hamid Karzai
was Washington's choice to run post-Taliban Afghanistan. Under UN
supervision, a conference of Afghans in Bonn had just nominated him
as the country's interim president.

Our other source of stories about the war around Kandahar was
what we could glean from trips to the Afghan border. This required
permission from the Pakistani authorities. You had to go to an office
in Quetta, fill out a form and return the next day for a No Objection
Certificate. Then followed a three-hour drive to the border from

Quetta, with police checkpoints all along the road to ensure no one went through without an up-to-date certificate. The Pakistanis rationed the permits among the large group of journalists in Quetta with the result that no one could go to the border on successive days. To make things worse, we were not supposed to spend the night in the Pakistani border town of Chaman but had to return to Quetta (though a few reporters, myself included, sometimes broke the rules by staying in one of Chaman's decrepit small hotels). Chaman was little more than a crossroads, crowded with stalls selling fruit and vegetables. The pungent smell of hashish hung in the air, and you never saw a woman younger than about fifty out in public, at least among those who wore hijab and showed their faces.

It was tantalizing to exert so much effort to reach the border and have such minimal reward. The road climbed a mountain range before reaching Chaman, which lay in the plain on the other side. From the highest point on the pass you could look across the desert haze into Afghanistan without being able to get there to report the momentous events we knew to be happening. Instead, we would roam around at the border crossing, interviewing drivers of trucks and taxis as they came through to the Pakistani side.

Two things became clear from the interviews. U.S. Special Forces were active inside Afghanistan. Shahzada, the driver of an oil tanker truck, told me how he had been sleeping in the desert with four other drivers after a journey of several hundred miles from the Iranian border. Suddenly they heard the sound of vehicles crossing the sand in the dark. "About seven or eight armed men surrounded us. They were talking English, and all had military uniforms," Shahzada recalled. Some of the intruders wore "big goggles," as he put it—sophisticated night-vision equipment. "They grabbed us and tied our hands behind our backs with very tough plastic," he said. The men, presumably U.S. Special Forces, put the drivers in four small armored vehicles and took them to a bleak spot in the desert about four miles from their trucks. One of the strangers could speak a few words in Persian, virtually the same as Dari, Afghanistan's main language. "He accused us of taking oil to terrorists, but we said it wasn't true. The oil is just for ordinary people," Shahzada said he told them. "I have been doing this work for fifteen years. We pick the oil up at the border with Iran near Zahedan, and deliver it here. It's my job. We saw one of the men making a telephone call. We didn't know what they were planning to do."

As the drivers sat fearfully in the dark wondering what their fate would be, they heard the sound of aircraft. A huge ball of fire lit up the desert. In horror the men realized what was going on. All five trucks had been hit by missiles or bombs. The attack over, the armed kidnappers took the men back to the wrecks of their tanker trucks and untied them. Then they disappeared. Shahzada acknowledged that the Americans had gone out of their way to save their lives by taking them off into the desert before sending in the strike aircraft to destroy their vehicles. But he did not see much reason for gratitude. "In a way they were protecting our lives," he said. "But they took away our livelihoods."

Our other finding in Chaman was the scale of the refugee exodus from Helmand and Kandahar, which was being caused by American bombing. Pakistan and Iran had closed their borders to new refugees in the days before the United States launched its air strikes in early October. From the Pakistani side of the border at Chaman, we could see a sea of tents in Spin Boldak, the Afghan town opposite. More than fifty thousand people were in four camps, supplied mainly by Arab charities, aid officials said. Emergency cases, women with sick children and elderly relatives, were being allowed through to camps on the Pakistani side that the UN refugee agency was running. Donkeys pulled carts laden with blankets and plastic pots and buckets through the entrance of one camp on an afternoon I was there. Two thousand emergency cases had been allowed to enter in the previous two days. "Some people have been walking with their wives and children for two weeks to escape the bombing," said Ahmad Azhar, the leader of a team of Malaysian aid workers.

Desperate to cross the border in the opposite direction in order to get the story of the Taliban's demise, the press pack in Quetta suddenly had a break. Word raced around the hotels that the consul-general of the Islamic Emirate of Afghanistan, as the Taliban called their state (not to be confused with the Northern Alliance's Islamic State of Afghanistan), was willing to give every journalist a visa, valid for a week. We rushed to the consulate to fill out applications and have our passports stamped. The Pakistanis relaxed their rules about needing permits to drive to the border, and a cavalcade of TV trucks, minivans and taxis stormed up to Chaman in order to cross to Spin Boldak.

Here at last was the chance to sense the twilight of the Taliban for ourselves. Sixty miles from Kandahar, Spin Boldak was the place where the Taliban had first emerged seven years earlier. Now it felt like the ragged fringe of a regime in its death throes. Pickup trucks laden with Chinese grenade-launchers raced up and down frantically and to no apparent purpose and young Taliban with rifles wandered around look- ing gloomy. Anxiety and tension seemed to swirl through their ranks as all-pervasively as the dust that blew off the desert through streets crowded with refugees from Kandahar. The mood varied from collec- tive anger to private angst as each man worried about his future. "I spit on America and Britain," said a middle-aged man as people with grime-matted hair and dusty turbans clustered around us, startled to see Western journalists in Taliban territory. "Psst," another man whis- pered into my translator Sharif's ear. "I'll tell you a secret. I'm on the side of the king."

It was November 19, and the movement appeared to be facing extinction. It had lost Kabul a week earlier and most of the north shortly before that. In Kandahar, Mullah Omar, the Taliban leader, was issuing orders to his troops not to give up, even as contacts were said to be under way with various Pashtun opponents about a deal to keep the city out of Northern Alliance hands. The United States was mount- ing the heaviest bombing the Kandahar region had ever seen. Yet the

Taliban chose this moment to open their gates to the press. If the aim was to show they still controlled Spin Boldak and the border crossing, they succeeded. If it was to prove their morale was undiminished, a verdict was harder to reach.

An afternoon during the annual fasting month of Ramadan was not the best time to judge people's moods. Ten hours after the pre-dawn meal and sometime before sunset when the next permitted meal, known as *iftar*, comes due, tempers tend to get frayed. But I sensed the tension of Spin Boldak had deeper causes. A mounting exodus seemed to be afoot, physical for the few who managed to escape to Pakistan, mental for many others.

The horde of journalists were taken to a guesthouse, described as belonging to the Foreign Ministry. It had only half a dozen rooms, but there was a large garden shaded by trees, running water, electricity and schools of cicadas chirping in the darkness. We hurried to the best spots and put down sleeping bags. The TV networks pitched small tents. The wall around the compound was only three feet high, and it was soon lined with children and teenagers, who watched in amazement as reporters sat on the lawn working at their laptops, set up satellite dishes or voiced stand-up stories in front of powerful arc lights. Armed Taliban guards occasionally drove the kids off, but they always reappeared as soon as the guards lost interest in the spectators. This was frequent as many of the guards themselves had never seen a TV set. They crouched excitedly around the editing screens and squealed with delight when they caught sight of themselves or their friends in the footage. It was one of the more astonishing clashes of culture I have ever witnessed.

The next day Taliban officials took us to one of the four refugee camps we had seen from the distance when we looked across the border from Chaman. We counted roughly 1,500 tents. With an average family size of six, this meant a total of 9,000 people, three times the estimate that UNHCR officials in Quetta had given. About two-thirds had fled from Kandahar, we were told by the camp's Taliban commander,

Mullah Mohammed Sayeed Haqqani. They had all arrived in the last three weeks.

Harehmutallah, a twenty-five-year-old man, told us his home was five hundred yards from the house of Kandahar's deputy governor. "The bombing is getting heavier and heavier. It goes on by day and not just at night. We couldn't take it any longer."

Sultan Mohamed, an elderly man with a deeply lined face, stood outside the small patch of desert, which he had staked out for his family by driving wooden poles into the sand and hanging blankets and pieces of sacking between them as a windbreak. Children sat on carpets inside his makeshift home. "We became so afraid of the loud sounds every night," his wife, Fatima Bibi, called out in a break in the tradition among uneducated Afghans, which prevents women from addressing male strangers, even in their husband's presence. Desperation bent the rules and she pleaded with us for help. "Even if the bombing stops, we will never go back to Kandahar again," she said. "Never. I am so afraid."

Camels wandered through parts of the camp, making it clear that some of the people were nomads who pasture their animals in the mountains in summer and return to the plains for winter. But Spin Boldak is not their normal resting place, and as one refugee from Kandahar said, "Even the nomads don't know where to go these days."

The camp offered no respite from the sounds, and memories, of war. As we walked around the tents, the rumble of a high-flying plane, probably on its way to or from Kandahar, cut through the air. Children who were eagerly following us around suddenly looked nervous.

But Mullah Haqqani insisted that the ferocious bombing was not having any political effect. He denied any talks were going on with Pashtun representatives of the former king, Zahir Shah, or local leaders opposed to the Taliban: "We don't know who these people are or how they intend to contact us. It's just American satellite TV channels they talk to. There is nothing to negotiate about."

Mullah Omar's message was repeated next day by Tayyeb Agha, one of his closest aides, who had managed to drive from Kandahar to meet us. A young man with fluent English that he said he had learned in a refugee camp in Pakistan during the Soviet occupation, he cut an odd sartorial figure. He wore a dark green Chinese Army jacket of the kind that the bazaars in Kabul and Kandahar sold. Over it he had draped a blanket. Constantly tugging at his black beard, he insisted that the Taliban movement was unbowed by forty-six days of U.S. bombing. (In early 2011, Tayyeb Agha would emerge as a key go-between for the Americans and Mullah Omar when the first U.S. overtures to the Taliban were made public.) Tayyeb Agha came across as authoritative, self-confident and intelligent. His reason for meeting us, he said, was primarily to reject recent reports that Pashtun leaders were negotiating with the Taliban about the surrender of Kandahar. "You may have heard reports of contacts. We can say this is also a kind of fighting by our enemies against us by means of propaganda," he said. "No elders have contacted us about transferring power. These elders were with us, are with us, and will be with us. They have made a lot of sacrifices to defend us." Although he repeatedly described the U.S.-led air strikes as a war on innocent civilians, the figures for dead and injured that he produced were not absurdly high. "Around 2,000" civilians were casualties of the bombing, a figure that most independent analysts would accept as probable after seven weeks of attacks. He would not give a figure of Taliban deaths, but said there had been "many."

He spoke of the United States in sorrow more than in anger. "Our Islamic system and Sharia law caused differences between our government and the United States. Gradually these differences, which were initially on paper, developed until they reached as far as a military attack on the Muslims of Afghanistan. It became an attack on us in the name of a strike on terrorism. Where was the UN when this attack started?" he asked. "The UN works under U.S. instructions. We cannot say the UN rules. America rules the UN." We were all eager to move forward to Kandahar, and we asked Agha whether he would authorize it, but it soon became clear that his visit to us was designed to give the international media the official line from Mullah Omar without having us in Kandahar city itself. No permission to travel to Kandahar was forthcoming. On the contrary the next day we were ordered to cross back into Pakistan and escorted to the border by armed Taliban guards.

With Taliban resistance continuing, the United States dispatched its first large contingent of ground troops on November 25. In an operation code-named Swift Freedom, up to a thousand marines flew in by helicopters and C-130 aircraft from aircraft carriers and amphibious assault ships in the Arabian Sea. They landed about thirty miles south of Kandahar city at a desert air strip at Dolangi, which Navy SEALs had captured a few days earlier and renamed Camp Rhino. The marines' mission, which was quickly accomplished, was to capture Kandahar's main airfield ten miles from the city for use as a new U.S. base to bring in more troops and supplies.

Around December 6, Mullah Omar and the rest of the Taliban leadership withdrew from Kandahar. U.S. forces moved in on December 7 without a shot being fired. Omar's retreat was the same tactic that Massoud had adopted in Kabul in 1996 when he withdrew in the face of the Taliban advance.

The Taliban's decision to abandon resistance followed a shift in U.S. bombing strategy. According to eyewitnesses in the city and to refugees pouring into the border area, bombing in the Kandahar region and along the main roads was massively stepped up. The aim appeared to be to create a free-fire zone around the city in which anything that moved would be treated as a legitimate military target. This would in effect cut the city of Kandahar off from the surrounding area and put pressure on the Taliban leadership to surrender. U.S. strikes also targeted the leaders' key buildings.

In Quetta we interviewed two journalists who had been allowed to work in Kandahar because they were not Westerners. Nisar Malik, a

Pakistani freelancer who spent five days in the city, said the Americans always targeted the same four or five places: Mullah Omar's two compounds, the madrassa next to the jail on the road to Herat, the headquarters of the religious police and the Foreign Ministry on the town's outskirts. Apart from these places, physical destruction in Kandahar was relatively light, he said. According to Yousuf al-Shouly, a correspondent for Al-Jazeera, the Qatar-based TV channel, the Americans were going for any moving target outside the city that they suspected of having military significance. The most damaging U.S. planes, he said, were F-14 Tomcats: "They are the real bastards. They hover like vultures looking for targets."

While many residents left Kandahar, a few others came in. "People who live in the typical walled family compounds on the outskirts moved into the city because the U.S. suspects they may be al Qaeda places or havens for the Taliban leadership," said Malik. Unlike ordinary people, business leaders had a voice in Kandahar, and it seemed they helped to persuade Mullah Omar to give up. As Malik put it: "The Pashtun are traders and businessmen. They calculate time, necessity and value. If the time is right, it necessitates a value decision. This may mean switching sides. People don't scream, 'Oh my God, he's a turncoat.' There's constant trading and constant battle. They coexist, and the cycle persists."

It was a wise summation of Afghan history—and only time would tell if the cycle would bring the Taliban around again.

[8] WHO KILLED ASAQ?

"Interrupting most of the country's international aid programs for three months only made matters worse."

—WESTERN HUMAN RIGHTS ANALYST

NOT ONE AMERICAN soldier or pilot was killed in toppling the Taliban. Two months after launching his attack on Afghanistan, Bush was able to celebrate one of the most one-sided triumphs in the history of warfare.

Afghan casualties, by contrast, numbered in the hundreds, civilian and combatant. But how were they to be counted with certainty? Would an accurate figure ever be found? While the U.S. bombing was under way, the Taliban allowed only a handful of reporters into Kabul and Kandahar. They were too busy and insecure to do much research on the issue. Meanwhile, U.S. authorities were not interested in keeping a toll of the human destruction they were wreaking.

Only when the guns fell silent was it possible to begin to piece the story together. It seemed important to try. The Afghan campaign was the first attempt by a Western state to achieve regime change in a poor country without losing the life of any of its own ground troops. It relied entirely on techniques of asymmetric warfare, massive and sustained bombing raids from the safety of the air as well as missile strikes from distant ships and submarines. Designed to terrorize and destroy an almost completely defenseless enemy, this new type of killing in which the attackers operated in a largely risk-free environment had a sanitized video-game quality, with warriors firing missiles from remote aircraft cockpits or sitting in front of screens in comfortable offices on the ground and using their computer mouse to direct a pilotless attack drone.

The story of what happened to the other side needed to be told.

Reporters for Western news organizations tried to reach a credible death toll by visiting the sites of large-scale U.S. bomb strikes and interviewing hospital officials and bereaved family members in January 2002. Carl Conetta of the Project for Defense Alternatives at the Commonwealth Institute, a think tank in Cambridge, Massachusetts, analyzed these reports and calculated that from October 7, 2001, to January 1, 2002, between 1,000 and 1,300 civilians were killed. On the basis of the amount of bombs dropped and missiles fired this meant the air campaign in Afghanistan was four times more deadly than NATO's bombing of Serbia and Kosovo in 1999. Although the Pentagon boasted it had used "smart weapons," Conetta argued that the campaign failed to set a new standard for accuracy because of the mix of weapons used, the unreliable nature of intelligence and the decision to bomb al Qaeda and Taliban leaders while they were at home. This meant that civilians died because either the house contained the al Qaeda or Taliban member's family, as was to be expected, or the wrong house was hit.

Marc Herold, a professor at the University of New Hampshire, used similar methodology and sources but added death reports from NGOs and non-Western media. Taking the end date as March 31, 2002, he calculated that since October 7, 2001, the start of Bush's Operation Enduring Freedom, between 3,000 and 3,400 Afghan civilians had been killed.

Cutting into this dry analysis a shooting star suddenly appeared.

Looking like a teenager and with a girlish shriek of a laugh, Marla Ruzicka, a twenty-five-year-old Californian, was not taken seriously when she arrived in Kabul on Christmas 2001 with a backpack and very little money. Bubbling with enthusiasm, she announced she had been sent by a San Francisco NGO, Global Exchange, to document civilian casualties.

Initially, people saw her as a classic war tourist or, worse, a war groupie. Unlike most aid workers, she cultivated journalists and wanted to know where the next party was. But her dedication and hard work soon convinced the doubters that Marla was not just a fly-by-night. Her self-proclaimed mission was a mixture of what each group was doing: getting facts and helping victims. The latter soon overtook the former. Her attempt to track the number of civilian deaths became an effort to aid bereaved and wounded survivors. In an essay sent to Human Rights Watch, she wrote: "A number is important not only to quantify the cost of the war, but, to me, each number is also a story of someone whose hopes, dreams and potential will never be realized, and who left behind a family."

I first met Marla in Kabul in June 2002, when she was hosting two American women who had each lost a sibling in the 9/11 attacks. They had come to share their grief with victims of the U.S. attack on Afghanistan and bring a message that not all Americans supported Bush's war or wanted revenge. By then, Marla's mission had developed still further. Using the argument that American 9/11 victims' families were getting compensation from the U.S. Government, she started campaigning for the United States to compensate Afghan victims too.

On the telephone, by email and through charm and personal engagement, she lobbied journalists and diplomats with equal persistence. But she loved nothing better than to sit with Afghan families after the media spotlight had gone elsewhere, record every detail of their stories, go out and campaign for official apologies and compensation—and then stay in touch to keep them informed.

She persuaded Senator Patrick Leahy of Vermont to add an amendment to a foreign aid bill giving $2.5 million to Afghan victims. It was

not described as compensation, since the United States did not wish
to take formal responsibility, but it passed. Marla visited families all
over Afghanistan, drew up lists of names and helped to ensure that the
money was distributed to the right people.

After Bush's invasion of Iraq, she moved to Baghdad to pursue
the same mission of help and compensation for Iraqi victims of U.S.
bombs. She was killed there in April 2005 when a car bomb aimed at a
convoy of foreign contractors detonated as she and her Iraqi coworker
were driving by. It was one of the cruelest deaths in a war of multiple
injustice.

My interest in Afghan casualties centered on the "indirect" victims
of U.S. bombs. The story of the "direct" victims had been done by others, Marla included. What kept recurring in my mind were images of
the waves of displaced and desperate Afghans I had seen in the camps in
Chaman and Spin Boldak. It was hard not to contrast the relatively little
attention they got in the Western media with the amount that Albanian
refugees from Kosovo had had during Slobodan Milosevic's ethnic
cleansing campaign two years earlier. With other reporters I spent days
in the Albanian town of Kukes in April and May 1999 just beyond the
Kosovan border interviewing refugees. It was not only that Kukes was
easier to work from than Chaman. The Albanian refugees were "con-
venient victims." The man responsible for their misery was the West's
enemy. Heartrending pictures of refugee columns crossing the border were grist for NATO's propaganda mill. They helped to maintain
Western support for the war in the former Yugoslavia. The refugees'
stories were not only shocking. They were useful. In Afghanistan, by
contrast, it was "our" side that was causing the refugees. They were
not fleeing from the Taliban but from the awesome sound and fury of
American missiles and bombs.

Had there been nightly TV interviews with these pitiful escapees,
Western support for the relentless air strikes on Afghanistan might have
been less strong. In the days after 9/11 the United States specifically

asked Pakistan to close its frontiers to Afghan refugees. Since Pakistan had hosted millions of Afghans who fled Soviet bombs in the 1980s and stayed for years before deciding to go home, it was happy to agree. The Bush administration was apparently anxious about the way people in the West would react to TV footage of huge flows of refugees. Better to have them wandering around out of sight inside Afghanistan than be filmed day after day arriving in Pakistan into the care of the UN High Commissioner for Refugees or the Islamic Red Crescent.

When Afghanistan opened up fully for reporters after the Taliban's overthrow, I wanted to investigate what had happened to them during the period when the air strikes prevented the UN and NGOs from delivering food and medicine.

Iran had also closed its borders when the U.S. bombing started. During the Soviet occupation and the civil war between mujahedin factions, hundreds of thousands of Afghans had fled to Tehran and other Iranian cities. By 2001 most had been in Iran for a decade or more. The Iranian Government did not want to receive a new mass exodus. Now, with the Taliban no longer in power, Iran was urging Afghans to leave, in particular the most recent arrivals.

In March 2002, I was in Tehran covering Iranian attitudes to regime change in Afghanistan as well as to the possibility of a U.S. attack on Saddam Hussein's Iraq, which was already being discussed as a serious option. After I finished that assignment the *Guardian* asked me to fly to Mashhad in northeastern Iran and cross into western Afghanistan and report from there. The border at Islam Qala was quiet and the road almost empty when I walked from the Iranian immigration sheds to the Afghan side and found a taxi for the two-hour drive to Herat, one of the finest medieval cities of Central Asia. The lack of returning refugees suggested the Iranian efforts at getting Afghans to go home were not having much success. Only a few Afghans were risking the journey home. Word had trickled out that even if the drought was ending and there was peace at last, living conditions in Afghanistan were dire. Few crops had been planted, livestock had been killed for meat, food aid was in short supply and jobs for urban families were scarce.

One morning soon after reaching Herat, I drove to the village of Ghorambay, where I found a few returnees. Seyd Mohammed and his family had decided Iran was too far off to flee to. Instead, soon after the United States started bombing, they had gone in search of food toward the nearest large town. The journey took them over mountains. Piling small children and a few possessions on the back of a donkey, he, his brothers and their wives traveled for four days on snow-covered tracks. They had no tents, and at night their only protection against the cold was a few blankets.

Before they set off, everyone in the extended family was already weak with hunger after three years of drought. The long trek was too much for the most vulnerable. They were in a state of exhaustion by the time they reached the town of Owbeh, and Seyd Mohammed's nephews, Asaq, who was just under two, and Abdul Rahman, his six-month-old brother, had lost the strength to recover.

Seyd Mohammed told me he believed the children would still be alive if the family had not been forced to flee. "We were hopeful they wouldn't have died if we had stayed here," he said sadly as he stood outside his home. Like every other house in the small settlement that straddled a main road, Seyd Mohammed's had a roof made of dried grass spread over a light frame. As the famine intensified, people became so desperate for cash to buy food that they took down the roof's original timbers to sell in the nearest town. Next to go were the window frames. By the time I saw it, the house resembled a prison, with rows of small branches propped up in every window like the bars of a cell.

The children's deaths could be blamed on drought, poverty, cold, the Taliban or the Americans or a combination of some or all of these factors. Sorting them out was not easy. Yet it had relevance in any attempt to calculate the human cost of the U.S. air strikes on Afghanistan.

U.S. bombing affected the humanitarian situation in three ways. It caused massive dislocation by prompting hundreds of thousands of Afghans to abandon their homes. It stopped aid supplies to drought victims. And it provoked an upsurge in fighting and turned a military stalemate into a situation of chaotic fluidity, leading yet more people to flee.

Counting the victims with accuracy was impossible. As Muslims, Afghans bury their dead within twenty-four hours, and the graves of those who died in the mountains as they fled their homes are only known to their closest relatives. No one had time to interview all survivors or check their stories. The only way to reach even an estimated figure was by extrapolation and intelligent guesswork.

The dislocation was massive. Just under a quarter of a million Afghans fled to Iran and Pakistan after 9/11 when it became clear the United States would attack. As both states had closed their official frontier crossings to Afghans this was no mean achievement, since it involved paying smugglers or bribing border guards.

In spite of these difficulties UNHCR, the UN refugee agency, estimated that around 160,000 Afghans had crossed into Pakistan by December 2001, often secretly in small groups. The number reaching the Iranian border was harder to estimate, but Iranian officials I interviewed in Zahedan in southeastern Iran in November 2001 talked of 60,000 Afghans crossing in the first month after the bombing. Another 9,000 set up camp on the Afghan side of the border.

In both cases, these refugees received some aid, either in established refugee and immigrant communities or official camps. The journey was the problem. An unknown number died on the way. Refugees intending to cross the border tended to be better-off people who knew they would have to pay and brought the funds to do it.

Those who fled within Afghanistan like Seyd Mohammed's extended family faced different problems. Alan Kresko, acting assistant secretary of the U.S. State Department's Bureau of Population, Migration and Refugees, estimated that 150,000 people were displaced after the

bombing started. Others put the figure higher. The UNHCR estimated
that 900,000 were already displaced inside Afghanistan before 9/11. In
March 2002 more than a million were still displaced. Subtracting those
who went home soon after the collapse of the Taliban and the end of
the bombing in December 2001 to try to plant seeds before the spring
rains, this still leaves a minimum of 200,000 and possibly more who fled
their homes after 9/11 but remained in Afghanistan away from their
homes.

The luckiest of these internally displaced people (IDPs) moved in
with relatives nearby. This was the case for many in Herat who escaped
the bombing to villages only a few miles away. There they continued
to have shelter and adequate supplies of food. The main problem was
trauma. "The bombing was very severe," Gholam Rassoul, a driver in
Herat, told me. "They mainly hit military targets but the force of the
explosions was so intense. It was terrible for children and people with
heart problems. My children used to rush to me, I could feel their hearts
pounding like a little bird in your hand."

The group most in danger were those who moved to areas of hunger and cold where they were at greater risk than if they had stayed at
home. Kate Stearman, head of communications at the British branch
of Care International, told me: "After September 11 there was widespread panic in Afghanistan with soaring food prices and mass flight
from cities. . . . The bombing and the deteriorating security situation
meant huge and largely unrecorded population movements. While the
expected one million–plus refugees in Pakistan did not appear, this in
itself was worrying because it indicated that many more were trapped
inside Afghanistan, their situation unknown."

With Minka Nijhuis, a Dutch reporter, and Habib, a local translator, I drove over the mountains from Herat to Qala-i Nau, the capital of
Badghis, one of the provinces most affected by three years of drought.
U.S. bombing had caused hundreds to flee the town. Faisal Danesh, a
worker for the charity World Vision, told us that in the countryside

people were closer to starvation than the urban dwellers, and villagers had no way to feed the newcomers. The bombing disrupted aid supplies, prompted expatriate aid workers to pull out of Afghanistan and stopped Afghan staff from giving aid and medical services in IDP camps, thereby exacerbating their plight. World Vision showed me their feeding center for children in Qala-i Nau. Abdul Kade had the spongy-soft cheeks of any normal toddler, but when his mother peeled off his trousers and lifted his sweater a shockingly different person emerged. His legs were matchsticks, his buttocks hung wrinkled and limp and his stomach was swollen by severe malnutrition. The image was out of Africa, so it seemed fitting that the two nurse nutritionists looking after Abdul and the other tiny Afghans in the center should be Africans. "Afghan children have round moon-faces so it's not like Africa, where sunken eyes and cheeks give starvation away immediately," said Jennifer Kisingula from Kenya, who had been in western Afghanistan for three months.

The remoteness of Afghanistan's mountain valleys meant many people with dying children failed to make the journey to the feeding center, which was attached to the local hospital, a sad building with a serious shortage of drugs. Such severe hunger had never struck the region before. "The distances are enormous. It's too far for them to walk to the nearest dirt road," Kisingula said.

In Kondolan, the first in a string of settlements ninety minutes' walk up the valley from Qala-i Nau, villagers took us around a new cemetery. They had started burials there four months before. We counted 112 graves covered in squares of turf or, more commonly, piles of neat round stones. Kondolan's remaining population numbered 250, said Mirza Behbut, a young farmer. That meant a death rate of around 30 percent. "My mother died," he said. "My sister died. So did the wife of my brother."

No one has exact figures on how much aid was lost as a result of the disruption caused by the months of bombing. In October 2001 national

deliveries were estimated to have gone down by 40 percent. As the
security situation improved, the main food-deliverer, the World Food
Programme, redoubled its efforts. Truckers agreed to take loads back
into Afghanistan in November and December, but it remained hard to
distribute it to camps and villages.

Before 9/11, Afghanistan already had one of the highest infant
mortality rates in the world and one of the lowest rates of overall life
expectancy. "Interrupting most of the country's international aid programs for three months only made matters worse," said one Western
human rights analyst who did not want his name published. "From
mid-September to mid-December it is possible to say that in areas with
already high levels of death from malnutrition and exposure, there
were likely increases in mortality rates. What these increases amount
to, no one can say, but the fact there were increases is not really in
dispute."

A further effect of the bombing was to heighten instability by
provoking the Taliban. Until 9/11 the Afghan civil war had been stale-
mated for almost three years. Except in parts of the central region near
Bamiyan, the front lines had not moved significantly.

Aid agencies delivered supplies to Taliban areas and those controlled by the opposition Northern Alliance with relatively little difficulty. There were shortages, but this was because Western governments
failed to respond adequately to UN appeals for aid to Afghanistan. For
rural Afghans the fact that most cities were controlled by the Taliban
was of marginal relevance. They barely saw the Pashtun fundamentalists. The village of Kondolan, where we had seen the new graves, was
Tajik, and rural women did not wear the burqa. It was not part of local
custom, and the Taliban never came to enforce it, villagers told us. The
Taliban ban on girls' education also had no effect, since there had been
no school of any kind in the village for the last twenty-five years. It was
a useful reminder that Taliban rule did not bring such extreme changes
as outsiders often imagined.

The U.S. intervention changed the dynamic. Deprived of food as American planes targeted their supply convoys, the Taliban began to loot warehouses in the towns and steal aid meant for drought victims. "Before September, the Taliban never looted. They were helped by Pakistan and some Arab countries," said Faisal Danesh of World Vision. "After September they faced difficulties in getting their own food."

The onset of the bombing also raised political tensions to danger level, turning peaceful communities into battlegrounds. In Ghorambay, the village where Seyd Mohammed and his small nephews had lived, the mujahedin appeared and handed out guns, urging villagers to ambush passing Taliban convoys. Acting on an informer's tip, the Taliban then raided the village for guns. They found nothing, but took five villagers away for interrogation. Frightened that the detained men would confess under torture (which they did), the remaining villagers fled into the mountains that night on the trek that led to the deaths of the two toddlers.

In the welter of anecdotal evidence, how could one calculate with any certainty the number of indirect casualties from U.S. bombing? The best approach was to investigate the death rates at the camps for the internally displaced. At the sprawling Maslakh camp outside Herat, workers for the humanitarian NGO Médecins du Monde kept itemized records of named people with the cause of death listed. These were compiled by fifteen Afghan health educators, who regularly visited every family to check their medical condition. Each educator concentrated on a small section of the vast camp. Some educators were women and therefore better able to win the trust of female IDPs and get accurate information.

Médecins du Monde assessed the death toll in Maslakh camp as averaging 145 per month for September, October, November and December, almost double the total of 79 for February 2002, a clear sign that things were worse in the period when aid convoys stopped during the bombing and in the run-up to it and in its immediate aftermath. The total of 580 deaths from September through December was compiled in the two main areas of the camp, which had an estimated population of 80,000. This produced a death rate of 1.8 per 1,000 people per month. Dr. David Hercot, a doctor from Belgium, told me, "We didn't have educators in Maslakh Three, the area where new arrivals came after 9/11. They lived in tents rather than brick shelters. We think their death toll could be higher."

Death rates at IDP camps in other parts of Afghanistan were above those at Maslakh, although statistics appeared to have been compiled less strictly. At Dehdadi south of Mazar-i Sharif, which sheltered 15,000 people, 230 people died between 9/11, when aid stopped, and January 11, 2002, according to Stephan Goetghebuer of another medical humanitarian NGO, Doctors Without Borders. This is a rate of around four per 1,000 per month, more than twice that at Maslakh. At Baghe Sherkat and Amirabad camps near Kunduz, the World Health Organization reported that 164 people out of a population of 25,000 IDPs died of hunger, cold and disease in a period of roughly two months—a rate of three per 1,000 per month. The death rate was lower at Dasht-e-Arzana camp outside Mazar-i Sharif. Officials said people were dying in early December 2001 at the rate of around 1.15 per 1,000 per month in a population of 21,000. At Nasaji camp in Balkh province with 14,500 IDPs, nineteen people died of malnutrition and exposure in November, a rate of 1.3 per 1,000 for that month.

Taking into account the difference in size among the camps, the average mortality rate comes to two per 1,000 per month. The camps covered by these figures contained about three-quarters of the total camp population of around 200,000. Extrapolating, this produces an average of 400 deaths in the camps every month, or 1,600 from September to the end of December.

What of the one million IDPs who never went to organized camps? It is hard to know whether they had comparable death rates. Assuming they did, the number of deaths would be 8,000 between September and

December in 2001, although it is very possible they were worse off. In addition, five million very poor Afghans who relied on aid remained at home during the bombing but found their drought relief deliveries disrupted. If their mortality rates were the same as those in the camps, one reaches an additional number of deaths from September to December 2001 of 40,000. These are maximum assumptions. Adding this figure to the 1,600 estimated deaths in the camps and the 8,000 deaths of IDPs outside the camps, the top figure would be 49,600.

How many of the post-9/11 deaths would have occurred anyway, even if there had been no bombing, given that so many Afghans were weakened by drought? All one can say is that the bombing caused a decline in aid deliveries to Afghanistan in October 2001 of 40 percent. Although deliveries to Afghanistan picked up sharply after the bombing stopped, distribution from the cities to outlying areas within the country was much harder than it had been before the bombing.

Taking 40 percent as a benchmark, one would conclude that the U.S. intervention caused around 40 percent of 49,600, the maximum number of assumed deaths. This amounts to 19,840 people. Even if one takes a conservative view of the data and halves the estimated percentage to 20 percent, a rough total of 10,000 died indirectly because of the U.S. campaign.

The range of estimates is broad, but it clearly exceeds the estimated number of direct victims of American bombs, which may have amounted to 3,400. No one will ever know the true figure and, as time has passed, the chances of reaching even a narrower estimate of the scale of death have receded. The nameless graves on Afghanistan's mountainsides, in patches of the desert and in obscure corners of abandoned camps are all but forgotten.

[9] BACK TO THE WARLORDS

"It's like a wolf that sees a sheep. He wants to eat it. We need the big powers to put all the wolves in a zoo."

—HAMIDULLAH, LOCAL OFFICIAL,
NORTHERN AFGHANISTAN, OCTOBER 2003

TEN DAYS BEFORE the Taliban lost power in Kandahar on December 6, 2001, the United Nations opened a conference in Germany where two dozen Afghans were asked to nominate a new government for their country. The Taliban had already withdrawn from Kabul, and it was accepted their time throughout Afghanistan would soon be up. After the fiasco of the mujahedin years and the failure to end the country's civil war after the Russians withdrew, there was a widely held view that a better effort must be made this time to include all strands of Afghan opinion in selecting an interim government. Its job would be to hold power for six months until a Loya Jirga, the traditional national gathering of tribal and other leaders, established a transitional authority that would lead the country to free elections for a new administration with a five-year term. A separate commission of Afghans, selected by the conference in Germany, would be tasked to draw up a new constitution.

The conference was held at the Hotel Petersberg, a luxury hilltop building outside the former West German capital of Bonn with a commanding view of the Rhine. The intentions were good, the results less so. The meeting failed to include representatives of several important sectors of Afghan society. Only four groups of Afghans received invitations, most of them exiles. This failure was one of the main reasons why the Taliban would mount resistance to the new setup, and quickly gain support little more than two years later.

The Northern Alliance had captured Kabul on November 13, and its leaders reached Bonn in a triumphant mood. They were determined to play a large role in the post-Taliban arrangements. Mainly representing Tajiks and Uzbeks, they were given eleven seats at the table. A delegation, known as the Rome group, represented former King Zahir Shah, who lived in the Italian capital. It was largely Pashtun although it contained a few people from other ethnicities. It too received eleven seats. A group representing other exiles and some former mujahedin fighters who had links with Iran were given five seats. They were known as the Cyprus group because they had held their first meetings there in October 2001. Iran had helped to arm the Northern Alliance in its struggle with the Taliban, and it was thought to be folly to exclude them from influence in the new setup. Finally five seats were also given to the Peshawar group, headed by Sayyid Ahmed Gailani, a Pashtun monarchist who used to lead one of the original mujahedin factions against the Russians in what was once known as the Peshawar Seven (discussed in Chapter Two). Some other mujahedin leaders from the Peshawar Seven were with the Northern Alliance delegation.

The absentees from Bonn's guest list were significant. There were no Pashtun Islamists or any Pashtun who represented the middle ground and had stayed in Afghanistan during the Taliban period. Absent too were representatives of Afghanistan's urban, secular, republican and nontribal professionals, the engineers, doctors, lawyers and other educated men and women who had avoided taking sides in the civil war and

wanted a chance to serve the country if it finally attained a unity government. Some of these men and women had lived abroad in the diaspora or grown up there since the Soviet invasion. Others had stayed in
Kabul in PDPA times, either as nonparty people or as junior members,
because it was hard to make a career without joining the PDPA. Finally
there were no invitations for former PDPA ministers even though they
had at least as much of a claim to a share in government as the mujahedin warlords, given the latter's internecine struggles in the 1990s, which
led to the destruction of Kabul and the rise of the Taliban.

Among all Afghans this group had the best education and were the
most attuned to modernity. They were firmly against Islamic fundamentalism and in favor of a separation of religion and the state. They
were eager to develop their country after a quarter of a century of civil
war. Regrettably, the former mujahedin leaders saw most of them as a
threat and were eager to exclude them. It was easy to label those who
had stayed in Kabul during the Soviet and Najibullah periods as communists even though most of them had never believed in the PDPA's
slogans or had demonstrably changed their minds since 1992, when the
PDPA lost power and they went into exile. Schooled during the Cold
War with its ideological simplicities and distortions about communism,
Bush and his neoconservative colleagues in the U.S. administration
were not likely to show any understanding of or sympathy for this large
group of men and women. But leaving them out of the equation at
Bonn and in the months afterward deprived Afghanistan of thousands
of professional people who could have helped to revive the country's
economy and administrative system.

The issue of potential Taliban representation at the Bonn conference was thorny. With hindsight, some analysts later argued that moderate Taliban should have been invited to Bonn. But it was hard to identify any. Before the invasion, some U.S. officials talked of trying to split
the movement, but once the attack was launched, U.S. policy turned
against that option. In an ominous signal for any potential defector,

at the request of the Bush administration, the Pakistani Government arrested the Taliban ambassador to Pakistan, Abdul Salam Zaeef, before the Taliban lost power and handed him over to U.S. custody. He was sent to the prison camp at Guantánamo and only released in 2005.

The Americans sent a relatively low-level delegation to Bonn, but everyone knew they called the shots. That was made clear on the opening day when delegates were called to silence and asked to look up to a speaker apparatus hanging above the conference table. A crackling voice was heard. It was Hamid Karzai, they were told, speaking by satellite phone from Uruzgan, where U.S. Special Forces were helping him to mount resistance to the crumbling Taliban.

Francesc Vendrell, who headed the UN mission to Afghanistan, saw a look of annoyance run across many delegates' faces and affecting their body language. Karzai was hardly a household name. Almost none of them had met him. The sacrifices he might have made in the struggle for a better Afghanistan were obscure.

Delegates felt they were being put under unfair pressure by this deus ex machina so early in the proceedings. Before the conference, there were rumors that the United States had already picked Karzai to lead the new government. His dramatic intervention, courtesy of U.S. force of arms, seemed to confirm them.

In the words of the official U.S. military history of the war in Afghanistan, Hamid Karzai is a Pashtun who is "both pro-Western and anti-Taliban, a rare combination." A member of the Popalzai clan, like former king Zahir Shah, Karzai was the son of a wealthy family from Kandahar. His father was elected to Parliament during the monarchy. The young Karzai went to secondary school in Kabul and university in Simla in India. Unlike his brothers and Ahmed Wali Karzai, his half-brother who emigrated to the United States and owned restaurants, Hamid Karzai stayed in Pakistan during the Soviet occupation of his country. In the jihad against the Soviets he was a fund-raiser but not a field commander for Sibghatullah Mojadeddi's pro-monarchist Afghan

National Liberation Front. During the period of mujahedin rule, he was briefly a deputy foreign minister. In that capacity he addressed the UN General Assembly in 1992 and briefly presided over its deliberations.

When the Taliban emerged in the mid-1990s, he initially supported them and was nominated to represent them at the UN. But after his father was assassinated in Pakistan in 1999, apparently by the Taliban, Karzai became a committed Taliban opponent. He participated in various meetings of exiles, forging links both with the Tajik leader, Ahmad Shah Massoud, and the Northern Alliance as well as the entourage of ex-king Zahir Shah.

In the first days after 9/11, Karzai took part in new negotiations between the Afghan monarchists and the Northern Alliance. This put him in line with U.S. policy for the post-Taliban setup. As Washington cast about for men who could be suitable to lead the country, Karzai's links to the king convinced the Americans he was not an Islamist. They felt Karzai could be a unifying figure who could straddle the Tajik/Pashtun divide. U.S. Special Forces were authorized to work closely with him against the Taliban, effectively creating a small army north of Kandahar from the thirty-five untrained friends and relatives that Karzai had managed to recruit. Within two days of their arrival the Special Forces saved Karzai from disaster by calling in close air support and bombing a large Taliban force that was advancing toward his group and could have overwhelmed it. As the number of his followers grew, the Americans brought in food, clothing, communications equipment and weapons.

Not everyone agreed with Washington's plan for Karzai to become president. The head of the Northern Alliance, Burhanuddin Rabbani, one of the original members of the mujahedin Peshawar Seven, was still the official leader of the internationally recognized Afghan government. He refused to attend the Bonn conference and after the Taliban withdrew from Kabul quickly moved back into Arg, the presidential palace there, in order to forestall any attempt to sideline him.

Lakhdar Brahimi, the UN secretary general's special envoy for Afghanistan, was the Bonn conference chairman. Along with U.S. diplomats at the conference, he found himself having to spend a great deal of time persuading the chief negotiator for the Northern Alliance, Yunus Qanuni, to phone Rabbani and persuade him to step down as president. Brahimi and the Americans used the argument that Afghanistan needed the man who had the best chance of creating national unity. They delicately hinted that he had to be a Pashtun since the Pashtun formed the country's largest ethnic group and it was important to win back the constituency that had initially followed the Taliban.

Members of the king's team were also unhappy at being railroaded into selecting Karzai. They knew and respected him as a fellow Pashtun but thought the king should lead Afghanistan again or at least have a major say in the choice of leader. They expressed their anger when the conference voted on candidates for the top post in the new interim government. To U.S. dismay the king's delegation gave only two votes to Karzai but nine votes to Abdul Satar Sirat, a relatively unknown figure who had served as justice minister during the king's reign. He was half Uzbek and half Tajik. The fact that so many of the king's men had not even voted for the Pashtun candidate, Karzai, was a clear signal of their fury.

Desperate U.S. diplomats wondered how they could redo the vote and get their desired result. They appealed to Qanuni to veto Sirat, but they had not done their homework. The two men's wives were sisters. Family loyalty is paramount in Afghanistan, and Qanuni was not prepared to create a scandal. He refused to veto his brother-in-law.

The Americans now turned to Gailani, and this time they were lucky. It had been agreed that any one of the heads of the conference's four constituent groups could cast a veto. Gailani duly vetoed Sirat. With a new vote scheduled, the king's team had to be persuaded to make the right choice. General Abdul Wali, Zahir Shah's son-in-law and his main fixer, consulted the monarch and came back to the Americans and the king's delegates with the message that the king's wishes had been misunderstood. When he had told his team before the first vote that he would leave the choice to them, what Zahir Shah really meant was that they were free to choose anyone as long as he was a Pashtun. This clarification knocked Sirat out, and the delegation duly plumped for Karzai.

Delegates might have preferred to delay the choice, but they had been warned to hurry. The U.S. and other foreign donors had summoned a conference for a date later in December to pledge money for Afghanistan's reconstruction and made clear that the pledging conference would not go ahead unless Bonn came up with the names of members of the transitional government. Donors needed to know whom their money was going to.

The other key decision the Afghan delegates in Bonn had to make was to ask for an international force to provide security. The United States intended to continue hunting for bin Laden in and around the Tora Bora mountains and was not in favor of taking part in any peacekeeping arrangements. But it agreed that some sort of non-Afghan security force was needed. The Americans and other foreign governments, as well as most Afghans, did not want the Northern Alliance troops to take charge of Kabul's security on their own. It was assumed the Northern Alliance could not be pushed aside altogether. The issue was whether foreign forces would be given the appropriate mandate and be large enough to keep the Northern Alliance under control.

In November, Brahimi had proposed to the Security Council that there be what he called a light footprint for peacekeepers and any international civilian advisers sent to Afghanistan so as to allow Afghans a strong decision-making role. The United States had been impressed by this phrase and the strategy it represented, and U.S. diplomats came to Bonn determined to press for it. During the Balkan crises of the mid-1990s, Clinton had authorized large U.S. contingents to join international peacekeeping forces in Bosnia and Kosovo, but Bush and his defense secretary, Donald Rumsfeld, wanted to keep the Pentagon's commitment in Afghanistan at a low level. Under the emerging Bush doctrine, the United States would no longer be engaged in nation building, and it did not seem eager for other states to nation build either. Barnett Rubin, a U.S. Afghan specialist who advised Brahimi at the conference, commented later: "The Bonn agreement had a time-table and benchmarks . . . but they were obligatory only for the Afghan government. There were no timetables and benchmarks for the inter-national community." Brahimi had been appointed over Vendrell's head as Kofi Annan's special representative in early October, appar-ently because the Americans felt they needed a high-profile Muslim diplomat with a ministerial background. Vendrell, who now found himself serving as Brahimi's deputy, disagreed with the light-footprint strategy. From experience in Cambodia and East Timor, he would have recommended a large UN force able to cover the country well beyond Kabul. "I also wanted the Security Council to pass a resolution saying that conquest of territory did not give the right to govern," he told me later. "The aim was to prevent the Northern Alliance taking over." Vendrell also felt the emphasis that the Bonn conference and the donors put on the process being "Afghan-led" was excessive. The phrase became a mantra, losing sight of the issue of which Afghans should lead it.

Support for the light-footprint strategy was also based on the dif-ficulties the Soviet Union had had in trying to pacify Afghanistan. Large non-Muslim armies were bound to provoke suspicion and hostility, it was argued. (The lesson was forgotten a few years later when the United States and Britain invaded Iraq.) This was why the United States and Britain initially floated the idea of having peacekeeping troops from Muslim countries such as Turkey and Bangladesh.

There were other, more pressing reasons for the U.S. reluctance to join a peacekeeping force in Afghanistan. Bush and Vice President Dick Cheney were already thinking of exploiting the war on terror in order to topple Saddam Hussein. For that adventure they would require large numbers of U.S. troops and the Pentagon needed to be sure it had enough.

As the moment of decision making approached, the United States abandoned the idea of leaving things to Muslim nations. It feared this would leave Afghanistan beyond its control. Instead, it pushed for a hybrid force under the command of NATO nations but without any U.S. participation. The Afghan delegates at Bonn duly approved this idea and asked the UN Security Council to endorse it.

On December 20 the Security Council authorized the peacekeeping force. The resolution was the first to give legal cover to the presence of foreign troops in Afghanistan, even though the Americans had already been there for more than two months. Designated as the International Security Assistance Force (ISAF), its command was unusual. It was neither a UN nor a NATO mission. Instead, ISAF was put under a single NATO member-nation's control for periods of six months. Britain would be in charge for the first half year, followed by Turkey. Although one nation would be in the lead and provide the largest troop contingent, other countries would also take part. ISAF's area of operations would be confined to Kabul. All other military units, including the Northern Alliance and Dostum's troops, were to be withdrawn from the city.

Although this arrangement amounted to much less than a full military occupation, there were already hints that resistance could develop if the Pashtuns felt excluded from the new arrangements and foreigners were seen to be running Afghanistan. On the eve of the Bonn conference and a few days before the Taliban retreat from Kandahar, I contacted Gulbuddin Hekmatyar, the Pashtun fundamentalist and member of the Peshawar Seven who had fought the Russians and then taken part in the mujahedin civil wars that destroyed Kabul. He was no friend of the Taliban and had fled to Iran when they captured Kabul in 1996. From my hotel in Quetta I faxed Hekmatyar a series of questions about his plans. He replied with a long and fiery denunciation of U.S. policy,

describing the Bonn conference as illegitimate: "It is not possible that
Afghans' problems will be solved with the establishment of a government that the US, Russia and their supporters make for Afghans, and
divide the cabinet into their dependent groups. The Afghan crisis has
just one solution: stop fighting, stop external interference, establishment of a people's representative council whose members are selected
by Afghans."

He warned Washington that resistance would develop in Afghanistan if the Taliban were overthrown. "Capturing the cities is an easy task
for the side having supremacy in technological equipment and weapons
but the main problem for the dominant side will start at the time [it
tries] to establish the desired system over the whole country. . . . We
say that the causes of US defeat in Afghanistan [are] possibly stronger
and more valid than the causes of Russian defeat in this country. The
possibility of resisting the US is very vivid." Hekmatyar acknowledged
one big difference from the time when the Russians invaded. At that
time Pakistan had kept its border open and aided the resistance. This
time Pakistan and Iran had closed their borders to Afghan refugees. But
Hekmatyar calculated that "if a change occurs in Pakistan that the US
wouldn't be able to use that country as a military base for an invasion
on Afghanistan, then Afghans can easily resist against the US." He was
right. As soon as the Taliban were toppled, Pakistan reopened the border. It resumed its training and arming of the Taliban and Hekmatyar's
own forces a year or so later.

As it turned out, the arrival of Western forces in Kabul was initially
met with broad approval. In 1979, Soviet forces had found a city that was
highly polarized. While secular and left-wing families welcomed the
overthrow of Hafizullah Amin and hoped the new government would
follow a path of moderate reforms, other Afghans saw them as invaders with a profoundly alien culture and ideology. Kabul in 2001 was less
divided. A decade of rule by the mujahedin and Taliban had discredited
the political Islamists. They were seen as corrupt and power-hungry

warlords, and most Kabulis hailed the incoming foreign troops as the only instrument for disarming them.

I decided to contact former members of the PDPA to get their views on the new army of foreigners. They had worked with the Soviet occupation and saw what ensued. Would they reject ISAF? In February 2002, I phoned Ahmad Sarwar, the PDPA's former ambassador in India who had become a German citizen after getting asylum in 1992. He was entirely positive and felt Afghanistan had a historic new opportunity. Germany had volunteered to contribute troops to ISAF in Kabul. "There was no other way to get rid of the Taliban," he told me. "I'm very happy that British and German troops are coming. They will bring discipline and hard work. Now is the chance for Afghans to rebuild their country and do something about the absolute lack of education. It's a chance which will not come again. We will learn. We will have to learn. We are a very poor country."

As I listened to him, I could not help feeling that history was being repeated, if in a slightly different form. Twenty years earlier the PDPA and other secular Afghan modernizers had seen a big power, the USSR, as their necessary allies in the struggle against local backwardness. Now the very same people were looking to Western Europeans and the United States to do the job.

Sarwar's subtext was that Afghans must work harder and do more for themselves. They should stop blaming foreigners for their problems but also stop looking to foreigners for solutions. Sarwar was impressed by the way Germans had rebuilt their country after 1945, literally moving rubble by hand and starting work from scratch. He kept returning to the point. Afghans had an obligation to their country. He acknowledged that it also applied to him, but he felt that now that he was in his early fifties with two daughters who were fully integrated into German life it was too late to make a new start. But he was sure every family in the diaspora would be thinking hard about whether to go back. Many had taken for granted that they would never see their homeland again.

Now there was a chance. He hoped it would not just be to reclaim land or property and make money or to get comfortable jobs in the new Afghan diplomatic service.

I asked Sarwar about his colleagues in the PDPA, most of whom were in Europe. As many as 5,000 former PDPA members were estimated to be living in Germany, and 15,000 in the Netherlands. He rattled off a list of senior figures from the Parcham wing and said he had heard they were holding private meetings to assess their options. But too many members of the leadership had become corrupt, he believed, and he was sure they could not go back and play any useful role. The younger generation realized the PDPA had made some very big mistakes. "They're driving taxis here. Engineers and teachers are doing manual work," he said. "They are keen to go back. The Afghan Government should invite them back."

Much would depend on security in Kabul, Sarwar thought. His elder brother was a doctor in San Diego, having emigrated there in 1982. On the phone his brother told him that Afghans in California were excited by the change but were deterred by the kidnapping and robberies they heard about. Professional people were particular targets.

A few days later, I consulted Zahir Tanin, who was once known as one of the PDPA's most reform-minded members. Arrested as a student leader under Taraki and Amin, he was only released when the Russians came in. He went on to edit a liberal and semi-independent weekly newspaper in Kabul and was elected to the party's Central Committee during the Najibullah period. After 1992, he found his way to Britain, taught himself English and joined the BBC Persian service. Through hard work and ability and thanks to his calm and balanced analysis of politics, he was now its head.

Tanin had just returned from a couple of weeks in Kabul. We sat on a faded leather sofa in the dowdy basement bar of Bush House, the BBC World Service's London headquarters, and he described his impressions. First the good news, he laughed. He found there were more people who spoke well of Najibullah than of the Northern Alliance. "More seriously, I see no place for a PDPA-type party now. New political parties must develop," he said. "Leftist groups have to think what kind of role they can play, but we certainly need a liberal group which is modern to counterbalance the right-wing Islamic groups. Many people round Karzai understand the need for this. Karzai is a Muslim. He prays five times a day and has a jihadi background but I don't think he's prejudiced against the PDPA.

"You can't just say it's an American-supported government, the new imperialism, etc.," he continued. But he was disappointed that something was preventing the United Nations, Karzai and the United States from stressing publicly that, because Afghanistan was so short of skills, there ought not to be prejudice against Afghans who happened to be leftists or preconditions for them to fulfill before coming back. He suspected Karzai and the West were giving way to the armed Islamic groups whom they wanted to dismantle gradually. They were afraid of alienating these groups by bringing so-called communists back. "There are mujahedin leaders who still want to portray people according to the logic of the Cold War," Tanin said, mentioning a media interview that Abdul Rahim Karimi, the new justice minister, had recently given in which he said all Afghans were welcome to return, except communists.

What worried Tanin was people's failure to distinguish prejudice from real issues of responsibility. It was regrettable that the PDPA's former leaders had not yet been able to produce a critical analysis of the Soviet invasion and what happened afterward, or distance themselves from it. But people who had only been rank-and-file members were not guilty, nor were people who worked for the PDPA government without being members. "They were inspired by the leftist ideas of the 1970s but basically they're secular modernizers. They are dispersed everywhere now, former army officers, civil servants, people in the professions. You can't ignore their expertise. It's too costly to import foreigners," he told me. (Four years later, in December 2006, Karzai would appoint Tanin as Afghanistan's UN representative.)

Two months later, I was back in Afghanistan, getting my first chance to see the country in its post-Taliban guise. I was in Herat, reporting on the indirect victims of the U.S. bombing campaign, as discussed in the previous chapter. My other assignment was to describe what Afghans felt about the new opportunities opening up with the departure of the Taliban.

Heratis have always prided themselves on living in the country's oldest and best-preserved city, once as famous in Central Asia as Samarkand. A mosque from the Timurid period, which lasted from 1370 to 1507, stands in ruins, but enough of its walls of magnificent turquoise tiles remain to hint at its former glory. On a hill above the city center, the dust-colored ramparts of the old citadel still dominate the crowded shopping streets below. In the better-off residential areas lined with pine trees, conversations centered on the return to power of a controversial governor, Ismail Khan. A mujahedin leader who had fought the Russians, he had lost much of his popularity in the following years because of his authoritarian and conservative rule. With his reappearance after a gap of six years Heratis were already wondering whether the fall of the Taliban was really going to provide democratic change, respect for women's rights and rule by qualified civilians rather than warlords—or would mean only a minor softening of Islamic fundamentalism.

Mohammed Rafiq Shahir, a lawyer who headed a recently founded association of professionals, invited me to meet some of them at his home. Over coffee on a balmy spring evening with the scent of jasmine wafting over the terrace, they explained their grievances and hopes. As intellectuals in a country where politics had for so long been dominated by men with guns, their sense of being beleaguered was palpable. They found it upsetting that the fighting of the last two decades had damaged their country's image to the point that you almost had to apologize for being an Afghan. "When you go to Cairo, shopkeepers are surprised to discover you are a doctor. They think every Afghan is a gunman or a heroin dealer," said Dr. Hassan Farid, a gynecologist. For Heratis who consider their city to be Afghanistan's cultural capital with a long history of music, poetry and miniature painting, encounters of this kind were particularly insulting.

With a membership of more than eight hundred engineers, architects, doctors, lawyers and teachers, their newly formed association included women as well as men, Shias as well as Sunnis. Most were neither former PDPA members nor supporters of the monarchy. They felt separate from the ideological tribalism of the last decades and proud to belong to the small band of educated and independent Afghans who had never joined the diaspora. Shahir had been a student leader when the PDPA came to power and was twice detained for a total of eighteen months. Farid lectured at Kabul University in the PDPA period before being appointed head of Herat's hospital. "I was not a member of the party but I stayed in the country. Now the jihadis say: 'You were a communist,'" he said angrily. "They say that of everyone who remained."

They had decided to create their organization in order to be able to address Ismail Khan with a strong and united voice. People had begun to enjoy the old freedoms again since the fall of the Taliban, but Khan was attempting to reverse them. He had just issued instructions, Shahir said, that no music be played in public during prayer time and that pinups of Bollywood actresses must be taken down from the scores of video shops that had reappeared since the Taliban's departure. Men who worked in government offices were ordered to grow their beards long. While the Western world applauded Afghanistan's apparent return to democracy, Shahir remained worried. "If leadership is not under the control of educated people, this country will not change. The gun must be replaced by education," he said. He had not given up hope, but there was an unmistakable hint of anxiety in his eyes.

Farid saw reasons for secular Afghans to feel optimism. He sensed that mullahs commanded less respect among the population than two decades before because of their weakness and opportunism. "They always go with whoever is in power, whether it is the communists, the Taliban or Ismail Khan." Farid said that the mujahedin leaders had also lost credibility: "People used to listen to the men in turbans. But the Islamic parties destroyed more than the communists, and created worse problems."

At the Mir Ali-Shir Navai high school, named after the medieval Herati poet who founded Turkic literature, female teachers were eagerly resuming professional work after the bans of the Taliban years. The headmistress allowed me to talk to a group in their common room. They were delighted to have their jobs back but worried about the politics of the new regime. Were Islamists going to remain a dominant force? How would the warlords be disarmed?

Mohsene Ahmedi, a math teacher, told me in excitement that it was her first day back at work. During the Taliban period she had taught girls in home schools. Even now she and her colleagues had to wear burqas, as they had done under the Taliban, because Ismail Khan's religious police and the local Ministry for the Elimination of Vice and the Promotion of Virtue insisted on it. Sixty percent of Herat's women would prefer not to wear the burqa, she claimed. She remembered the PDPA time when not even a head-scarf was considered necessary: "It was free then. No one bothered us. Now, even when I go out with my husband, I have to wear the burqa."

She wanted foreign peacekeepers to move out from Kabul and be deployed in Herat and other cities as well. "We want them to collect weapons," she said. "There are too many guns in the villages. Everyone has one." Her colleagues nodded in agreement.

When I reached Kabul in June 2002 on my first trip to the capital since the fall of the Taliban, the mood of concern I had come across in Herat was pervasive. A Loya Jirga had been mandated by the Bonn conference to be held six months after the installation of the interim government. It was about to open in Kabul, and my job was to cover it. Almost everyone I met was worried by the power and prominence of the old warlords as well as by the inadequate representation of Pashtuns. General Mohammed Qasim Fahim, the Tajik defense minister and an old Northern Alliance commander, was refusing to obey the provisions in the Bonn agreement that required all military units to withdraw from ISAF areas. Many of his estimated 300 tanks and 500 armored personnel carriers remained in Kabul. Others were based north of the city or in the Panjshir valley. At ministry headquarters he was putting his friends in charge of all key departments. His officers were seizing houses in the city to use for themselves. Barnett Rubin, the U.S. Afghan specialist, quoted Fahim as saying he did not believe in institutions and that it would be a long time "before *zawabit* [institutions] replaces *rawabit* [personal relations] in Afghanistan."

Fahim's activities undermined efforts to re-create national institutions, including a new Afghan National Army. Ninety of the 100 officers promoted by Fahim to positions in it were Tajiks from the Panjshir valley. All this inhibited other armed groups from handing in their weapons, as implementation of the Bonn agreement said they should. The armed groups' leaders saw no reason why they should give their weapons to another faction and let it have a monopoly of the country's legal weaponry.

Lakhdar Brahimi, the UN special envoy, was a key adviser at the Loya Jirga. As soon as he visited Kabul in January and observed Fahim's behavior, he realized his own light-footprint strategy was inadequate with its implication that foreign peacekeepers were needed only in Kabul. After talking to Afghans, he became an ardent supporter of the view that ISAF should move to other regions to disarm the warlords. The trouble was that the United States was not willing to go along.

Washington followed the "realist" argument that Afghanistan needed stability above everything else and any serious effort to disarm the warlords might provoke them into rebellion.

For Afghans who had been hoping that after the Taliban the country would be able to make a fresh start in which armed groups would not be the main decision makers, the U.S. preference for stability looked like a dramatic "walking-away" from Afghanistan and another betrayal. Before the war, Bush and Blair had repeatedly promised to install democracy after toppling the Taliban, but all they were doing was restoring the groups who had preceded the Taliban. As Wazhma Frogh, a human rights activist who won the 2009 International Woman of Courage Award, put it, "The Bonn agreement empowered the warlords. The Bonn 'democracy' included no justice."

If stability was the name of the game, then Pashtuns should be better represented in government so as to prevent them from feeling shut out. On his January 2002 visit, Brahimi urged Karzai to appoint more Pashtuns as ministers. He even argued that "moderate" Taliban should be included. Now that the Taliban were out of power, some former Taliban ministers no longer felt constrained by loyalty to the movement. They claimed to be ready to work with the new administration in a spirit of national unity. Brahimi felt they should be accommodated.

The best illustration of the prominence of warlords came at the Loya Jirga, which was supposed to pick a new transitional government until national elections were held. It was an extraordinary occasion. The German Government provided a vast white air-conditioned tent of the kind normally used for beer festivals in Bavaria. The paradox of housing an assembly of alcohol-refusers in a beer tent was only one of the Jirga's bizarre features. It was erected on the ruined campus of Kabul's Polytechnical University in the northwestern part of the city. Surrounded by burnt-out shells of lecture halls and faculty offices, I could not help thinking as I walked up to the tent that it would have been hard to choose a place that offered a more graphic legacy of

Kabul's destruction. Mujahedin factions had destroyed countless homes and public buildings when they launched rockets at each other in the urban civil war of the mid-1990s. Yet now, the guilty warlords were seated in rattan armchairs in the front row of the Jirga, flaunting themselves as heroes.

Some 1,050 Afghan delegates were selected to the Jirga in a process that was meant to be democratic and free. District assemblies would send names of candidates to provincial caucuses, where representatives used a secret ballot to choose the winners. But in areas where the selection process was unsupervised by independent observers, warlords would put forward their own slates and intimidate delegates to support them. To try to remedy this and broaden the representation, an extra 450 seats were given to women, other members of civil society and a few representatives from the diaspora. Initially, members of armed groups were excluded by a rule that invalidated people with histories of human rights abuse, but in the final days before the Jirga opened, the authorities turned a blind eye to this with the agreement of the UN and Western governments. An extra fifty seats were given to "leading personalities." This included provincial governors and tribal leaders and allowed warlords like Ismail Khan and Abdul Rashid Dostum to take part. On the eve of the Loya Jirga, Sam Zia-Zarifi, a senior researcher with Human Rights Watch, commented, "The degree to which the U.S. and the UN have compromised is shocking. It's odd to believe there can be kinder, gentler warlords. For the United States it's a strange position on which to base one's strategy in the first theater of the war on terror."

In spite of the warlords' dominance the Jirga broke new ground. It was probably the most democratic assembly Afghanistan has ever seen, before or since. People listened to its live proceedings on the radio avidly. Riveting clashes and major disagreements were aired in public. When the national anthem sounded, many Pashtuns refused to stand. They said it was a Tajik song from the Panjshir valley.

Around 210 women were in attendance, sitting in a block on the left of the huge conference tent, and several spoke forcefully. Sima Samar, the minister of women's affairs, said, "This is not a democracy. It's a rubber-stamp. Everything has already been decided by the people with power. This Jirga includes all the warlords. None is left out." We saw her deputy, Taj Kokar, and a group of women go up to former president Rabbani and ask him, "Why have you killed and raped our women? Why do we have so many widows in this country?" The startled politician had no reply. One woman, Massouda Jalal, put herself forward as a rival to Karzai in the selection for the country's presidency. A pediatrician and lecturer at Kabul University who lost her job after the Taliban took power, she called for social justice and equal rights as well as national unity. She talked about the country's massive unemployment and the huge number of orphans. "I am a Muslim woman and I have rights. For over two centuries there has been a cruel betrayal of women. This is a golden time for the people of Afghanistan," she told the delegates. "Now is the time to forget the clashes and conflicts of the past."

There was plenty of disappointment. I spoke to Adhitya Badghisi, a teacher from the north who was carrying her small daughter in her arms, when I caught up with her in a refreshment tent during a break in the conference. "I wanted to speak but I have given up hope. Our provincial delegates told me men have the priority. Until these warlords are disarmed or have their power reduced, the situation won't get better. ISAF should disarm them," she told me. It had been tough for her and her husband, who was not a delegate, to come to Kabul, and they had relied on the United Nations Children's Fund UNICEF) to organize a flight.

The topics that came up most frequently at the Jirga were whether the country should be described as an Islamic state, the need for unity after the ethnic tensions and fighting of recent years and in particular the need for a new Afghan National Army. Fatima Gailani, the daughter of Pir Gailani, one of the main mujahedin leaders, took a liberal view. "There's no open environment for delegates," she told me. "People who like to talk about the mystique of mujahedin leaders and the past conflict are not letting others speak. It's time to listen to those who are working for human rights. It's better not to have Islam in the state's official title. The name is exploited too much. For the last twenty-three years starting with the Soviet invasion it was good to have the reference to Islam, but it's unnecessary now. All our people are Muslims."

In spite of many disappointments, some delegates preferred to see the brighter side. Akbar Popal, the chancellor of Kabul University and a member of Rabbani's Jamiyat movement, defended the mujahedin leaders, even though his campus had been devastated by their fighting. "Most of Afghanistan was destroyed at some point. If we bring the past into the present, we won't have unity. The mujahedin did something significant during the Soviet occupation. We can't forget that. That's why people still respect them," he said. "Everybody lost loved ones. I lost several myself. Should we take up the gun against each other again? Blood cannot be washed away by blood."

Mohammed Rafiq Shahir, the lawyer I had met in Herat, was surprisingly positive. He had been selected as a delegate with several colleagues from his association of professionals. He described the Jirga as "a good step toward democracy" and said it would take time to build civil society. But he still wanted ISAF to expand and move to other Afghan cities.

The main decision the Jirga had to make was to pick a president. Before the meeting began, it was widely assumed this would be a straightforward process that would confirm Karzai since he was already the interim leader selected in Bonn. At Bonn it had also been decided that the king would open the Jirga. There was a large chair with gilded arms on the platform for him. But with everyone in the tent for the expected start at eleven a.m., nothing happened. The silence dragged on. Ten minutes, fifteen minutes, half an hour, and still no explanation.

Based on comments some of his staff and supporters had made the previous day, word began to circulate that the king was having second thoughts. He now wanted to be head of state again. There was panic among U.S. and UN officials as well as the Northern Alliance. Their fear was that when the king arrived in the tent some Pashtun delegates might call on the Loya Jirga to appoint him head of state by acclamation.

After an hour the Jirga was adjourned, with the announcement that it would reconvene for the formal opening sometime in the afternoon or perhaps the next morning. Journalists were told that Zalmay Khalilzad, the Afghan American who had been appointed as new U.S. ambassador in Kabul and had once been a consultant for Unocal, the American oil pipeline company that had negotiated with the Taliban, would hold a press conference later at the embassy. The media duly trooped there at the appointed time.

The U.S. embassy's transformation since the 1980s was dramatic. Instead of a single guard at the gate, the entrance was now heavily sandbagged. We had to walk down a narrow path between razor-wire while sniffer dogs put their muzzles against our equipment. Marine guards held their fingers ready at the triggers of automatic rifles.

Khalilzad was smooth and relaxed when he addressed us. His performance demonstrated how far the United States already dominated Afghan politics and made a mockery of Afghan sovereignty. With supreme self-confidence he blamed the media for the difficulties that were delaying the start of the Jirga. The media had broadcast statements "that indicated that the former king might be or is a candidate for the presidency. Since these statements were inconsistent with earlier statements by the king they caused some consternation and confusion among delegates." Khalilzad said he had talked to Zahir Shah the previous evening and again that morning "to ascertain his true intention." He was able to announce that Zahir Shah was definitely not a candidate to be head of state or president. It was unfortunate that an impression was created that Karzai and King Zahir Shah were political rivals. "He is not seeking the restoration of the monarchy nor is he a candidate for executive office," the ambassador stressed. Why hadn't the former king clarified the position himself rather than having the U.S. ambassador do it? a reporter asked. "He's going to make a statement shortly," Khalilzad replied.

With the press conference over, we rushed to the opulent villa where Zahir Shah was staying. There we watched the next act in his humiliation. On the terrace we found a single high-backed chair between a set of white plastic stackable garden chairs. Followed by three advisers the 87-year-old former monarch shuffled in, a stooped and tottering figure. He did not a speak a word. Hamid Siddiqi, his spokesman, said there would be no opportunity for questions. He would just read out what he said was His Majesty's statement. It matched Khalilzad's account almost verbatim, talking of confusion and the need for clarification "for the sake of my compatriots." The king did not seek the restoration of the monarchy nor to be president. His only purpose was to "serve the suffering people of Afghanistan." He fully supported Karzai's candidacy.

The cruel deed having been done, we were ushered out after barely ten minutes. When the Loya Jirga reconvened next morning, it was to watch Zahir Shah totter onto the stage and perform the only act he was allowed, which was to open the Loya Jirga formally. At least this time he read his remarks himself, but in a low voice that barely reached the microphone that an aide was holding to his lips. "By the will of God I am back in my country with my nation. My only wish is to bring peace in the country, national unity and reconciliation," he muttered. If any loyal delegates had wanted to propose the former king as head of state, they would know they were going against their leader.

Duly elected president by a huge margin over Massouda Jalal, the female pediatrician who had stood against him, Karzai asked the Jirga to confer on the king the title Father of the Nation. This was agreed, and Karzai went on to declare his happiness that after twenty-five years "all Afghans are gathering under one tent. The refugees are coming back. It is a proud moment for me."

The main job left was to negotiate a new cabinet and announce it. Mohammed Fahim, the Northern Alliance commander from the Panjshir valley, remained defense minister. Another Tajik from the same narrow area, Abdullah Abdullah, remained foreign minister. The only concession to the Pashtuns was that Yunus Qanuni, the Tajik interior minister who was also from the Panjshir, ceded his job to one of them. But Qanuni was given a specially created new post as presidential adviser on security. Although other Pashtuns received ministerial portfolios, the impression was reinforced that the government's key positions were held by Northern Alliance mujahedin. The fact that Karzai was a Pashtun was seen at best as irrelevant and at worst as proof that he was a prisoner of the Tajiks and a token designed to satisfy Pashtun pride.

As for the other best-known warlords, Ismail Khan and Dostum, they declined offers of cabinet seats, but this was not as encouraging as it first seemed. They were running their home areas like personal fiefdoms and enriching themselves with custom duties taken at the border and not passed to the national treasury. They preferred to stay as regional strongmen rather than risk a loss of power and money by taking an office job in Kabul.

Two days after the Loya Jirga ended, I went to see British Major General John McColl, the first commander of ISAF. Unlike the U.S. embassy, his headquarters seemed less well defended than an army base in Britain at that time, when the Irish Republican Army was still a threat. He invited me for tea in the garden in sight of the main gate. The high walls of Hesco barriers and watchtowers that today guard ISAF's Kabul headquarters were not yet needed.

General McColl indicated that, although the Loya Jirga had shown that the threat from men like General Fahim was political rather than military, this made them more dangerous. They symbolized the power of triumphant warlordism that was distorting the chances of honest civilian rule. The ISAF commander made it clear he was irritated by Fahim's refusal to withdraw his troops from Kabul, where there was no security threat other than the one they themselves offered. Fahim had twice as many troops and more heavy weapons than ISAF. The general pointed to a subtle difference in the text of the military-technical annex to the Bonn agreement. Whereas the English version said all military forces should be withdrawn from Kabul and its surroundings, the Dari text said "from the streets of Kabul." This allowed Fahim to argue that he was complying with the agreement since he kept his men, estimated at around 10,000, in barracks in Kabul.

McColl was shortly due to hand command over to a Turkish general, at which point the 1,500-strong British contingent would shrink to 300. I asked him about expanding ISAF across Afghanistan. "While it appears attractive in the short term, I think we will produce a better long-term solution by ensuring security sector reform and developing a multi-ethnic army," he told me, faithfully following the agreed U.S./U.K. script.

At that stage the U.S. plan was for an Afghan National Army of 60,000 men. This was considered fully adequate for protecting the country. Although no former PDPA men were invited to join the government, Lieutenant Colonel Kevin McDonnell, the U.S. Special Forces commander in charge of training the first volunteers, told me when I visited the base that no ideological bar was placed against officers or enlisted men from the former communist army joining up. They were better disciplined than the former mujahedin, he said. (Here, at least, was a sign of open-mindedness about the Soviet and Najibullah periods.) The only applicants rejected were those who could not swear they had not fought for the Taliban.

Away from the hothouse of the Loya Jirga, many Afghans still felt optimistic. Refugees were coming back from Pakistan in larger numbers than in 1992, when the mujahedin took over in Kabul. At that time, mujahedin leaders still had tight control over many camps and could virtually order families to go home since they had a vested interest in presenting an image of a new dawn after Najibullah's fall. In 1992, about 1.2 million Afghans came back from Pakistan, about a third of the total who were living there.

By 2002, more families had integrated themselves into Pakistani life, and conditions in the camps were freer. Nevertheless, the total number of Afghans who chose to return had reached a million by the middle of June. This was twice as fast a return as the UN refugee agency had counted after Najibullah's collapse in 1992, according to figures given to me at the agency's Pul-i-Charkhi reception center a few miles south of Kabul.

Trucks full of families and their belongings pulled into the parking lot every few minutes. In the welcome tents, they were given basic kits of plastic buckets, tarpaulin for shelter, blankets and food parcels. But so many refugees were returning and so little money was available from donor governments that food rations had been cut to a third of the previous level. The refugees paid about $10 each for the truck ride from Pakistan to Kabul. The UNHCR gave each family $20 a head for resettlement.

Families filed through another tent where an Afghan instructor explained the danger of the mines and unexploded cluster bombs they might see in their fields. But with several thousand people arriving every day, time was too short to get them to sit down and concentrate: they simply walked past the displays. For a third of the returnees this might not matter since they had already decided not to risk life in their villages but to stay in Kabul, mainly because it was seen as Afghanistan's safest place, in spite of its overcrowding.

To SEE HOW rural returnees were faring, I drove an hour north of Kabul to Istalif, a large, sprawling and once picturesque village on a ridge above the western edge of the Shomali plain. Over the centuries, potters here became famous for the distinctive blue-green glaze they used on their bowls and vases. Throughout the plain, which abuts on Bagram air base on its eastern side, people are Tajiks. Under Taliban rule, they were repeatedly attacked as suspected allies of the Northern Alliance, their homes destroyed and hundreds massacred.

Swallows were diving and soaring above fields of stunted vines. The apple trees were mainly leafless, thanks to Taliban destruction of the irrigation system. Istalif and its surrounding farms once had a population of 20,000. Now there were barely 4,000. "I'm happy to be back even though my house is a wreck," Sufi Shah Agha, a tailor, told me. His family and four others were living in tents in the yard.

The sound of hammering could be heard everywhere as villagers were putting up new roofs. Others were planting potatoes. Mohammed Khan, an elderly farmer, had placed a few branches from poplar trees across the damaged walls of his house to provide extra shelter. Only two of roughly half a dozen rooms had survived intact.

In a field in the upper part of the village, schoolchildren were sitting on blue tarpaulin laid out on the ground in four open tents that consisted of nothing more than a canvas roof held up by guy ropes. The gong that summoned the kids to class was an old artillery shell hanging from a tree. Only one wall of the old school was left standing. Incongruously, it was one with a map of Afghanistan painted on it. The message seemed to be that Afghanistan had survived decades of war as an abstract place but not much else.

With signs of battle all around them, it was hard to be confident that these children would really have a future of peace. Exactly ten years previously I had seen an earlier wave of Afghan refugees coming back to what they hoped would be a better life, only to be disappointed.

If the omens generally seemed more favorable this time, there were hints of trouble ahead. Six months after the Taliban had retreated, the problems that would allow them to return were mounting. The warlords were not being disarmed. ISAF was restricted to Kabul. Pashtuns were underrepresented in the new organs of power. U.S. control over Afghan politics in the capital, if not in the provinces, was humiliating. Western aid money was not flowing in the amounts that were needed.

In short, Bush's promise not to walk away was already close to broken.

[10] TALIBAN RESURGENT

"In an announcement marking a major victory in America's ongoing war on terror, Defense Secretary Donald H. Rumsfeld declared Thursday that 'major combat activity' has ended in Afghanistan."

—FOX NEWS, MAY 1, 2003

DEFENSE SECRETARY DONALD Rumsfeld's triumphant boast that major combat activity in Afghanistan was over coincided with the day of George W. Bush's appearance on the deck of the aircraft carrier, the USS *Abraham Lincoln,* off San Diego to announce with pride that "major combat operations have ended in Iraq." Both men's bombast was soon punctured. In Afghanistan little more than a month later a suicide bomber drove a taxi into a bus on the eastern outskirts of Kabul. The bus was carrying German soldiers from the International Security Assistance Force, which had been set up after the Taliban lost power. Four soldiers were torn apart in the blast. One Afghan bystander was killed and ten other Afghans suffered serious wounds.

The bombing shocked ISAF. It was the first suicide attack on foreign troops since they had arrived in Kabul eighteen months earlier. Although it was never confirmed whether the attacker was Afghan or of some other nationality, the murder suggested that the tactics of the

global jihad were about to become a grim new part of the struggle
going on inside Afghanistan. During the Soviet occupation and the
Taliban's battles against the mujahedin, suicide was never used as a
weapon. The change had alarming implications.

The ISAF bus bombing was just one of many signs of a recent revival
of violent activity against the U.S. and its allies in Afghanistan as well
as Afghan government forces. Separately from ISAF, which at that stage
operated only in Kabul, U.S. troops had been hunting al Qaeda fighters and their Taliban comrades in areas of eastern Afghanistan where
Osama bin Laden had once had his training camps. The Americans
reported that rockets and mortars were hitting their bases. Mines and
improvised explosive devices (IEDs) started to appear on the roads.

Initially, the Americans assumed this new offensive was by scattered
remnants of Taliban and al Qaeda who had not given up after U.S. air
strikes forced the Taliban regime to withdraw in December 2001. In
March 2002, the United States launched a major offensive, Operation
Anaconda, in eastern Afghanistan to try to finish the enemy off. The
operation was considered a success. But when several months later,
Afghan border posts in southern Afghanistan in Helmand and Kandahar,
areas that had always been the Taliban heartland, started coming under
frequent attack from the Pakistani side, the Americans realized they
were facing a new phenomenon. This was confirmed when Taliban
fighters were seen in groups as large as fifty during the spring of 2003,
often attacking Afghan police posts in the southern provinces. By the
summer, much of Zabul province had fallen under Taliban influence.

Taliban guerrillas were also hitting so-called soft targets. In March
2003, in Uruzgan (Mullah Omar's native province), a group led by
Mullah Dadullah, a senior Taliban commander, stopped a convoy of
vehicles belonging to the International Committee of the Red Cross,
and shot and killed one of the Red Cross workers, an engineer from
El Salvador. Over the next few months, other Afghan and foreign civilians working for the UN and various NGOs in Nimruz, Uruzgan and

Zabul provinces were assassinated. In September 2003, seven aid workers were murdered in Ghazni, Helmand and Nimruz provinces. The
situation became so grave that the UN announced a suspension of all
aid in Helmand and Nimruz, while in four districts of Kandahar province, aid workers were told not to continue with their projects unless
they had armed escorts.

What caused the Taliban resurgence? Some analysts have argued
that it was not a revival but simply a continuation of a civil war that
had never stopped. After all, the Taliban leadership had not surrendered
in 2001. All that happened was that they withdrew from Kabul and
Kandahar under the weight of ferocious U.S. bombing. The retreat was
not orderly: Mullah Omar, for example, jumped on a motorbike and
fled to his native province of Uruzgan before moving across the border
into Pakistan. Some analysts assert that because Taliban leaders would
never accept defeat, particularly at the hands of the United States, it was
only a matter of time before they reemerged in full force. There were
also now new grievances. The gross mistreatment of Taliban prisoners
captured by Dostum's forces in northern Afghanistan in the autumn of
2001 was a powerful recruiting tool. As many as 4,000 young men may
have died while being transported or held in overcrowded freight containers. Najibullah Lafraie, who had served as the mujahedin's foreign
minister from 1992 to 1996 and later moved to New Zealand to work as
a university lecturer in political science, believes "the tens of thousands
of revenge-seeking relatives of those victims provided a large pool of
potential recruits to the Taliban."

After the fall of the Taliban, Northern Alliance forces ethnically
cleansed several thousand Pashtun villagers in northern and western
Afghanistan. Some were killed. The rest fled south to Pakistan or the
Afghan border provinces, landless, homeless and jobless. They too
formed a pool of angry and disillusioned young men.

If the Karzai government and its U.S. backers had made a serious offer of reconciliation to the Taliban in 2002, they might have

defused the possibility of renewed fighting. Instead, they gave power in the southern provinces to regional strongmen who had lost out to the Taliban in 1994 and 1995 and remained vindictively anti-Taliban. In Helmand, it was Sher Mohammed Akhundzada from the Alizai tribe. In Kandahar, the strongman was Gul Agha Sherzai from the Barakzai tribe. Karzai also gave power to his half-brother, Ahmed Wali Karzai, who became the leading Popolzai enforcer in Kandahar. These men, and others like them, appointed governors and police chiefs who were from the same tribes and subtribes and used their positions to reward family members and followers.

These strongmen also got their hands on the reviving narco-business of opium and heroin. When it was in power, the Taliban had drastically reduced poppy production. In 2001, in all of Afghanistan, the harvest of raw opium was 190 metric tons. By 2003 it was 3,000 metric tons, around 60 percent of the world's supply. In the postwar and post-Taliban chaos, desperate farmers turned to poppy as the quickest crop from which to earn good money and in the knowledge that no one was going to prevent them. By 2007 annual production had risen to 8,200 metric tons, and had spread to every province, both inside and outside areas of Taliban control.

The government's poor record eased the way to the Taliban resurgence. Horiah Mosadiq, an Afghan working in London as a researcher for Amnesty International, put it graphically: "In 2001 most Pashtuns supported the overthrow of the Taliban. Insecurity increased after 2005 because the Taliban told people, 'Look, all the rapists are back in power, Sayyaf, Rabbani, Dostum.'"

Twenty years of war had shaken up the old social structures in the Afghan countryside. The tribal system could no longer give young people a social network or a sense of purpose. Tribal and village elders lost their authority, particularly for the thousands who had grown up in refugee camps. Local guerrilla commanders became the new role models for young men who returned to Afghanistan. Others turned to radical religious movements.

Madrassas in Pakistan played a big part in the revival of the Taliban. According to Antonio Giustozzi, a research fellow at the London School of Economics and one of the best-informed analysts on Afghanistan, Mullah Omar launched a recruitment drive in the second half of 2002 among madrassa students in Karachi and Baluchistan, whose capital city, Quetta, became his new base.

All these issues were little more than a cloud on the horizon when I flew to Kabul in October 2003. The *Guardian* was preparing a series of articles on Doctors Without Borders for the newspaper's annual Christmas appeal, and I was on my way to northern Afghanistan to look at some of their medical projects there.

Afghanistan in 2003 was a tale of two countries. People in the capital were aware that violence was brewing in the Pashtun heartlands in the south against the government and foreigners connected with it, but Kabul was calm and apparently making progress. Work was going on to draw up a new constitution and the UN was making plans to start registering Afghans for the presidential election of October 2004.

There was some trouble in the north, but it was caused by tension between rival warlords. The government was not the target, and people trusted ISAF to provide security. Armed clashes had occurred in Mazar, the capital of Balkh province, between Junbesh, the political movement loyal to the Uzbek General Dostum, and Jamiyat, loyal to Atta Mohammed Nur, the Tajik governor of Balkh province. The minister of the interior was trying to merge the two armies into a single corps and had sent 300 Kabul police to Mazar to do it. The local police could not be trusted, since they were biased in favor of one or the other warlord.

As a precaution against a breakdown in law and order, the United States had just given in to persistent demands from Karzai and many ordinary Afghans to extend ISAF's role beyond Kabul to the rest of the country. The new deployments would start in the north with 230 German troops going to a base in Kunduz. The United States had also agreed to strengthen ISAF by putting NATO in charge of the force's 5,000 troops, replacing the system of rotation whereby different countries held the top command positions and provided the bulk of the troops for six months.

The first Provincial Reconstruction Teams had been set up in Mazar and Kunduz. These were groups of foreign military and civilian advisers whose main tasks were to oversee the disarmament of militias and the behavior of the local police. The PRTs supervised the collection of weapons and their storage in armories. In Mazar they took part in a local security commission to which both warlords sent representatives. It was another mechanism to try to resolve disputes and prevent violence.

The PRTs were also designed to provide and supervise reconstruction and civilian aid. American and British military doctors would go into villages and set up one-day clinics to treat patients. At one level this was fine since the need was there, but it blurred distinctions in many Afghans' minds. They associated all aid work with the military presence, since the PRTs were fully integrated into the military's counterinsurgency strategies. Independent aid agencies like Oxfam and Doctors Without Borders were worried by the PRTs' move into hearts-and-minds work in health and education. As long as local people accepted ISAF, this was not a major problem, but as soon as tensions arose, it put aid workers at risk, making them targets, as was already happening in southern Afghanistan. The seeds had been sown for what was to be a major issue in the next phase of the war. By the end of 2003, there were already eight PRTs in provincial capitals with another four planned. It was a classic case of mission creep.

The Taliban revival owed much to Pakistan's intelligence agency, the ISI, which had helped to create the movement in the first place. The agency's motivation was the same as in the early 1990s: it saw Karzai as a pawn not just of the Americans but also of the Northern Alliance, whose Tajik leaders were thought to be too close to India, Iran and Russia. In this context the Taliban were a useful tool for Pakistan to put pressure on Kabul. Pakistan also wanted to be sure that if the Taliban ever returned to power across Afghanistan its leaders would feel a debt to Islamabad.

A key issue in the back of Pakistani minds was always Pashtunistan, the question whether the Pashtuns in southern Afghanistan and north-western Pakistan should form their own state. No Afghan government had been willing to accept the border drawn by the British in 1893, the Durand line, which divided the territory populated by the Pashtun tribes. Many Pashtun still considered Peshawar, Quetta and other parts of Pakistan's frontier regions to be Afghan and their annexation into British India in the nineteenth century to have been unjust. During their time in power, King Zahir Shah and particularly his cousin Daoud Khan advocated reclaiming these lands. Zahir Shah's return to Kabul in 2002, albeit in a purely ceremonial role, was a reminder that the issue was not dead. Ensuring that whoever ruled Kabul was Pakistan's client was a constant policy objective for Islamabad. It seemed the best way of preventing any Afghan government from reopening the border issue. Although it was unlikely that any Kabul government would go so far in Pakistan's direction as to abandon all territorial claims and recognize the Durand line as Afghanistan's official frontier, the next best thing from Pakistan's point of view was the status quo.

In 2004, the presidential election became a major focus for Taliban activity. The Taliban threatened to disrupt every stage of the proceedings from registration of voters to the conduct of the ballot. During the process they killed five Afghan army troops and fifteen election staff. By then, U.S. troops were operating not just in eastern Afghanistan but all across the south under the mandate of Operation Enduring Freedom, in the hunt for al Qaeda. American troops were separate from ISAF troops, who were still described as peacekeepers rather than war-fighters. The Pentagon was confident it would soon defeat the reviving Taliban, and in April 2004, General James Jones, the supreme allied commander in Europe, said, "We should not ever even think that there is going to be an insurrection of the type that we see in Iraq here. It's just not going to happen." He proved to be dramatically wrong.

By 2005, the Taliban were operating in large parts of southern Afghanistan, attacking government outposts and assassinating people who worked there. With its ground forces stretched in Afghanistan and Iraq, the Bush administration started to look to allies to contribute troops to the Afghan theater. In 2006, Britain took over from U.S. forces in Helmand under an ISAF plan that saw the whole of the south come under NATO control so that the Americans could concentrate on the eastern provinces, where al Qaeda and the Taliban were believed to be operating together. The ISAF contingent was to expand to 20,000 from its original 5,000 with large troop contributions in the south from Canada and the Netherlands as well as Britain.

Could the Taliban have been defeated had there been more U.S. troops to counter them in the early stages of their resurgence in 2003? Some analysts, like Ahmed Rashid, the Pakistani author and journalist, think they could, since the Taliban were far from popular and had little political control across the south at that stage. He and many other analysts accuse the United States of devoting too much attention and too many resources to Iraq when it could have succeeded in Afghanistan. Barack Obama has repeatedly leveled the same charge at the Bush administration.

Others doubt that more U.S. troops would have helped. U.S. pressure, backed by ISAF troops, could have been useful in disarming the warlords and persuading Karzai to install honest and efficient government representatives in the cities and provinces. This would have been good politics. But looking for a military solution against the Taliban was the wrong way to go. U.S. troops were not experienced in counterinsurgency

operations, as their performance in the early stages of the occupation of
Iraq in 2003 and 2004 had shown. Mass detentions of farmers, insensitive house searches and overreliance on air strikes provoked rather than
reduced resistance in the Iraqi countryside long before Sunni-versus-
Shia tensions changed the character of the war. Blanketing southern
Afghanistan with U.S. troops in 2003 and 2004 would have had a similar
effect of making the Taliban more, not less, popular. In the few areas
where they were operating, they were already alienating local Afghans.
As Barnett Rubin, the U.S. Afghan specialist who later became an adviser
to the Obama administration, put it in a 2004 interview: "Just as in Iraq,
but on a much lesser scale, when the United States forces undertake
house searches, when they arrest people, when they brutalize people in
captivity, this creates not only resentment but, in a tribal society, it also
creates obligations of revenge. So people will join the Taliban because
they now feel obligated to kill an American because Americans have
killed some of their relatives." But even if U.S. troops had behaved more
subtly, their very presence provoked resistance from Pashtuns who have
a centuries-long history of fighting foreign occupiers.

Twenty years earlier, the Soviets had found southern Afghanistan,
with its largely Pashtun population, the hardest region of the country
to pacify. Their control of Kandahar and Lashkar Gah, the capital of
Helmand, was never complete, unlike their control of Kabul and cities in the east and north like Jalalabad and Mazar. The Americans and
British were ploughing a similar furrow.

Washington's main problem in southern Afghanistan was that the
Karzai government and the provincial governors it appointed had minimal legitimacy in people's eyes. This was also true in large parts of the
north, but most of these places were not regions where insurgency and
armed resistance had a long tradition.

One indication of the loss of legitimacy was the drop in participation for national elections. Turnout across the country in the October
2004 presidential election, the first held since the fall of the Taliban,

was 75 percent. By the time of the parliamentary elections a year later, it was down to just over 50 percent. By 2009 it had collapsed altogether, totaling around 30 percent nationally in the first round of the presidential election. In many areas of Helmand and Kandahar it was less than 5 percent.

The presence of a large number of foreigners and Afghan expatriates in Kabul and other major cities helped to undermine the government's legitimacy, according to Najibullah Lafraie, the mujahedin's former foreign minister. The foreigners and returning expatriates brought with them increased alcohol consumption, prostitution, satellite and even domestic television programs that ran counter to Afghans' religious and cultural norms. Thus, the Karzai government seemed "un-Islamic" to many Afghans. Lafraie wrote that another major problem was "Karzai's perceived lack of autonomy and independence. From the author's experience during his trip to. Kabul, in everyday conversations, in religious talks in the mosques and even over the radio waves, one frequently comes across references to President Karzai as the 'contemporary Shah Shuja'—the notorious British-installed nineteenth-century Afghan king. Once Karzai is seen as a foreign agent and his government as un-Islamic, it would not be very difficult to portray him as an 'infidel,' as the Taliban try to do in their propaganda material."

In southern Afghanistan, where the Taliban has always been at its strongest, corruption of local officials, particularly the police, was a major factor in damaging the reputation of both local and central government. A British government poll in 2010 (discussed in Chapter One), which asked Helmandis about the justice system, revealed that people prefer the Taliban system because they do not have to bribe officials.

WHEN I MADE my next visit to Kabul in June 2007, four years after my previous one, the war in the south had become a full-scale conflict. The British troops who had been sent to Helmand a year earlier in a bid to contain it were taking heavy casualties. The number of foreign troops in Afghanistan as a whole was rising steadily from 30,000 in early 2006. By January 2009, when Obama took office, it was up to 64,000 and in the following two years would rise to 142,000.

Far from containing the insurgency by the Taliban and its allies, the Haqqani movement in eastern Afghanistan and Gulbuddin Hekmatyar's Hezb-i Islami, the addition of more troops served to strengthen it. It gave the Taliban a chance to pose as the country's defenders against yet another occupation by infidels. Whereas the population was largely supportive of the government from 2001 to 2005, public opinion in unstable areas began to shift in favor of anti-government elements in 2006–2007, according to Talatbek Masadykov, who worked as chief of the political affairs division, UN Assistance Mission for Afghanistan. Two years later the trend was even worse for the government. As he and two other analysts wrote in a research paper, "For the period late 2008–9, the population in unstable areas is voluntarily providing support to insurgents, and the population in stable areas is distancing itself from the Afghan government."

Civilian casualties began to soar. In the first six months of 2007, foreign forces had killed 292 Afghan civilians in offensive operations. Another thirty-nine died in so-called force protection operations, which meant that soldiers had shot them for coming too close to a convoy or patrol base, suspecting them of being suicide bombers. Armed opposition groups had killed 317 civilians over the same period, just under the combined total of 331 Afghan civilians killed by foreign forces.

In its first major study of civilian deaths by violence in 2007, Human Rights Watch published a searing account of the mounting toll of killings and maimings by insurgents. Suicide bombings were taking place at a rate of ten a month. In the words of Mohammad Yusef Aresh, who survived an attack in Kabul:

> *I passed the cart and a few seconds later the bomb exploded. It was like an earthquake. It blew me back about three or four meters. . . . I*

woke up and saw people and body parts everywhere: fingers, hands, feet, toes, almost everything. . . . People were screaming and others were screaming that another bomb would explode. . . . I was wearing a white suit that day and I saw that my suit was red. . . . I can't walk fast now. You know, I was a boxer. I can't box anymore. . . . My leg hurts everyday and I have a hard time walking. . . . When I think about these things it brings tears to my eyes. When I think about these things and put them all together it makes me want to leave this country.

I went to see Sima Samar, who headed the Afghan Independent Human Rights Commission, in her well-guarded office in a Kabul district still largely ruined from the days of mujahedin rule. "These suicide attacks are still very, very new for Afghans," she said. "It's only happened since the Iraq invasion. We're seeing the same tactic here now." In almost thirty years of war, Afghans had never known such random and unpredictable slaughter. The fact that young Afghans were strapping on suicide belts shocked older Afghans as a perversion of their warrior nation's patriotic traditions in which one died for one's tribe or country, not for Islam.

Although dozens of civilians were being killed by suicide bombers, the insurgents' primary targets at that stage were not civilians. In this there was a distinction from what was happening in Iraq, where Sunni jihadis were deliberately killing Shia civilians. The deaths of Afghan civilians occurred mainly because they happened to be passing when bombers struck Afghan police or coalition convoys or because bombs were badly made and handled and went off prematurely.

The political impact of the civilian deaths was different from what it was in Iraq, where public opinion turned strongly against sectarian death squads and their leaders. In Afghanistan in spite of the almost equal toll from insurgent attacks, the killing of civilians by NATO forces, in particular the Americans, generated much greater public anger. The Americans' arrival had at first been welcomed, but now people had become disappointed at the lack of economic progress and development. Worse still, they felt the troops' presence was generating instability, provoking armed resistance and producing unnecessary death and destruction.

Sima Samar reflected the change in attitude. A Hazara who had lived in exile in Quetta during the Taliban period, she said she had been delighted when the Americans removed the Taliban from power, but in June 2007 she was full of complaints. The Hazara heartland, Bamiyan, was secure and relatively peaceful, and for this she was happy. "But very little is being done to improve people's lives," she said to me. "We told the Americans several years ago to concentrate on the safe areas and put more money into development, in areas where there is not much opium poppy production, as a reward." But, she added, "Not much has happened."

As a human rights activist, Sima was also incensed with the killing of civilians in southern Afghanistan during American air strikes. She said that U.S. commanders requested so-called close air support too readily when their troops came under fire or they suspected resistance fighters were nearby. She blamed much of the problem on faulty intelligence and said the Americans often relied on "just one source" before acting too hastily. She cited as an example a recent investigation by her staff of a particularly serious incident. It was in Herat province at the end of April. American aircraft dropped bombs in support of U.S. Special Forces in the Zerkoh valley. Afghan Government officials counted forty-two civilians killed by the attacks. They said they found no evidence of Taliban forces in the area, and local residents were adamant there were no Taliban forces there at the time.

The incident caused such an outcry in the Afghan media that Karzai felt compelled to protest. It was one of the first times he publicly denounced U.S. tactics, though it would soon become a pattern. "We can no longer accept the civilian casualties the way they are occurring," he said. The issue never ceased to be a major political concern. Even when the number of deaths caused by suicide bombings by insurgents rose sharply, killings of Afghan civilians by U.S. troops continued to produce the greatest sense of outrage.

Initially NATO claimed that eighty-seven Taliban fighters had been killed in the Zerkoh valley case during a fourteen-hour-long battle and that there were no reports of civilian casualties. Later it said it would conduct an investigation. In May, Brigadier General Perry Wiggins, deputy operations director of the joint staff, reported on the findings and stated that U.S. ground forces were "continuously engaged by intense enemy fire after entering an area of known Taliban activity. . . . All targets were positively identified as hostile, [and] were under observation at the time of the engagement. The on-scene commander used appropriate level of force to respond to the continuous enemy threat and protect his unit." But Wiggins conceded that no accounting had been done of civilian casualties.

On that trip to Kabul in June 2007, I found that inflated promises of aid and development had caused a massive drop in the government's standing and that of foreigners. Afghans complained that they saw little direct benefit from all the aid that was delivered. They knew that much was siphoned off by government officials or spent on highly paid foreign consultants and advisers. Of course, in any country, aid delivery tends to be plagued by unrealistic expectations since people imagine the outsiders will make huge and rapid improvements. When they do not, people complain that nothing has been done. Nevertheless, the miserable state of the city's roads and the lack of basic urban infrastructure in Kabul remain shameful after years of involvement in Afghanistan by the world's richest nations.

Even today streets in the downtown area are full of potholes. Sidewalks for pedestrians are nonexistent on all but a few roads. Hundreds of thousands of Afghans have to put up with these hardships every day, lowering any pride they might have in their capital and constantly bolstering suspicions about foreigners' promises. Sidewalks are less important than drainage, sewerage and electricity, which large parts of Kabul are forced to go without. The capital city's population has quadrupled to well over three million since the 1980s, thanks to migration from insecure areas of the countryside, rural joblessness, returning refugees and natural growth. Every month new rows of poor mud-brick houses creep up the hillsides around the city center, the Central Asian equivalent of the favelas of Rio de Janeiro.

Jolyon Leslie, a South African architect who has worked in Afghanistan for a quarter of a century, sometimes for the UN and sometimes for NGOs, is one of Kabul's best-informed and hardest-working residents. He was intrigued by the country's beauty as well as its challenges when he passed through in the 1980s and is one of the few foreigners in the capital who have learned Dari. "People have become less tolerant of foreigners since about 2005. Before that they treated you as guests. It's a reaction to their out-of-touch Afghan Government," he told me in 2007. "There is more and more graft by the leadership and they seem unashamed. NGOs are perceived as complicit in this. People think we're just here to get money." His job at the time was director of the Agha Khan Trust for Culture, which was restoring mausoleums, mosques and sections of Kabul's Old City.

The trust was just putting the finishing touches to the restoration of Babur Gardens. In Asia's poorest capital city, which had no sewage system, no piped water, only a handful of hospitals and 60,000 street children, it might seem frivolous to spend close to two million dollars on re-creating a garden. Did a series of terraces and several rows of trees fill an urgent need? Wasn't this another example of foreign aid being wasted? "Not a bit of it," Leslie insisted. "On a Friday we get up to two thousand people in here, picnicking on the lawns, or enjoying the shade."

The garden's founder was the emperor Babur, who launched the Mughal dynasty. Even as he swept through northern India funding the designers who devised the stately arches that have become the subcontinent's best-known building style, Babur dreamed of this hill-side in Kabul. He wanted a garden to relax and eventually be buried in. Nowhere in India could match it.

When I first saw this ancient sloping garden in 1981 during the Soviet occupation, it was in a miserable state. The main attractions were an open-air swimming pool at the top, and a commanding view of the craggy hills that ring Kabul. Residents of the miserable shacks nearby had cut down most of the trees for firewood, and the grass was patchy. Even in that condition of scarce shade and dusty ground the garden provided weekend relief for families to lay out carpets, look for music channels on their transistor radios and get out their raisins and pomegranates. It was the largest park in Kabul. After the mujahedin captured the city in 1992 and started the internecine artillery battles that flattened several districts, the garden suffered particularly badly. Its irrigation pumps were destroyed and the remaining trees died.

But between 2004 and 2007, the Babur Gardens were transformed. Work started after consulting the community that lives on the steep hill-side above the garden. With cofunding from the German Government, the Agha Khan Trust paid for water pumps, storm drains and stone steps up the hill between the houses in place of uneven muddy paths. Thousands of local men were employed to remove the ruined swimming pool and erect a wall around the garden and the terraces. Working from Babur's original notes, the restorers planted walnut and plane trees on the outer edges of the site, and denser groups of mulberry, apricot, fig and almond trees near the garden's central axis.

The headstone on Babur's grave is scarred with mujahedin-era bullet holes, but the walls that once enclosed it were rebuilt according to nineteenth-century travelers' sketches, creating a tranquil precinct. The gardens' treasure is the white marble mosque dedicated during a visit to Kabul by Babur's descendant, Shah Jahan, in the same style as the Taj Mahal, which he built in Agra, India. The mosque is tiny but just as beautifully formed.

The resurrected garden offers Kabulis one of their few chances to escape the city's squalor and pollution, and also be reminded of their past. "This place is not just a garden," Leslie told me. "People are proud of it. It is part of their national identity."

Francesc Vendrell, the former UN envoy who negotiated with the Taliban and helped to organize the Bonn conference, is another Afghan enthusiast. He returned to Kabul as the European Union's special representative in Afghanistan. I found him in a pessimistic mood in June 2007. He had a list of complaints against the Karzai government and Western governments. He mentioned the appointment of bad provincial governors, widespread corruption including in the police and "ineffective reconstruction that hasn't reached ordinary people." Vendrell's only point of optimism sounded almost perverse. "I find it a sign of progress that the West now realizes Afghanistan is not a success," he told me. His hope was that they would change tactics and do better.

In fact, things continued to get worse. The toll of 629 Afghan civilians killed by coalition forces in 2007 showed a marked increase over the 2006 toll of 230. In 2008, it went up to 828. In response to mounting Afghan anger, General Stanley McChrystal, who became the commander of ISAF in June 2009, then tightened his troops' and pilots' rules of engagement to make sure they took greater care before shooting to kill. The toll of civilians killed by coalition forces dropped to 596 in 2009 and 440 in 2010. But the last figure was still almost double the death toll for 2006, showing how much the war had widened rather than diminished since the deployment of extra troops.

Evidence that these already high numbers of deaths did not tally with the truth emerged in a sensational way in July 2010. At the *Guardian*, we suddenly got access to an astonishing cache of official U.S. documents. They had apparently been leaked by Bradley Manning, a disillusioned young American soldier, to WikiLeaks, the international organization of activists who since 2006 had been publishing on their website hundreds of secret documents that whistle-blowers in governments, corporations and other powerful bodies took the risk to send them. On this occasion, WikiLeaks chose to share their new cache of documents with the *Guardian*. They consisted of intelligence reports on every military incident involving U.S. and allied troops in Iraq and Afghanistan, as well as a quarter of a million diplomatic cables sent between U.S. embassies around the world and the State Department in Washington. The Afghan logs, totaling 90,000 reports, covered the period from January 2004 to December 2009. They revealed, among a host of other important findings, that coalition forces in Afghanistan, mainly U.S. forces, had taken civilians' lives in dozens of incidents that had never previously been reported. In some cases, they had deliberately covered them up, or when the killings did emerge in the media at the time, U.S. forces knowingly gave false information in their public statements.

The treasure trove of documents, in particular the embassy cables, provided an extraordinarily vivid picture of the way governments operate. They also included devastatingly frank assessments by U.S. diplomats of foreign leaders and officials, complete with all their foibles and failings.

When I was first given access to them in the summer of 2010 in secure conditions in the *Guardian* office as part of a team of around a dozen specialist reporters, I was stunned by what I found myself reading. As I had covered the wars in Afghanistan and Iraq, my job was to concentrate on the diplomatic material on both conflicts as well as the war logs. Our team was faced with an extraordinary opportunity, mind-boggling in its implications. Not only were we privy to the biggest leak of official documents in world history. In case the British Government might seek court orders to send the police to seize the material, we had to hide, for more than three months, the fact we had this huge contemporary archive while we carefully read it, checked it against the public record, selected the most significant documents and wrote explanations of the background so that readers could evaluate their importance. None of our emails were supposed to contain any reference to the cache. Conversations about it in the office were forbidden except with the other reporters, editors and IT people who were working in secrecy together to index the mass of words and prepare our stories for publication.

Every journalist hopes at some point to be a fly on the wall at official meetings. Even off-the-record briefings when government officials claim to be reporting the true picture of what was said and decided, as with the sources on whom Bob Woodward's White House books rely, are vulnerable to the distortions of faulty memories and a natural desire by the informant to present his or her position in the best light. The leaked cables were much closer to the "real thing" in terms of truth, although they too consisted of diplomats' opinions in addition to facts and may in some cases have contained exaggerations and embellishments aimed at impressing officials higher up the chain.

The *Guardian* had managed to get exclusive access to the documents through fierce persistence by Nick Davies, one of its star investigative reporters who also broke the phone-hacking scandal at Rupert Murdoch's British tabloid, the News of the World. The editor-in-chief of WikiLeaks, Julian Assange, had spoken at a conference in Norway in March 2010 alongside David Leigh, another *Guardian* reporter. Afterward, Assange invited Leigh to his hotel room and revealed with excitement that he had been leaked a cockpit video from an AH-64 Apache helicopter as its U.S. crew killed a group of men in the Baghdad district of Sadr City. He showed Leigh the graphic footage of the killing in which two cameramen from the Reuters organization died and the occupants of a van which came to rescue the wounded were also shot. Leigh urged Assange to share the footage with the *Guardian,* arguing that it would have greater impact if it came out simultaneously on the *Guardian*'s website as well as on WikiLeaks. Assange said he would get back to Leigh but never did. Instead, he premiered the Apache video at the National Press Club in Washington on April 5, 2010. It made little impact, in part perhaps because of its tendentious title, "Collateral Murder."

Two months later, Nick Davies spotted a small news item saying that the *Daily Beast,* a U.S. news and opinion website, was reporting that Pentagon investigators were trying to track Assange down after military police arrested a U.S. soldier accused of leaking the Apache video. The *Daily Beast* was reporting that in addition to the video, the soldier was alleged to have given WikiLeaks 260,000 pages of confidential cables and intelligence assessments.

Intrigued, Davies started his own hunt for Assange, the elusive and mercurial founder of WikiLeaks, who traveled constantly but always refused to reveal his schedule. He declined to answer several email requests from Davies for a meeting until Davies caught up with him in a Brussels hotel on June 21, 2010. During a six-hour conversation Davies persuaded Assange, still upset by the minimal coverage for the Apache video, that collaboration with a major international paper with a reputation for high journalistic standards would vastly boost the impact of leaking the war logs and cables. Britain has weak laws to protect freedom of speech, and previous *Guardian* efforts to publish sensitive material had often been gagged by court injunctions, so Davies suggested it would be good to share the material with media organizations in the United States and continental Europe. He thought of the *New York Times,* the *Washington Post* and France's *Le Monde.*

Assange and Davies settled on offering it to the German news magazine *Der Spiegel* and the *New York Times.* They felt there was no way the Obama administration would dare to attack the most powerful Democratic-leaning U.S. newspaper. There was also the precedent of the paper's battle to get the right to publish the Pentagon papers during the Vietnam War. The agreement was made, Assange provided us with the CDs of leaked material and in the summer and autumn of 2010 we worked on collating it and selecting the most interesting elements. Initially, Assange would often come into the "bunker" at the *Guardian* where we were working and hover over our screens like a proud father as pregnancy with this amazing product approached its term. Volatile as always, he later fell out with the paper over a minor issue. But the agreement to share the sensational material stood, and WikiLeaks and the three news organizations released it in separate tranches, first the intelligence logs from the Afghan war, then similar logs from Iraq and finally the U.S. embassy cables.

Because of the ongoing war and the vast resources U.S. taxpayers were having to spend on it, public disclosure of the cables on Afghanistan and Pakistan was especially sensitive. The cables revealed U.S. Government anger over corruption and mismanagement in Kabul and the provinces, U.S. exasperation with Karzai, evidence of dishonesty by his family and doubts over the ability of the Afghan army and police to handle security. They also revealed disagreements between the United States and Britain over the war as well as secret U.S. efforts to split the Taliban. On Pakistan they showed how far its intelligence service had gone in aiding the Taliban.

On Afghanistan, the cables exposed corruption in a way that officials would never do on the record. In Helmand, for example, the Department of Agriculture, Irrigation and Livestock (DAIL) is one of the key agencies in an overwhelmingly rural province, but a November 2009 cable called it "corrupt and dysfunctional." Officials who are supposed to work in the district "sit in Lashkar Gah [the provincial capital], drink tea, and collect their salaries." Only 7 percent of DAIL's budget went to services for farmers, and the rest was eaten up by administrative salaries.

According to another cable in December 2009, "police corruption is perhaps the greatest impediment to the implementation of rule of law in Helmand." In Nad Ali/Marjah, where U.S. Marines conducted a major offensive against the Taliban in 2010, one cable said that "because of the revenue generated from the narcotics industry, the local police have long acted more as a private militia than a law enforcement body."

Two other cables provided graphic detail of colossal "wealth extraction" by the governors of two key provinces in eastern Afghanistan, areas where the Taliban get support because of massive distrust of local officials. Usman Usmani, governor of Ghazni, and Juma Khan Hamdard, governor of Paktiya, were accused of theft of public funds and extorting money from construction contractors on a regular basis. "The consistency and scope of explicit and detailed allegations lend veracity to charges that pervasive corruption defrauds the people of meaningful government services and significantly undermines popular support for the Afghan government."

The presidential election in 2009 offered Governor Usmani and several district governors he had appointed in the province ample opportunities for profit. Around $160,000 was dispatched to Usmani to pay local militias to guard polling places. According to the cables, Usmani kept $100,000 and divided the rest among the district governors, who produced fictitious lists of security guards. Since almost no voting took place in the districts, the American diplomat who wrote the cable said he doubted whether any guards worked at all. In another scam, land meant to be given to refugees from Ghazni who had decided to come home from Pakistan was divided into four sections. Two were on hillsides but the other two were on flat land near the city, ideal for building and development. The plots on the flat land were given to Ghazni government officials and their children as well as to fake refugees and then sold for profit.

In Paktiya province, the cables alleged that Governor Hamdard took bribes from contractors by sending in armed men who detained contractors at their job sites until the money was paid. According to one cable, "He allegedly has illicit contacts with insurgents in Parwan, Kunar, and Kabul provinces, as well as Pakistani intelligence (ISI) and Iranian operatives, through his business in Dubai."

The embezzling of cash was blatant. In one astonishing incident in October 2009, Karzai's then vice president, Ahmad Zia Massoud, was stopped and questioned in Dubai when he flew into the emirate with $52 million in cash, according to a cable sent by the U.S. ambassador in

Kabul, Karl Eikenberry. Massoud, the younger brother of the legendary anti-Soviet mujahedin leader Ahmad Shah Massoud, was detained by officials from the United States and the United Arab Emirates who were trying to stop money laundering. But the vice president was allowed to continue on his way without explaining where the money came from. The cable also detailed a colossal degree of capital flight from Afghanistan, often with the cash simply carried out on flights from Kabul to the UAE.

The WikiLeaks logs drew the veil away from a unit of U.S. Special Forces, known as Task Force 373, that was involved in extrajudicial killings and assassinations. Using bases in Kabul, Kandahar and Khost, it appeared to draw its troops from the Seventh Special Forces Group at Fort Bragg in North Carolina. Its mission was to hunt the more than 2,000 senior figures from the Taliban and al Qaeda whose details were held on a "kill or capture list," known in sanitized jargon as the Joint Prioritized Effects List, or JPEL.

A typical TF 373 engagement recorded in one of the war logs occurred on the night of Monday, June 11, 2007, when the unit set out with Afghan special forces to capture or kill a Taliban commander named Qarl ur-Rahman in a valley near Jalalabad. As they approached the target in the darkness, somebody shone a flashlight on them. A firefight developed, and the task force called in an AC-130 gunship, which strafed the area with cannon fire: "The original mission was aborted and TF 373 broke contact and returned to base. Follow-up Report: 7 x ANP KIA, 4 x WIA." In plain language, they discovered that the people they had been shooting in the dark were Afghan National Police (ANP) officers, seven of whom were now dead (KIA, killed in action) and four of whom were wounded.

The coalition issued a press release that referred to the firefight and the air support but failed to note that they had just killed or wounded eleven police officers. Evidently fearing that the truth might come out, to cover its back it added: "There was nothing during the firefight to indicate the opposing force was friendly. The individuals who fired on coalition forces were not in uniform." The involvement of TF 373 was not mentioned, and the story did not get out until WikiLeaks released the log.

Senior officers hurried to suppress the political damage. Next day, Lieutenant Colonel Gordon Phillips, commander of the Provincial Reconstruction Team, visited the provincial governor, Gul Agha Sherzai, who accepted that this was "an unfortunate incident that occurred among friends," according to the war log. They agreed to pay compensation to the bereaved families, and Phillips "reiterated our support to prevent these types of events from occurring again."

Yet, later that week, on June 17, as Sherzai hosted a *shura* (council meeting) of tribal leaders to reassure them about the safety of coalition operations, TF 373 launched a mission in Paktiya province against a notorious Libyan fighter, Abu Laith al-Libi. The unit was armed with a new weapon, known as the HIMARS (high-mobility artillery rocket system), a pod of six missiles on the back of a small truck. The plan was to launch rockets at targets in the village of Nangar Khel, where TF 373 believed Libi was hiding, and then to send in ground troops. The unit failed to find Libi but killed six Taliban fighters. When they approached the rubble of a school, however, they found the bodies of seven children who had been killed in the action. A U.S. medic cleared debris from the mouth of one child who was still alive and tried to revive him, but after twenty minutes the boy was pronounced dead. The coalition admitted in a press release that children had died but charged that Taliban fighters in the compound had used them as human shields. The war log had referred to an unnamed elder who "stated that the children were held against their will," but no one in the village said that there were any Taliban in the school where the children died. The rest of the press release was also misleading. It suggested that coalition forces had attacked the compound because of "nefarious activity" there when the reality was that they had gone there to kill or capture Libi. It made no mention of Libi, or of the mission's failure, which was revealed later by NBC News. Crucially, it failed to record that TF 373 had fired five of its six rockets, destroying the school and other buildings, before anybody had fired on them and that this looked like a mission to kill and not to capture. The war log made it clear that U.S. authorities wanted to suppress this fact. It was marked not only "secret" but also "Noforn," that is, not to be shared with the foreign elements of the coalition. "The knowledge that TF 373 conducted a HIMARS strike must be protected," it said.

The Taliban's revival is catalogued exhaustively in the war logs as the number of military incidents reported by U.S. intelligence grew consistently after 2004. The reports do not purport to provide reasons for the mounting local resistance to the U.S. occupation of southern Afghanistan. However, possible reasons are occasionally offered in the diplomatic cables such as the one, quoted above on Ghazni and Paktiya, which mentioned the decline in popular support for the government because of official corruption. Some analysts trace the Taliban resurgence to the availability of drug money and the growth of a narco-economy in southern Afghanistan. The argument is popular with ISAF officials, who say that the Taliban movement has virtually unlimited funds thanks to the increase in poppy production and the income they extract from it. At the village level, commanders of Taliban fighting units take 10 percent of farmer's poppy crop as tithe (*ushr*), according to Gretchen Peters, a U.S. journalist who worked for the Associated Press and ABC News. They give the farmers handwritten receipts. Each local commander pays a proportion to senior commanders. In addition, the Taliban control checkpoints to take taxes from drug smugglers and drug refineries located in the territories in which the Taliban operate. But commanders have other sources of funding and support in kind. They take tax in gasoline, mobile phone top-up cards and food. Captured Taliban commanders have told Afghan intelligence that proceeds from these various forms of ushr cover the bulk of their needs, including salaries for fighters. How much comes from drugs remains unclear.

Antonio Giustozzi takes a more cautious view of the role of the narcotics economy in funding the Taliban. He acknowledges that when the coalition promoted policies to eradicate poppy production, a move that upset many farmers, the Taliban in Helmand protected farmers. In Kandahar, they paid farmers compensation in exchange for support in resisting the government. He sees this as part of a wider Taliban strategy to exacerbate and exploit any differences between local people and the government. According to Giustozzi, the importance of drugs in financing the Taliban is limited for three reasons. The traffickers are unwilling to hand over too much of their profit. If large amounts of money were going to Taliban field commanders, they would be more independent, whereas, in fact, the Taliban remain remarkably cohesive. The final point is that the Taliban do not control the Afghan borders. Traffickers do not need their help in smuggling drugs into Pakistan, and it is more likely the traffickers bribe the border police and security forces.

The list of reasons why the Taliban revived is long: the feeling that the Pashtuns were marginalized by the Bonn agreement and the Karzai government which followed it; anger over the reappointment of mujahedin-era warlords; the deep sense of grievance felt by Pashtuns who were ethnically cleansed from their traditional communities in the north and west; interference by Pakistan, which trained and armed new recruits to the Taliban; the old Taliban leadership's desire for revenge; disappointment by ordinary people with the slow pace of reconstruction and development in Pashtun areas; anger at the corruption of local officials and ministers in the central government in Kabul; fury at the killing of civilians at intrusive house searches by foreign troops; and a patriotic desire to resist foreign occupation.

Most of these reasons were confirmed by a 2009 survey of what motivates people to join the Taliban, which the British government sponsored. Earlier studies had looked at the socioeconomic factors and found, unsurprisingly, that members of the armed opposition groups were angry young men. The presence in Afghan villages of large numbers of frustrated young males with few prospects of finding jobs and gathering the resources necessary to pay a bride's family and marry represented a stockpile of combustible material. Young returnees from Pakistan who grew up away from the influence of elders were particularly suitable for recruitment. The prospect of being issued a weapon and the status deriving from the role of mujahid were powerful motivations, just as they were in the Soviet period.

The 2009 study aimed at looking at the ideological reasons that brought men from this demographic group into becoming fighters, since by no means every young jobless male joined the Taliban or the Hezb-i Islami. An Afghan research organization, Cooperation of Peace and Unity (CPAU), undertook the field study, which involved interviewing members of armed groups. It found that most men are not radical or deeply religious when they join the Taliban or Hezb-i Islami. They may become radical afterward, depending on their commander. The survey also found that recruits were not primarily motivated by resentment over a perceived Western attack on Islam globally. There was little evidence of common cause being made with Islamist movements outside Afghanistan. What concerned them were two things: the presence and behavior of foreign forces in their country, and government corruption.

The government's failure to provide better basic services, such as health, water and sanitation, was not a major recruitment factor. These, of course, are the classic hearts-and-minds issues that coalition officials tend to stress, anxious not to admit that foreign occupation is a major problem. Taliban members recognized that the government provided services, albeit inadequately, in these areas as well as health care and education, and the Taliban provided none. So this was not an issue that made them take up arms.

By contrast, the government's poor record in providing security was important. "Although the Taliban don't deliver security (they attract fire by foreign forces and this endangers local populations) they do deliver justice. They are seen to do this reasonably well and attract support as a result," the study reported. Suspicion about coalition motives was also relevant: "Most respondents were unclear about what international forces are doing in Afghanistan. They do not believe it is to bring security, defeat the Taliban, support democracy or bring development, as they experience none of these. They argue the British are here for revenge and the Americans to pursue regional objectives."

The conclusion to be drawn from the study is that the best way to end the insurgency is not to pump money into the conflict zones through aid and development. If that had been tried in 2002 and 2003 right after the Taliban withdrew, it might have had some effect. Now it is too late as a game-changer. What has to be done is to reform Afghanistan's government system at local as well as central levels so as to reduce corruption and bribe-taking. Above all, there has to be a withdrawal of foreign forces. Their presence is the main recruitment tool, as it was during the Soviet period and throughout Afghan history.

[11] OBAMA AND KARZAI:
THE ODD COUPLE

"We must disabuse Karzai of the notion that we are just another imperialist force."

—Karl Eikenberry,
former U.S. Ambassador to Afghanistan

On June 30 and July 1, 2009, Karl Eikenberry, Washington's ambassador in Kabul, held as many as four separate meetings with President Hamid Karzai. A three-star general who had earlier been the supreme commander of U.S. forces in Afghanistan, Eikenberry found the series of encounters grueling and frustrating. The problem was not the issues, which were routine enough. The difficulty was the deep undercurrent of suspicion of U.S. motives and intentions running through Karzai's mind.

Back in the privacy of the fortified castle that the U.S. embassy in Kabul had become, Eikenberry wrote up his gloomy impressions and sent them to Hillary Clinton, his boss in Washington. Karzai would probably never break his habit of blaming the United States and its allies for Afghanistan's troubles and not addressing his own shortcomings, he told her. "Indeed," he wrote, "his inability to grasp the most rudimentary principles of state-building and his deep-seated insecurity as

a leader combine to make any admission of fault unlikely, in turn con-
founding our best efforts to find in Karzai a responsible partner."

There were two contrasting portraits of the Afghan president, the
ambassador wrote. "The first is of a paranoid and weak individual unfamiliar with the basics of nation-building and overly self-conscious that
his time in the spotlight of glowing reviews from the international community has passed. The other is that of an ever-shrewd politician who
sees himself as a nationalist hero who can save the country from being
divided by the decentralization-focused agenda of [his main challenger
in forthcoming presidential elections, Abdullah Abdullah], other political rivals, neighboring countries, and the US."

Translated into Russian, the Eikenberry cable could have mirrored
what Soviet ambassadors were telling their bosses in Moscow in the
early 1980s about Babrak Karmal, the difficult Afghan president they
had to deal with. He was constantly suspicious of the Kremlin's motives
and unsure of its loyalty. He too tried to present himself as a patriot
fighting a host of internal and external enemies, including the powerful
foreign state that was supposedly defending him.

The similarities between the two men were partly due to character.
Both Karzai and Karmal had volatile moods and stormy temperaments.
Karmal's successor, Mohammed Najibullah, by contrast, was tougher
and cooler. But the main reason for the similarity in the Karzai/Karmal
behavior was the almost identical context in which they both had to
operate as government leaders who were reliant on a foreign army for
their survival. Theirs was the classic relationship of colonial satrap and
metropolitan overlord, a balance that is inherently unstable because of
its inequality.

Karmal and Karzai were each handpicked by a superpower to preserve its strategic interests. They depended on that state economically,
politically and above all militarily. Without the imperial forces based in
Afghanistan, Karmal and Karzai knew they could not survive. Hence
their flashes of rage at the humiliation and impotence inherent in their

situation—and their desperate need to exert independence in small things, if not in anything that seriously mattered.

In Karzai's case, the cables sent to Washington and leaked to WikiLeaks in 2010 offered a fascinating insight into the unequal client-master relationship. The United States clearly had the upper hand in terms of leverage, but there was always the danger that Karzai, the ruler of a country that was theoretically sovereign, could ask them to leave. Eikenberry recognized the point in his cable to Clinton. "The danger of long-term damage to our relationship with and thus our influence over Karzai is real," he wrote, "but not irreversible."

The ambassador did not keep his concerns about Karzai within the close confines of secret cables to the State Department. The following day he told them to one of Karzai's ministers, a move that meant they were almost certain to get back to Karzai at some point. This may well have been Eikenberry's intention. "I told Interior Minister [Hanif] Atmar at our July 2 meeting that with his conspiratorial behavior, Karzai would run the risk of leaving USG [U.S. Government] interlocutors with the impression that we have accomplished very little here and that the Afghan government believed most of the failures lay with us," the ambassador informed the State Department. In the stern tones of a headmaster, he advised Atmar: "This is not a dialogue that will lead to an effective partnership. The US has been clear in its past shortcomings in Afghanistan, but we have yet to see Karzai admit to the serious shortcomings in his administration."

Atmar had been equally frank with the ambassador. He informed him of four "paranoias" that Karzai had. Karzai did not understand U.S. policy in the region. He suspected ulterior motives in its relationship with neighboring countries. He suspected the United States was contemplating a short-term strategy in Afghanistan that would result in disengagement within the next two years. And he felt the United States was plotting to divide and weaken Pashtuns on both sides of the Afghan-Pakistani border.

The trove of cables released by WikiLeaks that detail American conversations with Karzai number more than a hundred, most of them dating from 2008 and 2009. As well as firmly expressed lectures, they show the United States brandishing some tough weaponry in front of its client president. One was the threat of sanctions, if the United States did not immediately get its way or found Karzai and other Afghan ministers being resistant. The cables show how the threat was used. On December 14, 2009, Eikenberry went with Admiral Mike Mullen, the chairman of the Joint Chiefs of Staff, to see Karzai. It might be thought that the selection of ministers for Karzai's new cabinet would be a matter for Afghans to decide freely on their own without any American input. Not a bit of it. After various security matters had been discussed, Mullen left the meeting and the question of cabinet choices arose. Karzai mentioned that he wanted to keep the notorious Herati warlord, Ismail Khan, as minister of energy. Eikenberry made it clear he did not agree. The United States might be forced to cut its aid, he warned. Of course, he did not put his comment in the form of a threat. Instead, he fell back on the fact that, under the United States Constitution's separation of powers, aid has to be authorized by Congress. As though he and the Afghan president were on the same side, the ambassador told Karzai that the U.S. Congress could curb its funding for Afghanistan. Eikenberry had recently testified before Congress, and he told Karzai how they responded. "All members of the U.S. Congress expressed great concern over the long-term costs of Afghanistan, especially during the current financial crisis. If incompetent and corrupt ministers were appointed, it would provide a good reason for them to limit funding. The Ambassador urged Karzai to consider the tradeoffs," the cable reported him as saying. On this occasion the unmistakable threat failed to change Karzai's mind. He stuck with his decision to appoint Khan. The Afghan Parliament, which has the final word, then approved it.

On one occasion Karzai felt so angry that he threatened to go over to the armed insurgency. He told Parliament in April 2010 that he blamed foreigners for the election fraud the previous year. A member of Parliament from Nangarhar, Farooq Marenai, quoted him as saying, "If I come under foreign pressure, I might join the Taliban." Two other lawmakers confirmed the quote, saying Karzai repeated it twice.

At other times Karzai was ready to offer the United States huge concessions. Shortly before the 2009 presidential election, Eikenberry found the Afghan president "more coherent" and "less paranoid than in the past." Karzai offered to turn Bagram and Kandahar airfields, the biggest U.S. installations in Afghanistan, into permanent U.S. bases.

A permanent source of friction between Washington and Kabul was the issue of civilian casualties caused by U.S. air strikes. Karzai repeatedly urged the U.S. military to take more care. He was partly successful when General Stanley McChrystal, the U.S. commander in 2009 and 2010, changed the U.S. rules of engagement to give higher priority to the avoidance of casualties. But the issue was never resolved. General David Petraeus, who took over as ISAF commander in July 2010 after McChrystal resigned following a rash interview with *Rolling Stone* magazine, relaxed the rules again, though their text has not been disclosed and it is hard to be sure how big a change was made.

One of the worst arguments with Karzai erupted after an incident in February 2011 in Kunar province. Karzai's officials claimed that fifty people, including dozens of women and children, had been killed in a three- to four-day offensive in the Ghaziabad region, a particularly remote and inhospitable area of the country. U.S. officials said there was no evidence that a single civilian had died. After surveillance drones had tracked a number of insurgents, Apache helicopter gunships had been called in to strafe the area with rockets and Hellfire missiles. "I have reviewed the footage and found no evidence women and children were among the fighters. Again, no civilian structures were anywhere near where these engagements took place. It was at night and in very rugged terrain," said Rear Admiral Gregory J. Smith, the top U.S. military spokesman in Kabul. The provincial governor sent a fact-finding team to the valley next day. It came back with five children and two adults with burns and shrapnel wounds.

Because the discrepancy over casualties was so great, Petraeus visited Karzai and his National Security Council to explain the U.S. version of events. To their shock, Petraeus suggested that local people might have burned their own children to exaggerate claims of civilian casualties. "I was dizzy. My head was spinning. This was shocking," one participant at the meeting said afterwards. "Would any father do this to his children? This is really absurd."

Karzai's displeasure at the Kunar incident appears to have caused him to doubt the wisdom of the entire U.S. military operation in Afghanistan. On a visit to London three weeks later, he openly questioned the value of the counterinsurgency strategy and argued that the United States should stop operating in the Afghan countryside and focus on Pakistan. In an interview on British TV, he emphasized the fact that the United States was fighting two wars in his country, one against al Qaeda and a second against the Taliban and other insurgents. Only the first of these was legitimate, he said: "We would like military operations scaled down in Afghan villages because that's not where you can defeat terrorism or find terrorism," he said. "If the presence of international forces in Afghanistan is to fight an insurgency, that presence will not yield the result that we are seeking. That should be an Afghan matter and a matter for a political solution."

Four weeks later, he said he was giving the United States his "last warning" to stop air strikes on Afghan homes where suspected insurgents were hiding because the attacks killed so many civilians. "If they don't stop air strikes on Afghan homes," he said, "their presence in Afghanistan will be considered as an occupying force and against the will of the Afghan people. Such attacks will no longer be allowed." Leaders of regimes that depend on foreign armies are always trapped in an emotionally difficult position. In Karzai's case his temper and mood swings go back many years. His father singled him out among his five sons as "the mad one." His intellectual and at times dreamy quality finds expression in his passion for English poetry. He keeps a slim volume on his presidential desk. He also retains a schoolboy interest in railways. Afghanistan has only two functioning rail lines, short cross-border links to Turkmenistan and Uzbekistan, but Karzai would like to extend them as part of a grand scheme to enhance his country's role as the hub of Central Asia. He admires the two rusty steam engines that stand in the yard of the Kabul Museum, relics of the six-mile track that Amanullah Khan, the failed modernizer of the 1920s, laid down between Kabul and the European-style capital he started to build at Darulaman on Kabul's southwestern outskirts.

Not everyone who has met Karzai frequently are as unsympathetic as Eikenberry. Sherard Cowper-Coles, who served as Britain's ambassador in Kabul from 2007 to 2009 and a further year as the prime minister's special envoy to the region, describes the Afghan president as "neither hero nor zero." Cowper-Coles found him to be a man who preferred discussing strategy rather than detail. "He is a king, not a chief executive," he told me. "The Americans play him all wrong. They abuse him in public, then make up to him in private."

Ahmed Rashid, a Lahore-based veteran Pakistani analyst, is also relatively sympathetic to Karzai, having known him for almost thirty years. "From the Afghan president's perspective Washington treats him with a mixture of insult and confusion," he wrote in February 2011.

Karzai's relations with the White House were better under Bush than Obama. Even though Obama has given more sustained attention to Afghanistan than his predecessor, he seems to have spoiled his relationship with the Afghan president. Karzai is convinced that Obama and his entourage do not like or trust him. He was furious when General James Jones, Obama's national security adviser, briefed American reporters on Air Force One in March 2010 as it flew to Kabul that during his talks with Karzai, Obama was going to make a big issue of corruption. He was even more annoyed by Obama's next trip in early

December 2010. The U.S. president flew to Bagram air base to celebrate Thanksgiving with U.S. troops without coming on to Kabul at all. The official reason was that bad weather made it impossible for helicopters to fly but Obama should have ensured enough flexibility in his schedule to wait a few hours until it cleared. Karzai took the lack of a face-to-face meeting as a snub.

The Afghan president had not been happy with Bush for turning his attention to Iraq in 2002 and 2003. At that period, when the Taliban had not yet started their resurgence in a major way, more U.S. aid and development money in the Pashtun areas might have convinced Afghans that the forced departure of the Taliban had brought them visible benefit. Little was forthcoming. But Bush did maintain good relations with Karzai, telling him he could call at any time. Later, Bush used regular video conferences to keep in touch.

Karzai also liked the second U.S. ambassador, Afghan-born Zalmay Khalilzad, who had masterminded his emergence as president. Khalilzad's charm and astute use of flattery endeared him to Karzai, as did the ambassador's ability to get development money out of the U.S. administration and Congress. He ensured that the United States was fully behind the 2004 elections that put Karzai in power with a popular mandate for the first time. Khalilzad also broke the taboo of silence over Pakistan's behavior. He publicly criticized Pakistan's support for the Taliban and its failure to take action against their havens in the lawless frontier areas.

Obama's arrival in the White House changed the dynamic, according to Rashid. The new U.S. president was excessively demanding. He saw Afghanistan in terms of a laundry list of problems: nepotism, corruption, opium and heroin production and a lack of good governance. Richard Holbrooke, his adviser on Afghanistan and Pakistan, riled Karzai with his rude lectures. Six months later in August 2009 came Karzai's bid for a second term as president. This time, unlike 2004, Karzai felt the wind from Washington was icy. Instead of backing

him, the Americans did the correct thing of merely backing the process without saying publicly which candidate they supported. Karzai
suspected that Washington wanted to dump him in favor of his two
strongest-looking rivals, Abdullah Abdullah, the former foreign minister who was close to the Northern Alliance, and Ashraf Ghani, a
Pashtun who had spent years in Washington with the World Bank and
had served as Karzai's finance minister until 2004. Karzai believed the
United States was secretly funding the Abdullah campaign, according
to a WikiLeaks cable from Eikenberry.

Another cable revealed that the U.S. embassy was hearing sugges-
tions of deep anxiety in the Karzai camp. Before the election, they were
wondering about their personal safety and the potential need to flee
and seek asylum in case he lost. Francis Ricciardone, the U.S. deputy
ambassador in Kabul, cabled to Washington in August 2009: "Our contacts among Karzai's insiders report that Karzai's side is in some disarray. Karzai family and friends reportedly are keeping their families and
their funds out of the country and two of Karzai's brothers are preparing US refugee petitions. Their personal protection if violence occurs is
probably not the army, but instead the network of private security companies—especially the Asia Security Group, owned by Karzai's family."

To ensure his re-election Karzai and his supporters resorted to massive ballot-rigging. The so-called Independent Election Commission,
which was run by Karzai loyalists, set up around 1,500 ghost polling
places in areas of high insecurity where monitors and opposition agents
could not go. The polling centers were fictitious but election agents
working for Karzai were able to "count" hundreds of thousands of
votes which had allegedly been cast there. The fraud was clumsy and in
some of the centers Karzai won every single one of the supposed votes.
Karzai's opponents' suspicions were naturally raised.

Their complaints might have been brushed aside if Peter Galbraith,
a former US ambassador to Croatia who had become the UN's deputy
special representative to Afghanistan in March 2009, had not taken up

the issue publicly. Before the election he had already raised the question of the ghost centers with Kai Eide, a former Norwegian diplomat who served as his UN boss in Kabul. The UN was mandated to support Afghan institutions but Eide failed to act decisively to correct the threat of fraud. When the fraud became apparent after the election he persuaded the UN Secretary General Ban Ki-Moon to sack Galbraith. The row focused international scrutiny on the fraud and embarrassed Karzai as well as the UN.

It further soured the atmosphere between Karzai and Washington. Karzai was convinced he had enough votes to have won even if some votes were disputed but the Americans insisted the election must go to a second round after the Election Complaints Commission discarded the fraudulent ballots and reported that no one had crossed the 50 percent threshold. When Karzai reluctantly agreed to a second round, the United States further blotted its copybook in his eyes by urging Abdullah Abdullah, the runoff candidate, not to drop out. Eikenberry argued that the process had to be gone through to the end for the sake of democracy.

The chaos over the election and Karzai's anger almost led Eikenberry to lose faith in the war. During the administration's review of U.S. strategy in Afghanistan in the autumn of 2009, he sent two cables to Washington that clearly stated Karzai was no longer America's best partner. Separately from the later WikiLeaks cache, they were leaked to the *New York Times*. "President Karzai is not an adequate strategic partner," Eikenberry wrote. "He continues to shun responsibility for any sovereign burden, whether defense, governance or development. He and much of his circle do not want the US to leave and are only too happy to see us invest further. They assume we covet their territory for a never-ending 'war on terror' and for military bases to use against surrounding powers'."

Disappointed with the Afghan ruling elite, Eikenberry urged Obama not to send more forces. His fear was that enlarging the U.S.

investment of troops and treasure would only increase Afghan dependence and thereby delay a U.S. withdrawal.

It was a remarkable cable. It put him in the same category as the
Soviet generals who had advised Gorbachev that their Afghan allies,
Karmal and his successor, Najibullah, were unreliable, uncommitted
and unwilling to shoulder the responsibility of fighting and that therefore the war was unwinnable. No other U.S. military man took this view.
But Eikenberry had unrivaled experience. As U.S. senior commander,
he had seen the terrain on which U.S. troops were operating. As ambassador in Kabul, he understood the nature of Afghanistan's government
and the poor caliber of the men running it. "There is no political ruling
class that provides an overarching national identity that transcends local
affiliations and provides reliable partnership," Eikenberry wrote. "Even
if we could eradicate pervasive corruption, the country has few indige-
nous sources of revenue, few means to distribute services to its citizens,
and, most important, little to no political will or capacity to carry out
basic tasks of governance." Eikenberry survived the embarrassment of
having his cables disclosed, perhaps because they agreed with the views
of Vice President Joe Biden, who was also a war skeptic. But Karzai
found Eikenberry's survival insulting. It implied Obama cared little for
his feelings. He also felt angry at not being consulted during Obama's
strategy review and was stunned when the U.S. president announced
that some troops would start leaving Afghanistan in July 2011.

The Afghan president got on better with General McChrystal, who
flew him around the southern front in his helicopter to show him the
war and what U.S. troops were doing. Some leaders might have found
this patronizing and almost demeaning, as though he was the visitor in
someone else's country. Karzai appreciated that the experienced and
respected McChrystal sat cross-legged on the carpet during meetings
with tribal elders.

Although President Karzai relied on the U.S. military, he disap-
proved of the American and other foreign contractors. According to

the Pentagon in 2010, some 82 percent of the 112,000 private contractors employed by the U.S. military in Afghanistan were foreign. Other embassies and governments also employed hundreds of foreigners as security guards. In August 2010 Karzai announced he wanted to terminate their contracts. In this he was reflecting the views of most Afghans, who found their behavior high-handed, trigger-happy and arrogant. They were the ugly face of the occupation, a permanent reminder that Afghanistan's sovereignty was undermined. This was a difference from the Soviet occupation, which appeared more disciplined and less invasive of Afghan sensibilities. And the Soviets, of course, had never used private security forces.

Karzai's family's corruption was a major factor in spoiling his image, both in Afghanistan and Washington. According to a U.S. embassy cable, Umar Daudzai, Karzai's chief of staff, told the Americans he was "ashamed" of an incident in which the Afghan president pardoned five border policemen who had been caught transporting 124 kilograms of heroin in an official vehicle. The Americans assumed Karzai had freed the men because their extended family had contributed to his reelection campaign. Speaking generally about the release of drug traffickers, Mohammad Daud, deputy minister of interior with responsibility for tackling illegal drugs, is quoted in another cable as telling Anthony Wayne, the embassy's director for development and economic affairs, that he "some members of the president's family had been receiving money from those seeking the pardon and release of convicted traffickers."

Daud described the release of drug traffickers as a "big psychological blow" to him and the country's counter-narcotics police force. Masoon Stanekzai, a senior government official charged with disarming militias and helping Taliban defectors, is reported to have feared for his own life after defying Karzai's many demands to remove two provincial election candidates in Helmand from a blacklist. They were known drug traffickers and members of illegal militias.

Stanekzai told the U.S. embassy he had received threatening visits from the men, who on one occasion brought along a fifty-four-man militia that Stanekzai was supposed to have disbanded. Stanekzai thought Karzai was involved. According to the cable, "Karzai himself has made no overt threats but he [Stanekzai] believes the president is behind a litany of visits Stanekzai has had by known warlords, including the two narcotics traffickers." The embassy described the incident as "an example of Karzai meddling in the elections by using intimidation to protect known thugs."

In July 2010, a U.S.-led Afghan anti-corruption force arrested one of Karzai's closest advisers, Mohammed Zia Salehi, the head of the National Security Council, on charges of corruption. A phone tap allegedly heard him soliciting a car for his son as a bribe, in exchange for impeding an American-backed investigation into an Afghan company suspected of smuggling dollars out of the country. Apparently to spite the Americans, Karzai intervened and had Salehi released.

Other cables paint an unflattering picture of the president's half-brother, Ahmed Wali Karzai. They show that the United States was convinced the younger Karzai, a senior figure in Kandahar, was corrupt. The Nexus-Corruption Leadership Board, cochaired by a U.S. diplomat in the Kabul embassy and a U.S. intelligence general, met in February 2010 to discuss what measures to take "against criminal and corrupt Afghan officials in an effort to change their behavior ... and end tacit American support for corrupt Afghan officials." The aim was to show that the United States, often criticized for ignoring allegations that senior Afghan officials were involved in drug dealing and money laundering, was going "to change its policy on corruption." The cable said the board would recommend various measures, "including possible law enforcement actions against three prominent malign actors in southern Afghanistan, Abdul Razziq, Ahmed Wali Karzai, Asadullah Sherzad." Apart from prosecutions, the board would consider shunning corrupt officials, denying them photo opportunities with senior U.S. officials,

including visiting senators and representatives, refusing any exchanges
of gifts and blocking them from U.S.-funded travel, training or speaking
engagements.

A cable recounting a meeting with him at the end of September
2009 called Ahmed Wali Karzai corrupt. "While we must deal with
AWK as the head of the [Kandahar] Provincial Council, he is widely
understood to be corrupt and a narcotics trafficker," it said. Another
cable from Anthony Wayne, headed "Kandahar Politics complicate US
objectives in Afghanistan," described him as "the Kingpin of Kandahar."
Wayne told the State Department:

> It is important to understand the dynamics of political power and
> how fundamental Kandahar is to the fortunes of the Karzai regime.
> It is from Kandahar that President Karzai's claim to national
> legitimacy originates and from the province that the Karzai family's
> position as a semi-modern aristocracy stems. As the kingpin of
> Kandahar, the President's younger half-brother Ahmed Wali Karzai
> (AWK) dominates access to economic resources, patronage, and
> protection. Much of the real business of running Kandahar takes
> place out of public sight, where AWK operates, parallel to formal
> government structures, through a network of political clans that use
> state institutions to protect and enable licit and illicit enterprises. A
> dramatic example is the Arghandab river valley, an agriculturally rich
> and heavily populated district strategically located at the northern
> gate to Kandahar City, where the President's direct intervention in
> the Alikozai tribal succession increased Karzai's political dominance
> over two of the most valuable resources in Kandahar—fertile land and
> water. The tribal power structure in Kandahar seriously complicates
> our efforts to bring formal justice and modern governance to the region.

In his cable, Wayne described the province's tribal structure and said
President Karzai's true political base was the Durrani Popolzai tribe,
which he leads. "In Kandahar, political clans consisting of personal,

tribal, marriage and economic alliances engage in balance of power competition and cooperation," Wayne said. As for AWK, "the overriding purpose that unifies his political roles as chairman of the Kandahar provincial council and the President's personal representative to the South is the enrichment, extension and perpetuation of the Karzai clan, and along with it their branch of the Popolzai tribe. This applies equally to his entrepreneurial and his alleged criminal activities. AWK derives authority and legitimacy from his relationship to President Karzai, from the relative discipline and elite position of the Popalzai tribe and from his access to resources."

The region's clan network had "a caste-like division of labor. The Popalzai occupy the leadership pinnacle. The Barakzai, with Gul Agha Sherzai as their leader, compete for power and business, which includes, for example, contracting at Kandahar Air Field and transport on Highway 4 from the Pakistan border at Spin Boldak. The Noorzai occupy key positions in the ANSF [Afghan National Security Forces] and are the traditional racketeers (with ties to narcotics trafficking). The Achekzais along the border are the traditional smugglers, and the Alikozai are the traditional warriors." The cable ends with a damning conclusion: "In a land of popular strongmen, AWK is widely unpopular in Kandahar, because he rules exclusively rather than inclusively; he is not perceived as caring about the population at large but rather, as a traditional Pashtuns Khan using his power to 'feed his tribe'."

Describing a February 2010 meeting with Ahmed Wali Karzai, a U.S. diplomat reported that he was "eager to engage and rarely stopped talking in the two hour meeting. While he presented himself as a partner to the United States and is eager to be seen as helping the coalition, he also demonstrated that he will dissemble when it suits his needs. He appears not to understand the level of our knowledge of his activities, and that the coalition views many of his activities as malign, particularly relating to his influence over the police." In July 2011 Ahmed Wali Karzai was assassinated inside his fortified Kandahar compound by Sardar Mohammed, his long-time security chief. It was suggested he may have been acting on the Taliban's behalf. The assassin was shot by other guards and his body hanged in a public square in Kandahar in the same brutal way that the body of Najibullah had been paraded in 1996.

In spite of the massive flaws in Hamid Karzai's record, the United States could not easily remove him. He had won twice in national elections that, for all their problems, were certified by the UN and independent observers as fair. Washington could not behave as Moscow had done with Babrak Karmal and bully him into resigning on health grounds. The nearest the Americans might get would be to do what the Kremlin did to Najibullah in 1992: persuade him to go in order to make way for a coalition government as part of a peace deal.

Pending that possible outcome, Karzai seemed doomed to stay in office until the end of his second term in 2014. The United States would have to work with him, just as much as Karzai would have to work with Washington, however uncomfortable each side felt about the arrangement. There were times when each side wondered whether they could afford to break the link. "Can you manage without the United States?" the U.S. embassy reports Karzai asking his defense minister at one point, with the apparent idea of telling the United States to leave and seeing if Afghan security forces could run the counterinsurgency campaign against the Taliban on their own. The minister said he could not. Washington was in a similar bind. They could not manage without him, just as he could not manage without them. There was no obvious successor to Karzai.

The relationship was beautifully illustrated in a cable Eikenberry sent to Holbrooke on November 3, 2009. It described the tragic absurdity of Afghanistan's position, in part a sovereign state and in part a puppet in the hands of foreign occupiers. The cable outlined the U.S. embassy's recommendation for a conference of foreign ministers to be held in Kabul a few months after Karzai's inauguration in early 2010. Unlike earlier international conferences on Afghanistan that took place abroad, "the Kabul setting is an essential backdrop to our efforts to emphasize Afghan ownership of their destiny; the venue will capture their people's pride, imagination, and sense of national ownership."

Eikenberry went on to say that the conference "should be conditioned on the new Karzai government enacting several key steps that show a real commitment to reform: the appointment of a clean and competent cabinet; detailed planning for the implementation of elements of the inauguration speech . . . ; taking action against high-ranking officials accused of corruption; and avoidance of previous missteps such as pardoning narco-traffickers, terrorists or other serious criminals."

The irony of using a conference to emphasize Afghan "ownership" of the country's future only so long as it was conditioned on Karzai fulfilling U.S. demands seemed to be lost on Eikenberry. He was, after all, Washington's overlord in Kabul, and those who help to run empires usually fail to see the world from a different perspective.

[12] TALKING TO THE TALIBAN: HOW THE WAR ENDS

"Every war has to end with talks and negotiations. Afghans need peace like oxygen."

—SHUKRIA BARAKZAI,
MEMBER OF THE AFGHAN PARLIAMENT

THE NOTION OF American exceptionalism is as old as the writings of Alexis de Tocqueville, the first analyst to describe the United States' significant differences from European states. He pointed to its love affair with liberty, its deep-seated commercialism, its revolutionary birth as a "new nation" and its zeal for technological modernization sitting alongside widespread religiosity.

The concept was quickly taken up by American politicians to highlight what they saw as their country's manifest destiny and its special role as the model for an envious world. Over time dozens of other writers, American and foreign, added to the list of America's unique attributes.

Almost invariably they focused on American life within its shores. Yet there is one important "exception" that relates to foreign policy. The United States has had the good fortune to crown almost every war it has fought with victory. The First World War ended with Germany's defeat, the second with two enemies' unconditional surrender. America's Civil War ended with the South's defeat and surrender.

Only two wars came to a halt with something less than victory, and they are not remembered in the United States with any enthusiasm. In Korea the belligerents reached an armistice that was never followed by full-scale talks, as a result of which the two Korean states still face each other today across a tense demilitarized zone without a peace treaty. The Vietnam War concluded after five years of negotiations in Paris, but the peace accords were violated, mainly by North Vietnam, which sent its forces into the south across the cease-fire lines. Two years after the Paris accords, America's South Vietnamese allies were defeated, leaving U.S. diplomats to make a humiliating escape by helicopter from the roof of the Saigon embassy in full view of the cameras.

This tarnished history of peace talks and cease-fire agreements appears to have imbued U.S. decision makers and the American electorate with a deep prejudice against them. Americans tend to see negotiations as defeatist, unnecessary and prone to disaster because the other side will always obstruct or cheat. Since freedom must not be compromised, the notion that a war to safeguard and spread liberty should give way to talks sounds weak and unworthy of a nation that is the world's sole superpower and whose sacred self-appointed mission is to prevail.

The U.S. experience runs against that of the rest of the world, where it is generally acknowledged that a war may end more quickly and at less cost through political compromise and agreement. The belligerents on all sides realize that victory is impossible, the war is essentially a stalemate and the demands for which they took up arms are not going to be achieved in full. It may take years of bloodshed and destruction to reach this judgment, but in the end the hard truth takes hold that something less than the other side's defeat will have to be accepted.

That was true in recent times in El Salvador as well as Bosnia, in Sudan as well as Northern Ireland. The British, in particular, have a

long history of being forced to make deals with resistance groups, guerrilla armies and opposition politicians whom they had once detained,
in India, Cyprus, Kenya and Rhodesia/Zimbabwe, to name just a few.

Afghanistan has become the latest test of the proposition that civil
wars are more likely to end in long-term peace if there is an inclusive
political settlement. Thirty-five years of fighting have seen several
changes of regime in Kabul but no end to war. No group has been able
to take control of the whole country and douse the embers of armed
resistance for the long term. They have always flared up again.

Efforts by the Kremlin to seek a political deal with the mujahedin
in the 1980s foundered on their intransigence, backed by Pakistan and
the United States. Similar efforts by the Najibullah regime suffered the
same fate. After the Taliban retreat in 2001, the Bonn conference of
Afghan leaders was meant to usher in an era of peace. It came to nothing, in large part because the Taliban were excluded from negotiations,
and the short-lived peace dividend was not spread to the Pashtun.

Whether the Obama administration is prepared to put serious
backing behind peace talks between the Kabul government and the
insurgents and take a direct role itself in ending the country's civil war
has become the biggest U.S. foreign policy issue of 2011 and 2012. It is
likely to play a major role in Obama's reelection campaign. A majority
of Americans have turned against the war, and they want to know how
soon U.S. troops are going to be withdrawn and whether it will be done
with honor. Taking a longer perspective Afghans want to know whether
the withdrawal will bring them the peace that eluded them when the
Russians left. The dramatic attack on Osama bin Laden's Pakistani compound by U.S. Navy SEALS on May 2, 2011, and the death of the iconic al
Qaeda leader strengthened the pressure for an early end to U.S. involvement in Afghanistan. It gave Americans a sense that an important battle
for justice had been won and that to continue the fight against al Qaeda
required action in Pakistan rather than Afghanistan. President Karzai
made the same point emphatically a few hours after bin Laden's killing

was announced. The al Qaeda leader's discovery in Pakistan showed the West's entire military strategy was wrong, Karzai said. Speaking in front of a packed hall in his palace in Kabul, he declared, "Year after year, day after day, we have said the fighting against terrorism is not in the villages of Afghanistan, not among the poor people of Afghanistan. The fight against terrorism is in safe havens. It proves that Afghanistan was right."

In light of the historic difference between British and U.S. attitudes to negotiating with colonial resistance movements, it was not a surprise that the first senior Western politician to propose talks with the Taliban was David Miliband, Britain's then foreign secretary. He deliberately chose a venue in the United States to air the proposal. "The idea of political engagement with those who would directly or indirectly attack our troops is difficult," he said in a speech at the Massachusetts Institute of Technology in March 2010. "We have no more right to betray our own values than those of the Afghan people who pray that the Taliban never come back. But dialogue is not appeasement and [giving the Taliban] political space is not the same as veto power or domination."

At the time, Miliband's argument received a frosty reception in Washington. Clinton was on record as a strong critic of the Taliban's treatment of women and was seen as a hawk on the issue of the Taliban's future. In London, Miliband's views were also shelved by his colleagues. They were not taken up by Prime Minister Gordon Brown or by his successor, David Cameron, who won the May 2010 election. The new British Government echoed the line, pushed by Obama and Karzai for several months, that any political solution to the Afghan war had to be based on the Afghan Government's reintegration and reconciliation program, which offered incentives for Taliban leaders and fighters, either individually or in groups, to lay down their arms and return to civilian life. Launched at an international conference in London in January 2010, the program was a relaunch, or indeed a re-relaunch of a program that had been repeatedly tried since the end of Taliban rule in 2001 and with minimal success. It amounted to little more than an invitation to surrender.

Up to 2007, only twelve of the 142 senior Taliban figures who had been put on the United Nations sanctions list as people subject to travel bans and asset freezes had applied for amnesty. They included men like Arsala Rahmani, the former Taliban minister for Islamic affairs who returned to Kabul and was appointed by Karzai as a senator (see Chapter Six for more on his views). Another was Abdul Salam Zaeef, the former Taliban ambassador in Islamabad, who had spent four years in the U.S. prison at Guantánamo. Important though these men had been when the Taliban ruled Afghanistan, neither of them, nor any of the other ten who came back to Kabul, were involved in the post-2001 insurgency. The reintegration program also failed to attract more than a handful of active middle-level Taliban commanders. So there was no reason to expect that the new reintegration program, announced with great fanfare at the London conference in 2010, would have better success.

In theory, there was supposed to be a difference between reintegration and reconciliation. The former offered incentives such as vocational training to young men or help for community projects in a village if foot soldiers or field commanders from that village left the Taliban, put down their arms and went home. (The government did not want to pay individual Taliban for stopping fighting since this would look like rewarding people for having been insurgents.) The latter was geared to more senior people whose opposition to the Karzai government rested on political disagreement. In practice both parts of the policy amounted to the same thing. Like reintegration, reconciliation was a one-sided offer from the government to the insurgents. There was no direct promise that the government was prepared to make political concessions to the insurgents. Indeed, in diplomatic circles at the time, there was much talk of a distinction between so-called reconcilables and irreconcilables. Some Taliban, it was argued, could be won to the government side. Others like Mullah Omar and the core of the last Taliban government, now in refuge in Quetta, were considered to be too extreme to be worth approaching. Western analysts compared the reconciliation strategy to the successful U.S. effort led by Petraeus when he was U.S. commander in Iraq in 2007 and 2008, where the armed Sunni resistance split into pro– and anti–al Qaeda forces and Washington helped to widen the split by making cash payments to the latter group, known as al Sahwa or the Awakening. American officials continued to repeat the mantra that they knew there had to be a political solution to the war. But it was a hollow claim. "Talking to the Taliban" was not intended as a genuine move toward negotiations. It was a weapon of war and a counterinsurgency tool, designed to undermine the Taliban by encouraging defections and breaking the movement into more easily defeatable fragments.

As I went through the diplomatic cables obtained by WikiLeaks and helped the rest of the *Guardian* team select which ones to highlight, I found a mass of evidence that the reconciliation strategy in Afghanistan was a device to split the Taliban and that the U.S. and Afghan governments' dominant strategy was to step up pressure on the Taliban. A message from the U.S. embassy in Kabul to Washington in January 2010 summarized a conversation between Karzai and Richard Holbrooke, the U.S. special representative for Afghanistan and Pakistan, shortly before the London conference. Karzai told Holbrooke that previous efforts to persuade Taliban leaders to defect had not worked. The U.S. and Afghan governments must avoid "the same vicious cycle of trial, failure, trial, partial success," he said. What was vitally needed, he insisted, was that Pakistan be brought on board. As long as it gave the top Taliban leaders safe haven, there was no chance of success.

Karzai revealed in another cable that he had recently approached Saudi Arabia for cash to pay lower-level Taliban commanders to switch sides. The Saudi Government responded favorably and offered to give defectors free trips for the hajj, the pilgrimage to Mecca.

Barnett Rubin, the U.S. Afghan expert who had become an adviser to Holbrooke and attended the meeting with Holbrooke, approved the idea, saying it would "offer a strong religious motivation and undercut the Taliban. . . . Holbrooke assured Karzai that Afghanistan's current reintegration draft policy has the backing of the U.S. and seems to have strong Gulf buy-in, which Karzai flagged as crucial to psychologically undermining the Taliban. The U.S. would not prevent this from happening as it had in the past, Holbrooke said; on the contrary we plan to help fund the plan."

A few days earlier, the Afghan president was explicit about surrender. He told visiting U.S. senators that reconciliation was not a matter of negotiations with the Taliban but of getting them to give up, according to another cable from the U.S. embassy in Kabul. To reinforce the point to his American partners, he mentioned the American Civil War as a useful analogy. "Karzai said he could refer to American history and the 'lenient' terms extended to members of the Confederate Army, including General Robert E. Lee, when they surrendered," a cable reported. Reconciliation would not just be offered to Taliban foot soldiers but to senior leaders who gave up. But there was no question of offering reconciliation to Mullah Omar, the cable reported him as saying.

Karl Eikenberry, the U.S. ambassador in Kabul, had doubts about the plan, according to a secret cable he sent to Washington. But these did not include criticism of its basic thrust of rejecting negotiations with the top Taliban. Rather, his doubts focused on the reaction of non-Pashtuns. The powerful Tajik and Uzbek leaders in Karzai's government who had always been fiercely anti-Taliban needed to be convinced that Karzai was not selling out to the Taliban. There must be "buy-in from non-Pashtuns" who might otherwise be suspicious of what might look like a separate peace between Karzai, a Pashtun, and the largely Pashtun Taliban, Eikenberry's cable said. He warned the Afghan Government that the United States would withhold aid money for the reintegration strategy if Kabul stepped over Washington's "red lines."

The leaked cables showed that Obama's most senior advisers were initially united on the issue of not negotiating with top Taliban. One message summarized a conversation Holbrooke had with the Indian foreign secretary, Nirupama Rao, on January 18, 2010. "There will be no power-sharing with elements of the Taliban," Holbrooke stressed. He explained this was because of their "unpalatable social programs" and their links with al Qaeda.

General Petraeus, who had taken charge of U.S. Central Command after leaving Iraq, was also shown to be a firm opponent of any deal with Mullah Omar. As the architect of the surge of extra U.S. troops to Iraq in 2007 he prided himself on having reduced Sunni violence. The claim was inflated because there were several reasons, unconnected to the surge, which explained the lessening of Sunni-Shia tensions and the splits among Sunni tribal, religious and political leaders between supporters and opponents of al Qaeda in Iraq. But, as the focus switched to Afghanistan, Petraeus continued to fight the last war, like many another general in history. He hoped to split the Taliban just as he imagined he had split the Sunni resistance in Iraq.

In January 2009, according to a leaked cable, Petraeus in his capacity as Centcom commander visited Kazakhstan for a meeting with its president, Nursultan Nazarbayev. When Nazarbayev suggested it would be highly dangerous to take reconciliation so far as to bring the Taliban into the Afghan Government, Petraeus agreed. "We have no illusion that Mullah Omar could ever join the government," he told the Kazakh leader. The White House confirmed the point in March 2009 in its White Paper, "A New Strategy for Afghanistan and Pakistan": "Mullah Omar and the Taliban's hard core that have aligned themselves with al Qaeda are not reconcilable and we cannot make a deal that includes them."

Was this also the view of Afghans? With the Taliban revival continuing to gain strength, I had my first chance to test the mood in Kabul in March 2010. This time I was in the Afghan capital for the BBC rather than the *Guardian*. The BBC World Service Trust had invited me to take three weeks out to give professional training to some of their Afghan journalists. The team of roughly forty-five scriptwriters and broadcasters included almost twenty women. Working closely with them gave me the opportunity to hear what educated Afghan women felt about the controversial idea of having their government negotiate with the Taliban. They were the people who had suffered most from the Taliban's brutal form of male chauvinism.

During the first weeks after the Taliban came to power in Kabul in 1996, I had heard a surprising number of women say they welcomed the Taliban victory because their families were at last safe from the shells and rockets that rained down during the civil war. This more than made up for the Taliban's repression of women, they argued. Many changed their views later, but at the time the calculus of security-versus-rights was coming down in favor of the former.

My interviews in Kabul in March 2010 suggested a similar calculus was emerging again. It was a remarkable change since 2007 when the Taliban comeback was still young and defeating them was the watchword of the day. There had been a tectonic shift in Afghanistan's public mood since then. It was prompted by a host of factors: growing disappointment with Western governments and the ineffectiveness of billions of dollars in aid that seemed to go nowhere except into the bank accounts of foreign consultants or local politicians; a sense that foreigners were deliberately prolonging the new civil war; grief and despair over the mounting toll of civilian casualties, many caused by U.S. air strikes; rising nationalist anger and a feeling of humiliation; and a desire to return to an Afghan consensus in which Afghans found their own solutions.

Over two afternoons, I sat down over tea with six women journalists from the group I was training. In varying degrees they all favored negotiations. They did not want their names used, so I will identify them by the letters A to F. A was a Pashtun. She was already a refugee in Pakistan when the Taliban took over, having fled in 1993 at the height of the civil war. She only returned to Kabul after the Taliban were overthrown. B, also a Pashtun, lived under Taliban rule. She felt the United States, Pakistan and other foreigners were manipulating the war and even had the elusive Taliban leader, Mullah Omar, under their influence. I encountered this sense of the Taliban as puppets, even victims, in numerous other conversations with Afghan men as well as women.

"It's an excuse for foreigners to occupy Afghanistan and stay here," said A. "That's why the war continues. It's not a war against the Taliban. It's a war for their own objectives." B said Taliban rule had positive as well as negative sides. As a woman, you couldn't work, "but if you were walking in the street no one could kidnap you. We felt safer than now, when there are all these security guards and other people with guns who can abduct a woman at any time."

C, a Tajik, mentioned bin Laden. "There is something going on behind the curtain. It's politics. They could find Saddam, but they can't find bin Laden. When they wanted to find Saddam, they did." C was thirteen when the Taliban captured Kabul and sent all schoolgirls back home. Because of a health emergency her father took the family to Karachi for a year. She recalled her fear when a Taliban militiaman stopped their taxi on the way and found a pinup of a young woman stuck to the back of the mirror. He beat the driver mercilessly. When the family returned to Kabul, she could not go to school for four years. Yet, in spite of these bitter memories she now supported negotiations with the Taliban.

D, another Pashtun, spent the Taliban period as a refugee in Pakistan. "When we were there, we were afraid of the Taliban. I came back here in 2002 and just didn't want the Taliban to exist," she told me. "Then I began to realize they are also Afghans and Pakistan is using them." A key question was whether the Taliban leadership's eight years out of power have changed their thinking. Would they really try to turn the clock back for women a second time? E, a Pashtun, answered that there were always good and bad Taliban. "Some were educated and religious, but others joined them from Pakistan, and then criminals piled in." F, a Tajik, said she had noticed Taliban members presenting themselves as nationalists more than Islamists these days. "There are two kinds of Taliban: those who want a strict implementation of Sharia law, and those who want to get rid of U.S. forces," she said.

I visited Shukria Barakzai, one of the most remarkable independent woman members of the Afghan Parliament, in her home in the Kabul district of Wazir Akbar Khan. She was regularly approached by journalists and diplomats, and I had to wait my turn in the hall before she took me into her reception room. Exhibiting extraordinary courage, she stayed in Afghanistan throughout the Soviet occupation, the four-year rule by mujahideen warlords and the Taliban period. She found the mujahedin time the worst. She lost a son and a daughter during their shelling of Kabul. Her antipathy to the former mujahedin warlords carried over into Parliament, where she frequently criticized them for blocking reforms, particularly of women's rights, and suffered death threats for speaking out. "I've tried to break the chains of traditions," she told me. Her memories of Taliban rule were also overwhelmingly negative. On one occasion during their rule she felt ill and went to the doctor. When the Taliban's religious police found her on the street without her husband, they beat her with sticks. In spite of these experiences, she told me she now favored talks with the Taliban. "I changed my view three years ago when I realized Afghanistan is on its own," she said. "It's not that the international community doesn't support us. They just don't understand us. Everybody has been trying to kill the Taliban, but they're still there, stronger than ever. They are part of our population. They have different ideas, but as democrats we have to accept that. Every war has to end with talks and negotiations. Afghans need peace like oxygen. People want to keep their villages free of violence and suicide bombers."

As popular pressure rose within Afghanistan for an end to the war, Karzai's attitude appeared to change during the spring of 2010. He talked of negotiating with "our disaffected brothers" and sometimes, as we have seen, even suggested he would go and join them, though it was hard to tell whether his words were serious or another sign of emotional volatility.

In June 2010, Karzi invited around 1,600 Afghans to take part in a consultative peace Jirga in Kabul, which endorsed plans for discussions with elements of the Taliban and other armed insurgents. Its final resolutions described them as "angry brothers." The Jirga did not clarify the confusion over whether talks were aimed at getting the insurgents to see the error of their ways and surrender (a process of reintegration) or were designed to listen to grievances and lead to mutual concessions (a process of accommodation). But senior Tajiks were alarmed. Abdullah Abdullah, who was foreign minister during Karzai's first presidential term and challenged him in the 2009 election, expressed alarm at Karzai's language. Abdullah is half Pashtun but has spent his entire career in Tajik circles. During Karzai's recent visits to Kandahar, his home province, the president's references to the Taliban had gone well beyond the fraternal, he said. "It's not just the language he has used for months about 'disaffected brothers'; now he says, 'Talib-jan,' which is like calling them 'darling'."

After the Jirga, Karzai appointed a High Peace Council to be in charge of the negotiations. Its seventy members included around a dozen former Taliban ministers and officials from the pre-2002 period. Its chairman was a former Afghan president, Burhanuddin Rabbani, a Tajik former mujahedin leader and fierce opponent of the Taliban. Analysts were divided over what this all meant. Some said it was important to have non-Pashtuns on board if any deal with the Taliban was not to reignite civil war on an ethnic basis. Others said Rabbani would use his position to block any accommodation with the Taliban. The best that might be hoped for was that the peace council could prepare the way for talks by calling for some Taliban detainees to be released.

David Miliband's cautious proposal for talks with the Taliban in March 2010 was in large part the brainchild of Sherard Cowper-Coles, Britain's special representative for Afghanistan and Pakistan, Holbrooke's British counterpart. Cowper-Coles had become a strong advocate of negotiations with the Taliban. His frequent visits to Helmand and his close contacts with the U.S. and British military had convinced him that they were exaggerating the progress they were making. The tactical gains they boasted of did not amount to a winning strategy, he felt. He saw no alternative but to talk to the Taliban at the top level and had persuaded Miliband, his boss, to make the point publicly in his speech at MIT. Having watched the British Government's peace process in Northern Ireland, Cowper-Coles understood that civil wars are best ended through political agreement. The other side must be treated as a legitimate player with demands and grievances that have to be addressed seriously, whatever one thinks of their use of violence and terrorism. At the British embassy in Kabul, where he was based for a few months in the spring of 2010, he told me: "There will have to be some form of power-sharing, probably involving constitutional changes. We've been pushing for this but the U.S. won't take it seriously." As for the hope of splitting the Taliban, he described it as nonsense and wishful thinking.

Cowper-Coles told me that the U.S. policy of boycotting Mullah Omar and the Taliban leadership in Quetta (the twelve-man council known as the Quetta Shura) was so firm that the Obama administration had not even started to prepare the way for a possible change of policy. The White House had not authorized the CIA even to make secret low-level contacts with them of the kind that could plausibly be denied, if news leaked out.

Although the Miliband speech put down a useful marker, it came at the wrong moment for a policy rethink in Washington. The extra troops that Obama had authorized in December 2009 for Afghanistan were still deploying in the spring of 2010 and the U.S. military was determined to use them to try to knock the Taliban back. If there was any notion of eventually negotiating, it would have to be when the Taliban would sue for peace from a position of weakness.

When Petraeus took over as ISAF commander in July, he stepped up the U.S. military's night raids aimed at assassinating Taliban commanders. It was clear he still preferred to use force to try to push the Taliban back and create a perception of U.S. military success, at least while he was in direct charge of the war. His reputation as a general depended in large part on highly debatable claims of success in Iraq, and he wanted to reinforce that image by arguing that two surges of extra U.S. troops to Afghanistan had also achieved progress. If the alleged progress evaporated or Obama later moved toward a strategy of negotiations, Petraeus could always fall back on the Vietnam-era claim that others had snatched defeat from the jaws of victory.

The notion of talks with the Taliban seemed to take a further knock in the autumn of 2010. Reports emerged that agents for MI6, Britain's foreign espionage service, had worked with a senior Taliban leader, given him safe overland passage from Pakistan and flown him secretly to Kabul for meetings with Karzai earlier in the year. It turned out that the man was nothing more than a shopkeeper from Quetta and an impostor. As well as humiliating MI6, the story embarrassed General Stanley McChrystal, the then U.S. commander in Afghanistan, who had asked the British to develop the contacts since the CIA was not permitted to have its own links with the Taliban.

In the State Department, the first tentative discussions of a shift in policy were being held. Cowper-Coles told me in June 2010 that Richard Holbrooke had come around to the view that talks should take place with the Taliban. Holbrooke, after all, was renowned for his success in running the negotiations at the Dayton conference in 1995, which brought the war in Bosnia to an end. But Holbrooke was on his own. Secretary of State Hillary Clinton had yet to be persuaded.

Members of the British House of Commons Foreign Affairs Committee who visited Washington for talks with administration officials in the autumn of 2010 reported that "although we heard repeated references to the number of insurgents killed, captured or considering 're-integration,' we heard little recognition within military circles of the importance of higher-level political reconciliation." In evidence taken in London, Gilles Dorronsoro, an expert on Afghanistan's politics at the Carr Center for Human Rights Policy at Harvard University's Kennedy School, told the committee that reconciliation "is not supported by the US military." Their dynamic was "never to say, 'OK, we have to negotiate,' it's always to ask for more resources" and Obama "doesn't seem able to stop these demands."

Holbrooke's sudden death on December 13, 2010, seemed, paradoxically, to lead Clinton to take his views more seriously. In February 2011 in a speech praising Holbrooke's contribution to U.S. foreign policy over the years, Clinton told the Asia Society in New York: "I know that reconciling with an adversary that can be as brutal as the Taliban sounds distasteful, even unimaginable. And diplomacy would be easy if we only had to talk to our friends. But that is not how one makes peace." It was time, she said, "to get serious about a responsible reconciliation process, led by Afghans and supported by intense regional diplomacy and strong U.S.-backing." Crucially, she dropped the preconditions that before any reconciliation occurred the Taliban must renounce violence, abandon their alliance with al Qaeda and abide by the Afghan constitution, with its support for women's rights. These issues were "necessary outcomes of any negotiation," she said. But there were still contradictory notes. Clinton praised the surge as designed to "break the Taliban." "Weakening the insurgents" would prepare the ground for a political process, she said.

Nevertheless, some hints of forward movement followed. In May 2011, the *New York Times* reported that Tayyeb Agha, the aide to Mullah Omar who had spoken on behalf of the Taliban leader at their last conference before retreating from Kandahar in December 2011 (see Chapter Seven), had met U.S. officials three times, first in Qatar in the first weeks of 2011 and twice in Germany since then. It later emerged that the U.S. officials were Frank Ruggiero, a deputy to Marc Grossman, Holbrooke's successor, and Jeff W. Hayes, an official of the Defense Intelligence Agency who was working on the National Security Council. In another potential signal, in June 2011 the UN Security Council voted with U.S. support to divide its sanctions list into two, separating al Qaeda and Taliban leaders. The move was hailed by some as making it easier to lift sanctions on Taliban leaders and offer them safety to meet diplomats, mediators and negotiators as well as to travel from their hideouts.

Obama's speech on June 22 announcing a withdrawal of 33,000 troops by the end of September 2012 was designed to satisfy both hawks and doves in the United States. It was meant to signal a substantial drawdown before the 2012 election without offering the prospect of a complete withdrawal at any foreseeable time. The administration had started to try to negotiate a "strategic partnership agreement" with the Afghan Government that would allow the United States to keep troops in the country indefinitely. They would not be designated as combat troops but trainers, advisers and logistics specialists. The long-term presence of U.S. bases would, however, make nonsense of any Afghan aspiration of neutrality for their country.

On negotiating with the Taliban, the Obama speech was disappointing. It offered no advance toward negotiations and seemed more cautious than Hillary Clinton's speech to the Asia Society. Although the president said, "We do know that peace cannot come to a land that has known so much war without a political settlement" and "America will join initiatives that reconcile the Afghan people, including the Taliban," he trumpeted the claim that "we've inflicted serious losses on the

Taliban and taken a number of its strongholds." He insisted that any talks "must be led by the Afghan government, and those who want to be a part of a peaceful Afghanistan must break from al Qaeda, abandon violence, and abide by the Afghan constitution." This sounded like the old formula of demanding the Taliban surrender rather than any presidential endorsement of the view that the war had reached a strategic stalemate and there was an urgent need for talks without preconditions.

The U.S. military had hoped Obama would take fewer troops out. But they went on with their efforts to decapitate the Taliban by assassinating as many of their field commanders as possible. Some analysts argued that since the new wave of Taliban commanders who took over tended to be more hard-line than their predecessors, the assassination strategy would make negotiations harder to start. This may have been Petraeus's intention. Other analysts, including Michael Semple, took the opposite view. Semple worked for Francesc Vendrell, the European Union special representative, and hit the headlines in December 2007 when Karzai ordered him expelled from Afghanistan over a misunderstanding after he had talked to Taliban field commanders about reintegration. He later wrote that Taliban fighters might switch sides if they thought NATO was going to win. "War in Afghanistan has developed its own peculiar rules, style and logic. One of these rules is side with the winner," he argued. "Afghanistan's recent history is replete with examples of commanders choosing to flip rather than fight."

The reverse is also true. Members of the Afghan National Army and the police have flipped and joined the Taliban. Indeed, the U.S. strategy of building up Afghan security forces so that they can gradually take responsibility from ISAF is highly problematic. The army is only 3 percent Pashtun, so that in southern Afghanistan, where resistance is strongest, people see the Afghan army as a force that is just as foreign as the British and Americans. The idea that the Afghan army and police will be ready to take the lead in counterinsurgency by 2015, Obama's notional date for a withdrawal of U.S. combat troops, seems fanciful.

As Gilles Dorronsoro told British lawmakers, "If you think of the Afghan national army as a way to contain the Taliban, it's not going to work because the Taliban are already penetrating the Afghan national army and Afghan national police. What we have seen in a district north of Ghazni recently . . . is that the whole district went to the Taliban, joined up to the Taliban. That kind of thing can happen again and again. . . . Second, the ethnic composition of the army is a real serious problem."

Even when soldiers do not switch to the Taliban, thousands desert and go home. Lieutenant General William Caldwell, the U.S. commander in charge of NATO's training mission in Afghanistan, told a press conference in Kabul in March 2011 that although 110,000 men had been recruited in 2010, attrition rates meant that the total increase in manpower was just 70,000.

The Afghan police are equally poor as a foundation on which to build a counterinsurgency strategy in southern and eastern Afghanistan. "The police are widely seen as a Tajik-dominated service. . . . it's very hard for those who don't speak Pashto to do the job that the police are meant to do, which is to integrate themselves with the community and establish co-operative mechanisms," according to Gerard Russell, a former British diplomat who served as a senior political adviser at the United Nations political mission in Afghanistan from 2007 to 2009.

In addition to the national force, Afghanistan now has a new set of police. Karzai signed a decree setting up the Afghan Local Police (ALP) in August 2010. The idea came from Petraeus, who modeled it on the Sons of Iraq program, which he devised when he was the senior U.S. commander in Iraq. Under the Iraq scheme Sunni tribal leaders provided men for a series of local militias whose aim was to confront al Qaeda militants. In Afghanistan the new force is trained by U.S. Special Forces and is meant to be supervised by the Interior Ministry so as to prevent its men from being rivals to the national police. The plan was to recruit as many as 15,000 men in 61 districts within six months.

The haste with which the new units were created raised questions about the adequacy of their training and whether they were little more than yet another undisciplined tribal militia of the kind that Afghanistan has already had in plenty in the past. A United Nations report on the ALP said in March 2011 that Afghanistan had "a long history of past negative experiences with similar local defense groups which were abusive to local communities." It expressed concern that the new units were likely to be more loyal to their tribal and ethnic leaders and local power brokers than to the national police. Other tribes might see them as an alien force and this "could lead to increased communal violence." The report mentioned a case where a local ALP commander invited elders from various villages in a district of Uruzgan province to a meeting. He then asked the elders either to provide men for the ALP or pay 15,000 Afghanis (roughly $300). Several elders refused and were detained by the commander. They were released ten days later after reportedly paying an unspecified amount of money.

In spite of these criticisms, the U.S. military wants to expand the ALP and has in some cases bypassed the Interior Ministry and given weapons directly to the police. It has also used the ALP to try to capture insurgents, sometimes crossing provincial boundaries, and thereby converting them into small armies answerable only to their commander or the United States. The U.S. military's enthusiasm for the new force was further proof that the Pentagon remained highly skeptical of any peace talks.

Whether talks get under way depends on the insurgents as much as the governments of Afghan and the United States. The Taliban leadership's reaction to Obama's June 2011 speech was uncompromising. They continued to reject talks with the Karzai government until all foreign troops had left Afghanistan.

Assessing the mood among Taliban commanders and fighters with any accuracy is virtually impossible, given the lack of easy access to them. Member of Parliament Shukria Barakzai's willingness to support talks with the Taliban stemmed in part from her view that they could not win power in Kabul again and were in no position to dictate the terms of any peace deal. "They no longer have the support and reputation they had back then [when they first came to power in 1996]. Taliban is an ideology. It's no longer a united force," she told me in March 2010. Her position mirrored the findings of a Pentagon report, "State of the Taliban 2009," classified as secret. Cowper-Coles summarized its findings to British lawmakers on November 9, 2010. The study was based on interviews with dozens of detained Taliban insurgents. Such interviews have to be treated with caution since prisoners may tailor their true opinions to what they think the interrogators want to hear, and the Pentagon may have skewed the results. Nevertheless, these showed that the Taliban were tired of fighting but remained confident they were winning. They hated foreigners, a category which, they said, included Arabs and Pakistanis as well as American and British. They wanted an honorable recognition that they were pushed aside but not defeated in 2001. They wanted to be brought back into the political equation.

At ground level the Taliban movement is a loose structure, in which field commanders have considerable autonomy. This stems in large part from the necessities of asymmetric warfare, which requires Taliban units to be mobile and keep their communications tight as the Americans have the technology to listen to everything as well as watch them by day. They include tribal strongmen, landlords, drug dealers, farmers and unemployed young people. Michael Semple describes them as neither "a terrorist organization, a tribal movement, nor a modern party. Rather, they are best considered a vanguardist brotherhood." He defines "vanguardist" as meaning the Taliban assert moral authority over the general population, and "brotherhood" as meaning they have a strong awareness of identity and solidarity.

At the leadership level, the armed insurgency has three components: Hezb-i Islami under Gulbuddin Hekmatyar, the Haqqani movement and the Taliban's Quetta Shura. Hezb-i Islami operates in Kunar, Laghman and Nangarhar provinces in eastern Afghanistan. One of the cruelest mujahedin warlords in the mid-1990s, Hekmatyar fled to Tehran when the Taliban captured Kabul. But as foreign pressures mounted on the Taliban, he started to criticize the Iranian Government for its links with the Northern Alliance. After the U.S. attack on Afghanistan in 2001, he went further and denounced Iran for having given it tacit support.

In early 2002, the Iranians asked Hekmatyar to leave. Not surprisingly, he moved to a safe haven in Pakistan from where he revived his guerrilla army for attacks on U.S. and Afghan facilities in Afghanistan, as he had warned he would do in an interview I had done with him by fax in 2001.

Hekmatyar's group has claimed responsibility for some of the most deadly and spectacular attacks in Kabul, including an attempt to assassinate Karzai during a military parade in 2008. But Hekmatyar was always a politician more than a military leader. Hezb-i Islami, a party which took the same name as his, was legalized and won seats in the Afghan Parliament in 2005. More than a third of the provincial governors were linked to it, and though before the election they claimed to have broken with Hekmatyar, it is likely he could use their influence if bargaining over a peace settlement becomes a reality. Hekmatyar is said to be willing to support peace talks. He has set the precondition that the Americans must first announce a timetable for withdrawal but is not insisting on a withdrawal before talks can start.

In October 2002, Hekmatyar wrote an emotional open letter to Bush and the U.S. Congress, saying the Afghan people resented the U.S. presence, that Karzai's government did not have people's loyalty and that the Afghan people were being persecuted by American soldiers who were insensitive to their religious beliefs and practices. "No wise and well-informed person could consider the invasion of Afghanistan a success," he said.

After Obama's election and before the inauguration, he wrote to the president-elect, urging him to change course: "Wasn't it enough

killing 800 thousand Iraqis and Afghans to avenge those killed on
September 11, 2001? Two hundred and sixty Afghan and Iraqi people
were killed for every American killed in those events." He criticized
Iran and said Tehran's aim was to keep the war running and block
access for oil and gas to flow from the markets of Central Asia through
Afghanistan to Europe and other world markets, and thereby maintain
markets for Iran's own oil.

Hekmatyar also made several overtures to Karzai, and in March
2010 Karzai agreed to meet a delegation representing him. Haroun
Zarghoun, its spokesman, said the delegates presented a fifteen-point
plan, including a call for foreign troops to withdraw from Afghanistan
within six months, starting in July. Six months after that, an interim government would be appointed and preparations made for fresh elections.
Analysts described the plan as an opening position since Hekmatyar
must have known it would not be accepted. They found it remarkable
that such senior insurgent leaders were allowed to move freely around
Kabul. The meeting looked like part of Karzai's strategy to split the
insurgency rather than negotiate seriously.

The insurgency's second wing is the network loyal to Jalaluddin
Haqqani and his son Sirajuddin. Jalaluddin was part of the mujahedin
resistance to the Soviets, but, unlike Hekmatyar, he joined the Taliban
government and became minister for tribal affairs. Now elderly, he has
handed over most of the group's activity to his son though he appears
to be the network's main link with Mullah Omar and the Quetta Shura.
The Haqqanis stem from Paktiya in southeastern Afghanistan but have
their base in Pakistan's north Waziristan region, where they have close
links to al Qaeda. They also have good ties with Pakistan's ISI. Their
proximity to al Qaeda has led some analysts to see them as hostile to
peace talks, but others say that if the ISI developed an interest in talks
the Haqqanis would have to go along with them.

The heart of the insurgency's leadership remains the Quetta Shura
with Mullah Omar as its leader. They have consistently refused to hold

talks until foreign forces leave Afghanistan, but many analysts see this as a public position that conceals options for flexibility behind the scenes. This view was strengthened in late January 2010, when the Pakistanis arrested Mullah Abdul Ghani Baradar, a member of the twelve-man *shura,* during a raid on a madrassa near Karachi. Baradar was thought to be one of the more moderate voices in the shura and perhaps more open to the idea of peace talks. According to Cowper-Coles, Baradar had long-standing contacts with the Karzai family in Kandahar and had made a "protection" deal with them not to attack Karzai interests in return for payments.

The CIA was anxious to interrogate Baradar after his capture, but Pakistan's intelligence agency, the ISI, denied it access for several weeks. The ISI apparently wanted to keep control over Baradar so that if talks did get under way, the ISI would have a veto over the agenda. Pakistan's own homegrown Taliban were becoming an increasing threat within Pakistan, and the weight of opinion in Islamabad was moving toward supporting negotiations on Afghanistan so as to end the cross-border war and get the Afghan Taliban leadership to go home. Once that happened, it would be easier for Islamabad to concentrate on trying to crush the insurgency in Pakistan.

The Quetta Shura has made its political goals clear. It wants the unconditional departure of foreign forces and the establishment of an Islamic system in Afghanistan. It seeks normal relations with all neighboring states and promises to pose no threat to any other state. "The fear that Afghanistan may turn out to be a threat to world peace must be put out of your minds as it is mere baseless propaganda," the Taliban said in an appeal to the U.S. Congress in November 2010. This statement and others like it are usually interpreted as meaning the Taliban are a nationalist movement whose goals are confined to changing Afghanistan. They do not share al Qaeda's ideology and intend to take no part in its global jihad. But the Taliban have been reluctant to spell this out explicitly. Separation from al Qaeda is a bargaining chip which they do not want to put on the table too early in any negotiation process, although bin Laden's death must make it much easier for Omar to break with al Qaeda. The original link between the two movements was very much a personal deal between two strong leaders. With his onetime guest and supporter dead, Omar may feel less bound to stay connected with the movement that bin Laden founded.

On the face of it, the Quetta Shura's rejection of peace talks until all foreign forces have left Afghanistan would seem to undermine any realistic hope of negotiations. It looked like the mirror image of the argument, used by Senator John McCain and other U.S. hawks, that any U.S. talk of a complete withdrawal of American troops or even the setting of deadlines would undermine the prospect of serious negotiations since all the Taliban have to do is to sit back and wait until the Americans have gone.

But there have been signs that the Taliban were willing to negotiate even while troops remain in Afghanistan. In an interview in October 2010 on the official website of the Islamic Emirate of Afghanistan (the name they called Afghanistan when they were in power in Kandahar and which they still retain for their communications), Mullah Abdul Kabir, a member of the *shura* who is described as the coordinating chief of the eastern provinces, appeared to be taking the movement's standard hard line. "Peace talks in conditions of the presence of foreign forces are meaningless and futile," he said. He denounced Karzai's High Peace Council, saying it consisted of people who "practically support the Americans." They might once have been mujahedin, but "by siding with the American invaders, they have forfeited the credibility in the eyes of the Afghans which they once enjoyed during the era of the former Soviet Union's invasion of Afghanistan."

Abdul Kabir also poured scorn on the former Taliban ministers and officials who now live under guard in Kabul: "They have been given membership in the peace council but are not in the capacity to represent the Islamic Emirate. They are living under the eyes and surveillance of the Americans." He denied that any talks with authorized Taliban representatives had taken place anywhere.

Yet when Abdul Kabir answered a second question on peace talks, he offered clear hints of flexibility. "In Afghanistan, in the current condition, only those efforts of peace and reconciliation are pragmatic which surely lead to withdrawal of the foreign invading forces from Afghanistan and pave the way for establishment of an Islamic system in the country," he said. "This objective can't be achieved in conditions of presence of foreign forces in the country." He appeared to be saying that an Islamic system cannot be set up in Afghanistan as long as there are foreign forces there. He was not ruling out "efforts of peace and reconciliation which lead to a withdrawal of foreign forces." These "efforts" presumably could include talks. He defined this as pragmatism.

Why would the Taliban become more pragmatic? One reason is that they realize they cannot capture Kabul and the north again as they did in 1996 and the succeeding years. The Afghan National Army has been built up to the point where, although it is too weak to defeat the Taliban, it is too strong to lose the capital and the Tajik and Uzbek areas to the north. The Taliban can take over the Pashtun south, but if it wants any say in what happens elsewhere in Afghanistan it will have to take the route of negotiations and power-sharing.

Another reason is that the Taliban must calculate that waiting until 2015 when the United States has said its combat mission will end offers no certainty that the United States will ever leave the country completely. The Obama administration has suggested that it will keep residual forces in Afghan land and air bases from which it can always emerge to strike insurgents, just as it has done in Iraq. By reducing the death toll of U.S. troops, this will lower political pressure in the United States for a complete withdrawal. The only way for the Taliban to ensure a total departure of U.S. forces is to enter a process of talks. This is likely to end with a clear Taliban break from al Qaeda and agreement on a new and more decentralized Afghan constitution.

The Taliban must also take into account the risk that, as time goes on without an end to the war, the role of the Tajiks in the Kabul government may increase. They are less willing to negotiate a deal than Karzai is. For all his inadequacies and the corruption of his family Karzai is a better negotiating partner than any of the likely alternatives. The final factor that could push the Taliban toward talks is the growing pressure from Pakistan for a political settlement and an end to the Taliban's safe havens in Quetta. The embarrassment that enveloped the Pakistani authorities and its intelligence service when it was discovered that bin Laden was hiding so close to Islamabad was bound to raise questions in Washington about whether the Pakistanis were shielding Mullah Omar. Perhaps he was not near Quetta at all. He might be in Karachi or some other city far from the Afghan border. Either way, Pakistan might well feel, after the fiasco over their role in the bin Laden case, that they had better loosen their ties to the Taliban leadership and get them to leave.

How can the logjam be broken? Two things are needed. One is a clear statement from Obama that he wants no long-term bases or U.S. troop presence in Afghanistan, is prepared to let his representatives sit down with the Taliban and discuss their demand for a complete withdrawal in the context of an end to the country's civil war and that a priority item on the agenda for talks would be a cease-fire by all sides. The other is the establishment of a neutral space to which Taliban envoys can travel safely without fear of arrest and meet informally with their counterparts from the Karzai government, Pakistan, Iran, India, the United States and other relevant states. This could in time lead to formal negotiations. Cowper-Coles has argued that a military base in Abu Dhabi would be an appropriate venue. He used the analogy of Laneside, a safe house south of Belfast in Northern Ireland, where the IRA and British emissaries met secretly for months in 1974 for an "exchange of views," long before formal negotiations began. The Turkish Government has offered to provide a place on its territory.

Given that the Taliban are fragmented with much of the daily decision making in the hands of field commanders, any process of dialogue must take place at multiple levels: the local, the national, the regional and the international. Because of the high level of mutual distrust, negotiations between the United States and the Taliban will take time to start and even longer to bear fruit. In the interim, there is a case for trying to negotiate local cease-fires with Taliban commanders. But the purpose must not be the old one of trying to split the Taliban and get men to defect to the government side. The aim must be to protect civilians and give them security by creating demilitarized "islands" of peace that can, it is hoped, be enlarged as confidence increases.

The British tried this in Musa Qala, a town in the rocky hills of northern Helmand province, in October 2006. The town had been the scene of fierce fighting until local elders struck a deal with the Taliban not to come in if the British withdrew three miles from the town. The deal had the backing of Britain's General David Richards, the then commander of the ISAF. The Americans criticized it as a concession to the Taliban and briefed against the British, accusing them of weakness.

The Musa Qala agreement went to the heart of doctrinal differences among NATO allies. According to one senior British officer, "the Americans favor a 'kinetic approach,' a lot less carrot, a lot more stick and considerably more projectiles." Three months later, a raid by an American B-1B Stealth bomber just outside the three-mile exclusion zone around the town narrowly missed Mullah Ghaffour, the local Taliban commander, but killed his brother and twenty followers. It looked as though the Americans were trying to sabotage the cease-fire. Whether that was true or not, the bombing raid had the effect of ending the cease-fire. Incensed and suspecting that the elders had given away his hiding place to the Americans, Ghaffour's men regrouped and recaptured the town. The British were forced to change tactics, and a few months later, aided by the U.S. Eighty-second Airborne Division, thousands of ISAF troops retook Musa Qala. A brief experiment was over and has not yet been repeated.

Several U.S. think tanks have endorsed the concept of peace talks with the Taliban. Some have also recommended the United States revisit the light-footprint strategy proposed by the UN's Lakhdar Brahimi, which Washington originally favored after the Taliban withdrew from Kandahar in December 2001. At that time, the Bush administration assumed the Taliban were finished. Now that the Taliban have managed to reemerge, a light footprint would mean organizing local cease-fires and pulling back to concentrate on defending the main Afghan cities rather than seeking to "take the fight to the enemy" and control the villages. This is what the Soviet Union did in the final years of its occupation.

Proposals along these lines were eloquently put forward in August 2010 by the ad hoc Afghanistan Study Group, made up of some thirty analysts from several U.S. think tanks in a report titled "A New Way Forward: Rethinking U.S. Strategy in Afghanistan": "Protecting our interests does not require a U.S. military victory over the Taliban. A Taliban takeover is unlikely even if the United States reduces its military commitment. The Taliban is a rural insurgency rooted primarily in Afghanistan's Pashtun population, and succeeded due in some part to the disenfranchisement of rural Pashtuns. The Taliban's seizure of power in the 1990s was due to an unusual set of circumstances that no longer exist and are unlikely to be repeated. . . . Non-Pashtun Afghans now have ample experience with Taliban rule, and they are bound to resist any Taliban efforts to regain control in Kabul." The group argued that the continuation of an ambitious U.S. military campaign in Afghanistan was likely to work against U.S. interests. A large American presence fostered local, and especially Pashtun, resentment and aided Taliban recruiting.

As for the threat from al Qaeda, they said the movement would probably not be invited back to Afghanistan even if the Taliban were to regain power in some provinces. They concluded, "Al Qaeda sympathizers are now present in many locations globally, and defeating the Taliban will have little effect on Al Qaeda's global reach. The ongoing threat from Al Qaeda is better met via specific counter-terrorism measures, a reduced U.S. military 'footprint' in the Islamic world, and diplomatic efforts to improve America's overall image and undermine international support for militant extremism."

Robert Blackwill, who served in 2003 and 2004 as deputy to Condoleezza Rice, at the time George W. Bush's national security adviser, has also argued that the al Qaeda threat from Afghanistan is virtually at an end. "The CIA now thinks there are barely 50–100 al-Qaeda fighters left in Afghanistan, facing 100,000 U.S. troops," he wrote in July 2010. "The original Afghan objective was to destroy al-Qaeda, not fight the Taliban. That has largely been accomplished. Even if the Afghan Taliban invited al-Qaeda to join them in greater numbers, the estimated 300 or so al-Qaeda fighters in Pakistan moving across the border would not substantially increase the threat. Is it worth an indefinite ground war, and thousands more US and allied casualties, to try to prevent that happening?"

One of the most powerful statements of the case for a political settlement came in March 2011 from an international panel chaired by Thomas Pickering, one of Washington's most experienced former diplomats, and Lakhdar Brahimi, the veteran UN negotiator and convenor of the 2001 Bonn conference. They argued that the war was a stalemate that neither the U.S. military nor the Taliban would be able to break. They poured cold water on the U.S. and U.K. policy of reintegration that tried to get Taliban leaders and commanders to defect: "Securing defections of insurgents or trying to co-opt senior-level Taliban to join the Kabul regime is unlikely to be sufficient to bring peace; reconciliation with the insurgents will eventually have to involve creating a broader political framework to end the war." They suggested the Taliban were becoming more willing to talk as they realized they could not regain total control over Afghanistan: "For their part, the Taliban have encountered increasing resistance from the population in areas beyond their most dedicated base when they have sought to re-impose the stern morality code of the years when the Taliban were in power in Kabul and Kandahar. Moreover, the improved living standards that international aid has brought to many Afghans contrasts sharply with those under Taliban rule. Taliban leaders are also feeling pressure to explore a negotiating track from the new ambivalence that many detect in Pakistan." They pointed out that the ban on music that the Taliban enforced in the mid-1990s had become so unpopular in recent years that Mullah Omar was forced to issue a fatwa giving local field commanders discretion on enforcing the emirate's social edicts, and that most opted for a relatively relaxed attitude.

Pickering and Brahimi argued that the complexity of the issues and the need to get Afghanistan's neighbors to agree to any deal that included a withdrawal of U.S. forces meant that talks would benefit from a UN-appointed facilitator. It sounded like a replay of the process that ended the Soviet occupation, thanks to Diego Cordovez, a former foreign minister of Ecuador, who facilitated the Geneva agreements of 1988 by acting as a UN-appointed mediator.

In an important departure from the usual top-down approach, the Brahimi-Pickering report recommended local cease-fires as part of a confidence-building process that could start before full-scale talks got under way. They suggested a trade-off in which the United States ended its assassination of Taliban commanders and the Taliban ended its placing of roadside bombs and the assassination of government officials.

Other confidence-building measures would be the release of Taliban and other insurgent detainees from U.S. and Afghan custody and the removal of more Taliban from the UN sanctions list which no longer lumps them together with al Qaeda. The latter would allow them to travel freely again. The report endorsed the idea of providing a safe location where Taliban emissaries could meet the facilitator and representatives of the Karzai government and the United States, though it did not suggest a specific place.

On some relatively simple issues it has already been possible to negotiate successfully with the Quetta Shura. In September 2009 the International Committee of the Red Cross won the Taliban's endorsement for a three-day polio vaccination drive that included access by medics to Taliban-controlled areas. A letter of support from the Taliban contained Mullah Omar's signature. Negotiating a comprehensive peace deal would be a much more complex and time-consuming endeavor, but the Red Cross precedent shows that contact can be made with the Taliban leadership through intermediaries. At some stage they would have to be followed by direct talks with Taliban representatives and eventually with the top leadership.

In Britain, pressure has been growing for the government to accept talks as the best exit strategy. The British Government has not yet publicly supported it, but the influential Foreign Affairs Committee of the House of Commons declared in March 2011 that "there is evidence to suggest that the core foreign policy justification for the UK's continued presence in Afghanistan, namely that it is necessary in the interests of UK national security, may have been achieved some time ago, given the apparently limited strength of al Qaeda in Afghanistan." That meant, they argued, that Britain should reconsider the need for a major military presence and focus on achieving a political settlement.

While the general case for a negotiated settlement with the Taliban is strong, two key issues will need to be addressed as talks proceed. First, how would a compromise deal that produced a power-sharing arrangement with the Taliban affect the rights of Afghan women? And second, are Afghanistan's neighbors willing to join negotiations and what kind of deal would they be prepared to accept?

The next two chapters will discuss these questions.

[13] THE GIRL WITH THE MISSING NOSE

"Nobody wants to abandon the women of Afghanistan, but most Americans don't want to keep fighting there for years and years. The grim reality is that, despite all of the talk about promoting women's rights, things are going to have to give."

—SENIOR U.S. OFFICIAL

IT MAY HAVE been the most horrendous cover picture in *Time* magazine's history. Published in July 2010 it showed a very young woman with dark eyes and a lock of black hair falling fetchingly over her forehead from behind a purple veil. The shock was her nose, or rather the gaping hole where her nose should have been. Beside the picture a headline proclaimed: "What Happens If We Leave Afghanistan." There was no question mark.

Inside, an article described how the girl, Bibi Aisha, an eighteen-year-old from the southern province of Uruzgan, had fled from her husband's house because of constant abuse by her in-laws. Her husband caught her. He was a Taliban commander, *Time* reported, and because she had run away he resolved to punish her and deter other young women from doing the same. He flung her down, cut off her ears and nose and left her bleeding on a hillside. Somehow she found the strength to walk off and find help.

Almost as terrible as her injuries was the story of Aisha's marriage, though *Time* did not recount this. It had been reported some months earlier in the *Daily Beast*. At the age of twelve she and her younger sister were awarded to her husband's family under a tribal custom for settling disputes known as *baad*, which treats young girls as voiceless commodities. They are offered in compensation for unpaid debts or if a member of another family has been killed. In Aisha's case, her uncle had murdered one of her future husband's relatives. In order to settle the blood debt her father gave the two girls to the victim's family. When Aisha reached puberty, there was a formal marriage and she became his wife against her will.

In an editorial accompanying the cover picture, *Time* claimed it was not being published either to support or to oppose the presence of U.S. troops in Afghanistan. But in highlighting the fact that the brutal husband was a Taliban commander and ignoring the ancient practice of *baad*, which long pre-dated the Taliban, *Time*'s story and its cover headline ("What Happens If We Leave Afghanistan") were a clear piece of propaganda in favor of keeping U.S. troops in Afghanistan and preventing the Taliban from returning to power. *Time* criticized the notion of talks with the Taliban and wrote, "For Afghanistan's women, an early withdrawal of international forces could be disastrous."

Some critics called the picture "war porn." Others took issue with the article, denouncing it as "emotional blackmail." "Feminists have long argued that invoking the condition of women to justify occupation is a cynical ploy and the *Time* cover stands accused of it," wrote Priyamvada Gopal, a lecturer in the Faculty of English at Cambridge University.

Three months later the centerpiece of *Time*'s argument collapsed. Abdul Ghafar Stanikzai, who heads the branch of Afghanistan's Independent Human Rights Committee in the province of Uruzgan, told the BBC that reports that the Taliban initiated Aisha's grotesque maltreatment were untrue. Her mutilation was not linked to Taliban ideology but was part of traditional Afghan male culture, which goes back centuries. "We have found out that the Taliban were not behind this. This was a case of family violence, not the Taliban," he said. Aisha's husband, the Taliban commander, did not disfigure her on his own. Haji Suleman, her father-in-law, helped to hold Aisha down while her husband and other members of his family cut off her nose. Uruzgan's police chief, Juma Gul Herat, said his men had arrested Suleman for questioning, but Aisha's husband was at large, apparently having fled to Pakistan. Suleman had told police his family became angry with Aisha after she criticized her new marital home and spent too much time in her father's house. Meanwhile, the Taliban condemned the incident as "barbaric" and denied having anything to do with it.

The controversy over the *Time* article was important because it goes to the heart of one of the key issues surrounding the question of possible talks with the Taliban. The Taliban attitude to women is cited as a good reason for trying to defeat the Taliban and rejecting any talks with them. Others say talks are necessary, but, if they are held, negotiators should ensure there are certain "red lines" on human rights and gender equality, beyond which no concessions or compromises must be made. This is the position of some Afghan human rights organizations as well as of international groups like Amnesty International and Human Rights Watch.

The basis of any discussion has to be clarity about the situation of Afghan women before and after the Taliban. Was the Taliban period uniquely bad for women? If so, how much worse than the time before? Since the Taliban withdrew from Kabul and Kandahar in 2001, how far have things changed for the better? At that time George Bush and Tony Blair brought their wives in on the celebrations. The American First Lady and the British Spouse of the Prime Minister enthusiastically proclaimed the Taliban's exit as the arrival of a new dawn for Afghan women: liberation from the burqa and the chance for education and work again. Has it really worked out like that?

MYTH NUMBER TWELVE:

The Taliban are uniquely harsh oppressors of Afghan women.

Afghanistan has a long history of honor killings and honor mutilation, going back before the Taliban period and continuing until today. They occur in every part of the country and are not confined to the culture of the Pashtun, the ethnic group from which most Taliban come. "For sure, we have hundreds of Bibi Aishas in Afghanistan," Ahmad Fahim Hakim, the deputy chairman of the Independent Human Rights Commission, told reporters in Kabul in December 2010 at the launch of a report by the United Nations Assistance Mission in Afghanistan (UNAMA) on traditional practices that violate women's rights. In one of the secret cables released by WikiLeaks in 2010, Ambassador Karl Eikenberry also called the Bibi Aisha case one "of domestic violence, not a political act."

On the wider issue of gender rights, the Taliban are rightly accused of relegating Afghan women to second-class citizenship. But to single the Taliban out as uniquely oppressive is not accurate. Violence against women has a long pedigree in all communities in Afghanistan, among the Hazara Shias and the northern Tajiks as well as the Pashtun Sunnis.

Underage marriage is common across Afghanistan, in all regions and among all ethnic groups. According to UNIFEM (the United Nations Development Fund for Women) and the Afghan Independent Human Rights Commission, 57 percent of Afghan marriages are child marriages—where one partner is under the age of sixteen. In a study of 200 underage wives, 40 percent had been married between the ages of ten and thirteen, 32.5 percent at fourteen, and 27.5 percent at fifteen. Girls as young as four are sometimes promised to men, often to ones who are decades older. It may be for money or as part of *baad*.

UNAMA discovered some terrible cases. A twenty-year-old woman, from Takhar province in northern Afghanistan, who was engaged under *baad* at the age of four, sought protection from the Department of Women's Affairs in Taloqan in January 2009 to avoid being officially married. After two months of threats from local community elders and politicians, the department's officials sent the young woman to the district court for a decision on the legality of the marriage. As the court session was about to start, a group of some three hundred people who supported the forced marriage attacked the court compound, abducted the woman and forcibly took her to her in-laws' house. All efforts by UNAMA to contact the woman failed and her whereabouts remained unknown.

In October 2009, a sixteen-year-old girl from Logar province was forcibly engaged to a sixty-five-year-old man. According to the girl, the man insisted on visiting her at her family home prior to the marriage, claiming he had given the girl's father a vast amount of money and was entitled to see her. During this time, the girl phoned a local radio station and discussed her problem with the male host. They became friends and continued to call each other. Later they both fled to Laghman province where they intended to get married, but police arrested them on charges of *zina*, sexual intercourse outside marriage. The man was convicted and sentenced to thirteen years' imprisonment and the girl to five years, and she was reportedly raped while in detention. UNAMA learned that the sixty-five-year-old man demanded another girl in compensation, and the girl's father then gave him his younger daughter, who was about fourteen.

Although, under *baad*, the girl is supposed to be transferred from one family to another as compensation, experience shows that girls given in *baad* may endure a lifetime of misery. They may be treated as virtual slaves, suffering constant mistreatment, physical violence and humiliation. If a formal marriage takes place, it is done without any large ceremony, and the stigma of having been given in *baad* stays with the girl forever. Insults and beatings are common, and, in some cases, the husband's family denies the girl all contact with her parents and siblings. A group of Pashtun women in Faryab province told UNAMA researchers: "The girl is never respected by her new family as they associate her with her male relative who committed the crime and accuse her equally of being a criminal. The girl is treated like a servant as a means of revenge. Sometimes she is forced to sleep with the animals in the barn."

Baad may also be practiced where a newlywed husband discovers that his wife is not a virgin. He returns the bride to her father's house and receives her virgin sister as compensation.

Baad is forbidden under Sharia law, which insists that marriage be covered by the principle of consent and women may not be treated as property. The practice is also illegal under Afghan law as well as Afghanistan's international human rights obligations. Yet it continues to be enshrined in Pashtunwali, the traditional Pashtun code of conduct, as well as in the customs of other Afghan communities that stress the importance of maintaining tribal and family honor and prefer reconciliation over Sharia's respect for individual justice.

"Without *baad*, we would have conflict between the families, with murder and revenge. *Baad* is a good thing. Killing and enmity are prohibited in Islam," said Nadira, a female member of a family in the northern city of Mazar-i Sharif who had accepted Nilab, a two-year-old from another family. The toddler was traded away because her uncle was found guilty of having sex with a cousin whose husband had been away working in Iran for several months. The cousin became pregnant. Her father-in-law accused the uncle, and the two families agreed to take the issue to the council of tribal elders. Their judgment was that Nilab, the toddler, should become the bride of the betrayed husband's six-year-old brother. Two children were thereby married without their consent. Yet a relative commented: "This is a very good decision. Peace has been restored to the two families. Their enmity has turned to friendship."

As Bibi Aisha discovered, running away from a forced marriage rarely leads to safety. There are few places where a young woman can get protection. If she takes refuge in a neighbor's house, the police may prosecute her for the intention of having sexual intercourse outside marriage or for having created the opportunity for it. If she escapes to a police station, the police often return her to her husband's house where she may be viciously punished or killed. Even if she is sent back to her own family, a young woman may suffer there too, for allegedly having sullied the family's honor.

To escape these horrors, some Afghan women turn to self-immolation and suicide. Kerosene is used for cooking in many households, and women set themselves alight with it, mistakenly thinking it will provide a quick and easy death. In reality, death is not immediate or guaranteed, and women may have to endure pain from appalling burns for several days before they die. A few survive with grotesque scars.

The Afghan Government estimates that 2,400 women immolate themselves every year. In a typical case in Nimruz province in May 2009, a thirteen-year-old girl set herself on fire after three years of an unbearable marriage. She took three days to die. Health authorities in Herat, a city in western Afghanistan where Taliban influence is minimal, established a special burns unit in 2007. It handled eight to ten self-immolation cases a month in 2010, 40 percent more than the previous year. Doctors estimated there were probably an equal number of cases they did not see because they took place far from the city, or because the victims were simply left to die at home without being brought to the hospital.

Self-immolation is often more sinister than it seems. Burn cases are homicides masquerading as suicides, according to doctors, nurses and human rights workers. "We have two women here right now who were burned by their mothers-in-law and husbands," Dr. Arif Jalali, the Herat hospital's senior surgeon, told the *New York Times*. "Violence in the lives of Afghanistan's women comes from everywhere: from her father or brother, from her husband, from her father-in-law, from her mother-in-law and sister-in-law," said Dr. Shafiqa Eanin, a plastic surgeon at the same hospital.

One reason for the prevalence of child marriage is the custom of bride price. In theory, this might appear to increase respect for women. In practice, it is another powerful factor in turning them into commodities or chattels that families can buy and sell. Poverty may encourage fathers to get rid of their daughters, even when they are still small, and marriage becomes a transaction in which women are sold to the highest bidder. In some cases the need to pay a bride price encourages fathers to marry off severely underage daughters in order to gather money for older sons to buy a wife. Sometimes bride price can reach thousands of dollars, especially in towns and villages where people live off the proceeds of the drug business. Kabul has seen massive bride price inflation in recent years. Gaudy new wedding palaces dot the streets of better-off suburbs.

Once they are married, social pressure on young brides to bear children immediately is huge. Most child brides are poor and have had little or no schooling. They rarely have information on family planning or any services to help them. Girls who become pregnant before the age of fifteen, when their bodies are immature, are five times more likely to die before or during childbirth than women in their twenties. Afghanistan has the worst maternal mortality rate in the world, with around 24,000 deaths a year, and an estimated rate of 1,400 deaths for every 100,000 live births, compared with twenty-four per 100,000 in the United States and twelve per 100,000 in Britain. In 2009 this figure of maternal deaths in Afghanistan was ten times higher than the number of civilians killed in conflict.

Early marriage harms not only the girl child but also the infant she bears. Premature birth, low birth weight and poor mental and physical growth are frequent characteristics of babies born to young mothers. A child born to a girl under the age of eighteen has a 60 percent greater chance of dying in the first year of life.

MYTH NUMBER THIRTEEN:

Banning girls from school is a Taliban trademark.

A right as basic as the freedom to go out of the house can, if denied, lead to a host of other disabilities. Women are forbidden from taking jobs. Girls are prevented from going to school. In the minds of Western politicians and the media, these prohibitions are often associated exclusively with the Taliban. Yet the claim that the Taliban were the first or only Afghan group to ban girls' education and jobs for women is too facile. The forced isolation of women by keeping them confined within the house or family compound is a deep-seated part of Afghan rural culture. It is also found in poorer parts of the major cities.

In November 2003 I spent a week reporting on the work of Doctors Without Borders in and around Sar-e Pul, a mainly Uzbek and Tajik town in northern Afghanistan. One day we followed a group of Afghan health educators as they rode rickety bicycles from a clinic to a local village. With small cool-boxes full of vaccine against tuberculosis strapped behind their saddles, they pedaled along dusty roads where donkeys and camels provided the commonest form of transport. They often had to dismount and walk because of the quantity of stones on the road. Arriving in the village, one of the vaccinators climbed a ladder to the roof of a mosque. Through a bullhorn he invited people to bring their babies for injection. His colleague laid a carpet on the ground under an almond tree and took out papers to prepare to register the children. Coming for injections seemed to require little propaganda. Their value was clearly well understood, and a crowd soon gathered in the yard of the mosque. But a large section of the village population was conspicuously absent. There were no adult women. The babies were brought in by sisters up to the age of around ten and older brothers. A few young fathers also turned up with infants in their arms. From the clumsy way they fumbled to find the buttons of babies' cardigans and shawls, it was clear that child care was not one of their regular chores.

Conservative attitudes were also apparent in a health clinic we visited in the small town of Tibir. Male doctors described how restricted they were in examining female patients even with a male relative in the room. Some women declined to remove the all-encompassing burqa from their faces, making it impossible to look into their throats, eyes or ears. Even women who were prepared to lift the veil usually drew the line at having stethoscopes applied to their stomachs. Gynecological examinations were completely rejected, so that male doctors had to work entirely on the basis of the woman's statement of her symptoms.

Yet women came to the clinic eagerly, outnumbering men by almost two to one. The need for medical help is one of the few legitimate reasons for a woman to be allowed to leave the home. Doctors find that when female patients have very minor complaints their primary aim in coming to the clinic is to get tea, sympathy and some conversation and companionship in the women-only waiting room. Who can blame them?

I came across other examples of the forced seclusion of women when I spent three weeks in Kabul in March 2010 giving journalistic training to staff at the Afghan Education Project (AEP), a radio service founded and supervised by the British Broadcasting Corporation. They put out children's dramas and adult educational programs in Dari and Pashto on health, hygiene and agriculture. These include documentaries on how to grow better crops and mitigate the effects of a severe drought as well as a soap opera, *New Home, New Life,* in which the characters discuss the issues that affect ordinary rural households and their families. The channel is popular, in part because of its lively format but also because it keeps up-to-date with the full range of farmers' concerns about crop diseases and unexpected weather changes and the dangers of unexploded mines. Women's rights are promoted in *Shoulder to Shoulder,* a program that shows how men can work with women to share tasks and responsibilities. Another soap opera is geared to urban listeners. The soap operas are the channel's most popular productions and some characters have become household names across Afghanistan.

In order to keep these public-service broadcasts topical and relevant, AEP's researchers and scriptwriters go out of Kabul roughly once a month to a randomly selected village to meet listeners and get ideas for future programs. Men and women together pile into a minivan and set out from Kabul for a day's work in the country. What would be a relaxed experience in other countries is highly problematic in Afghanistan. Security is so poor in most provinces, even those close to Kabul, that it is better not to give any sign that you are a member of Kabul's small professional class. Danger may come not just from Taliban or police roadblocks but from armed bandits and vehicle hijackers. So, the team tries to look like a bunch of friends going on a picnic rather than broadcasters or journalists.

The team's problems do not end once they arrive at their chosen village. Making phone contact with local elders in advance may alert the wrong people, so they turn up unannounced. At the checkpoint that most settlements mount at the village entrance, they explain their business to the guard. If all goes well, he will contact the elders, and they will be invited in for a few hours of discussion. Inevitably, it will be an all-male affair on the villagers' side. "Men often don't let their wives leave the house or family compound," I was told by one AEP woman journalist. "Even when two women reporters ask to talk to women in their homes, that is often not permitted." For security reasons, the team only visits villages not frequented by the Taliban, so these rules are not connected with Taliban demands. They stem from the conservatism of traditional Afghan life.

A central theme in these soap operas and documentaries is the benefit of letting girls go to school. Thousands of Afghan fathers forbid their daughters from attending school, either because they misunderstand the Qur'an or out of security concerns. They are afraid of what may be going on at school or what may happen on the way if she does not have an older brother or other male relative to escort her. Children often walk for an hour or more on rough mountain paths.

When the Taliban held power in most of Afghanistan's provinces in the 1990s, they clamped down heavily on girls' education. But their bans on girls going to school and receiving higher education were never absolute, as mentioned in Chapter Six. Since they resumed their insurgency and particularly over the last two years, Taliban policy has become more pragmatic and fluid. Girls' schools and health clinics that have women staff are largely spared from attack.

In Helmand in 2010, Western officials told me that most Taliban commanders recognized that people wanted schools and health clinics and to destroy them was bad for their image and their hopes of getting villagers' support. Commanders who were more hard-line blew schools up, regardless of local people's views. But other commanders even tried to win credit by telling local elders that the Taliban presence forced the foreigners to pay to build schools as a way of competing with the Taliban. According to Brett Rapley, the Provincial Reconstruction Team's education adviser, "There is huge pressure in newly cleared areas to open schools and we only do it with buy-in from the local population. The Taliban haven't been active in attacking schools. There have been no attacks on girls' school in Lashkar Gah since 2005. There was one in Gereshk in April this year."

Other evidence has emerged of Taliban flexibility. When a Taliban leader was quoted by Afghan media in April 2011 as saying the movement would protect schools in areas they controlled, President Karzai told university graduates: "If it is proved that Mullah Omar has really ordered the Taliban not to prevent children from accessing education, I will thank him." In a telephone interview with a reporter from the Institute of War and Peace Reporting, Taliban spokesman Zabiullah Mojahed said his movement was not against education and wanted to have popular support: "The Taliban are the children of the people; they have emerged from among the people. The Taliban have always tried to be close to their people and to get their support."

People living in areas under Taliban control reported a relaxation of the rules in 2010 and 2011. In Ghazni province, Rahimullah, a father in the Andar district, said he had been forced to move from the area to get education for his children after their school was closed by the Taliban. He was able to return in early 2011 because schools had been allowed to start operating again. "The elders asked the Taliban to reopen the schools," he said. Ali Khan, a teacher in the Sayed Abad district of Wardak province, fled his home for fear of being targeted. In 2011 he returned to his job. "We don't know why the Taliban have become so flexible. I left my home because I was scared. Now the Taliban are encouraging us to go into school and teach."

Health clinics had also started to be spared. "Before I came here," said Dr. Jonathan Cox, the PRT medical adviser and a colonel in the British Army, "I thought the Taliban would be burning clinics down. That's not the case. They seem not to burn them down or blow them up. They don't even do it to clinics we've built." According to Rapley, the PRT education specialist, "women teachers who live in Taliban-influenced areas outside the security bubble and come in to work are sometimes intimidated." Medical staff appeared to be better off. "There is surprisingly little intimidation of health and clinic workers in lonely places," said Dr. Cox. "If it's a local [as opposed to an out-of-area or foreign] insurgent, he must know his family must be using that clinic and when the war is over he will need one himself."

How much has women's situation in Afghanistan improved since the Taliban lost power? The 2004 constitution declared that "the citizens of Afghanistan—whether man or woman—have equal rights and duties before the law," but this blanket statement needed to be fleshed out with legislation. It was not until August 2009 that the Afghan Parliament, under foreign pressure, passed a law to eliminate violence against women. Described as a big step forward in ending child marriage and the mistreatment of women, the law has suffered from minimal implementation and ambiguous instructions given to police and prosecutors. The law itself has loopholes. It failed to criminalize honor killings or clarify the distinction between rape and consensual sex outside marriage.

A separate bill governing family life for the Shia minority and signed into law by Karzai, also in August 2009, allows a man to withhold food from his wife if she refuses his sexual demands. A woman must get her husband's permission to work, and fathers and grandfathers are given exclusive custody of children.

Over 80 percent of Afghan women, particularly in rural areas, are illiterate and have very little or no awareness about their human rights, including the right to a fair trial. For a woman to refer a case of domestic violence to the police or a prosecutor is widely believed to be pointless. Allegations are usually not taken seriously, properly recorded or acted upon.

New rules drafted by the Ministry of Justice in early 2011 would dramatically change the operating procedures of some fourteen shelters for runaway and battered women and make treatment for women harder. The shelters were the first independent refuges for Afghan women, but the draft regulations would require women to undergo a medical examination before being admitted and bar them from leaving the grounds of the safe house except with permission from a government official to visit relatives. Further medical tests would be carried out monthly, and women would be ejected if their families said they would take them back or for marriage. The guidelines did not clarify if this included abusive families they had fled or forced marriages they were trying to avoid.

Some officials have claimed the fourteen shelters for runaway and battered women were involved in prostitution and drug use, an accusation reflecting suspicion about Western influence. Human Rights Watch said the draft illustrated the growing strength of conservative factions within Karzai's government and was an effort by him to improve his

Islamic credentials. The proposed rules would bring the shelters—funded by international organizations, Western governments and private donors—under the direct control of the Afghan Government.

One of NATO's favorite measures of change since Taliban times is the number of girls attending school. According to UNICEF, 2.5 million are in school, a huge rise from the 839,000 recorded in 2002. But many of these are in Kabul, and the official figures for the provinces tend to be inflated. Uruzgan, Mullah Omar's home province, with a total population of around 320,000, officially has 220 schools, but only twenty-one of them are functioning. Only one is a girls' school, and it is in the provincial capital, Tarin Kowt.

For girls to be permitted and able to go to school is a benefit, but what happens when they leave school? Where are the jobs, and what are U.S. and British aid programs doing to encourage female employment? To find out, I asked PRT officials in Helmand to arrange for me to see a group of women in Lashkar Gah in October 2010. We met in the Department of Women's Affairs, the only neutral venue they considered safe. They refused to come to the PRT fortress for fear of reprisals. About a dozen turned up—all teachers from various Helmand districts. The overriding problem for other women was jobs, they said. But even in downtown Lashkar Gah, the most modern part of the province, many women were kept permanently at home. In one of the city's poorer quarters, husbands even forbade their wives from going to the doctor.

Even when husbands or fathers allowed women out of the house, however, there were few jobs available apart from teaching. Rahela Safi, the deputy headmistress of a high school in Lashkar Gah, told me she had an enrollment of almost 10,000 girls. They studied for only two or three hours a day because teachers had to get through three shifts of students. Some pupils were already in their early twenties, having missed out during the Taliban period. But, though they studied subjects from math to biology and computer sciences, most ended up—if they found a job at all—teaching the next generation of girls. The cycle is hard to break. The hope must be that even if they get no paid work, the growing numbers of educated women in Afghanistan will have a greater chance of breaking through the walls of conservative male prejudice.

On my trip there, I learned that the Provincial Education Department in Lashkar Gah employed seventy people, but none were women. Officials said money was being allocated to set up a women's education unit to be staffed by women. This would be a step forward, even if it was still a case of women only working with and for other women rather than for the community as a whole. The PRT itself employed no women interpreters. When I asked the reason, a (female) British civilian adviser suggested the question was culturally insensitive since it assumed there were women available who had language skills and permission from their families to work alongside men. I suggested that the PRT could get the facts by advertising on the radio in Kabul or Lashkar Gah and seeing what responses they received. The provincial council in Lashkar Gah had three women members, but only one of Helmand province's district community councils, selected by local elders under U.S. and U.K. supervision and with U.S. and U.K. funding, had any female representatives.

The impression I came away with was that Washington and London were happy to try to alter Afghan culture when it came to the economy and business practice. When that culture restricted women's rights, there was less energy for reform. "Is it our goal to change Afghan society or deliver basic services and security and make it able to have a representative government?" said Arthur Snell, a British diplomat who served as the Lashkar Gah PRT's deputy head. "It would play into the Taliban's hands if they could say the foreigners are here to undermine Afghan traditional society. You have to strike a careful balance in getting things right."

His cautious attitude seemed to reflect a general retreat by American and British officials from pushing for equal rights for women in recent years. They have been giving up on nation building in favor of a strategy of leaving things to the Afghans, justifying this as part of the transition to Afghan sovereignty. Some critics say it is a concession to Karzai and the former mujahedin warlords who surround him and on whose political support he depends. Others see it as part of Petraeus's counterinsurgency tactics of trying to undermine rural resistance to the foreign occupation.

In a further sign of the trend of downgrading women's rights, the U.S. Agency for International Development (USAID) deleted most of its gender equality provisions from a $140 million program for land reform. When the agency sought bids for the huge program in March 2010, it had insisted that the winning contractor meet specific goals to promote women's rights. The number of deeds granting women title to land had to increase by 50 percent. There would have to be regular media coverage on women's land rights. Teaching materials for secondary schools and universities would have to include material on women's rights. A legal-aid system for women had to be set up and registrars had to be given incentives for ensuring that marital property is registered in the names of both spouses. USAID said "women in Afghanistan have few rights to inherit, obtain or transfer land," and the new program was "expressly designed to enhance and improve land use and ownership rights of women."

But before the contract was awarded, USAID stripped out all the targets. Under the new bidding rules, the contractor would only have to perform "a written evaluation of Afghan inheritance laws," assemble "summaries of input from women's groups" and draft amendments to the country's civil code. And this was not the only such case. A $600 million municipal government program which USAID awarded in 2010 also had women's rights requirements removed. "If you're targeting an issue, you need to target it in a way you can achieve those objectives," said J. Alexander Thier, director of USAID's Office of Afghanistan and Pakistan Affairs. "The women's issue is one where we need hardheaded realism. There are things we can do, and do well. But if we become unrealistic and overfocused . . . we get ourselves in trouble." Another senior U.S. official told the *Washington Post*, "Gender issues are going to have to take a back seat to other priorities. There's no way we can be successful if we maintain every special interest and pet project. All those pet rocks in our rucksack were taking us down."

If and when serious talks with the Taliban and the other armed insurgents get under way, it is right that women's rights are part of the agenda. It is also important that the negotiations are as transparent as possible with regular feedback to the Afghan Parliament, media and public so as to avoid having unfair deals made behind the Afghan people's backs. The negotiations will require compromises on all sides, including by the Taliban.

One can understand why *Time* magazine, with its Bibi Aisha story, should be upset about the treatment of Afghan women. Only the most hard-hearted would not feel concern for their plight. But it is too simple to blame the Taliban for the problem and thereby imagine that defeating the Taliban is a quick fix for solving it. Nor does it follow that making a deal with the Taliban is automatically a step backward.

The Afghan women professionals whom I interviewed in Kabul (see Chapter Twelve) took the view, in spite of their bitter experience of Taliban oppression, that security was the greatest human right. Gender equality was not the top priority at this stage in Afghan history.

The oppression of women in Afghanistan is an ancient and deep-seated ill that will take decades to cure. The prospects for improvement are greater in peacetime than in the midst of war.

[14] A DANGEROUS NEIGHBORHOOD

"Victory is impossible in Afghanistan. Obama is right to pull the troops out. No matter how difficult it will be. But what's the alternative— another Vietnam? Sending in half a million troops? That wouldn't work."

—MIKHAIL GORBACHEV, OCTOBER 2010

JULY 2009, OBAMA'S first visit to Moscow. Before the summit his administration announces that the "reset button" on Russian-American relations has already been pressed. Hopes are high and prove not to be in vain. The U.S. president and Dmitry Medvedev, his Kremlin counterpart, agree to cut their nuclear arsenals by almost half. They also issue a pledge to cooperate on anti-ballistic missile defense.

The surprise is item number three. Russia promises to let American military cargo, destined for Afghanistan, pass through its territory, both by air and overland. The offer is unprecedented, marking a level of military cooperation between Washington and Moscow that has not been seen since World War II.

Normally, both countries guard their sovereignty with enormous sensitivity. Now, less than twenty years since the Cold War ended, the two countries are allies in a joint battle against radical Islam. Nor is

Russia's offer merely symbolic. The United States plans to benefit from its unprecedented partnership with Russia by making as many as 4,500 flights to Afghanistan through Russian airspace every year as well as using freight trains for other cargo.

Cynics might have thought the Russians would enjoy America's discomfiture in Afghanistan. After all, many U.S. politicians aided the mujahedin in the 1980s since "we have a chance to give the Soviets their Vietnam," as Zbigniew Brzezinski put it. But if there were temptations for schadenfreude, Russian officials banished them long ago. The Kremlin felt Afghanistan posed just as much of a threat to Russia as it did to the United States. They wanted the Americans to succeed.

Drug trafficking and the increase in heroin addiction among Russians as well as the danger of the spread of Islamic fundamentalism were not issues that prompted Brezhnev and his colleagues to invade the country in 1979. Their fear was that chaos in Afghanistan would be exploited by the United States to take the country over. Much had changed in the intervening years. By 2001, two wars in Chechnya, turbulence in the northern Caucasus and countless terrorist bomb attacks by suspected Islamists had taken more lives in Moscow and other Russian cities than were lost in the United States on 9/11. Russia was not a direct al Qaeda target, but it was a victim of numerous atrocities by home-grown jihadis in its own southern republics as well as in the independent Central Asian states that used to be part of the Soviet Union.

After the Soviet collapse, Russians initially turned their backs on Afghanistan, where they had spilled so much blood. The "new Russia" under Boris Yeltsin stopped sending funds and fuel to Kabul, leading to the fall of the Najibullah regime. It was one of the ironies of Afghan history that Najibullah's collapse was achieved not by the mujahedin but by the Kremlin.

There were further ironies to come. After the Taliban captured Kabul in 1996, Moscow started to aid and arm the forces of Ahmad Shah Massoud, the Tajik warlord whose men had killed thousands of

Soviet soldiers during their army's failed offensives in the Panjshir valley. Their old enemy had become their new ally.

The reason was simple. Moscow wanted to prevent the Taliban from taking control of the whole of Afghanistan and in particular the provinces bordering on Uzbekistan and Tajikistan. As a leader of the Northern Alliance, Massoud was rightly seen as less extreme than the Taliban and a bulwark against the spread of radical Islamic movements into Central Asia. Unlike the Taliban he did not accept Chechen fighters in his ranks.

Russia continued to aid and arm the Northern Alliance throughout the 1990s, and its diplomats often met Massoud. Vladimir Putin was one of the first world leaders to send condolences to Bush after 9/11, and he strongly welcomed Operation Enduring Freedom, the U.S. attack that toppled the Taliban in 2001. Since the International Security Assistance Force coalition began in 2002, Russian Mi-8 and Mi-26 troop-carrying helicopters have been in active service in Afghanistan again, though flown by freelance Russian and Ukrainian pilots. The dreaded Mi-24 Hind helicopter gunships, which did so much damage during the Soviet occupation, now operate against the Taliban, mainly with Afghan pilots.

Where Moscow has drawn the line is on sending any ground troops back to Afghanistan. Joining the ISAF would be a step too far. Russian memories of their own Afghan war are still too raw. Their suspicion that the American war may also be doomed is deep. The comments from Gorbachev that head this chapter reflect the views of many ordinary Russians, but the Russian government has not voiced a similar opinion. Whatever doubts they may have about the chances of the United States winning the war, Medvedev and Vladimir Putin would prefer to see the Americans remaining engaged in Afghanistan than risk the chance of a Taliban victory.

The main Russian goal is a stable Afghanistan that is neutral, at peace with its neighbors and has no ambitions or plans to interfere. If they were convinced that an end to the civil war could be reached without the Taliban seizing power, they would support it. At the moment they feel uneasy. They fear that talks with the Taliban would be appeasement and might lead to a Taliban takeover of Kabul again. They would rather keep Karzai in power with the Uzbek and Tajik warlords who support him.

It is vital, therefore, that any negotiating process has a regional dimension. Afghanistan's neighbors must be kept informed of any discussions with the Taliban. They also need to meet regularly to work out a regional agreement on non-interference and respect for Afghan neutrality which could be signed in parallel with a settlement of the civil war.

The Russian preference for the Americans over the Taliban is firmly shared by Uzbekistan and Kyrgyzstan. On the eve of Operation Enduring Freedom, they agreed to lease two Soviet-era bases to the United States to help prepare for the attack. Although there have been periodic disputes over how much rent the United States should pay for the Manas base in Kyrgyzstan, it remains at U.S. disposal. In southern Uzbekistan the United States used the Karshi-Khanabad air base for several years, but after Washington condemned the Uzbek authorities for a harsh police crackdown on protesters in the town of Andijan in May 2005, permission was withdrawn. The row soon blew over, and the Uzbek regime has granted the United States transit rights to supply its forces in Afghanistan.

The regimes in Uzbekistan and Kyrgyzstan see more than a financial advantage in working with the United States. They believe it helps them to reduce Russia's historically large influence in their countries. This strategy of "re-balancing" their foreign policy since independence from the Soviet Union has also led them to improve relations with China.

While the Taliban were in power, Uzbekistan faced problems from a local armed fundamentalist group, the Islamic Movement of

Uzbekistan, which also operated in Tajikistan and Kyrgyzstan and was supported by the Taliban. Since 2001 the IMU has been much less active, especially after its leader, Juma Namagani, was killed.

The U.S. military also has transit agreements with the other three Central Asian states, Kazakhstan, Tajikistan and Turkmenistan. This helps to relieve pressure on the alternative route through Pakistan, which has frequently been attacked and sabotaged.

The Shanghai Co-operation Organization, a new regional body to which Russia, China and four of the Central Asian states belong, has called on the United States to close its bases in the region on the grounds that they were meant as a temporary facility in the initial attack on the Taliban. But they have never pressed hard to have this demand fulfilled. They still see benefit for themselves in the U.S. struggle against the Taliban.

Among Afghanistan's neighbors, Iran's role has been the most complex. Iran armed and aided the Northern Alliance for some years before 2001. After 9/11 it supported the U.S. attack on the Taliban. But it has understandable concerns about seeing a major U.S. air base at Shindand in western Afghanistan close to its border. With U.S. bases in Iraq and in the Persian Gulf, it feels surrounded. "Five Islamic countries are against the bases," Mustafa Mohammad Najjar, Iran's interior minister, said during a visit to Kabul in March 2011. "The arrival of foreign forces in the region, their presence and their bases are not in the interest of our government and our nation. Foreign forces have brought insecurity and terrorists to the region."

In recent years, Tehran's strategy has been to maintain contacts with, and put money on, every horse in the Afghan race, including the Taliban. In some cases, their investment has literally been cash. "They do give us bags of money—yes, yes, it is done," Karzai told a Kabul news conference in October 2010. "We are grateful to the Iranians for this. Patriotism has a price." He was responding to questions about a report that Iran sends regular cash payments to his chief of staff, Umar

Daudzai. Karzai discounted their importance, claiming the cash transfers, which amounted to about $1 million once or twice a year, were well-known, and that he had even disclosed them to then president Bush during a meeting at Camp David. "The United States is doing the same thing. They are providing cash to some of our offices," he said. Asked what he did in return for the Iranian money, Karzai said, "They have asked for good relations in return and for lots of other things in return."

NATO officials have regularly accused Iran of arming and financing the Taliban, and even of running training camps in Iran for Afghan fighters. They claim the evidence of arms supplies comes from intercepts. In March 2011, Mark Sedwill, NATO's senior civilian representative to Afghanistan, said alliance troops had seized forty-eight 122mm rockets which can be fired up to thirteen miles from a target, and explode in a burst up to 80 feet wide. This was double the power of the 107mm rockets allegedly provided by Iran to the Taliban since 2006. The rockets had no Iranian markings or serial numbers, but an intelligence official told an Associated Press reporter their technical details matched other Iranian models.

Whatever the level of Iranian military support to the Taliban may be, Tehran sees its strategic interest better served by the Karzai government than by a fundamentalist Sunni movement like the Taliban, with whom it had poor relations when it was in power. Arming the Taliban may be an insurance policy toward guaranteeing good relations in case they return to power. It is also a way of denying the United States any chance of a quick victory in Afghanistan, which might embolden Washington's hawks to turn their attention to attacking Iran. Like Russia, Iran also has anxieties over the traffic of heroin from Afghanistan through its territory. It has strengthened its border police to try to counter smuggling.

India is not a major element in the current Afghan equation. Its position on Afghanistan's future is mainly seen in terms of denial.

The Indians do not want a government in Kabul that is a close ally of Pakistan. The same is true of Pakistan's desires, only in reverse. This zero-sum logic has not changed from the time of the Daoud Khan regime and the subsequent Soviet occupation to Obama's war today.

During the Soviet and Najibullah periods, the Indians were close to Kabul's communist governments because they saw their opponents, the mujahedin, as tools of Pakistan and fundamentalist Islam. Once the mujahedin took power, India kept polite relations with Kabul until the Taliban victory. They kept contact with the ousted Northern Alliance, preferring to see them in power rather than the Taliban, a position that still holds today. India will have an important role to play in any talks on a regional agreement, provided it does not allow its dispute with Pakistan over Kashmir to distort the agenda or delay a solution.

Pakistan remains the key outside player in any process of ending the Afghan war. Second only to the United States, it plays the central role in whether there can be reconciliation between the Afghan parties. It may even hold a veto on whether talks even start. Anne Patterson, the U.S. ambassador in Islamabad until October 2010, understood this well when she cabled Washington in September 2009 that no amount of U.S. aid to Pakistan would buy it off supporting the Taliban's war in Afghanistan (or its support for armed groups in Kashmir). According to a document released by WikiLeaks to the *Guardian*, she wrote, "There is no chance that Pakistan will view enhanced [U.S.] assistance levels in any field as sufficient compensation for abandoning support to these groups, which it sees as an important part of its national security apparatus against India. The only way to achieve a cessation of such support is to change the Pakistan government's own perception of its security requirements." The main security concern, as the cable stated, was Pakistan's obsession with India, which it fears would use a "pro-India" government in Afghanistan to run a proxy war against Pakistan.

The Pakistani Government and Army would like to see a stable non-Taliban government in Afghanistan as long as it was predominantly

Pashtun, Patterson stated. It feared the Afghan Tajiks and Uzbeks were too close to India. But in the absence of such a government, Pakistan would continue to support the Taliban (although they publicly deny supporting them) as the lesser of two evils. Patterson told Washington that Pakistan was worried about any talk of reducing the U.S. military presence or of deadlines for a U.S. withdrawal from Afghanistan. "In such a scenario, the Pakistan establishment will dramatically increase support for Taliban groups in Pakistan and Afghanistan, which they see either as ultimately likely to take over the Afghan government or at least an important counter-weight to an Indian-controlled Northern Alliance."

Patterson made it clear that the Pakistani Government and Army were worried about instability in their own country. They were concerned by the threat posed by the Pakistani Taliban who operated from the areas along the Afghan border, the so-called Federally Administered Tribal Areas (FATAs). This was a largely ungoverned space in which al Qaeda had safe haven.

The Pakistani Taliban, known as Tehrik-i-Taliban Pakistan (TTP), is a group which began in the south Waziristan region of Pakistan in 2006 or 2007, mainly in response to U.S. activities in Afghanistan and attacks by the American and Pakistani forces on suspected al Qaeda strongholds in the Pakistani tribal belt. The TTP are less ideologically motivated and less well organized than the Afghan Taliban, though their commanders come from similar backgrounds—young mujahedin who fought the Russians in Afghanistan. If they have a clear goal, it is to convert Pakistan into an Islamic state. Their most conspicuous success so far was the incursion into Pakistan's Swat valley, but they were driven out by an army offensive in 2009. They are mainly located in north Waziristan but continue to pose a threat elsewhere.

Patterson warned Washington in her cables that rooting out the Pakistani Taliban had to be a long-term process in which the United States and the Pakistani security forces and law enforcement agencies worked together. American strikes from unmanned Predator drones were not the way to go since they only alienated Pakistani opinion and strengthened support for al Qaeda and the TTP. Her last point, a criticism of current Pentagon and White House policy, was phrased in suitably low-key terms: "Increased unilateral operations in these areas risk destabilizing the Pakistani state, alienating both the civilian government and military leadership, and provoking a broader governance crisis in Pakistan without finally achieving the goal."

There are two issues that Patterson's many leaked cables do not mention. One is Pashtunistan (described in Chapter Ten). Although rarely mentioned in diplomatic circles since it is not a live topic at the moment, it is deeply embedded in Afghan and Pakistani consciences. Several Pashtun Afghans have said to me, "Of course Peshawar is an Afghan city," or words to that effect. Pakistan's keen interest in what happens in its neighbor to the north is based on fears of Afghan territorial claims. The Pakistanis want to be sure that Afghan governments do not raise them. Hence their desire to have strong influence in Kabul to ensure the Pashtunistan issue remains dormant. Ideally, the issue should be settled permanently during talks on an end to the Afghan civil war. At the least, in return for pledges of non-interference from Pakistan, Afghanistan would promise not to raise the issue for a stipulated period of time, preferably decades, but continue to accept the present border as the de facto international frontier. But it may be that the weight of other more pressing issues will keep border disputes off the agenda. Burdening the negotiations with Pashtunistan might risk destroying everything.

The second subject Patterson did not mention was Islamabad's attitude to peace talks for Afghanistan. While the main thrust of the Pakistani intelligence service's policy has been to support the Taliban's war, signs appeared in 2010 that Pakistan might be coming under pressure to favor a negotiated settlement. In January 2010 a Pakistani intelligence team arrested Mullah Abdul Ghani Baradar, one of the twelve members of the Quetta Shura. Baradar was known as an advocate of peace talks with the Afghan Government and the Americans. There was immediate speculation that the Pakistanis wanted to hold him so as to control the agenda and timing of any peace negotiations. Another shift in the environment was the growth of the Pakistani Taliban. This could encourage Islamabad to feel it would be better to have a settlement in neighboring Afghanistan so as to clear the way for a full-scale military campaign against the Pakistani Taliban. Pakistani embarrassment over U.S. suspicions after bin Laden's discovery and death that Pakistani intelligence services had been sheltering bin Laden all along could also strengthen the case for them to get the Afghan Taliban to go home. That would require pushing the Taliban leadership toward accepting peace talks with the Afghan Government and the Americans.

Gerard Russell, the former British diplomat who worked for the UN in Afghanistan, shares Patterson's assessment that Pakistan would prefer a non-Taliban government in Kabul provided it is dominated by Pashtuns. He believes, moreover, that Pakistan fears a Taliban victory would not lead to lasting stability and would irritate China, one of Pakistan's main allies. The Chinese need a settlement in Afghanistan so they can develop the copper and other mining interests they have there. That requires bringing all the various Afghan groups on board so as to end the long-running civil war that has held development back.

New indications that Pakistan was coming around to the view that peace talks were the best solution in Afghanistan emerged in April 2011. The two states upgraded a peace commission they had set up in January and agreed it should meet regularly at prime ministerial or presidential level. One of its mandates would be to keep each side informed about talks with the Taliban. After meeting Karzai in Kabul, Pakistan's Prime Minister Yousuf Gilani told reporters, "Pakistan stands strongly behind efforts to make peace with the Taliban and while the US will play a role in any reconciliation, Kabul should set the parameters for any talks to end the war." Karzai told the same press conference that if members of the Taliban who were interested in negotiating peace were in Pakistan, they should be "given protection and they should not be treated otherwise." His remarks seemed to be a mild rebuke to Pakistan for arresting Mullah Baradar or at least a plea to Pakistan to treat him well and let him take part in peace talks.

It is clear that the regional picture is complex. Russia and the Central Asian states are broadly satisfied with the U.S. presence remaining indefinitely in Afghanistan as long as the Taliban do not regain power in Kabul. Iran and India have not got a fixed position, while Pakistan and China are leaning toward a peace deal in which the Taliban are involved.

But there is a factor that could unify them all. If Afghanistan's neutrality or non-alignment is made part of an international settlement, along with the withdrawal of all foreign troops and bases, the neighbors could accept it. This means that the Afghan parties would have to break formally with al Qaeda and pledge that Afghanistan will not allow its territory to be used to threaten any other state. Osama bin Laden's death has made that an easier proposition. By the same token, other states would pledge to respect Afghanistan's integrity and not interfere in its internal affairs. And of course there could be no U.S. or other state's troops or military bases in the country. The time for trying to exert influence over Afghanistan through Great Games must end.

CONCLUSION:
THE WAY FORWARD

"Any future Defense Secretary who advises the president to again send a big American land army into Asia or into the Middle East or Africa should have his head examined."

—Robert Gates, former U.S. Defense Secretary,
West Point, February 2011

In their burqas and sandals a group of women sit on the ground chopping carrots and boiling rice over a wood fire. Men with long white beards wait patiently nearby. The Afghans are real, but not the village. It is a replica, set up at a British Army camp in southern England.

Chinook helicopters swoop down to off-load a platoon of troops, who will drink tea with the "elders" and chat with them via a Pashtun interpreter. The soldiers will soon be off to Helmand for their first mission in Afghanistan, and this is part of their "familiarization" routine. At German Army bases, similar role-playing goes on for German troops who are to deploy to Kunduz in the north.

However useful the exercises may be in terms of troop training, they carry within them a tragic irony. Many of the amateur actors have never been to Afghanistan. They are children of the diaspora, sons and daughters of men and women who have had to flee their country at some point in its last thirty-five years of unending war. Yet now for money (and in these straitened times some can find no other paid work) they put on national dress to teach the culture and traditions of a country they themselves have never known to young foreigners who are about to go to it with military uniforms and guns. The horror of Afghanistan's modern history has many faces, but this vignette is one of the most painful I have yet come across. It involves no blood, no wounds, no death, only the humiliation of displacement and exile.

Hundreds of thousands of Afghan refugees live in the diaspora in Europe and North America. They are less poor than the one and a half million in camps in Pakistan, but their sense of loss of homeland is just as great. In terms of security they are certainly better off than the thirty million Afghans in Afghanistan, cursed by its misery, underdevelopment and recent decades of war and blessed only in that they live in their own country where they have their roots.

Afghanistan ranks 135 out of 135 countries on the UN's Human Poverty Index. Life expectancy at 44.6 years is the lowest in the world. One out of every five children dies before the age of five, and Afghanistan has the highest infant mortality rate in the world. Seventy-three percent of the population have no access to safe drinking water.

If the country were to return to peace, these dramatic statistics could not but change. Afghanistan has the potential to prosper. It is rich in natural resources, which the long years of conflict have kept from exploitation. Mineral deposits, mainly of iron and copper, are thought to be worth close to $1 trillion. In 2006, the United States Geological Survey estimated that northern Afghanistan had 1,596 million barrels of crude oil, and 15,687 billion cubic feet of natural gas.

In 2007, the state-owned China Metallurgical Group bid $3.4 billion to win the right to mine the vast copper deposits at Aynak. The royalties China paid to the Afghan state constituted the government's largest single revenue source. China is also showing interest in newly discovered deposits of lithium, which is needed to make mobile phones and electric car batteries.

Countries in the region have already held talks on tying Afghanistan into a larger regional economy through new road, rail and pipeline links. This could allow Afghanistan to become a gateway for trade to and from Central Asia, South Asia and Iran. The Afghanistan-Pakistan Transit Trade Agreement permits goods from Afghanistan to transit Pakistani territory en route to India, although plans for Indian goods destined for Afghanistan to pass through Pakistan were not yet complete by the spring of 2011. Pakistan will be able to export goods to Central Asia via Afghanistan.

Plans have been revived for a natural gas pipeline that would cross through Turkmenistan, Afghanistan, Pakistan and India. The Asian Development Bank is sponsoring and financing the project. The Silk Road Initiative, a regional program led by the United Nations Development Programme (UNDP), aims to engage countries that have historic links with Afghanistan but are not direct neighbors. It focuses on facilitating public/private partnerships in investment, trade and tourism.

It has not been this book's purpose to outline Afghanistan's economic future, though it is important to recognize the potential good news that awaits a settlement of its long-running civil war. Afghanistan is not an inherently poor country that will need development aid for decades. The prospect of long-term peace is the top priority rather than long-term foreign cash.

What I have tried to do is to reveal the "ghosts"—the specters of past mistakes that haunt the Americans and British in Afghanistan today. The ghosts of the Soviet misadventure in Afghanistan point the way. The Kremlin should not have taken military action to achieve regime change in Kabul. It acted from a desire for revenge and a false reading of how best to protect national security. It failed to consider the consequences of a non-Muslim state inserting troops into a country with a long history of defying invaders. What was intended as a quick in-and-out invasion soon suffered mission creep. Regime change turned into nation building and an occupation that lasted nine years. The comparison with U.S. policy is clear, except that Washington's occupation remains unfinished after ten years.

It was not as if American policy makers were ignorant of Afghanistan before they went in. The United States played a key role in exploiting the Kremlin's blunders by arming rebels during the Soviet period, many of whom—including Osama bin Laden—wanted to impose a fundamentalist version of Sharia law that was not part of Afghan tradition. In 2001 hubris led Washington to think it would be able to do a better job of providing stability and progress than the Soviets had done.

My second aim is to highlight the one enormously important difference between the Soviet and American record. A new leader came to power in the Kremlin, abandoned hopes of victory and tried hard to achieve a negotiated settlement with his Afghan enemies. He urged his allies in Kabul to reach out to opposition forces, whether they were the secular nationalists around the exiled former Afghan king or the mujahedin fighting from sanctuaries in Pakistan. He encouraged them to offer political compromises that could lead to a cease-fire and a peace treaty.

At the end of July 2011, after Obama's announcement of an end to the U.S. troop surge, I went to Moscow to see Gorbachev. It was twenty years since the Soviet Union's collapse and I found him remarkably cheerful at the age of eighty. He had had plenty of time to reflect on his extraordinary legacy and confessed to making many mistakes, including not having resigned from the Communist party when it became an obstacle to reform. Among other issues, I wanted to know what lessons he felt the Americans could learn from his own Afghan experience. This was an issue on which he said he had no second thoughts. The Soviet withdrawal had been right. Should the Americans talk to the Taliban, I asked him. "They should talk to everyone. We talked to everyone, including the people fighting against us," he replied. "I say withdraw the troops. Help the Afghans create a political situation that would be more democratic and make it possible to shape some kind of government, a central government and provincial governments, taking into account their tribal allegiances because without taking that into account success is impossible. Support the business community, religious leaders. I tried to do all that. Then work out some arrangement and start pulling out and put an end to this epic story."

While Gorbachev's efforts were serious and sustained, the successor regime of Mohammed Najibullah also made overtures to the rebels after the Russians withdrew their troops. He offered sweeping concessions in the hope of reaching a political agreement that could last.

Regrettably, both efforts came to nothing, thanks in large part to opposition from the West. The problem was not that the West "walked away" from Afghanistan after the Russians withdrew in 1989, as one of the oldest myths has it. The West stayed in the game and maintained the wrong strategy, cynically blocking every chance for a negotiated end to the Afghan civil war. The United States bears a heavy burden of guilt for that policy, and has suffered greatly from the blowback of its shortsighted support for the fundamentalists who became al Qaeda and for the mujahedin who turned into the Taliban. But the largest number of victims, of course, are in Afghanistan itself.

The lesson for today is clear. This time there must be negotiations. For the Obama administration to put its weight behind a serious effort to end the Afghan civil war would atone, in part, for the U.S. policy of sustaining and enlarging it in the 1990s. Polls show that a majority of Afghans see ceasefires and talks as the only way to end the bloodshed, and they want the United States to wholeheartedly support them. At a summit in Lisbon in November 2010, the governments of the forty-eight states contributing to the International Security Assistance

Force set a goal of December 2014 for asking Afghan troops to take the lead in combat throughout the country. The implication was that foreign forces would then depart. The move was widely welcomed in Afghanistan. As Jolyon Leslie, a former UN negotiator and one of the most experienced foreign residents of Kabul, put it: "We shouldn't forget that the 2014 date was immensely relieving to the Afghan people. It didn't come across to the people with whom I live and work as a harbinger of 'Oh my God, they are cutting and running.' It came across as 'Thank Goodness, we can get beyond this and we can work things out for ourselves.'"

The Obama administration is planning to keep hundreds of troops in Afghanistan as advisers and trainers after 2014 on a long-term basis, Robert Gates, the former U.S. defense secretary, told Afghanistan's Tolo News in June 2011. Ryan Crocker, the new U.S. ambassador in Kabul, said at his confirmation hearings in the Senate that the strategic partnership agreement that the United States wants to sign with Karzai's government would "provide a road map for our political, economic and security cooperation." Although U.S. troops would be quartered on nominally Afghan bases, these plans undermine the prospect of Afghan independence and threaten to make a peace deal impossible. Neither the Afghan resistance, which has fought long and hard to remove foreign troops, nor Afghanistan's regional neighbors will accept this. Rather than keeping U.S. troops in Afghanistan indefinitely, Washington should plan for a complete withdrawal as part of an agreement that finally ends the country's more than thirty years of civil war. If Washington rushes ahead to negotiate a bilateral document on long-term strategic relations with the Karzai government before trying to negotiate a deal with the Taliban and the other resistance groups, it will be sabotaging the chance for a comprehensive peace.

The killing of Osama bin Laden in Pakistan on May 2, 2011, has removed the main plank that was used to justify Operation Enduring Freedom, the attack on Afghanistan, in October 2001. Long before his death, it was clear that al Qaeda's operations in south Asia were conducted from Pakistan, not Afghanistan. It was also clear that the Taliban's goals were separate from those of al Qaeda. Now that bin Laden is dead, public opinion in the United States and Britain is understandably swinging away from keeping troops in Afghanistan any longer.

Even as public impatience justifiably increases, the option of withdrawing from Afghanistan without a negotiated settlement, as the Soviets did, is not the best one. It is preferable to staying in the country in a futile search for military victory, but its results could be dire. They were spelled out graphically by Francesc Vendrell, the former UN and European Union envoy. "Having failed dismally to make the Afghan people our allies," he wrote in 2011, "we will inevitably abandon them to a combination of Taliban in the south and the warlords in the north and—having somehow redefined success—we will go home convinced that it is the Afghan people who have failed us."

That scenario must be avoided at all costs. Any process of negotiations will be prolonged and difficult. They will be harder than the talks that ended the Soviet occupation because the pro-government side contains powerful players who lost power to the Taliban in 1996 and want to concede as little as possible to the Taliban today. Leaders of the largely Tajik Northern Alliance may try to sabotage the talks altogether.

It will also be important to take on board the rights of women and find space in the negotiations for representatives of the cadre of secular professionals who make up the bulk of the Afghan diaspora. They provide the best hope for progressive administration but have been shut out of every Afghan regime since the fall of Najibullah. The mujahedin and the Taliban marginalized them deliberately. The arrangements set up at the Bonn conference in 2001 offered them some room to express their views but little decision-making power. The Karzai-led governments of the last decade have all been dominated by warlords and their cronies or corrupt tribal appointees.

   The social regression of recent years in Afghanistan will be hard to reverse. After three decades of war, too many of its people have been traumatized by the loss of loved ones and years spent as refugees. The country is full of men with guns who have spent much of their lives in official or unofficial armed units and know nothing of normal social and economic exchange. A peace deal is only the first step in what will have to be a long process of healing and repair. But local cease-fires and negotiations, between Afghans and the foreigners and among Afghans themselves, are the only way to start the process. They will give the people of Afghanistan a sense of physical security that so few of them have ever known.

ACKNOWLEDGMENTS

MUCH OF THE material in this book was collected while I was on various assignments in Afghanistan for the *Guardian* over the past thirty years, and I am grateful to the foreign editors who sent me, including Campbell Page, Martin Woollacott, Paul Webster, Simon Tisdall and Ed Pilkington. My most recent trip to Helmand was commissioned by Clare Margetson, the editor of the paper's G2 section.

I have also benefited greatly from conversation and discussion with Afghan and English friends. The late Fred Halliday, professor of International Relations at the London School of Economics, was a valued source of support in the 1980s, when the number of Western analysts and journalists who were willing to put the Cold War aside and write about the Soviet occupation calmly and without prejudice was minute.

The dozens of Afghans I interviewed at different times in their country or outside it are identified in the text by name, and I am grateful to them all. I am particularly thankful to those who read parts of the book and suggested changes. They include Ahmad Sarwar and Shirazuddin Siddiqi. My former *Guardian* colleague, John Gittings, and John Kampfner also made valuable comments. Anthony Sheil, my literary agent, was as encouraging with this book as he has been on all my previous ones.

I want to thank the many people who read chapters and provided appreciative comments, some of which appear on this book's cover. They include Jon Lee Anderson, Sherard Cowper-Coles, Lyse Doucet, Peter Galbraith, Selig S. Harrison, Seymour M. Hersh, Simon Jenkins, Mary Kaldor, Jolyon Leslie, Mark Malloch Brown and Jon Snow.

I am indebted to the teams at Counterpoint Press in Berkeley and Portobello in London, in particular Jack Shoemaker and Philip Gwyn Jones. I only met Norman MacAfee, my copy editor in New York City, electronically, but he was immensely thorough and thoughtful.

Above all, I am grateful to my wife, Ruth, who read the entire script, pointed out errors and offered numerous ideas for improvement. As always, she was a source of unwavering support.

NOTES

ANATOMY OF AFGHAN SOCIETY

9   *Estimates of the population of Afghanistan:* "Population of Afghanistan," CIA, *The World Factbook*, 2010.

9   *The last official census, in 1979: Afghanistan Country Study.* Illinois Institute of Technology, pp. 105–106.

9   *Ethnic Groups (in percent):* Wikipedia, World Factbook, Library of Congress Country Studies.

9   *Languages (in percent):* Central Intelligence Agency, The World Factbook, Afghanistan.

10   *It ranks 135 out of 135 countries:* UN Human Development Report 2009, Country Fact Sheets: Afghanistan.

10   *per capita income is $906, and its GDP is:* "Afghanistan," International Monetary Fund.

10   *Afghans' life expectancy at birth:* "The Real Wealth of Nations: Pathways to Human Development," UN Human Development Report 2010, November 2010, available at http://hdrstats.undp.org/en/countries/profiles/AFG.html.

10   *Twenty percent of the children die:* USAID, "Afghanistan: Health," Fall 2009, www.usaid.org.

10   *Education: Mean years of schooling:* UN Human Development Report 2010, available at http://hdrstats.undp.org/en/countries/profiles/AFG.html.

10   *American geologists and Pentagon officials estimated:* James Risen, "U.S. Identifies Vast Mineral Riches in Afghanistan," *New York Times,* June 13, 2010, available at http://www.nytimes.com/2010/06/14/world/asia/14minerals.html.

INTRODUCTION

13   *Epigraph: A confused silence greeted:* Bob Woodward, *Obama's Wars* (New York: Simon and Schuster, 2010), p. 97.

[1] WHERE ARE WE NOW?

19   *Epigraph: "What we figured out is":* Unnamed official on the decision to withdraw troops from the Pech valley in Kunar province, eastern Afghanistan, quoted in C. J. Chivers, Alissa J. Rubin and Wesley Morgan, "U.S. Pulling Back in Afghan Valley It Called Vital to War," *New York Times,* February 24, 2011.

25   *Munshi Abdul Majid, the provincial governor:* Joshua Partlow, "In Letter, Petraeus Offers Optimistic Assessment of Afghan War," *Washington Post,* January 26, 2011.

25   *Two United Nations maps:* Yaroslav Trofimov, "UN Maps Out Afghan Security," *Wall Street Journal,* December 26, 2010.

25   *Pentagon's annual report to Congress:* Available at www.defense.gov/pubs /November_1230_Report_FINAL.pdf.

26   *A poll conducted in July 2010:* "Afghanistan: The Relationship Gap," International Council on Security and Development, London, July 2010.

26   *Freight convoys between Afghanistan's:* U.S. Senate Armed Services Committee, Inquiry into the Role and Oversight of Private Security Contractors in Afghanistan. Report published on September 28, 2010.

31   *According to a U.S. diplomatic cable:* Available at *Guardian* website: http://www .guardian.co.uk/world/us-embassy-cables-documents/187068.

32   *The Taliban replied by spreading allegations:* Sebastian Abbott, "Villagers Claim Deaths, Complicating Afghan Push," Associated Press, November 26, 2010.

32   *"The people say we don't need any help":* Ibid.

33   *A BBC reporter wondered whether:* Ben Anderson, BBC News, January 31, 2011.

34   *A few months later, reporters found:* Elisabeth Bumiller, "Some Skeptics Questioning Rosy Reports on War Zone," *New York Times,* November 7, 2010.

34   *A year after Operation Mushtarak:* Available at www.isaf.nato.int and then 0423-11_Marjah_LR_en.pdf.

35   *Similar complexities prevail in Kandahar:* Yaroslav Trofimov, "Afghan Offensive Pushes Militants to Kandahar, Back in Home City Taliban Use Bombs, Threats to Undermine Local Officials," *Wall Street Journal,* November 3, 2010.

35   *"Nobody wants to work with me":* Ibid.

35   *The general's murder came four days after:* Tom A. Peter, "Assassinated Kandahar
      Police Chief Was Optimistic About Security," *Christian Science Monitor,* April 15,
      2011.

39   *In April 2011, General David Petraeus said:* Deb Riechmann, "Petraeus: Al Qaeda
      Is Not on Rise in Afghanistan," Associated Press, April 10, 2011.

39   *On March 27, 2009:* Available at http://www.whitehouse.gov/the-press-office
      /remarks-president-a-new-strategy-afghanistan-and-pakistan.

40   *In his book* Obama's Wars: Bob Woodward, *Obama's Wars* (New York: Simon
      and Schuster, 2010), passim.

40   *"'Ghosts,' Obama whispered":* Ibid., p. 97.

43   *The results, published in 2010:* Helmand Justice Mapping Study, PO 5272, pro-
      duced by Coffey International Development Ltd., Reading, Berkshire, U.K.,
      2010.

45   *Sherard Cowper-Coles, Britain's special:* Sherard Cowper-Coles, Oral evidence
      given to House of Commons Foreign Affairs Committee on November 9, 2010,
      published on March 2, 2011, p. 123.

45   *According to Nick Abbott:* Interview with author, London, September 2010.

46   *There were 225 aid workers killed:* Data from the Aid Worker Security Database
      (www.aidworkersecurity.org). For analysis of motives, see A. Stoddard, A.
      Harmer, D. DiDomenico, "Providing Aid in Insecure Environments: 2009
      Update," Humanitarian Policy Group, Policy Paper 34, London, April 2009.

47   *Since mid-2008, the risks for NGOs:* Yaroslav Trofimov and Habib Khan Totakhil,
      "Aid Groups Seek Safety Pacts with Taliban; Agencies Tout Their Neutrality to
      Get Permission to Operate," *Wall Street Journal,* November 22, 2010.

49   *"It's a matter of life and death":* Tarek El-Tablawy, "NATO: $20 Billion
      Over 2 Years for Afghan Training," Associated Press, January 5, 2011,
      available at http://news.yahoo.com/s/ap/20110105/ap_on_re_as
      /as_afghan_nato_training.

50   *Petraeus told Congress in March 2011:* Thom Shanker, "General Sees Joint Bases
      for Afghans After 2014," *New York Times,* March 15, 2011.

50   *General Ronald Burgess, the director:* Available at Defense Intelligence Agency site:
      http://www.dia.mil/public-affairs/testimonies/2011-03-10.html.

50   *Major General Phil Jones:* Alissa J. Rubin, "Few Taliban Leaders Take Afghan
      Offer to Switch Sides," *New York Times,* June 19, 2011.

51   *A 2009 survey commissioned by the DFID:* "Testing Hypotheses on Radicalisation,"
      Sarah Ladbury in collaboration with Co-operation for Peace and Unity (CPAU),
      Kabul, August 2009. The report was on the DFID website but has been taken
      down.

[2] THE SOVIET INVASION

53   *Epigraph: "We have carefully studied all aspects":* Woodrow Wilson Center
      for International Scholars, Cold War International History Project, Virtual
      Archive: Collection: Soviet Invasion of Afghanistan: Meeting of Kosygin,
      Gromyko, Ustinov, and Ponomarev with Taraki in Moscow, March
      20, 1979. Available at http://www.wilsoncenter.org/index.cfm?topic_
      id=1409&fuseaction=va2.document&identifier=5034DBE7-96B6-175C
      -981ACBCBC6932105&sort=Collection&item=Soviet%20Invasion%20of%
      20Afghanistan.

63   *"Kabul, thank goodness, I was there":* Artyom Borovik, *The Hidden War* (London:
      Faber and Faber, 1991), p. 239.

66   *"no one knows who killed him":* Abdul Karim Misaq interview with author,
      London, March 2011.

69   *"afraid Daoud would arrest them too," Ahmad Sarwar recalled:* Interview with
      author, Wesseling, January 2011.

69   *Babrak Karmal, the Parcham leader, later said:* Interview with Vladimir Snegirev,
      Trud, October 24, 1991.

69   *Aleksandr Puzanov, the Soviet ambassador in Kabul:* Odd Arne Westad, "Prelude
      to Invasion: The Soviet Union and the Afghan Communists 1978–79,"
      International History Review, Simon Fraser University, Volume XVI, Number
      1, February 1994. This long essay, which is based on access to Soviet archive
      materials, provides the most detailed and documented account of the Soviet
      invasion.

72   *"After more than forty years":* Zeary interview with author, London, March 2011.

74   *Transparency International in its 2010 report:* Report available at http://www
      .transparency.org/policy_research/surveys_indices/cpi/2010/in_detail.

74   *"In the first three months after":* Keshtmand interview with author, November
      2010.

75   *Summoned to Moscow in March 1979:* Woodrow Wilson Center for
      International Scholars, Cold War International History Project, Virtual
      Archive: Collection: Soviet Invasion of Afghanistan: Meeting of Kosygin,
      Gromyko, Ustinov, and Ponomarev with Taraki in Moscow, March

20, 1979. Available at http://www.wilsoncenter.org/index.cfm?topic_
id=1409&fuseaction=va2.document&identifier=5034DBE7-96B6-175C
-981ACBCBC6932105&sort=Collection&item=Soviet%20Invasion%20of%
20Afghanistan.

75   *Taraki's murder infuriated Brezhnev:* Giles Dorronsoro, *Revolution Unending*
      (London: Hurst, 2005), p. 96.

77   *Rumors about Amin's loyalty:* Rodric Braithwaite, *Afgantsy* (London: Profile
      Books, 2011), p. 40. Braithwaite sources the information to General Aleksandr
      Lyakhovski whose book *Tragediya i Doblest Afgana* is a record of interviews with
      Soviet officers. Lyakhovski himself served for five years in Afghanistan.

80   *In his memoirs, Robert Gates:* Robert Gates, *From the Shadows: The Ultimate
      Insider's Story of Five Presidents and How They Won the Cold War* (New York:
      Simon and Schuster, 1996), pp. 142–149.

80   *Brzezinski remains pleased to have done so:* "Brzezinski and the Afghan War Pt2,"
      YouTube: http://www.youtube.com/watch?v=RGjAsQJh7OM&feature=
      channel.

80   *Mohammed Dost, the foreign minister, insisted:* Interview with author, Kabul,
      November 1981.

83   *"You can't just say Afghans":* Interview with author, Kabul, November 1981.

85   *One afternoon in November 1981:* Yuri Volkov interview with author, Kabul,
      November 1981.

87   *During their time there, Soviet advisers:* Cold War International History
      Project, available at http://www.wilsoncenter.org/index.cfm?topic_
      id=1409&fuseaction=va2.browse&sort=Collection&item=Soviet%20
      Invasion%20of%20Afghanistan.

90   *As Morton Abramowitz, who directed:* Interview with CNN Cold War project,
      August 1997, unpublished transcript in possession of author.

90   *Suggesting that the mujahedin were not winning:* Doris Lessing, *The Wind Blows
      Away Our Words* (London: Picador, 1986), p. 74.

[3] THE GORBACHEV EFFECT

93   *Epigraph: Nikolai Ryzhkov, Soviet prime minister, January 1987:* Notes from
      Politburo session. Available at National Security Archive, "an independent, non-
      governmental research institute and library located at The George Washington
      University, Washington, DC." http://www.gwu.edu/~nsarchiv/NSAEBB/
      NSAEBB272/.

96   *In a Moscow bookshop ... anthology of letters and poems:* Pyotr Tkachenko, *My Darlings ... Letters from Afghanistan* (Moscow: Profizdat, 1991).

97   *Every so often I came across:* Ibid., p. 34.

97   *Private Sergei Bolotnikov, a farmworker:* Ibid., pp. 49–50.

98   *At the time he was selected:* Anatoly Chernyayev, *Sovestnyi iskhod: Dnevnik dvukh epokh Rosspen* (Moscow, 2008), pp. 570–571.

99   *After Chernenko's funeral, Gorbachev:* National Security Archive Electronic Briefing Book no. 272 NSAEBB 272. Available at http://www.gwu .edu/~nsarchiv/NSAEBB/NSAEBB272/.

99   *A month later, in his private diary:* Chernyayev, *Sovestnyi iskhod,* pp. 570–571.

99   *There were arguments against withdrawal:* Quoted from Politburo documents in Artemy Kalinovsky, "Decision-Making and the Soviet War in Afghanistan," *Journal of Cold War Studies,* Volume 11, Number 4, Fall 2009.

100   *a damning report from General Valentin Varennikov:* ibid., p. 61.

101   *Edward Girardet of the* Christian Science Monitor: Edward Girardet. *Afghanistan: The Soviet War* (London: Croom Helm, 1985), pp. 33–34.

102   *Ahmad Sarwar, the former Afghan chargé:* Interview with author, Wesseling, January 2011.

102   *The massive hardship their tactics:* Paul Robinson, "Soviet Hearts-and-Minds Operations in Afghanistan," *The Historian,* Volume 72, Issue 1, Spring 2010, available online at http://onlinelibrary.wiley.com/doi/10.1111 /j.1540-6563.2009.00254.x/full.

103   *The war involved appalling brutality:* Vitaly Krivenko, *Ekipazh mashiny boevoi* (St. Petersburg, 2004), p. 372, quoted in Rodric Braithwaite, *Afgantsy* (London: Profile Books, 2011), p. 230. *Afgantsy* contains a wealth of eyewitness accounts and graphic reminiscences from Soviet troops, officers and advisers.

103   *Andrei Greshnov interviewed Mohamed Hamid:* Andrei Greshnov, *Afganistan: Zalozhniki vremeni* (Moscow, 2006), p. 133, quoted in Braithwaite, *Afgantsy,* p. 233.

104   *As Chernyayev put it in his diary:* Available at http://www.gwu.edu/~nsarchiv /NSAEBB/NSAEBB272/.

106   *"With or without Karmal we will follow":* Ibid.

107   *In 1980s Moscow things were different:* Cold War International History Project. Available at http://wilsoncenter.org/index.cfm?topic_ id=1409&fuseaction=va2.document&identifier=5034DF42-96B6-175C

-94B37A1064349E42&sort=Collection&item=Soviet%20Invasion%20of%20 Afghanistan.

107   *Marshal Sergei Sokolov's turn to sound:* Cold War International History Project: Publications Index, p. 15, Document number 181.

110   *army chaplain, Reverend G. R. Gleig:* Quoted in William Dalrymple, "As the Great Game Repeats Itself, India Must Wake Up to Karzai's New Moves," available at http://www.outlookindia.com/article.aspx?266767.

112   *According to one U.S. Government estimate:* Selig Harrison and Diego Cordovez, *Out of Afghanistan* (New York: Oxford University Press, 1995), p. 199.

113   *The best study of the Stingers issue:* Alan J. Kuperman, "The Stinger Missile and U.S. Intervention in Afghanistan," *Political Science Quarterly,* Summer 1999, Volume 114, Number 2, pp. 219–263. Available at http://links.jstor.org /sici?sici=0032-3195%28199922%29114%3A2%3C219%3ATSMAUI%3E2 .0.CO%3B2-V.

114   *Eduard Shevardnadze, the Soviet foreign minister:* Cold War International History Project: Publications Index, p. 15, Document number 181.

114   *article in the Moscow weekly* Literaturnaya Gazeta: Aleksandr Prokhanov, *Literaturnaya Gazeta,* February 17, 1988.

117   *According to the version Karmal:* Interview with Vladimir Snegirev, *Trud,* October 24, 1991.

119   *Soviet thinking was evolving fast:* Notes from Politburo session, available at http://www.gwu.edu/~nsarchiv/NSAEBB/NSAEBB272/.

121   *Cordovez complained that Western governments:* Harrison and Cordovez, *Out of Afghanistan,* p. 283.

122   *As Khalis put it, "If we accepted":* "Rebels Outline Plan for Afghan Regime— Some Kabul Officials Could Be Included," *Washington Post,* February 24, 1988.

124   *Shultz later admitted that Shevardnadze felt betrayed:* Harrison and Cordovez, *Out of Afghanistan,* p. 263.

125   *"Zahir Shah simply failed to gather":* Ibid., p. 369.

128   *The Americans claimed that they were sure of victory:* Jonathan Steele, "Kabul at the Crossroads: The Najib Government's Chances of Independent Survival," *Guardian,* April 23, 1988.

[4] RECONCILIATION FAILS

131   Epigraph: "The only thing I question": Charles Cogan, Interview for CNN Cold
       War series, August 1997. Unpublished transcript in possession of author.

131   Epigraph: "The Soviet-backed government of Najibullah": "Understanding
       Afghanistan," Report by the Recovery and Development Consortium for the
       U.K. Department for International Development, November 2008, p. 26. "The
       views expressed in the report are those of the authors and do not represent UK
       government policy."

133   Staffan de Mistura, who was working for the United Nations: Interview with author,
       Kabul, March 2010.

133   Sultan Ali Keshtmand, one of the most experienced administrators: Interview with
       author, London, November 2010.

134   "Once again due to Cold War logic": De Mistura interview with author, Kabul,
       March 2010.

134   Najibullah made a virtue out of necessity: Jonathan Steele, "The Lamb Stands
       Up to the Lion: The Afghan Government Is Proving a Power to Be Reckoned
       With," Guardian, February 25, 1989.

138   "I thought they were going to lose Jalalabad": Ahmad Sarwar interview with
       author, Wesseling, January 2011.

139   "I told him they had three options": Ibid.

140   Karmal had been the first leader: Antonio Giustozzi, Empires of Mud (London:
       Hurst, 2009).

142   The expansion of the militias created: Ibid., p. 54.

144   The dramatic switch in Kremlin policy: Jonathan Steele, "Afghan Leader Feels
       Moscow Draught," Guardian, November 19, 1991.

[5] MUJAHEDIN DISASTER

151   Epigraph: "The key problem": Charles Dunbar, interview for CNN Cold War
       Project, August 1977. Unpublished transcript in possession of author.

151   Shirazuddin Siddiqi remembers well the doubts: Conversation with author, March
       2010.

[6] TALIBAN TAKEOVER

167   *Epigraph: "It is not in the interests"*: Closed-door speech to UN, quoted by Ahmed Rashid in *Taliban* (London: I. B.Tauris, 2010), p. 178.

201   *Anders Fänge of the Swedish Committee*: Interview with author, Kabul, March 2010.

202   *"They didn't have good management"*: Arsala Rahmani interview with author, Kabul, March 2010.

206   *State Department cables released after 9/11*: Available at National Security Archive, http://www.gwu.edu/~nsarchiv/NSAEBB/NSAEBB134/index.htm.

207   *bin Laden was "being kept under restriction"*: Ibid.

208   *Malinowski described the unexpected call*: State Department cable on the phone call can be accessed at http://www.gwu.edu/~nsarchiv/NSAEBB/NSAEBB343/osama_bin_laden_file07.pdf.

209   *"you go in and have your say," Brahimi told me later*: Conversation with author, London, October 2001.

210   *Brahimi concluded that the Taliban leader*: Ibid.

211   *Vendrell's lot was not an easy*: Vendrell interview with author, London, September 2010.

[7] TALIBAN TOPPLED

215   *Epigraph: "America has never sought"*: Pamela Constable, "U.S. Ambassador to Afghanistan Counters Karzai's Criticism," *Washington Post*, June 20, 2011.

215   *In New York the World Trade Center*: Abdul Salam Zaeef, *My Life with the Taliban* (London: Hurst, 2010), p. 141.

216   *next morning the ambassador called a press conference*: Ibid., p. 144.

216   *Zaeef wrote a long letter to Bush*: Ibid., p. 146.

218   *I put the question to Francesc Vendrell*: Interview with author, London, September 2010.

220   *As Naik told me in a phone interview*: Jonathan Steele, Ewen MacAskill, Richard Norton-Taylor, and Ed Harriman, "Threat of US Strikes Passed to Taliban Weeks Before NY Attack," *Guardian*, September 22, 2001.

221   *Jonathan Powell . . . later joked*: Conversation with author, London, December 2010.

226   *Under international law, war cannot be justified:* George W. Bush, *Decision Points* (New York: Crown, 2010), p. 128.

227   *Representative Barbara Lee:* Available at http://www.wagingpeace.org /articles/2001/09/14_lee-speech.htm.

230   *"We'll encourage our friends":* Jonathan Steele and Julian Borger, "Attack on Afghanistan: Allies Rush to Fix Deal on Future of Kabul: Rebel Successes Force Pace over Postwar Plan," *Guardian,* November 12, 2001.

230   *Secretary of State Powell said:* Ibid.

[8] WHO KILLED ASAQ?

241   *Epigraph: "Interrupting most of":* Interview with author, Herat, March 2002. The analyst did not wish to have his name published.

242   *Reporters for Western news organizations tried:* Carl Conetta, "Operation Enduring Freedom: Why a Higher Rate of Civilian Casualties?" Project on Defense Alternatives, available at www.comw.org/pda/0201oef.html.

242   *Marc Herold, a professor at the University of New Hampshire:* Marc W. Herold, "A Dossier on Civilian Victims of United States' Aerial Bombing of Afghanistan: A Comprehensive Accounting [revised]," University of New Hampshire, 2002.

243   *In an essay sent to Human Rights Watch:* Available at http://www.hrw.org/en /news/2005/04/17/civilian-war-victims-advocate-marla-ruzicka-mourned.

248   *Kate Stearman . . . at the British branch of Care International:* Interview with author, London, November 2001.

250   *Before 9/11, Afghanistan already had one:* Interview with author, Herat, March 2002.

[9] BACK TO THE WARLORDS

255   *Epigraph: "It's like a wolf that sees":* Hamidullah interview with author, Sar-e Pul, October 2003.

258   *Francesc Vendrell, who headed the UN mission:* Interview with author, London, September 2010.

258   *In the words of the official U.S. military history:* Operation Enduring Freedom, p. 21, available at http://www.history.army.mil/brochures/Afghanistan /Operation%20Enduring%20Freedom.htm.

262   *Barnett Rubin, a U.S. Afghan specialist who advised Brahimi:* Barnett Rubin, speech
       made at a Delhi Policy Group conference in Delhi in 2005, reported in "Peace
       Agreements and After," a Delhi Policy Group publication, 2006.

262   *"I also wanted the Security Council":* Vendrell interview with author, London,
       September 2010.

263   *I faxed Hekmatyar a series of questions:* Text in possession of author.

265   *Ahmad Sarwar, the PDPA's former ambassador in India:* Phone interview with
       author, Wesseling, February 2002.

271   *Rubin . . . quoted Fahim:* Barnett Rubin, interview with Asia Society, New
       York, May 28, 2003. Available at http://asiasociety.org/policy-politics
       /strategic-challenges/us-asia/barnett-rubin-afghanistan-vicious-cycle.

272   *Wazhma Frogh, a human rights activist:* Speech at meeting at the London School
       of Economics, March 2010.

273   *Sam Zia-Zarifi . . . with Human Rights Watch:* Interview with author, Kabul, June
       2002.

[10] TALIBAN RESURGENT

285   *Najibullah Lafraie, who had served as the mujahedin's foreign minister:* Najibullah
       Lafraie, "Resurgence of the Taliban Insurgency in Afghanistan: How and
       Why?" *International Politics* (2009), Volume 46, Number 1, pp. 102–113.

286   *Horiah Mosadiq, an Afghan working:* Speech at London School of Economics,
       March 2010.

287   *Madrassas in Pakistan played a big part:* Antonio Giustozzi, *Koran, Kalashnikov
       and Laptop* (London: Hurst, 2007), p. 37.

290   *By 2005 the Taliban were operating:* Gareth Porter, "How Afghanistan Became a
       War for NATO," Inter Press Service, Washington, DC, January 3, 2011.

290   *Could the Taliban have been defeated:* Ahmed Rashid, *Taliban* (London: I. B.Tauris,
       2010), p. 225.

291   *As Barnett Rubin, the U.S. Afghan specialist:* Barnett Rubin, interview for
       Council on Foreign Relations, available at http://www.cfr.org/world
       /rubin-us-must-confront-warlords-deal-taliban/p7191.

292   *Lafraie wrote that another major problem:* Lafraie, "Resurgence of the Taliban
       Insurgency in Afghanistan," p. 109.

293   *As he and two other analysts:* Talatbek Masadykov, principal author of
"Negotiating with the Taliban: Toward a Solution for the Afghan Conflict,"
London School of Economics Crisis States Research Centre, coauthored with
Antonio Giustozzi and James Michael Page, London, Working Paper Number
66, January 2010, p. 4.

293   *In the words of Mohammad Yusef Aresh:* Human Rights Watch, "The Human
Cost: The Consequences of Insurgent Attacks in Afghanistan," New York, April
2007, p. 2.

295   *The incident caused such an outcry:* Human Rights Watch, "Troops in Contact:
Airstrikes and Civilian Deaths in Afghanistan," September 2008, p. 18.

296   *In May, Brigadier General Perry Wiggins:* Ibid.

307   *At the village level, commanders of Taliban fighting units:* Gretchen Peters, "The
Taliban and the Opium Trade," in *Decoding the New Taliban*, edited by Antonio
Giustozzi (London: Hurst, 2009), p. 8.

308   *Antonio Giustozzi takes a more cautious view:* Giustozzi, *Koran, Kalashnikov and
Laptop*, p. 87.

308   *Most of these reasons were confirmed by:* Sarah Ladbury, "Testing Hypotheses on
Radicalization in Afghanistan: Why Do Men Join the Taliban and Hizb-i Islami?
How Much Do Local Communities Support Them?" Independent Report for
the Department for International Development, August 14, 2009.

[11] OBAMA AND KARZAI: THE ODD COUPLE

311   *Epigraph: "We must disabuse Karzai":* Cable sent to State Department, September
1, 2009. Available at *Guardian* website: http://www.guardian.co.uk/world
/us-embassy-cables-documents/223183.

311   *Back in the privacy of the fortified castle:* Cable sent to State Department, July
7, 2009. Available at *Guardian* website: http://www.guardian.co.uk/world
/us-embassy-cables-documents/215470.

313   *The ambassador did not keep his concerns:* Ibid.

314   *The Ambassador urged Karzai to consider:* Cable sent to State Department,
December 16, 2009. Available at *Guardian* website: http://www.guardian
.co.uk/world/us-embassy-cables-documents/240103.

314   *On one occasion Karzai felt so angry:* Amir Shah and Christopher Boden,
"Lawmakers: Afghan Leader Threatens to Join Taliban," Associated Press,
April 5, 2010.

315 *At other times Karzai was ready:* Available at *Guardian* website: http://www
.guardian.co.uk/world/2010/dec/02/wikileaks-cables-panic-afghan-elections.

315 *rash interview with* Rolling Stone *magazine:* Michael Hastings, "The Runaway
General," *Rolling Stone,* June 22, 2010.

315 *One of the worst arguments with:* Joshua Partlow, "Petraeus's Comments on
Coalition Attack Reportedly Offend Karzai Government," *Washington Post,*
February 21, 2011.

316 *To their shock, Petraeus suggested that:* Ibid.

316 *Karzai's displeasure at the Kunar:* March 2, 2011, interview, available on
Channel 4 website: http://www.channel4.com/news/hamid-karzai
-on-the-taliban-corruption-and-wikileaks.

316 *Four weeks later, he said:* Tom A. Peter, "Afghan President Karzai Demands
NATO Stop Airstrikes on Homes," *Christian Science Monitor,* May 31, 2011.

317 *Sherard Cowper-Coles, who served as Britain's ambassador:* Conversation with
author, London, June 2010.

317 *Ahmed Rashid, a Lahore-based veteran Pakistani analyst:* Ahmed Rashid, "How
Obama Lost Karzai," *Foreign Policy,* New York, February 22, 2011.

319 *Karzai believed the United States was secretly funding:* Cable sent to State
Department, September 3, 2009. Available at http://www.guardian.co.uk
/world/us-embassy-cables-documents/223517.

319 *Another cable revealed that the U.S. embassy:* Cable sent to State Department,
August 28, 2009. Available at *Guardian* website: http://www.guardian.co.uk
/world/us-embassy-cables-documents/222682.

320 *Separately from the later WikiLeaks cache:* Eric Schmitt, "U.S. Envoy's Cables Show
Worries on Afghan Plans," *New York Times,* January 25, 2010.

321 *It was a remarkable cable:* Ibid.

322 *Karzai's family's corruption was a major factor:* Cable sent to State Department,
August 6, 2009. Available at *Guardian* website: http://www.guardian.co.uk
/world/us-embassy-cables-documents/219677.

322 *Speaking generally about the release of drug traffickers:* http://www.guardian
.co.uk/world/2010/dec/02/wikileaks-cables-hamid-karzai-erratic.

323 *Stanekzai told the U.S. embassy:* Ibid.

323 *Apparently to spite the Americans:* Rod Nordland, "Afghans Drop Corruption
Case Against Karzai Aide," *New York Times,* November 9, 2010.

323   *The Nexus-Corruption Leadership Board:* Cable sent to State Department,
       February 15, 2010. Available at *Guardian* website: http://www.guardian.co.uk
       /world/us-embassy-cables-documents/248828.

323   *A cable recounting a meeting:* Available at http://www.nytimes.com/2010
       /11/29/world/29cables.html?pagewanted=4.

324   *Another cable from Anthony Wayne:* Cable sent to State Department, December
       6, 2009. Available at *Guardian* website: http://www.guardian.co.uk/world
       /us-embassy-cables-documents/238320.

325   *Describing a February 2010 meeting:* Cable sent to State Department, February
       25, 2010. Available at http://www.nytimes.com/2010/11/29/world/29cables
       .html?pagewanted=4.

326   *The relationship was beautifully illustrated:* Available at *Guardian* website:
       http://www.guardian.co.uk/world/2010/dec/02/wikileaks-cables
       -panic-afghan-elections.

[12] TALKING TO THE TALIBAN: HOW THE WAR ENDS

329   *Epigraph: "Every war":* Interview with author, Kabul, March 2010.

332   *Speaking in front of a packed hall:* Jon Boone, "Osama bin Laden Dead: US
       Strategy Misconceived, Says Hamid Karzai," *Guardian,* May 2, 2011.

332   *In light of the historic difference between:* David Miliband, MIT speech, March
       10, 2010, available at http://www.fco.gov.uk/en/news/latest-news
       /?view=News&id=21866339.

334   *Karzai revealed in another cable:* Available on *Guardian* website: http://www
       .guardian.co.uk/world/us-embassy-cables-documents/244047.

335   *"Karzai said he could refer to American history":* Ibid.

335   *Karl Eikenberry, the U.S. ambassador:* Available at *Guardian* website: http://www
       .guardian.co.uk/world/us-embassy-cables-documents/243317.

336   *The leaked cables showed that:* Available at *Guardian* website: http://www
       .guardian.co.uk/world/us-embassy-cables-documents/245980.

336   *In January 2009, according to:* Available at *Guardian* website: http://www
       .guardian.co.uk/world/us-embassy-cables-documents/187794.

336   *The White House confirmed the point:* Available at http://www.whitehouse.gov
       /blog/2009/03/27/a-new-strategy-afghanistan-and-pakistan.

340   *During Karzai's recent visits to Kandahar:* Laura King, "Ethnic Divide Threatens
       in Afghanistan," *Los Angeles Times,* July 7, 2010.

343　*Members of the British House of Commons Foreign Affairs Committee:* Evidence to House of Commons Foreign Affairs Committee, published on March 2, 2011, p. 55.

343　*Gilles Dorronsoro, an expert on Afghanistan's politics:* Ibid.

343　*In February 2011 in a speech:* Hillary Clinton, Asia Society speech, February 18, 2011, available at www.state.gov/secretary/rm/2011/02/156815.htm.

345　*Other analysts, including Michael Semple:* Fotini Christia and Michael Semple, "Flipping the Taliban: How to Win in Afghanistan," *Foreign Affairs,* July/August 2009.

346　*As Gilles Dorronsoro told British lawmakers:* Dorronsoro, Evidence to House of Commons Foreign Affairs Committee, p. 128.

346　*Lieutenant General William Caldwell, the U.S. commander:* Caroline Wyatt, "Can Afghan National Army Survive NATO Exit?" BBC, March 9, 2011.

346　*The Afghan police are equally poor:* Gerard Russell, Evidence to House of Commons Foreign Affairs Committee, p. 128.

347　*A United Nations report on the ALP:* United Nations Assistance Mission in Afghanistan and Afghanistan Independent Human Rights Commission, Annual Report 2010, "Protection of Civilians in Armed Conflict," Kabul, March 2011, p. 41.

347　*Shukria Barakzai's willingness to support talks:* Interview with author, Kabul, March 2010.

348　*Cowper-Coles summarized its findings:* Evidence to House of Commons Foreign Affairs Committee, p. 124.

348　*Michael Semple describes them as:* Michael Semple, *Reconciliation in Afghanistan* (Washington, DC: U.S. Institute for Peace, 2009), p. 46.

349　*In October 2002, Hekmatyar wrote:* Available at http://www.enotes.com/america-helping-article.

349　*After Obama's election and before the inauguration:* Available at http://www.cbsnews.com/8301-502684_162-4684702-502684.html.

350　*Hekmatyar also made several overtures to Karzai:* Jon Boone, "President Meets Militant Group Officials to Discuss Warlord's 15-Point Peace Plan for Troops to Withdraw from Afghanistan," *Guardian,* March 22, 2010.

351　*According to Cowper-Coles:* Conversation with author, Kabul, March 2010.

351　*The Quetta Shura has made its:* Lynne O'Donnell, "Taliban Call on US to Send Fact-finding Team to Afghanistan," Agence France Presse, November 7, 2010.

352 *But there have been signs:* Available at http://www.shahamat.info/english /index.php?option=com_content&view=article&id=2435:peace-talks-in -conditions-of-the-presence-of-foreign-forces-are-meaningless-and-futile -&catid=4:statements&Itemid=4.

354 *Cowper-Coles has argued that a military base:* Conversation with author, London, November 2010.

355 *The Musa Qala agreement went:* Jason Burke, "Musa Qala's Fall Jeopardized the Entire UK Strategy. Now a Fight Is On to Take It Back," *The Observer,* London, February 4, 2007.

356 *Proposals along these lines were:* "A New Way Forward: Rethinking U.S. Strategy in Afghanistan," Report of the Afghanistan Study Group, available at www .afghanistanstudygroup.com.

357 *Robert Blackwill, who served in:* Robert Blackwill, "America Must Give the South to the Taliban," *Financial Times,* July 21, 2010.

357 *One of the most powerful statements:* Thomas Pickering and Lakhdar Brahimi, *Afghanistan: Negotiating Peace—The Report of The Century Foundation International Task Force on Afghanistan in Its Regional and Multilateral Dimensions* (New York: The Century Foundation Press, 2011), p. 2.

359 *In Britain, pressure has been growing:* House of Commons Foreign Affairs Committee, p. 78.

[13] THE GIRL WITH THE MISSING NOSE

361 *Epigraph: "Nobody wants to abandon the women":* Rajiv Chandrasekaran, "In Afghanistan, U.S. Shifts Strategy on Women's Rights as It Eyes Wider Priorities," *Washington Post,* March 5, 2011.

361 *It may have been the most horrendous cover picture:* "The Plight of Afghan Women: A Disturbing Picture," *Time,* July 29, 2010.

362 *In an editorial accompanying the cover:* Ibid.

362 *"Feminists have long argued that":* Priyamvada Gopal, "Burqas and Bikinis," *Guardian,* August 3, 2010.

362 *Three months later the centerpiece:* Julius Cavendish, "Justice for the Symbol of Afghan Cruelty: Former Father-in-Law 'Confesses' to Mutilation That Shocked the World," *Independent on Sunday,* December 9, 2010.

364   *"For sure, we have hundreds of Bibi"*: Jon Boone, "Afghan Women Still Suffer Horrendous Abuse, Says UN Report," *Guardian,* December 10, 2010.

364   *In one of the secret cables:* Cable sent to State Department, January 10, 2010. Available at *Guardian* website: http://www.guardian.co.uk/world /us-embassy-cables-documents/243011.

364   *According to UNIFEM:* Quoted in United Nations Assistance Mission in Afghanistan, "Harmful Traditional Practices and Implementation of the Law on Elimination of Violence Against Women in Afghanistan," Kabul, December 9, 2010, p. 18.

364   *In a study of 200 underage:* Ibid.

366   *"The girl is never respected by":* Ibid., p. 14.

366   *"Without* baad, *we would have conflict":* Institute for War and Peace Reporting, "Afghan Girls Suffer for Sins of Male Relatives," ARR No. 317, March 26, 2009, available at http://www.unhcr.org/refworld/docid/49dc4b201c.html.

367   *Self-immolation is often more sinister:* Alissa J. Rubin, "For Afghan Wives, a Desperate, Fiery Way Out," *New York Times,* November 7, 2010.

368   *Afghanistan has the worst maternal mortality rate:* Figures available from the World Health Organization at http://apps.who.int/ghodata/?vid=250.

372   *According to Brett Rapley:* Interview with author, Lashkar Gah, October 2010.

372   *Other evidence has emerged of Taliban flexibility:* Khan Mohammad Danishju, "Allowing Schools to Reopen and Reconstruction Projects to Go Ahead Seen as Sign of Pragmatic Attempt to Win Public Favor," Institute for War and Peace Reporting, April 8, 2011.

373   *People living in areas under Taliban:* Ibid.

373   *"Before I came here," said Dr. Jonathan Cox:* Interview with author, Lashkar Gah, October 2010.

377   *In a further sign of the trend:* Rajiv Chandrasekaran, "In Afghanistan, U.S. Shifts Strategy on Women's Rights as It Eyes Wider Priorities," *Washington Post,* March 5, 2011.

377   *"If you're targeting an issue":* Ibid.

378   *Another senior U.S. official told:* Ibid.

[14] A DANGEROUS NEIGHBORHOOD

379   *Epigraph: "Victory is impossible in Afghanistan":* Mikhail Gorbachev interview
       with BBC News, October 27, 2010, available at http://www.bbc.co.uk/news
       /world-south-asia-11633646.

383   *"Five Islamic countries are against the bases":* "No Evidence to Prove Iran's
       Interference in Afghanistan," Bakhtar News Agency, March 9, 2011.

383   *In recent years, Tehran's strategy:* Dexter Filkins and Alissa Rubin, "Afghan Leader
       Admits His Office Gets Cash from Iran," *New York Times,* October 25, 2010.

384   *NATO officials have regularly accused Iran:* Kimberly Dozier, "NATO Forces Seize
       Rockets from Iran in Afghanistan," Associated Press, March 9, 2011.

385   *she wrote, "There is no chance that Pakistan":* Available at http://www.guardian
       .co.uk/world/us-embassy-cables-documents/226531.

385   *The Pakistani Government and Army would like:* Ibid.

386   *Patterson warned Washington in her cables:* Ibid.

388   *Pakistan's Prime Minister Yousuf Gilani told reporters:* Deb Riechmann, "Pakistan
       Says It Firmly Backs Taliban Peace Talks," Associated Press, April 16, 2011.

388   *Karzai told the same press conference:* Ibid.

CONCLUSION: THE WAY FORWARD

391   *Epigraph: "Any future Defense Secretary who advises":* David S. Cloud, "Gates
       Warns Against Future Land Wars Like Iraq, Afghanistan," *Los Angeles Times,*
       February 25, 2011.

392   *Afghanistan ranks 135 out of 135:* UN Human Development Report 2009,
       Country Fact Sheets: Afghanistan.

392   *Life expectancy at 44.6 years:* "The Real Wealth of Nations: Pathways to Human
       Development," UN Human Development Report 2010, November 2010.

392   *One out of every five children dies:* USAID, "Afghanistan: Health," Fall 2009,
       www.usaid.org.

392   *Seventy-three percent of the population:* "Afghanistan Country Overview 2010,"
       World Bank, www.worldbank.org.af.

392   *Mineral deposits, mainly of iron and copper:* James Risen, "U.S. Identifies Vast
       Mineral Riches in Afghanistan," *New York Times,* June 13, 2010, http://www
       .nytimes.com/2010/06/14/world/asia/14minerals.html.

392   *In 2006, the United States Geological Survey estimated:* Arne Straud, Mohammad Hakim, Sediqa Newrozi, Akbar Sarwari and Aled Williams, "Afghan Hydrocarbons: A Source for Development or for Conflict?" Chr. Michelsen Institute, 2010, p. 8.

392   *In 2007, the state-owned China Metallurgical Group:* Michael Wines, "China Willing to Spend Big on Afghan Commerce," *New York Times,* December 29, 2009.

394   *At the end of July 2011:* Available at http://www.guardian.co.uk/world/2011/aug/16/gorbachev-guardian-interview?INTCMP=SRCH

395   *Polls show that a majority of Afghans:* Eighty-three percent of respondents supported the government's attempts to address the security situation through negotiation and reconciliation with armed anti-government elements, compared to 71 percent in 2009, according to the Asia Foundation: "Afghanistan in 2010: a Survey of the Afghan People," available at http://asiafoundation.org/country/afghanistan/2010-poll.php.

395   *As Jolyon Leslie, a former UN negotiator:* Evidence to House of Commons Foreign Affairs Committee, p. 99.

396   *The Obama administration is planning to keep:* Karen DeYoung, "U.S. Wants 'Joint Bases' in Afghanistan, Gates Says," *Washington Post,* June 9, 2011.

396   *Ryan Crocker, the new U.S. ambassador:* Ibid.

397   *spelled out graphically by Francesc Vendrell:* As quoted in "Divided We Stand," *The Age,* June 23, 2010, available at http://www.theage.com.au/world/divided-we-stand-20100622-yvpv.html.

BIBLIOGRAPHY

Anwar, Raja, *The Tragedy of Afghanistan* (London: Verso, 1988)

Arnold, Anthony, *Afghanistan's Two-Party Communism* (Stanford, CA: Hoover Institution Press, 1983)

Borovik, Artyom, *The Hidden War* (London: Faber and Faber, 1991)

Bradsher, Henry, *Afghan Communism and Soviet Intervention* (Oxford: Oxford University Press, 1999)

Braithwaite, Rodric, *Afgantsy* (London: Profile Books, 2011)

Chernyayev, Anatoly, *Shest Let s Gorbachëvym* (Moscow, 1993)

———, *Sovmestny Iskhod: Dnevnik Dvukh Epokh 1972–1991 gody* (Moscow, 2008)

Cooley, John, *Unholy Wars* (London: Pluto Press, 1999)

Cordovez, Diego and Harrison, Selig, *Out of Afghanistan* (Oxford: Oxford University Press, 1995)

Cowper-Coles, Sherard, *Cables from Kabul: The Inside Story of the West's Afghanistan Campaign* (London: HarperPress, 2011)

Crews, Robert and Tarzi, Amin, *The Taliban and the Crisis of Afghanistan* (Cambridge, MA: Harvard University Press, 2008)

Crile, George, *Charlie Wilson's War* (New York: Grove Press, 2003)

Derber, Charles and Magrass, Yale R., *Morality Wars: How Empires, the Born Again, and the Politically Correct Do Evil in the Name of Good* (Boulder, CO: Paradigm, 2008)

Dorronsoro, Gilles, *Revolution Unending* (London: Hurst, 2005)

Elphinstone, Mountstuart, *An Account of the Kingdom of Caubul* (London: Bentley, 1815)

Fergusson, James, *Taliban* (London: Bantam, 2010)

Gates, Robert, *From the Shadows* (New York: Simon and Schuster, 1996)

Ghani, Ashraf and Lockhart, Clare, *Fixing Failed States* (Oxford: Oxford University Press, 2008)

Girardet, Edward, *Afghanistan: The Soviet War* (London: Croom Helm, 1985)

Giustozzi, Antonio, *Koran, Kalashnikov and Laptop* (London: Hurst, 2007)

———, *Decoding the New Taliban* (London: Hurst, 2009)

———, *Empires of Mud* (London: Hurst, 2009)

Gorbachev, Mikhail, *Memoirs* (London: Doubleday, 1996)

Grachev, Andrei, *Gorbachev's Gamble* (Cambridge: Polity Press, 2008)

Greshnov, Andrei, *Afganistan: Zalozhniki Vremeni* (Moscow, 2006)

Grey, Stephen, *Operation Snakebite* (London: Viking [Penguin], 2009)

Griffin, Michael, *Reaping the Whirlwind* (London: Pluto Press, 2003)

Hopkirk, Peter, *The Great Game* (London: Murray, 1990)

Hosseini, Khaled, *The Kite Runner* (London: Bloomsbury, 2003)

Hyman, Anthony, *Afghanistan under Soviet Domination 1964–81* (London: Macmillan, 1982)

Johnson, Chris and Leslie, Jolyon, *Afghanistan: The Mirage of Democracy* (London: Zed Books, 2005)

Krivenko, Vitaly, *Ekipazh Mashiny Boevoi* (St. Petersburg, 2004)

Lessing, Doris, *The Wind Blows Away Our Words* (London: Picador, 1986)

Loyn, David, *Butcher and Bolt* (London: Hutchinson, 2008)

Lyakhovski, Aleksandr, *Tragediya i Doblest Afgana* (Moscow, 1995)

Maley, William, *Fundamentalism Reborn? Afghanistan and the Taliban* (London: Hurst, 1998)

———, *Rescuing Afghanistan* (London: Hurst, 2006)

Marsden, Peter, *Afghanistan: Aid, Armies and Empires* (London: I. B. Tauris, 2009)

Rashid, Ahmed, *Taliban* (London: I. B. Tauris, 2010)

Roy, Olivier, *Islam and Resistance in Afghanistan* (Cambridge: Cambridge University Press, 1986)

Semple, Michael, *Reconciliation in Afghanistan* (Washington, DC: United States Institute of Peace Press, 2009)

Steele, Jonathan, *The Limits of Soviet Power* (London: Penguin, 1985)

———, *Eternal Russia* (London: Faber and Faber; Cambridge, MA: Harvard University Press, 1994)

Stewart, Rory, *The Places in Between* (London: Picador, 2004)

Tkachenko, Pyotr, *Dorogiye Moi* (Moscow: Profizdat, 1991)

Tomsen, Peter, *The Wars of Afghanistan*, (New York: PublicAffairs, 2011)

Turse, Nick, *The Case for Withdrawal from Afghanistan* (London: Verso, 2010)

Urban, Mark, *War in Afghanistan* (London: Macmillan, 1988)

Woodward, Bob, *Obama's Wars* (New York: Simon and Schuster, 2010)

Zaeef, Abdul Salam, *My Life with the Taliban* (London: Hurst, 2010)

INDEX